D1738230

Southern California's Spanish Heritage

AN ANTHOLOGY

In Commemoration of the Quincentenary
of the Voyage of Christopher Columbus
to the New World

QUINTO CENTENARIO

Southern California's Spanish Heritage

AN ANTHOLOGY

Introduced and Edited by
Doyce B. Nunis, Jr.

Foreword by
Honorable Señor Eduardo Garrigues
Consul General of Spain

Compiled from the
Southern California Quarterly
the publication of the
Historical Society of Southern California

LOS ANGELES
HISTORICAL SOCIETY OF SOUTHERN CALIFORNIA
1992

DOYCE BLACKMAN NUNIS, JR.

THE DIRECTORS of the Historical Society of
Southern California are pleased to take this
opportunity to publicly recognize the thirty
years of distinguished service that Dr. Nunis
has given the Society as editor of the
Southern California Quarterly.
Since becoming editor in 1962, Dr. Nunis
has transformed the *Quarterly* into one of the
leading interpreters of the Spanish experience in Southern California and throughout
the state. The selection of articles which follows, taken from the *Quarterly*, will stand
as a lasting testimony to his vision and
energy as historian.

Therefore, it is appropriate that

Southern California's Heritage: An Anthology

be dedicated to

DOYCE BLACKMAN NUNIS, JR.,

a Fellow of the Historical Society
and a wonderfully gifted servant of history
to Los Angeles and Southern California.

Foreword

IT IS WITH GREAT PLEASURE that I write this foreword to the anthology of southern California's Spanish heritage, compiled from various articles published in the *Southern California Quarterly*, and now appearing in a single volume in commemoration of the Quincentenary of Cristobal Colón's voyage to the New World. In my double capacity as Consul General of Spain in southern California and historian "aficionado" with a special interest in the Southwest, I consider it a great honor to have these few pages published in the illustrious company of some of the professional historians who have devoted the best part of their lives exploring the Spanish past of California.

Allow me to congratulate Dr. Doyce B. Nunis, Jr., editor of the *Quarterly*, and of this volume in particular, for his splendid selection of articles, addressing some of the most interesting topics related to the Spanish influence in California. From the early explorations, to the naming of Los Angeles — a subject often raised in social conversations, and frequently misinterpreted — to such delicate and essential topics as the missionary approach to the Indians, the rich facets of Spanish rule in California are embodied in this volume with accuracy and objectivity. One cannot underscore enough the importance of this anthology for the historian and layman alike, as it will be impossible to understand what California is today without a general knowledge of the Spanish period. In this respect, I am at a loss trying to pinpoint which is the most fascinating topic in this anthology: the economic dimension, the study of the California ranchos, the artistic or architectural analysis concerning the missions and the adobes, or the originality of contributions like "No Settlement Without Women," which certainly destroys more than one cliché regarding the sole importance of soldiers and priests in the colonization of California.

As the controversy over the Quincentenary, mentioned by Dr.

Nunis in his introduction, appears to have the effect of blurring history in a halo of passion — when it seems that the lapse of five hundred years should give us the advantage of historical perspective — the professional historian has to start by fighting the political mythology and by reasserting historical reality.

In the U.S.A., the critics of the Discovery and the Spanish legacy have found well-oiled machinery in die-hard anti-Spanish feelings, rooted first in the colonial rivalry between England and Spain, and later nurtured in the Anglo-Saxon hostility toward the Spanish heritage, a cultural barrier encountered in America's expansion westward, especially on the Southwestern frontier. In fact, it is not surprising to hear Black Legend clichés being uttered during the Spanish-American War of 1898.

As Oxford scholar Felipe Fernández-Armesto, author of a recent book on Columbus, points out, "Myths are believed because they make people feel good — usually by confirming prejudices or reinforcing convictions of moral superiority. Conventional thinkers in a post-imperialist and ecologically conscious age can take comfort from indicting conquistadors who destroyed subject cultures and raped the conquered environment." Although between the early exploration of the Caribbean and the late colonization of California, the political system and the approach to the natives from the Spanish colonizers had evolved substantially, the critics of the Discovery engulf all in the same sweeping condemnation of events which occurred two hundred years apart.

In fact, the best proof that Spanish colonization was not quite so bad must be sought among the very critics of the system who lived at that time. Bartolomé de Las Casas, who denounced the *encomienda* practice and excoriated his own compatriots for their treatment of the natives, was promoted to the rank of bishop and became a counselor to the Crown. What would have happened if a U.S. Army chaplain in the Old West had set about openly attacking the conduct of his superiors in their dealings with the Indian tribes? How long would it have taken for him to be stripped of his post and punished for his insubordination? As historian Fernández-Armesto writes: "No empire has ever legislated more persistently for the alleviation of injustice to its subject peoples. Where cruelties and atrocities occurred, historians know of them precisely because of the sixteenth-century Spanish passion for justice, for they were condemned by moralists or recorded and punished in the courts."

No matter how negative one can be toward Columbus and his Spanish successors, they can hardly be blamed for the human and natural disasters which occurred in North America about 400 years after the first voyage of Discovery. In California, for example, while some place responsibility on the Spanish colonization and the mission system for the decline of population in the Indian tribes, the real tragedy of the Indian came with the Gold Rush and the great American invasion. In the book *The Destruction of the California Indians*, anthropologist Robert F. Heizer estimates that between 1848 and 1870 about 50,000 California Indians died. And although the Treaty of Guadalupe Hidalgo guaranteed Spanish and Mexican *Californios* the rights to their land grants, according to research by historian Patricia Limerick, author of *The Legacy of Conquest*, 80 percent of those land grants eventually fell into the hands of American lawyers and settlers. Then, perhaps, in a well aimed attempt to eradicate the obnoxious "lust for gold" from the Spanish descendants' soul, California passed the Foreign Miners' Tax in 1850, driving Hispanics out of the mines.

Personally, I have always wondered why, while the Spanish conquerors were accused of being "gold crazed," the forty-niners were described with the poetical term of "argonauts" and their exploits praised in folklore and songs. It is true that the first Spanish *entrada* into the Southwest was prompted by the lure of the "Seven Golden Cities of Cíbola," but the journey of Francisco Vásquez Coronado, covered in a golden armor and leaving behind a beautiful "Dulcinea" in northern Mexico in search of a mythical El Dorado across the barren plains, has a quixotic texture which is difficult to find in the accounts of his prosaic followers of the mid-nineteenth century. Even Hernando Cortés, after sacking the Aztec Empire, spent most of his fortune in five explorations to the mythical California, all of them ending in failure, except for the geographical discovery of the Sea of Cortes, the peninsula of

California and some islands in the Pacific.

Although Coronado and his men were the first Europeans to scout the Colorado River, the Grand Canyon, and the first to see the vast herds of buffaloes — called "cibolos" in memory of their vain pursuit — neither they nor their descendants could be blamed for the slaughter of the big herds, which were decimated between 1825 and 1883, after Spain withdrew from the American mainland. According to historians and ecologists, the destruction of the buffalo, combined with their replacement by cattle and the settlement of farmers from the East in the western plains, disrupted the native ecology and originated an environmental catastrophe without precedent.

In fact, the long presence of Spain in the Southwest affected in a limited way the native population and the natural resources. This is because of, among other reasons, the very limited means the Spanish settlers had at their disposal to fight the hostile environment and the wild tribes. When the heroic yarns about American pioneers were still fashionable in Hollywood, there was not a single movie portraying the endurance and courage of the Spanish pioneers, who fought their way in the wild West with practically the same tools and weapons as the Indians they encountered. The conquest of the desert by Anza or the fabulous itineraries of Kino and Garcés should be known to the California schoolboy with the same perspective as the exploits of Frémont and Kit Carson.

To come to terms with the Spanish heritage in California is essential for the vast population of this beautiful state, including the important minority of Spanish-speaking immigrants which, without probably knowing it, came following in the steps of Alarcón, Coronado, Anza, and Garcés.

EDUARDO GARRIGUES
Consul General of Spain in Los Angeles

Acknowledgments

THE Historical Society of Southern California is pleased to acknowledge The Ahmanson Foundation and the Spring Street Foundation as BENEFACTORS, the Comisión Nacional Quinto Centenario and the Consulate General of Spain in Los Angeles as PATRONS, and the Los Angeles 200 Committee as SPONSOR, of this *Anthology*.

In addition to this generous financial support, Lee Walcott of the Ahmanson Foundation, Winston Morrow of the Spring Street Foundation, and the Honorable Eduardo Garrigues, Consul General of Spain in Los Angeles, have provided considerable encouragement throughout the publication process.

The vision and tireless editorial work of Doyce B. Nunis, Jr., the detailed indexing of William Heckman, the impeccable artistic design of Ward Ritchie, and the careful supervision by Dana Cordrey at each stage of the process, have enabled this *Anthology* to meet the high standards of both the Historical Society and the donors to the publication.

To all involved, the Board of Directors expresses its sincere thanks for this opportunity to share the deep and richly textured Spanish Heritage of Southern California.

Introduction

THE YEAR 1992 marks the quincentenary of the effective discovery of the New World by Christopher Columbus and his gallant band of mariners who dared to undertake that epic-making voyage. No serious historian will deny that North America was undoubtedly visited first by Norsemen in their Viking ships in the eleventh century. Solid archeological evidence along with some documentation establishes these early visitors' presence in southern Greenland and as far south as the present state of Maine. There are some who would say Massachusetts. However, their discovery went unnoticed and remained obscure until centuries after their first appearance in North America. It had no impact at all on the long course of history.

There is also the school of thought that it may well be that Central America may have had earlier alien contact, visitors supposedly from North Africa, mayhap Egyptians. This hypothesis would help explain the use of pyramid architecture in the Mayan and Aztec nations, as well as the high degree of astronomical knowledge which was widespread in these two Meso-American cultures. Up to the present no written records or solid archeological evidence has been brought to light either to prove or disprove this supposed North African contact. And decades ago the supposed visitation of Chinese navigators to the west coast of North America was branded pure fiction, even though this fantasy continues to pop up now and then in the tabloid press seeking to capitalize on sheer ignorance, as does the story that visitors from space may have also dropped in on the New World eons of ages ago.

However, there is no dispute on the fact that the Columbus discovery radically altered the course of history, both for Europeans and the inhabitants of the New World. That fact is undeniable. Today, in marking this event as one of the turning points in world history, arguments are heard loud and clear as to the dire effects that the Columbian discovery had on the indigenous New World inhabitants. The Eurocentric view is heavily criticized by those who would rewrite history to accommodate a certain mindset, a strident passion, or a given political agenda. Such critics of the discovery fail to look at the other side, namely the impact the discovery of the New World had, first on Europeans, later Africans and Asians. No one on earth escaped being touched by the end results of the effective European discovery of the New World, and the expansion that followed when Europeans began to make their presence felt from the St. Lawrence to the Rio de Plata, from the Atlantic to the Pacific shores. Though it would take some four hundred years to redirect the way of life for the native inhabitants and the same length of time to impact on Europe, Africa, and Asia, the process certainly dates from October 12, 1492 when Columbus and his three small ships, flying the flag of Spain, spied the first landfall in the eastern Caribbean. Although the exact landfall has not been fixed with certainty, the date, according to the Julian calendar, is not disputed.

That Spain was the harbinger of what was to fashion a sea of changes — cultural, economic, political, and religious, changes that simply altered the course of human history — was by pure happenstance, unless one believes in divine intervention. The irony of the discovery is that Columbus was trying to reach Japan and China by sailing due west, not knowing that an entire New World lay astride his track. When reality finally dawned, Spain moved quickly to establish its physical presence in the new-found lands. It could do so because of several fortuitous circumstances. First, it entered the New World at its most advantageous geographical point, the Caribbean and Central America where the continents, North and South, are joined by the narrowest land mass, a land mass easily reached by the many islands scattered as stepping stones in the Caribbean, stretching from Florida to Venezuela. Second, the sailing pattern into the Caribbean was a mariner's dream: the lovely central Atlantic Ocean trade winds blowing westward, and the marvelous Gulf Stream with its steady currents and winds eastward. Thus one had a perfect water highway, favored by currents to propel the ships along and generous winds to supply the sails with sustained power. The geographic and maritime advantages were Spain's by sheer coincidence. And Spain capitalized on those advantages to the fullest. This is why it was able to move so swiftly in its thrust into the New World.

Another Spanish advantage was that the first native peoples encountered were urban dwellers. Lacking domesticated animals, notably horses and mules, the only viable transportation was by water, which was certainly used, though less prevalent in Central America than in North and South America. Modern armaments and horses gave the Spanish the decided military edge in all confrontations. That power, coupled with a surplus army which had accrued to Spain in its 800 years of struggle to rid the Iberian Peninsula of the Saracens, proved indomitable in the abrupt conquest of those lands entered by Spain on a permanent basis. Unhappily, this overriding military force was further empowered by the invisible enemy all Europeans brought to the New World, their infectious diseases. The germs which traveled with the Europeans took a dreadful toll on the indigenous people who lacked immunity to the most commonplace diseases to which Europeans had long become accustomed. Devoid of any prior biological accommodation, they perished in the hundreds of thousands, devastating the cities because of human contact, the primary transmission of most infectious diseases. Although the Western medical arts were at best primitive, at the time no one understood the germ theory let alone how to prevent or treat such diseases. Such knowledge did not begin to emerge until the middle of the nineteenth century in Europe. Disease proved a formidable ally in conquering the native peoples of the New World.

On another front, the Spanish lucked out more than any other New World colonizer. In Mexico, when it fell to them in 1521, they hit a jackpot, for the country was rich in gold and silver deposits. A second precious metals bonanza was found when Peru was subjugated in 1535. These two conquests only spurred more effort. It was in that endeavor to find new riches that California began to figure, although as yet unnamed. The man who pointed the way was none other than Hernando Cortés, the conqueror of Mexico.

In 1535–37, he undertook the colonization of Baja California in hopes of discovering new gold lands and rich pearl fisheries, inspired by a romance of chivalry, the *Adventures of Esplandían*, published in Madrid probably in the very early sixteenth century. Written by Garcí Ordóñez de Montalvo, it spun a tale of an island ruled by Queen Califia, a nation of black Amazons, who wore gold armor. This fictional tale proved Cortés's undoing: his colonial venture failed miserably. He had to sustain the enormous financial losses incurred in that vain effort. But he did leave an important legacy behind him — the place name California.

In 1539 Cortés sponsored the voyage of Francisco de Ulloa to explore what became known as the Vermillion Sea, later the Sea of Cortes, now the Gulf of Baja California. Ulloa clearly discerned that Baja California was a peninsula, although it took 200 years for this to become fact in geography and cartography. It may well be that he was also the first European to visit Alta California for he sailed into the mouth of the Colorado River, although it is uncertain how far north he sailed into the estuary, and there is no record of his landing on the river's western bank. In all likelihood, he did not actually reach Upper California. We know he sailed down the east coast of Baja California, then around Cabo San Lucas, pushing as far north as Cedros Island, which he discovered. In this vicinity, his two surviving ships — one had been lost earlier in foul weather — were forced to retreat in the face of severe storms. As to Ulloa's fate, that has yet to be finally determined.

Francisco Vásquez de Coronado's southwestern expedition of 1540–42 might well have sent one of its columns into southern California. It is well established that one column, under the command of Hernando de Alarcón, got as far as the Colorado River, and there is some likelihood that column may have sent a detachment across to reconnoiter the western bank; there are those who argue that brief. But from a purely documentary point of view, the honor of being the first recorded European to reach the present state of California falls to Juan Rodríguez Cabrillo. On September 28, 1542, he "discovered a very closed port in 34° 20′, which they named 'San Miguel.'" Later this port would be renamed San Diego by Sebastián Vizcaíno in 1602, the second

European to visit it. While there, though the language barrier was insurmountable, the Spaniards learned "that some people like us, that is bearded, dressed and armed like those on board the vessels, were going about inland. They showed by signs that these carried cross-bows and swords; . . . and further showed by signs that these were killing many of the native Indians." On October 8th, the expedition reached "a large bay, which they named 'Bahia de los Fumos' [Bay of Smokes] on account of the many smokes [fires] they saw there." This was either San Pedro or Santa Monica Bay, take your pick since the landfall is arguable. Again, what was first learned at San Miguel was confirmed by the Indians previously encountered, namely, "that men like the Spaniards, wearing clothes and having beards, were going around on the mainland." These two reports confirm that the coastal Indians had knowledge of the Coronado column that may or may not have pushed across the Colorado River into southern California, the only indirect evidence — granted hearsay — to make the case. But the point which is not disputable: here is the beginning of the written record of Spanish contact with southern California, the seeding of its Spanish heritage.

Another point to be made is singular: the use of the Spanish language for place names, beginning with San Miguel, later San Diego. One of the most enduring aspects of southern California's history is the survival of such place names. And these are legion: San Diego, San Juan Capistrano, San Luis Rey, Santa Monica, San Pedro, Los Angeles, Santa Barbara, etc. The use of such names stretches from Santa Rosa south to the border. Not only do cities and towns carry Spanish names, but also geographic features ranging from bays, canyons, deserts, mountains, rivers, and streams. Thus Los Angeles is ringed by the Santa Monica, San Gabriel, and San Bernardino mountains, to observe the obvious. Nor should one forget the impact of such place names on California geology — the San Andreas Fault being one. In addition, Spanish names dot many a city and town directory and map — business establishments (Taco Bell), parks, streets, subdivisions, not to mention churches, institutions (El Camino College), and missions. And again the obvious: many of these place names reflect the influence of the Catholic Church on Spanish culture, which in turn flavored southern California's historic heritage. This heritage dates from 1542 and is still in vogue with real estate developers and businessmen who are not always accurate in their modern usage of the language since there are blooper names in abundance, especially street names.

However, the effective discovery of California in 1542 by Cabrillo was not taken seriously by the Spanish until the reign of King Charles III. The primary reasons for this neglect was that the two major expeditions sent to California, Cabrillo in 1542, Vizcaíno in 1602, failed to find anything of material value which would stimulate Spanish interest. There was no discernible gold or silver, let alone pearls. Little did they know the rich treasure trove that lay dormant, awaiting discovery in the foothills of the Sierra Nevada Mountains.

Spain was finally galvanized into occupying its long neglected territorial claim to California in the late 1760s. In 1768 the "Sacred Expedition," as it was christened, was formulated and promulgated by José de Gálvez, Visitor General to New Spain (Mexico), while on a protracted visit to Baja California. Sending out three ships, one of which disappeared, and two expeditions by land via Baja California, the formal occupation of southern California was launched with the arrival of the *San Antonio* at San Diego on April 11, 1769; the *San Carlos* arrived on April 29. Finally, part of the land contingent made its appearance on May 14. The first permanent settlement was effected on May 17 at the foot of the present Presidio Hill. The second overland party reached San Diego on July 1, including Fray Junípero Serra, founder of the first Franciscan missions, beginning with Mission San Diego de Alcalá on July 16. Thus did the long task of fashioning a mission and a presidial system commence. By 1821, the end of Spanish rule, there were twenty missions scattered along El Camino Real, the King's Highway, and four royal presidios: San Diego, Monterey, Santa Barbara, San Francisco. Monterey was selected as the provincial capital in 1775. The culminating event came in early 1776, the year the American Revolution commenced on the Atlantic seaboard: the first civilian settlers were brought overland from Sonora by

Juan Bautista de Anza, 240 colonists in all, accompanied by 700 mules and horses, and over 300 cattle. Such was the beginning of the civilian population in Spanish California, one that numbered only about 3,000 by 1821, as well as laying the foundation of ranching in California, a feature so predominant in the life of the southland for much of its early decades. To cap matters, on June 1, 1779, Governor Felipe de Neve drafted his *"Reglamento."* This document was approved by the king on October 24, 1780 and provided for a complete code of legislation for California. Under its provision the pueblo of San Jose, founded in 1777, was reorganized, and the pueblo of Los Angeles was established on September 4, 1781.

One of the great ironies of history is that California was the last imperial colony established by Spain. It was founded during the budding American revolt against British colonial rule, 1768–81. What provoked Spain to undertake this last colonial venture? Pure and simple, the founding of California was motivated solely by the policy of defensive expansion. Rumors were abroad that the Russians in Unalaska were intent on pushing down the western Pacific coast, with California one of their intended objectives. Although this threat was at best rumor, it stimulated the Spanish government to action to implement its long held claim to California, one established by Cabrillo in 1542–43. Besides, if Russia moved into California, who knows, perhaps Mexico would be the next target of opportunity. Frankly, the Russians were not capable of undertaking such action due to their extraordinary supply problems. Unalaska could only receive supplies sent overland from Russia to Siberia's maritime provinces, then from thence, placed on ships for the final leg of a journey that measured in the thousands of miles. It was impossible to resupply from Baltic ports, for the distance was even greater than the land-ship route via Siberia. So the extended supply line proved a severe deterrent to any Russian dream of further North American expansion, other than the abortive and limited intrusion into Spanish California in 1810 at Bodega Bay and subsequently at nearby Fort Ross. However, this penetration was purely logistical and never had as one of its objectives providing a beachhead for Russian acquisition of California. Besides, the Russian timing was excellent: Spain was caught in the grips of the Napoleonic struggle for European dominion. Distracted and finally defeated, Spain never even attempted to purge California of the Russian presence, since it was soon recognized as posing no menace to the security of the province.

Up until the Napoleonic conflict, one which actually devoured sovereign Spain for several years, Spanish rule in California went unchallenged by settlers or the few foreign visitors who began to call at San Diego, San Pedro, Monterey, and San Francisco, beginning with the 1786 La Pérouse expedition, the first non-Spanish visitors to visit California, that is until 1818. Southern California received even fewer visitors, mostly American sailing ships, than the northland did. But none of these visitors actually posed a threat until the privateering expedition of Hippolyte Bouchard, flying the revolutionary flag of Buenos Aires, appeared on the coast in 1818. In late November, the two frigates after successfully attacking, capturing, and sacking Monterey, headed south for Santa Barbara. There on December 2, after plundering Rancho Refugio near Dos Pueblos, where resistance was offered by the alerted military authorities, the privateers anchored at Santa Barbara on December 6 to exchange prisoners, but did not attack the presidio. Sailing south, Bouchard landed at San Juan Capistrano on December 14, burned a few Indian dwellings, and then sailed the next day, leaving California without further ado.

But this introduction is not meant to recap the history of Spanish California in full. Rather, that history is best told and revealed in the essays which follow. These first appeared as articles in the *Southern California Quarterly* and are reprinted here since they detail the more important topics which highlight various aspects of the Spanish era in the southland. Written by recognized scholars in the field, they are multi-dimensional in content, displaying many of the rich facets which reflect Spanish rule in southern California's history. When originally published, the articles were annotated. A variety of considerations dictated that the notes be deleted from this anthology, but the curious reader can easily turn to the original issues and find the documentation. In addition, a biographical sketch of each contributor is included in the appendix along with reference to the specific issue of the quarterly in which the article originally appeared.

The Historical Society of Southern California is pleased to sponsor this quincentenary tribute to the Columbian discovery. In doing so, the Society recognizes that the history of the state owes much to its Spanish heritage, a heritage that was planted and nurtured in the course of several centuries, culminating in California becoming Spain's last colony. The era of Spanish rule, 1542–1821, especially from 1769, left indelible footprints on the Golden State's history and a remarkable legacy, one that is explored and elucidated in this anthology, *Southern California's Spanish Heritage*.

DOYCE B. NUNIS, JR.

Table of Contents

Southern California's
Spanish Heritage
AN ANTHOLOGY

The California Armada of Juan Rodríguez Cabrillo

BY HARRY KELSEY

JUAN RODRÍGUEZ CABRILLO brought the first European visitors to the shores of upper California in 1542. He was a soldier, sailor, shipbuilder, government administrator, and possibly even the first published author in California. Yet his expedition is poorly documented and his own considerable accomplishments are almost unknown. In order to understand the accomplishments of Juan Rodríguez, as he was usually called, it is necessary to look at the numerous original sources that comment on his expedition and to learn a bit about the armadas that belonged to his friend and commander, Don Pedro de Alvarado.

During the 1530s Alvarado, *adelantado* of Guatemala, assembled two large fleets with the intention of discovering and colonizing new lands for Spain. His long term goal was a voyage to the Moluccas and other islands in the Western Pacific, but these plans were often sidetracked, as we shall see.

On September 1, 1532, Alvarado reported to the king that he had just finished building eight ships which he intended to take on a voyage to Peru. The flagship was a galleon of three hundred tons. Three others were half that size. In addition there were three caravels of fifty or sixty tons, as well as a tender to serve all the ships.

Alvarado later confessed in an unusually frank moment that these were poor ships. He called them *navíos flacos* and resolved never again to command such a sorry fleet.

Moreover, the flagship was too large and ungainly for the extremely shallow and hazardous Guatemalan harbors, the best of which were little better than open roadsteads. Alvarado lost two vessels in these treacherous waters, before he finally decided to move his fleet to a better anchorage in the Gulf of Fonseca. It was here in March 1534 that Juan Rodríguez met the *adelantado*, bringing important messages and presumably sailing in his own ship.

Several of the vessels in that early armada did not belong to Alvarado. One in particular, the *San Antonio*, was the property of Juan Rodríguez Cabrillo. Two other ships in the armada belonged to Hernán Ponce and to the partners Pedro Bravo and Cristóbal Burgos. Another seems to have belonged to the late Governor Pedro Árias de Ávila, two to Gabriel de Rojas, and perhaps one to Cristobal Rodríguez.

Scarcely five months after the meeting in the Gulf of Fonseca, Alvarado had most of his fleet in Peru, though Juan Rodríguez and the *San Antonio* were not with him. In August 1534, Alvarado sold six of his ships to Diego de Almagro. He later claimed that Almagro paid him only a fraction of their value, but they can hardly have been worth a great deal.

Back home in Guatemala Juan Rodríguez Cabrillo had *San Antonio* in the river near Acajutla, rigging the ship and loading it with horses and trade goods for another trip to Peru. But before Rodríquez could put to sea, Alvarado returned from Peru and seized the ship for his own suddenly dwindling fleet. This pattern of mixing his own ships with those of his friends and lieutenants is precisely the practice Alvarado followed in his second armada, which included the ships sent to California with Cabrillo.

By late 1536 Alvarado was able to report to the king that he had the beginnings of a brand new fleet. He had bought "two ships of moderate burden and one large *bergantín*," all three of which were "already built and in the water." In addition Alvarado said he was "beginning to build in the shipyard three galleons of a hundred tons burden each and one galley, all of them equipped with oars." In a separate letter Bishop Francisco Marroquín of Santiago, Guatemala, wrote to the king, saying that Alvarado's newest ships were "built the best of any that sail the sea."

Cabrillo was not a novice shipbuilder. His experience extended back to the beginning of the Conquest, when he helped furnish materials for the *bergantines* used by Cortés in the final capture of Mexico City. Juan Rodríguez then went to Guatemala with Alvarado and was one of the first citizens of the new capital, Santiago.

It is not certain he was in charge of building the fleet for Alvarado in 1532, though this seems likely. By 1534, however, he was using the shipfitting facilities at Acajutla, Guatemala. After 1538, when Alvarado received royal permission to undertake explorations to the north and west, Cabrillo was the man responsible for building and refitting the ships of the armada. The port of Istapa became the base of operations, while the shipyard remained at Girabaltique.

Cabrillo had full authority to do whatever might be necessary to make the fleet seaworthy. Alvarado made him *justicia mayor* of Istapa, conferring on him the *vara de justicia* as the symbol of his office. This meant that he was administrative head of the municipal government and that he presided over the *cabildo* as deputy to the governor.

During much of this time, Alvarado himself was in Spain, leaving Juan Rodríguez at home to build the ships, and leaving his *mayordomo*, Álvaro de Paz, with instructions to furnish any materials or funds that might be needed for the project. When he returned, Alvarado brought with him a new wife and a whole retinue of servants and marriageable ladies, plus iron, sail cloth, and other supplies for the new fleet.

Years later Antonio de Remesal wrote that huge numbers of Indians were forced to work on the shipbuilding project, cutting timber, building a road, and carrying sails and iron overland from Puerto de Caballos in the Gulf of Mexico to Istapa on the Pacific Coast. Bartolomé de Las Casas, who saw it all, said:

He killed an infinite number of people in building the ships; from the north to the south sea a hundred and thirty leagues the Indians carried anchors of three and four *quintales*, which cut furrows into the shoulders and loins of some of them. And he carried in the same way much artillery on the shoulders of these sad naked people; and I saw many loaded with artillery on those anguished roads. He broke up homes, taking the

5

women and girls and giving them to the soldiers and sailors in order to keep them satisfied and bring them into his fleets.

There is much more to the story, but this passage says enough about the character of the men in the armada. Juan Rodríguez, the man in charge of building the fleet, was responsible for a great part of this villainy.

By midsummer of 1540 a fleet of a dozen ships was ready to sail, while one more ship was under construction and nearly finished. Three quarters of a century later Remesal said the fleet was one of the finest ever built on the coast of Central America. García de Palacio thought differently, calling the vessels "very small ships." Probably both statements were true. Ships of a hundred or two hundred tons were indeed small. But if cost is any indication of quality, the fleet should have been a good one. It was widely rumored to have been one of the most costly ever constructed. Bernal Díaz, who was there, said that eighty vessels could have been built in Spain for the same price.

For various reasons historians have been confused about the names and numbers of the ships in Alvarado's fleet. Henry Raup Wagner quoted sources that seemed to set the number of ships at thirteen. Hubert Howe Bancroft, using the same sources, plus a few others, said there could have been as few as ten. The differences between the sources may be more apparent than real. In most cases the variations are accounted for by the fact that there were different numbers of ships present at different times.

For example, in November 1540, Alvarado claimed ownership of twelve vessels: nine large ships, a galley, a *fusta*, and a *fragata*. Four months later, in March 1541, he reported only eleven vessels in his fleet: nine large ships, a galley, and a fusta. He did not count the fragata, because she was on the way back to Guatulco, as Pilot Luis González later reported.

The fragata was named *San Miguel*. This small vessel later rejoined the fleet, but without González, who stayed in Guatemala, perhaps because of the terrible earthquake that occurred there in September 1541.

Bernaldo de Molina, who saw the fleet at Acajutla in August

1540, told the chronicler Oviedo that the fleet consisted of three galleons of more than two hundred tons, seven other ships of a hundred tons or more, a very beautiful *galera*, and two *fustas*. Moreover, Molina had a painting of the fleet which he showed to Oviedo before he took it to Spain, having been dispatched with a report from Alvarado to the king.

None of this contradicts Alvarado's statement in November 1540 that he had twelve ships in the harbor at Santiago, plus another *que se hace de nuevo*. Nor does it contradict the testimony of several contemporary witnesses, who all reported that Alvarado had a fleet of thirteen vessels. The total never changed, though the number present for duty in one place sometimes varied.

None of these ships was larger than two hundred tons burden. The three-hundred-ton vessel Alvarado had owned in 1532 was simply too large for the shallow harbors on the west coast of New Spain, as the navigator and shipbuilder García de Palacio reported some years later.

The thirteen vessels in Alvarado's armada were:

1. *Santiago*, a galleon, and the *capitana* or flagship
2. *San Salvador*, a galleon, and the *almiranta* or ship of the officer second in command of the fleet; also called *Juan Rodríguez*
3. *Diosdado*, a galleon
4. *San Jorge*
5. *San Antonio*
6. *San Francisco*
7. *San Juan de Letrán*
8. *Figueroa*
9. *Alvar Nuñez* — one of these was probably also called *Victoria*
10. *Anton Hernández*
11. *San Christóval*, a galera
12. *San Marín*, a fusta
13. *San Míguel*, a fragata

Just as Alvarado had convinced Juan Rodríguez Cabrillo to build and equip the fleet, he also convinced him to sail north as *almirante*, or second in command of the armada. Doubtless, one reason the almirante accepted the command was that his own ship,

7

San Salvador, had been requisitioned by Alvarado to accompany the fleet.

Sailing north from Guatemala, Alvarado took his fleet first to Guatulco to pick up additional supplies. There he met emissaries from Viceroy Mendoza who told him the supplies could be made available only at the port of Santiago in the province of Colima. Since Mendoza was by royal edict a one-third partner in the enterprise and a man to be consulted in the operations thereof, Alvarado had little choice but to sail north as he was told.

Luis González, who joined the fleet in Guatulco, has left some interesting information about the fleet and Juan Rodríguez. His testimony, given in 1560, was recorded in the third person, as was common Spanish practice in that era.

The witness was in the port of Guatulco and he saw the armada of the said adelantado enter [the port] and it went on up to the coast of Colima of New Spain for the said voyage [of discovery] and the said Johan Rs Cabrillo went in his own ship which flew the banner of an almirante from the foretopmast as almirantes of the sea are accustomed to do.

From Guatulco the fleet sailed on to Acapulco. *San Míguel,* with Pilot Luis González aboard, then turned around and sailed back to Guatulco, and ultimately to Guatemala, probably carrying dispatches. The rest of the fleet went on to Santiago, Colima, where the viceroy's agents tried to negotiate a new agreement with Alvarado, who insisted that he would only deal with the viceroy himself.

Finally, on November 29, 1540, Alvarado and Mendoza signed a document which gave the viceroy a half interest in Alvarado's fleet, plus half of any profits that might be made from his expedition. Alvarado received in return a half interest in Mendoza's own fleet and in his expedition to Cíbola as well. Since Alvarado did not own all the ships listed in his contract with the viceroy, he was actually giving little or nothing away, even though the viceroy made him a partner in the expected profits from the expedition of Francisco Vásquez de Coronado. Once the bargain was made the partners moved their fleets to Navidad, a nearby port discovered by Cabrillo near Santiago on the Colima coast.

The almirante's own feeling about the contract between Alvarado and Mendoza was summed up very nicely in a statement he made on September 1, 1541, just a few months before leaving for California.

It may be six years, more or less, when the aforesaid governor went to Spain and at the time he was going he charged me with building an armada for him in the meantime and then I built it and served in making the said armada which is the one he brought to this port of la navidad and with my own means I built a ship named sant salvador which is anchored in this port and at my own expense without the governor or his stewards' putting anything whatever into it.

The new partners soon made preparations for sending out several naval expeditions. One, under Ruy López de Villalobos, a protegé of Mendoza, would have taken three ships and a galera to the Moluccas. Another under Juan de Alvarado, nephew of the adelantado, was to have taken five ships and a fusta to explore the coast of California.

During the next few months there was great scurrying around Navidad (where the fleet was stationed), Acapulco (the supply base), and Girabaltique (the partners' shipyard, where another ship was under construction). Since the partners were now sending out several armadas, there was a good deal of new work to be done.

On April 29, 1541, Alvarado and Mendoza met in Mexico City to issue orders for an expedition to sail north along the coast of California, though the land did not then have that name. The fleet was to be commanded by Diego López de Zúñiga, Mendoza's lieutenant governor. Among the five vessels in the proposed armada were "the ship of Juan Rodríguez" and another called simply "the black galleon." The context seems to imply that Juan Rodríguez's ship was to be the almiranta again.

A month later, on May 31, 1541, Mendoza ordered Hernando de Alarcón to prepare his own three vessels for another voyage up the Gulf of California.

Before either of these armadas could leave, an Indian war in the interior of Mexico reached such a crisis that Mendoza had to ask

Alvarado for help. The old conquistador promptly stripped men, supplies, and guns from his fleet, appointed Almirante Juan Rodríguez Cabrillo to command his fleet and men at Navidad, and departed for the scene of the fighting. A few weeks later Don Pedro de Alvarado was dead. All the great plans for exploration and conquest were suddenly thrown into a state of uncertainty and suspense.

Faced with an Indian war of increasingly serious proportions, Mendoza changed his mind about the voyage up the California coast. Instead of sending López de Zúñiga with five ships, he decided to dispatch Francisco de Bolaños as commander of a smaller fleet.

Since Alvarado had taken most of the men and supplies with him, the remaining ships were no longer prepared for a long sea voyage. It is unlikely that they remained idly at anchor in Navidad, but just as unlikely that any of them strayed very far from familiar coastal areas.

Bernal Díaz del Castillo, who was then living in Guatemala, said that all the ships of the armada scattered as soon as the commanders received word of Alvarado's death. Juan Rodríguez Cabrillo himself seems to have waited at Navidad long enough to see the other ships safely out to sea. Bolaños and his armada of three ships departed on September 8, 1541. Alarcón had been sent off for duty at Autlán with the men and guns from his three ships. Nonetheless, he seems also to have come back to Navidad in time to take his ships to sea on September 8, 1541. Without proper supplies, he probably made only a brief trip up the coast and accomplished little or nothing.

Events in Guatemala also helped to thwart the exploration plans. On the tenth of September 1541, an earthquake and flood destroyed the city of Santiago, where more than a thousand perished. Men from Alvarado's force who had not already gone back to Guatemala would certainly have done so at this point. Juan Rodríguez very likely returned home at this time. He could hardly have kept his men and ships idle in the port of Navidad, when they were so sorely needed in Guatemala.

In fact, a little pamphlet printed in Mexico City in the last part of 1541 and signed *Juan Rodríguez, escribano*, says that very thing: "The *Señores* of the whole land have come here, concerned about what has happened."

The name of the document in question is *Relación del espantable terremoto que agora nuevamente acontecido en las yndias en una ciudad llamada Guatimala*. Juan Rodríguez Cabrillo is not known definitely to be the author of this document, though he easily could have been.

He was always known in Guatemalan records simply as Juan Rodríguez. This was common Spanish practice. The use of the name Cabrillo would not have been necessary unless there were another prominent Juan Rodríguez in the neighborhood with whom he could have been confused.

The printed *Relación* probably originated in a letter or report from Juan Rodríguez to someone in Mexico City. There is good reason to suppose that the addressee was Juan de Alvarado, vice commander of the adelantado's military forces. He apparently had a copy of the *Relación* as early as November 1541, when Bishop Marroquín reported him as having departed for Spain. On a stopover in Cuba Juan de Alvarado gave a copy of the *Relación* to Juan de Lobera, who sent it on to Oviedo in Santo Domingo, where it arrived before the end of January 1542.

These circumstances make Juan de Alvarado a likely prospect as the man who had the *Relación* printed in Mexico City in late 1541. They also give an indication of the way in which Juan Rodríguez came to be called escribano, a term perhaps selected by the printer Juan Pablos to indicate the name of the man who wrote the letter. In addition the little pamphlet helps to explain what Juan Rodríguez was doing in the year that elapsed between the time of Alvarado's injury and death in early July 1541, and the departure of the armada for California in late June 1542.

While all this was going on, Viceroy Mendoza had taken personal command of the troops that were attempting to suppress the Indian uprising. It was not until the spring of 1542 that he was able to begin thinking again about the expeditions he and Alvarado had planned. By that time all the work of preparation had to be done again.

11

Not only were the ships scattered in various ports, there had also been some bad luck with the three vessels in the Bolaños armada. The capitana and the almiranta had broken their masts and were laid up somewhere in Lower California. The viceroy told Bolaños to bring these ships back to Navidad.

By March 10, 1542, Mendoza had ordered someone— presumably Juan Rodríguez—to prepare two other vessels for another voyage up the California coast. He had three additional ships and a *galeota* that he intended to send to the Moluccas under the command of Ruy López de Villalobos, and their refitting was also entrusted to Juan Rodríguez.

The work went so well that Mendoza was able to send six vessels to the Moluccas, including the two that had returned from the Bolaños expedition with broken masts. The flagship on the Moluccas voyage was *Santiago*, the ship Alvarado had used as his own flagship and doubtless one of his two-hundred-ton galleons. The other three ships were *San Jorge* and *San Antonio*, two of Alvarado's hundred- ton vessels, and *San Juan de Letrán*, also a hundred tonner and perhaps the ship *que se hace de nuevo* in the words of his letter of March 1541.

None of the ships in this armada or in the one sent to California belonged to Mendoza himself. Alvarado in his will had ordered his heirs to carry out the terms of his agreement with Mendoza. Because of the huge debts incurred in building the fleet, no one would step forward to claim the estate. Mendoza apparently felt he was helping the creditors by sending these vessels to sea where there might be some potential for profit—perhaps another Mexico or another Peru.

Bishop Marroquín, Alvarado's executor, knew how slim these chances were. Still, he could do little beyond ordering that the three vessels belonging to Juan Rodríguez, Santos de Figueroa and his partners, and the heirs of Antonio Diosdado be paid for out of any proceeds that might accrue to the estate.

After the armada for the Moluccas voyage had been chosen, there were still seven ships from which Juan Rodríguez could select his own fleet. All sources seem to agree that his flagship was *San Salvador*, which was probably a galleon and one of Alvarado's three vessels of two-hundred tons burden.

The seventeenth century Spanish historian Herrera seems to say one of the ships was a two-hundred-ton vessel. His evidence is not always reliable, but in this case his account is supported by the testimony of the sixteenth century Spanish chronicler, Oviedo, who talked to a witness and also saw a picture of the fleet.

Herrera did his research nearly three quarters of a century after the fact, but he apparently had access to original documents not now available. Therefore, his undocumented assertion that one of the ships was named *Victoria* is doubtless reliable, because there is no evidence to the contrary. However, Herrera also says there were only two ships on the journey to California; there is good reason to think he was mistaken in this case, as we shall see later.

Two men who sailed to California with this armada gave brief accounts of the journey in response to questions prepared by Juan Rodríguez *el mozo*, son and heir of the explorer. Their testimony was given at Santiago de Guatemala on April 26, 1560.

Lázaro de Cárdenas said that after Alvarado's death Ruy López de Villalobos was made captain general of the armada. Following a trip to Mexico City, Ruy López brought back orders making Juan Rodríguez captain general of a three-ship armada to explore the coast. Cárdenas remembered the details because he had accompanied Ruy López on the journey from Mexico City: "Ruylopez brought here an order from the viceroy and the royal *audiencia* in which they made Johan Rs. Cabrillo Captain general of one ship [his own] and of two other ships for discovering the coast." Francisco de Vargas, the other member of the expedition, agreed that there were three ships in the armada, which he said also included a small escort vessel or bergantín.

The testimony offered by these two men was not limited to their own personal experience. As was common practice in Spanish legal proceedings, they could also testify to facts that were "common knowledge" (*público y notorio*) in the community. They took their oaths on April 19, 1560, then had several days to discuss their recollections of events, as they doubtless had done on many occasions since 1543. When these men said there were three ships in the armada, they were giving not only their own recollections of

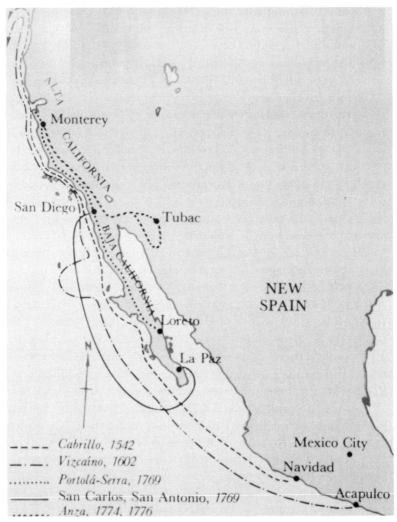

The major Spanish-sponsored expeditions sent to Alta California are indicated on this map, beginning with the Cabrillo expedition. *Courtesy Copley Press.*

events, they were also recording the reports of other participants that were "common knowledge" in Guatemala at that time. The interrogator knew in advance that the answers would agree with the questions that had been proposed. The notary simply summarized their responses in the third person, frequently noting only that the respondent had affirmed the information in the question.

There are other sixteenth century sources that say something about the size of this fleet. One of these is Viceroy Mendoza's *interrogatorio* of January 8, 1547. In this document the viceroy said that when the expedition returned from California, he sent the sailors off again to Peru with three ships, presumably the very same ones they had sailed for Juan Rodríguez Cabrillo. Several facts emerge from this document. First, the crews were large enough to handle three ships. Moreover, there was room on board those ships for the original crew of Juan Rodríguez, plus the horses and supplies Mendoza was sending to Peru for trade.

Additional information about the size of the armada comes from the set of instructions prepared by Mendoza and Alvarado on April 29, 1541. These papers described an expedition of six sailing vessels. The armada was to explore and colonize the coast of California. If a good place for a settlement were found, the commander was to remain there with three of the vessels. His almirante would then complete the exploration of the coast, using "the ship of Juan Rodríguez, the galleon *prieto* and the fusta."

This was a sizable armada. Bolaños had three ships in his own less ambitious armada, and since there were still seven vessels left for use by Juan Rodríguez, it is unlikely that Juan Rodríguez, almirante of the entire fleet, would have been sent to explore a longer stretch of coast with only one small ship and a single escort vessel.

In the face of all this evidence to the contrary, it seems surprising that so many historians have accepted the story that only two vessels made the voyage to California in 1542–43. The only evidence to support such a claim is a brief summary that appeared seventy years later in a general history of Spanish discoveries in the New World. This is the account written by Antonio de Herrera. It appears to be based on the original documents, though none of them are specified. In any case, it is clearly not firsthand testimony.

A similar but much longer account was prepared in 1543 by Juan Páez. This man lived in Guatemala, knew Juan Rodríguez and the others, and may even have gone with the fleet to Colima, where his married daughter had her home. It is even possible that Páez went to California as official notary of one of the ships, but this is not certain.

One thing is certain. Both Herrera and the Páez accounts refer in several places to more than two ships. Since these two texts have been so widely used by historians writing about the expedition, it might be well to take a closer look at each of them.

In the Juan Páez account the entry for Wednesday, November 1, 1542, says: *"Los del otro navio pasaron más trabajo y rriesgo q los de la capitana por ser el navio peqeño y no tener puente."* The meaning here is that one of the ships was small and did not have a sterncastle (puente), unlike the flagship (capitana), which seemingly did have a sterncastle.

For Wednesday, February 28, 1543, a similar entry reads: *"Las mares . . . pasaban por encima de los nabios que a no tener puentes."* Here the meaning is that the seas washed over the ships that had no sterncastles. Obviously, more than one ship did not have a sterncastle. Thus it appears from the Páez journal that while the capitana had a sterncastle, at least two others did not.

A number of writers—Richard Stuart Evans, Alexander Smith Taylor, George Davidson, and Herbert E. Bolton—have thought that a ship without a puente had no deck at all; it was simply an open boat. Henry Raup Wagner knew the meaning of the term but could not bring himself to use it properly. Obviously, there is confusion not only about the numbers of ships but about their size and superstructure as well.

The problem arises from the use of the words puente and *cubierta*, both of which mean "deck," but each in a somewhat different manner. Herrera, who wrote the first published account of the voyage, said in one place: *"El un Navio alijó todo lo que llevaba, sobre cubierta."* The storm was so bad that one of the ships lost all the cargo that was being carried on deck.

A further statement made it clear that the ship in question was not the flagship. As the author explained, the ship was a *navio pequeño*, or a small ship: *"Como no tenia Puente, havia alijado todo lo de cubierta, i hacia mucha Agua."* Since it had no puente, it had lost everything carried on the cubierta.

Obviously the meaning of the words puente and cubierta are important to an understanding of the Herrera and Páez accounts. In the *Instrucción Náutica* of 1587, Diego García de Palacio gave a careful description of the construction and terminology used in ships of the time. The lowest level of a ship was called the *plan.* Each deck above that, including the main deck, was called a cubierta. The sterncastle or aftercabin was called a puente.

Herrera and Páez, who both apparently saw the same original accounts of the expedition, agree that all the ships in the fleet had decks (*cubiertas*). They both also seem to agree that at least one of the ships had a sterncastle (puente), while one or more other vessels did not.

Páez wrote his account in 1542. He may have been a member of the expedition, though this is not certain. However, he does agree with the two known participants, Vargas and Cárdenas, that there were three ships in the expedition. Herrera, who wrote three quarters of a century later, apparently had not talked to participants.

Nonetheless, there are enough similarities in their accounts to lead to the conclusion that both Páez and Herrera saw the same original reports. One of these was perhaps the missing relación written by Juan Rodríguez Cabrillo. The others could have been the accounts written by Cárdenas or Vargas. And all the evidence seems to say that there were three ships. The failure of Cárdenas to mention a bergantín is not particularly significant. It was common practice in those days to send one or more small vessels along with every fleet. The boat could be a fusta, a galeota, or even a bergantín. The terms were almost interchangeable; any of the vessels could be propelled by oars or sails, depending on the need.

In his letter of November 1539, Alvarado reported that he had a bergantín with thirteen banks of oars. The Juan Páez summary journal makes no reference to a bergantín. However, it does refer to a *batel*, in fact to more than one batel.

Bateles were commonly twenty or twenty-five feet in length, with seven banks of oars. Every ship had one, to set the anchor or bring it in, to load or discharge cargo, to tow the ship into or out of port. Bateles could be relatively large; bergantines could be very small. Even men familiar with the sea could mix them up. Perhaps the larger of the bateles was the bergantín reported by Francisco de Vargas.

Statements in the Páez summary journal make it certain that all three of the ships were square-rigged and had topsails on both the foremast and the mainmast. This is clear from the description of the way in which his ships ran before a storm with only a lower sail on the foremast.

On February 27 the ships ran all day to the west-northwest *con los trinquetes baxos*. Some days later, with the storm still raging, the ships ran before the wind *con los trinquetes baxitos*. Both these phrases refer to the lower sails on the foremast.

The following Sunday, still in the grip of the storm, they sailed before the wind *con sendos papos de velas en los trinquetes*. This means that each ship had a small stormsail on the foremast.

Herrera gave a similar description of the rigging used during the storm: *en cinco Dias corrieron docientas leguas, con los Papahigos de los trinquetes*. In five days they sailed two hundred leagues with only the lower sails on the foremasts.

There is additional evidence about the rigging of the flagship *San Salvador*. Luis González, who was pilot on one of Alvarado's vessels, later testified as follows concerning this matter: "Johan Rs. Cabrillo went in his own ship which flew the banner of an almirante from its foretopmast . . . and this witness spoke with his pilot and knew it to be his ship."

All these references mean that each of the ships, large and small alike, was square-rigged. The foremast was rigged with a topmast. The mainmast, therefore, had a similar rig, and there must have been a mizzenmast, perhaps with a lateen rig.

Having discovered the names of all the ships in Alvarado's fleet, and having studied the size and rig of John Rodríguez Cabrillo's armada, it is possible to make some close estimates about names and tonnages in the fleet he brought to California.

San Salvador and *Victoria* were certainly two of the ships. The third vessel could have been *San Francisco* or one of the three vessels that we know only by their secular names.

Common Spanish practice in those days gave a vessel a religious name, which was its official title. In daily usage, however, a ship was called by the name of its owner or commander. Thus, *San Salvador* was also called *Juan Rodríguez*. The religious names of *Diosdado*, *Figueroa*, *Alvar Nuñez*, and *Anton Hernández* are not known.

In all probability *Diosdado* was not in the California fleet. She was a galleon and thus too large to be one of the smaller vessels brought to California.

This leaves *San Francisco*, *Figueroa*, *Alvar Nuñez*, and *Anton Hernández*. One of the latter three may have had the religious name *Victoria*, the ship listed by Herrera as the second vessel on the expedition. Two of these four ships apparently made the trip to California, but it is unclear which two did so.

The bergantín or fragata was doubtless *San Míguel*, the only other escort vessel in Alvarado's fleet. She had a single mast and a lateen sail. During long runs bateles were either towed by the ship or stowed on her deck. If this fragata were a batel, she would have been handled the same way.

San Míguel was probably the fragata mentioned by Alvarado in November 1540, when she was beached for repairs in the port of Acapulco. On the voyage to California Juan Rodríguez also had to put this small vessel ashore for repairs to her hull.

The flagship, *San Salvador*, was a galleon about a hundred feet in length, with a sterncastle and a forecastle. She had a relatively slim hull—about twenty-five feet of beam—a square stern, and a good deal of taper from main deck to the top of the sterncastle.

The other two ships were uncastled but square-rigged like *San Salvador*. They were probably carracks, round-bellied vessels that easily fit Alvarado's description, *novíos gruesos*.

These were sound ships, well equipped and well manned. Remesal said the fleet was "larger and better than any that sailed the South Sea up to that time or for many years thereafter." Everyone who saw the fleet held the same opinion, a tribute to the skill and ability of Juan Rodríguez Cabrillo as sailor, administrator, and manager of Alvarado's shipyard.

The events of the journey to California are well known, at least so far as they are revealed in the report of Juan Páez. The vessels sailed up the coast of California, well past Monterey. But they did not reach the Moluccas or the Spice Islands or any other rich lands. Moreover, the men suffered terribly from the cold and wet and from Indian assaults on their winter camp. Finally, the commander himself, Juan Rodríguez Cabrillo, was injured and died, and his men decided to return home. Within months there was nothing left of the great fleet Juan Rodríguez had built for Alvarado. Remesal says: "The entire fleet perished, some ships eaten by shipworms, others scattered to different ports in disorder, because the Adelantado had died."

A report was prepared and sent to Spain, where a minor official read it and wrote on the cover: "No ymporta." It was simply not significant enough to be brought to the attention of the Council of the Indies. Instead, it was sent along to the archives to be stored with the records of countless other forgotten expeditions to the frontiers of New Spain.

Symbolic Acts of Sovereignty in Spanish California

BY MANUEL P. SERVÍN

SPANISH CALIFORNIA, like the rest of the Spanish territories in the Americas, was originally claimed by the crown of Castile by means of symbolic acts of sovereignty. These symbolic acts, first used by the Portuguese in claiming their discoveries of the islands and the coasts of Africa and later introduced by Columbus in the discovery of the New World, consisted in general of four different parts: the religious ceremony, the proclamation claiming the territory, the symbolic ritual by which ownership or sovereignty was obtained, and the formal attestation taken by a notary. With few exceptions, either the complete symbolic ceremony or portions of it were used by various navigators and explorers of the great colonial powers of Europe — Spain, Portugal, England, and France — in establishing their nation's claim to American territories. But of greater importance than the practice of establishing claim by symbolic acts in newly discovered lands was the fact that "such discovery with symbolic taking possession constituted legal title to *terra nullius* in North America prior to 1700." Thus, California, at least from the southern tip of the peninsula of Lower California to the area of southern California, became Spanish territory by virtue of possession-taking, before it was permanently settled.

Notwithstanding the importance of symbolic acts of sovereignty in establishing Spain's claim to California, this aspect of the province's history has been virtually neglected. Furthermore, the students of the state's history who have an organized knowledge of possession-taking activities in California appear to be few indeed.

Possession-taking activities in California began with the *Con-*

21

quistador, Hernán Cortés. Cortés, having heard of a legendary "island entirely populated by women . . . which is very rich in pearls and gold," determined as early as 1524 to explore this apparently wealthy area. This project was, however, delayed until 1532 when he sent his exploratory expedition of two ships under Diego Hurtado de Mendoza. This expedition failed, and in the following year Cortés dispatched a second one under the command of Diego Becerra de Mendoza and Hernando Grijalva. While Grijalva and his crew discovered and solemnly claimed the Revillagigedo Islands by an act of possession, Becerra was killed and supplanted by Fortún Jiménez de Bertandoña. Jiménez, the mutineer, leading his ship across off the Gulf of California, became the effective discoverer of La Paz, and therefore of California. He, however, failed to claim the territory on behalf of Castile, and thus allowed Cortés this distinction.

The failure of Cortés' two previous expeditions, coupled with Jiménez' report of the "abundance of pearls at La Paz," moved the Conquistador to lead the next expedition personally. Recruiting men and obtaining supplies for the establishment of a permanent settlement, Cortés sailed for La Paz with about a third of the party. Landing at La Paz Bay on May 3, 1535, the feast day of the Finding of the Holy Cross, he renamed the port Santa Cruz (Holy Cross) and proceeded to claim the area by the first symbolic act of sovereignty performed in California. This act, as the *procèsverbal* that follows reveals, presented an impressive picture:

On the third day of May in the year one thousand five hundred and thirty-five of Our Lord, which is this day and which more or less could be noon, the Very Illustrious Señor, Don Fernando Cortés, Marqués del Valle de Oaxaca, Captain General of New Spain and of the South Sea for His Majesty, etc., arrived at a port and bay of a land newly discovered on the aforesaid South Sea by means of a ship and an armada of the aforementioned Señor Marqués. His Lordship arrived at the aforesaid port with ships and an armada; and having arrived, he jumped on land, accompanied by his men and horses. Standing on it at the beach, in the presence of me, Martín de Castro, notary of His Majesty and of the aforementioned Señor Marqués' government, he explained by word of mouth and said that on behalf of His Majesty and by virtue of the latter's royal provision and in fulfillment of what had been contracted with His Majesty concerning the discovery of the aforesaid South Sea, he had discovered the aforesaid land by means of his ship and armada; that in order to conquer and colonize and pursue the aforesaid discovery, he had come with his armada and men; that therefore he wishes to take possession of the aforesaid land and of all the other lands which from it may continue, be found, and discovered; and that therefore he was asking, did ask, and ordered of me, the aforementioned notary, to give testimony of what he had said and of what would take place.

Then the aforementioned Señor Marqués, taking the aforesaid possession in the name of His Majesty and by virtue of the aforesaid provisions and contracts, said that he takes and seizes on behalf of His Majesty the possession of the aforesaid newly discovered land where we now are and of all the other lands which are contiguous and which are situated in those territories and delimitations, so that using this land as a beginning he may pursue the discovery, conquest, and colonization of them in His Majesty's name. As a sign and act of the aforesaid possession, the aforementioned Señor Marqués named the aforesaid port and bay, Puerto y Bahía de Santa Cruz; and he walked back and forth on the aforesaid land, throwing sand from one place to another; and with his sword in hand he cut certain trees that were there; and he ordered the men who were present to acknowledge him as His Majesty's governor of those aforesaid lands; and he performed other acts of possession. While his Lordship was doing this, he said that in behalf of His Majesty and by virtue of the aforesaid provisions and contracts, he is acknowledged and was acknowledged as having obtained and as having received the occupancy and possession of this aforesaid land where we now are, with all the other lands which are near and within its territory and which, in the pursuance of the aforesaid discovery, he may discover and find, with the intention of pursuing their conquest and colonization. All this took place peacefully and without the contradiction of anyone who may have been or appeared there. The aforementioned Señor Marqués ordered that it be attested to in a legal instrument, and I, the notary, gave him the abovesaid, which I witnessed, on the aforesaid day, month, and year. That witnesses, who were present at what has been related, are Dr. Valdesbieso, *alcalde mayor*, and Juan de Gaso, and Alonso de Navarette, and Fernán Darías de Saavedra, and Bernardino de Castillo, and Francisco de Ulloa, and many others of the aforesaid army and armada — I, Martín de Castro, His Majesty's notary, affix my notarial mark under these circumstances in testimony of the truth — Martín de Castro, notary.

23

Unfortunately, Cortés was not as successful in establishing a colony and in finding pearls as he was in performing the ceremony of possession-taking. Despite the three unsuccessful expeditions to the "island" of California, he determined to embark on a fourth venture in search of the fabled Seven Cities of Cíbola. Prevented by his rival, Viceroy Antonio de Mendoza, from travelling overland to present-day New Mexico, Cortés dispatched an expedition under Francisco de Ulloa in hopes of reaching Cíbola from the sea. Ulloa sailed up the Gulf of California to its head, ascertained the peninsularity of California, and solemnly took possession in the area of the mouth of the Colorado River with this very brief act translated by Henry R. Wagner:

I, Pedro de Palencia, notary public of this armada, bear true witness to all to whose eyes these presents shall come (whom God, Our Lord, honor and preserve from evil) that on the twenty eighth day of the month of September of the year fifteen hundred and thirty-nine the very magnificent Señor Francisco de Ulloa, governor's lieutenant and captain of this armada for the very illustrious Señor Marques del Valle de Oaxaca in the Ancon de San Andres and Mar Bermejo, which is on the coast of this New Spain, toward the north, in latitude $33^{1}/2°$, took possession for the said Señor Marques del Valle in the name of the emperor, our master, king of Castile, actually and in reality; placing his hand upon his sword, saying that if any person disputed it, he was ready to defend it, with his sword cutting trees, pulling up grass, moving stones from one place to another, and from there to another, and taking water from the sea and throwing it upon the land, all in token of the said possession.

Witnesses who were present when this was done, Reverend Fathers of the Order of Saint Francis, Father fray Raimundo, Father fray Antonio de Meno; Francisco de Terrazas, inspector; Diego de Haro, Gabriel Marques.

Done this day, month and year aforesaid.

And I, Pedro de Palencia, notary public of this armada, recorded it as it occurred in my presence and in conclusion made here this, my notarial mark, in testimony of the truth.

Pedro de Palencia, notary public.

Frater Raimundus Anyelibus. Frater Antonio de Meno. Gabriel Marques. Diego de Haro. Francisco de Terrazas.

Ulloa, having thus taken possession, sailed down the cape, around the tip of the peninsula, and up the western coast as far north as Isla de Cedros. During the rest of the voyage Ulloa took solemn possession of the peninsula by four other acts: two in the gulf areas of Bahía de los Angeles and of Loreto, and two in the Pacific Ocean regions of Isla de Santa Margarita and of Isla de Cedros. Thus by 1539 Cortés, as the result of Ulloa's voyage, had extended Spain's territorial claims on the western coast of North America to the mouth of the Colorado River on the gulf and to the Isla de Cedros on the shores of the Pacific.

Ulloa's voyage marked an end to Cortés' discoveries and possession-taking activities in North America and in California. Viceroy Mendoza, however, continued where the Conquistador stopped. By April 1541, Mendoza, with his unscrupulous partner Pedro de Alvarado, prepared instructions for Diego López de Zúñiga and Gonzalo de Ovalle for a proposed voyage northward along the "coast of the South Sea." Although there is much uncertainty regarding the execution of the voyage, the instructions are important because they reveal both the official Spanish attitude to possession-taking and the Viceroy's interest in enlarging New Spain's territory by discovery and symbolic acts of sovereignty. Article VII of the instructions, which treats the performance of symbolic acts, stated:

Having received the fleet in this manner and having made sail, you will follow the coast of New Spain to Chiametla, . . . thence following the coast in quest of the Isla de Cedros where you will provide yourself with wood and water. Then, with the aid of Our Lord, following the coast closely as it opens up, you will from there onward all along make stops and take possession according to the minute which for that purpose you carry with you, so that all the coast you leave behind may be inspected and known and notice be had of what there is, so that it may be ascertained which is the best. . . .

The instruction to "make stops and take possession according to the minute" apparently was not carried out. The expedition, damaged by storms, did not sail beyond, nor reach, the Isla de Cedros where Ulloa had previously taken solemn possession. Mendoza, however, was not dissuaded by the failure, for preparations for another voyage were begun immediately.

Chosen as head of the new expedition for the voyage was the seasoned mariner Juan Rodríguez Cabrillo, future discoverer of Upper California. Rodríguez Cabrillo, who in all probability received orders similar to those of Zúñiga, departed from Navidad on June 27, 1542, sailed up the western coast of the peninsula, but did not begin performing symbolic acts of sovereignty until he passed the Isla de Cedros. Rodríguez Cabrillo landed and first took possession at San Quintín, which he named Puerto de la Posesión. (Unfortunately, his instruments of possession-taking have not been found, and therefore the actual ceremony he performed is still unknown.) Continuing north along the coast of the peninsula, he again landed and took possession first in the area of present-day Cabo Colnett and Santo Tomás which was (perhaps erroneously) named San Martín, and then in present-day Ensenada which he named San Mateo. Sailing from San Mateo, Rodríguez Cabrillo "discovered a port, closed and very good, which they named San Miguel," and thus became the discoverer of Upper California. Despite his stay of six days at San Diego, Cabrillo did not perform any possession-taking ceremonies. Not until his arrival at Pueblo de las Canoas, possibly in the area of Mugu Lagoon just south of Ventura, did Cabrillo formally take possession of the newly discovered territory. Although he may have also taken possession at San Miguel Island on the Santa Barbara Channel and did attempt to perform an act of sovereignty probably at Monterey (Bahía de los Pinos), neither Cabrillo nor his successor Bartolomé Ferrer, who commanded the expedition perhaps as far north as the Oregon boundary, ever took possession of the country above the Channel Islands. Thus Rodríguez Cabrillo, despite his discovery and exploration of the western coast of Upper California, failed to establish a Spanish claim to the area of central and northern California.

Actually, the English, through Francis Drake's possession-taking activities, first attempted to establish a claim to this territory. The intrepid Drake, a consummate navigator and an unscrupulous pirate, arrived in the area north of San Francisco after successfully plundering Valparaíso and Callao, and capturing the treasure galleon *Cacafuego.* Landing in "a faire and good Baye," Drake not only performed an act of sovereignty establishing England's claim by nailing his famous brass plate, but also initiated California's most prolonged and acrimonious historical discussion — the location of Drake's landing. Whether Drake landed at the specific spot of Bodega, Drake's, or San Francisco Bay, is not of essential importance at this time. What is essential is the fact that the

... Generall set up a monument of our being there; as also of her Maiesties right and title to the same, namely a plate nailed to a faire great poste, whereupon was ingrauen her Maiesties name, the day and yeere of our arriual there, with free giuing up of the prouince and the people into her Maiesties hands, together with her highnes picture and armes, in a piece of six pence of current English money under the plate, where under was also written the name of our Generall.

The General's plate, discovered in 1936 by Beryle Shinn, supposedly proves Drake's intention of formally claiming the area for England. [However, it should be noted that the authenticity of Drake's plate has been recently challenged, effectively so. It is still quoted here for it correctly reflects the kind of possession-taking device Drake used.–ED.] The plate bears the following inscription:

> BEE IT KNOWNE VNTO ALL MEN BY THESE
> PRESENTS
> IVNE. 17. 1579.
> BY THE GRACE OF GOD AND IN THE NAME OF
> HERR MAIESTY QVEEN ELIZABETH OF ENG-
> LAND AND HERR SVCCESSORS FOREVER I TAKE
> POSSESSION OF THIS KINGDOME WHOSE KING
> AND PEOPLE FREELY RESIGNE THEIR RIGHT
> AND TITLE IN THE WHOLE LAND VNTO HERR
> MAIESTIES KEEPEING NOW NAMED BY ME AN
> TO BEE KNOWNE VNTO ALL MEN AS NOVA
> ALBION.
> > FRANCIS DRAKE

27

Obviously, Drake's claim to Nova Albion, because of the piratical nature of his voyage, could not be acknowledged by the virginal Queen. Understandably, Elizabeth at this time rejected the validity of symbolic acts for obtaining sovereignty over previously unclaimed territories. Her rejection, however, did not establish a precedent, for England continued to maintain and to defend her claims and rights, based upon symbolic acts, to New Netherlands, the Hudson Bay area, the Falkland Islands, and numerous Pacific and Antarctic islands.

Insofar as Spain was concerned, Drake's act of possession in the Bay area had little or no influence on the activities of her subjects; her navigators simply continued their possession-taking activities in Upper California. Pedro de Unamuno, enroute from Macao to Acapulco in 1587, "put in at the first bay he encountered on the California Coast, probably at Morro Bay." Here Unamuno took solemn possession of the area. Eight years later, Sebastián Rodríguez Cermeño, who had been commissioned by the Viceroy Luis Velasco to explore the Upper California coast for relief ports for the Manila Galleon, landed and performed an act of sovereignty at Drake's Bay which he called San Francisco.

Cermeño's act at Drake's Bay in 1595 appears to be the last possession-taking ceremony performed in Upper California until the province was permanently settled by the Sacred Expedition of 1769. Sebastián Vizcaíno, who in 1596 had taken possession of the areas of La Ventana and of La Paz, followed Cermeño in 1602–3 and explored the Upper California coast as far north as Cape Mendocino. Vizcaíno, however, did not perform any possession-taking ceremonies, notwithstanding his questionable practice of changing the geographic names that his predecessors had bestowed on the coast of the Californias.

Although Upper California was entirely neglected for over one hundred and fifty years after Vizcaíno's voyage of 1602–3, Lower California continued to be the scene of Spanish explorations and possession-taking activities. Following Vizcaíno's voyage of 1596 to Lower California were the subsequent pearl-fishing expeditions of Nicolás Cardona (1615), Francisco Ortega (1632–6), Pedro Porter y Casanate (1648–9), Bernardo Bernal Piñadero (1663–8), and

The founding of San Diego, July 16, 1769. An artist's conception of how it would have looked at Mission San Diego de Alcalá. *Courtesy Copley Press.*

Francisco Lucenilla (1668). Of these five expeditions, only two appear to have formally claimed the territory — Cardona's and Porter's. Cardona's expedition, led by Juan Iturbi, set out from Mazatlán to the peninsula and took possession at least once at an undetermined landing point. Porter's expedition, of which little is known, sailed up the coast of Lower California and enacted possession-claiming acts at various unknown ports and harbors.

Possession-taking activities in still uncolonized Lower California did not, however, end with Porter's acts. In January of 1683, Isidro de Atondo y Antillón, accompanied by the scholarly and devout Eusebio Kino, S.J., began his voyage of colonization. "On April 1 anchor was cast and a formal proclamation issued.... On the fifth all disembarked with the royal standard, a salute was fired, three *vivas* were shouted for Charles II, and the admiral took possession for the king, calling the province Santísima Trinidad de California. At the same time Fathers Kino and Goñi took

The founding of Monterey in 1769. An artist's conception of the ceremony which was an act of sovereignty. *Courtesy Copley Press.*

ecclesiastical possession." Unfortunately for Atondo, the La Paz settlement proved unsuccessful, and he found it necessary to begin anew at San Bruno where possession was again formally taken. San Bruno, which was abandoned within two years (1685), had the distinction of being the last local area to be formally claimed before the establishment (and possession-taking) of the first permanent Hispanic settlement in Lower California, Mission Loreto (1697).

With Father Juan María Salvatierra's establishment of Loreto in 1697, the gradual permanent occupation of Lower California began, and consequently the peninsula's northern frontier advanced. Maritime exploratory and possession-taking expeditions, however, were at this time curtailed, not as the result of the overland northward advance but rather as the result of the Spanish government's shortsighted policy. Thus, a lull of nearly three-quarters of a century occurred in Spain's possession-taking activities.

Spain's prolonged lull was finally broken by the ambitions of José de Gálvez, the Visitor General of New Spain. Gálvez, seeking advancement and prestige, conceived and directed the occupation of Monterey and Upper California by the Sacred Expedition of 1769. Among the instructions which the Visitor General gave Gaspar de Portolá was the specific order to take possession upon arrival at Monterey:

8. After the governor and his expedition has succeeded in reaching Monterey, ... he must formally perform a solemn act of possession in His Majesty's name, drawing up the corresponding instrument which he will forward to His Excellency the Viceroy....

Portolá, as every student of California history well knows, carried out his instructions on Pentecost Sunday, June 3, 1770, after the celebration of High Mass. His instrument of possession read:

Don Gaspar de Portolá, Captain of Dragoons of the Regiment of Spain, Governor of California and Commander-in-Chief of the Expedition of the ports of San Diego and Monterey, situated in thirty-three and thirty-seven degrees, in accordance with the Royal Decree:

By these presents be it known that in the Camp and Port of Monterey on the third day of the month of June of this year, in fulfillment of the orders which I bear from the Most Illustrious Señor Inspector General Don Joseph de Gálvez of the Council and Cabinet of His Majesty in the Royal and Supreme Council of the Indies, as appears from the decree which he was pleased to give me, naming me Commander-in-Chief of said expedition in virtue of his having the vice-regal powers, finding among the chapters of the orders which I had to execute, that as soon as I should arrive at the Port of Monterey, I should take possession in the name of his Catholic Majesty, I ordered the officers of the sea and land to assemble, and begged the Reverend Fathers to please attend, in obedience to the said order, commanding the troops to be at arms, and notifying them of what had been thus ordered, and having made these preliminary arrangements, and having set up the triumphant standard of the

31

holy Cross as the primary care of the Catholic, Christian and pious zeal of His Majesty, as is manifested by the superior orders and is known, far and wide, from the fact that his royal treasury is open for the purpose of gathering the evangelical harvest which is being undertaken for the sake of the many gentiles who inhabit this country. I proceeded to take possession in the name of His Majesty, in the form provided by the decree, going through the ceremony of throwing earth and stones to the four Winds and proclaiming possession in the Royal name of His Catholic Majesty Don Carlos Third, may God guard him, who must be recognized as sovereign of said Port of Monterey and such other lands as is right and fitting. And in order that it may be known for all time, I sign this and the officers sign it as witnesses. And since it is the duty of the sea officers to understand the affairs of ports better than those of land, I desire that the captain of the ship named *El Príncipe*, which is in said Port, Don Juan Pérez and his pilot, Don Miguel del Pino, and other land officers, shall be witnesses in order that they may give fuller faith and credence.

Gaspar de Portola (Rubrica)

With Portolá's act at Monterey in 1770, possession-taking came to an end in the California areas effectively occupied by Spain. Although the validity of symbolic acts of sovereignty was no longer recognized when Monterey was occupied, it is evident that Spain had maintained her rights of ownership over Lower and Upper California prior to their permanent colonization due to the performance of such acts.

Juan Crespí: Southern California's First Chronicler

BY RAYMUND F. WOOD

IF YOU WERE TO ASK the average well-informed Californian, even a man who prided himself on his general knowledge of California history, if all of the following statements were true, it is almost certain that you would receive an affirmative reply: first, that Father Junípero Serra led the initial group of Franciscan friars into Alta California in 1769, and specifically that he led them to San Diego; second, that the mission he founded there on July 17, 1769, was the first of a long series of missions founded by himself and by those who succeeded him; third, that he then led the march northward up the coast (accompanied of course by some military forces) as far as Monterey, where he founded Mission San Carlos in June 1770; and fourth, that a few years later, specifically in 1776, he founded a mission at the place that was to become the future city of San Francisco.

Actually, not one of these statements is true.

As to the first point, that Father Serra led the initial group of Franciscans into Alta California, the new land that was assigned to them for their mission field, north of the northernmost Jesuit mission in Baja California, the plain fact is that Father Serra was the fifth Franciscan to arrive at San Diego, being preceded by Fathers Gómez, Parrón and Vizcaíno, who came by sea, and by Fr. Juan Crespí, who came by the land route from Baja California.

As to the second point, the mission which Fr. Serra founded at

San Diego on July 17, 1769, was not the first to be founded by him. On May 14 of that same year Fr. Serra had founded his first mission, calling it San Fernando de Velicatá, at an Indian *rancheria* about 235 miles south of San Diego, in present-day Baja California, a place that had been visited by the Jesuits from nearby Santa María, but which had not had a regular mission there. San Diego was therefore Fr. Serra's second mission.

As to the third point, Fr. Serra did not proceed from San Diego to Monterey by land, and he had nothing to do with the bestowal of any of the place names which were given by the Spaniards on the trip northward from San Diego. Fr. Serra went by ship to Monterey.

As to the fourth point (though on this matter the affirmative response might not have been given quite so readily), Fr. Serra did not found either the city or the mission of San Francisco. The founding of the city was accomplished when Captain Juan Bautista de Anza, in the spring of 1776, carefully plotted the sites for a presidio, for a mission (though in this matter he left the precise location to Fr. Font, chaplain and diarist of the expedition, who chose a site on the small stream called Nuestra Señora de los Dolores), and for homes for future settlers; these latter arrived, under the guidance of Anza's lieutenant Moraga, later on in the summer of the same year, at which time the mission, already located by Fr. Font, was founded by Fr. Francisco Palóu. Fr. Serra did not even visit San Francisco until the end of September 1777.

The reasons for attributing to the great Father Serra honors to which he was not strictly entitled are not far to seek. First, by analogy with military affairs, wherein accomplishments of soldiers, or of those under obedience, are commonly attributed to the commanding officer, Fr. Serra was the "President" or spiritual leader of the Franciscans assigned to take over the former Jesuit missions, and then to found more missions to the north of the Jesuits' northernmost line of advance. In a sense, therefore, anything achieved by any Franciscan after 1768 in either Baja or Alta California could be attributed to the leader, Junípero Serra, since it could be presumed to have been done under his direction or command. Still, this is not quite the same thing as accomplishing it himself.

Secondly, and perhaps more importantly, Americans of the twentieth century have been bombarded by a barrage of books, articles, and pamphlets, written by authors zealous for the cause of Fr. Serra, so that the image of the great Fray Junípero overshadows all others — even his friend Francisco Palóu, who began the trend of adulation by the publication of the *Life and Apostolic Labors of the Venerable Padre Fray Junípero Serra* as long ago as 1787.

Most of these lives of Serra, if read carefully, will not of themselves make deliberately false statements regarding their hero, but they do tend to give the impression that he single-handedly established the first nine missions of California, up to the year of his death, 1784. A 1960 booklet, for example, published by the Native Sons of the Golden West, makes no mention of how Fr. Serra went from San Diego to Monterey in 1770. With regard to San Francisco, the author does not explicitly state that he personally founded the mission there, but he uses wording that implies it. "Within two and a half years of his return (from Mexico City), Mission San Francisco was founded...." And a sentence or two later, "Thus, within eight years of his coming, Serra had effectuated as many missions." This somewhat misleading impression is reinforced by words employed a sentence or two later, " . . . the physical founding of nine missions...." To cite yet one more example of misleading information the *Diccionario Enciclopedico U.T.E.H.A.* (Union Tipográfico Editorial Hispano Americana), of Mexico (c. 1964), vol. 2, p. 740, refers to "el ilustre Fray Junípero Serra, fundador de San Francisco."

Other writers, both historians and novelists, tend to create in the minds of their readers the same general impression. They would have us believe that Serra alone was zealous, energetic, pious, indefatigable, and so on. The truth of the matter is that there were several other Franciscans in Alta California during the late eighteenth century who were also zealous, energetic, pious, indefatigable, and so on. One of them is the man who gave Los Angeles its name, Fray Juan Crespí, a Franciscan missionary-explorer who has dwelt too long in the shadow of his illustrious superior.

The man who was to be known in California as Fray Juan Crespí was born at Palma, on the Balearic island of Majorca, a territory then, as now, a part of the Spanish realm, on March 1, 1721, the son of Joan Crespí and of his wife Joana (Fiol), members of the parish of San Jaume. He was baptized shortly afterwards, the form of the name which appears in the document being the Majorcan spelling, Joan Baptista. An additional name, Martí, was also given at this time. Joan Baptista Martí Crespí attended elementary school in Palma, where he became acquainted with a fellow pupil, nearly two years younger than himself, by the name of Francesch Miquel Palóu, who was also to gain fame in California in later years, he too being better known by the Castilian form of his name, in this case Francisco Miguel.

Joan Baptista entered the Franciscan order on January 4, 1738, two months short of his seventeenth birthday, finished the usual one-year novitiate, and made his profession in the Order on January 9, 1739, at the Convent of San Francisco in Palma. He at once began his classical and philosophical studies, and in the following September was assigned to classes in philosophy being taught by a new professor, Fray Junípero Serra. Fray Junípero was also a Majorcan, who had entered the Order some nine years earlier and, after the usual course of philosophy and theology, had recently passed his Lectorate examinations which qualified him to teach. In November of the same year young Joan Baptista was delighted to have as a new classmate his old friend from grammar school days, Francisco Palóu, who had entered the Order the previous year, at a different Franciscan convent, and who now caught up with his friend Joan in the philosophy course at San Francisco in Palma. The two young men studied together for nearly three years under Fr. Serra, and towards the end of their course they found that the same holy man was to be their teacher also in theology, he having in the meantime finished his academic work for the degree of Doctor of Sacred Theology. In January 1744 Doctor Serra was assigned as principal professor in one of the three chairs of theology at the Lullian University, Palma, which the Franciscans of the Convent of San Francisco, Crespí and Palóu among them, attended for their theological studies. All three friars therefore

became well known to each other long before they found themselves fellow missionaries in far-off California.

Both young Franciscans, upon completion of their theological
training in 1746, were ordained to the priesthood, and assigned to
various duties within the Order, Palóu to advanced studies in philosophy (he passed his competitive Lectorate examinations in
1749), and Crespí to religious or teaching duties at the Novitiate of
Santa María de los Angeles, outside of Palma.

Some time in 1748 or early in 1749, Fr. Serra began to petition
his superiors in the Order for permission to give up his successful
teaching career at the university in order to go as a missionary to
the heathens in the Indies, as indeed many of his fellow Franciscans were doing at that time. Though reluctant to allow this outstanding teacher and popular preacher to leave the Province of
Majorca, his superiors finally acceded to his wishes, and Fr. Serra
received the formal permission on Palm Sunday, 1749. He had
already persuaded both Fr. Crespí and Fr. Palóu to apply for the
same mission, and both young men, fired with zeal for souls and
inspired by the example of their beloved teacher, had gladly
requested the same permission to leave Majorca for the New
World. Fr. Serra and Fr. Palóu sailed for Cadiz on April 13, while
Fr. Crespí did not sail until September 4. Upon their arrival in
New Spain about the end of 1749, all three were assigned to the
College of San Fernando in Mexico City for some rest and for some
additional training before being sent out to the rigors of missionary life. After a few months, however, all were given specific
assignments among the Pame Indians of the Sierra Gorda, about
175 miles north of Mexico City, in the present state of Querétaro — Serra and Palóu to the mission of Santiago at Jalpan, the
principal town of the Pames, and Crespí to San Francisco de
Tilaco, a small native community on the eastern border of the
mission country.

These three friends worked in the Sierra Gorda, along with several other Franciscan missionaries already there, for a period of
eight years, learning the Indian language and building some fine
churches for their partly civilized charges, before a massacre of

some Franciscans in Texas brought a partial termination to their activities. Fr. Serra was recalled to Mexico City, and Fr. Palóu was ordered to ready himself for departure, so that these two could be sent as replacements for the murdered missionaries in Texas. This plan did not mature, however, so Fr. Palóu remained as Superior at Jalpan, and Fr. Serra remained at the College of San Fernando where he was employed as Novice Master, choir director, and spiritual adviser to the community, as well as being in some demand as a preacher in the churches of the city. Fr. Crespí was not directly affected by these changes, but continued at his mission of Tilaco in the Sierra Gorda for another eight years.

In 1767 an event occurred which was to have a profound effect on all of New Spain, including particularly those portions of New Spain which afterwards became the states of California and Arizona. The king of Spain, Carlos III, for reasons which, he said, "he kept locked in his royal heart," suddenly and without warning ordered all the Jesuits then in the kingdom of Spain and its overseas dominions to be arrested and sent out of the country. This decree made no exceptions, and applied to all Jesuit schools, colleges, churches, and even missions. The decree of expulsion was to be put into effect in Mexico on June 24, 1767.

For about seventy years the Jesuits had been slowly and painfully establishing a chain of missions on the peninsula of Baja California, from Cape San Lucas to a point about 290 airline miles south of present-day San Diego, the northernmost Jesuit mission being one named St. Mary of the Angels, established on May 7, 1767, only a few months before their expulsion. All of these missions were now to be turned over to the Franciscans of the Missionary College of San Fernando, and Fray Junípero Serra had already been selected as their superior.

The plans for the expulsion of the Jesuits from Baja California (as well as from Sinaloa, Sonora, Arizona, and other misson lands) were carefully laid by José de Gálvez, a man who had been appointed Visitador General, with powers almost equal to those of the viceroy himself. Gálvez ordered the arrest of all the Jesuits at the same time, those on the mainland of New Spain as well as those in Baja California, but the difficulty of crossing the gulf caused some delay in the arrest of those on the peninsula. For this latter operation he commissioned Gaspar de Portolá to proceed with fifty soldiers to arrest the sixteen Jesuits on the peninsula, and to send them to the mainland under guard. Gálvez gave specific orders to accomplish all this by surprise, so as not to give the Jesuits any opportunity to hide any evidence of the treason they were alleged to have plotted against the king. Portolá's soldiers did as they were bid, landing at Cape San Lucas in October; but it took several months for all the Jesuits in the eight-hundred-mile-long peninsula to be apprised of the fact that they were under arrest and were to be expelled from their adopted land. By February 13, 1768, the last of them had been assembled at Loreto, had celebrated their last Masses for their weeping Indian converts, and had been sent into exile. No evidence of treason was found, nor, incidentally, was any treasure found, despite the eager expectations of the soldiers.

In the meantime the sixteen Franciscans who were to take over the Jesuit missions, under the leadership of Junípero Serra, and with Palóu and Crespí among them, were making the journey from Mexico City to San Blas. There they waited for some time until, about the first week of March of 1768, the ship arrived from Loreto with the Jesuits aboard. There was little time for any intercommunication between the two groups of missionaries, for the Franciscans were ordered to board the ship as soon as the Jesuits disembarked; and so Fr. Serra, and Fr. Palóu, and Fr. Crespí, and thirteen other padres, came to California, arriving at Loreto on Good Friday, April 1, 1768.

While all this had been going on, other and far more significant events were taking place in Madrid and Mexico City, events which were to have far reaching consequences for the land of California. The "Russian Bear" was beginning to growl, and the Spanish ambassador at the Russian court was sending alarming notes to Madrid, saying in effect that Russia was not going to stop with its occupation of the Aleutian Islands, but intended to set up bases at Sitka and other points on the mainland, and would undoubtedly move as far south as to the legendary bay of San Francisco, or perhaps to the equally legendary bay of Monterey, which had been claimed for the Spanish throne nearly two hundred years earlier, but which had not yet been occupied.

This situation gave the Visitador General, José de Gálvez, the necessary urgency to his half-formulated plan to establish a Spanish foothold of some kind at Monterey, and he had little trouble in persuading Viceroy Francisco de Croix to approve the plan in principle, and to obtain a royal order for its execution. The precise wording of Croix's original letter to Gálvez has not been published (though it still exists in the archives), but a subsequent letter, referring to this earlier one, has been translated and reads in part as follows: "I . . . transmitted the order of the court to the *visitador,* bidding him to make an expedition by sea toward the threatened port (Monterey). The visitador, bethinking himself of the difficulties of a maritime expedition, and being desirous of exploring the province, sent two expeditions, one by sea and the other by land." These words, taken from Chapman's *History of California, the Spanish Period,* p. 218, clearly indicate that neither the Spanish royal order, nor Croix's letter of transmittal of the same, specifically ordered a second expedition by land, nor, for that matter, did the original instructions say anything about founding presidios or missions.

Gálvez had no sooner received official sanction for his plans than he started to put them into execution. He gave orders for two separate expeditions to be prepared, one to proceed by land and one by sea, both of them to meet in Alta California for the purpose of founding two colonies (missions protected by soldiery, after the Jesuit pattern), one at San Diego and one at Monterey. Both of these places had been seen and partially explored by Spanish ships over a hundred years earlier; their latitudes and general configurations were known, and Gálvez thought they could be identified. But he was playing it safe when he ordered the expeditions to proceed separately, by land and by sea; and to be still more safe he split each one into two parts. So in reality four separate expeditions started from Baja California for San Diego in the spring of 1769, though the contemporary accounts generally refer to them as two.

Junípero Serra, President, or Superior, of the band of sixteen

Franciscans, was naturally chosen to be the superior of the padres who were to found the missions in the new land, and Gaspar de Portolá, who was already in Baja California rounding up the Jesuits, was ordered to take command of the troops for this new venture.

So, while the first of the two ships which were to carry some of the soldiers, two blacksmiths, a cook, a baker, a surgeon, and some missionaries, was being readied for sailing from La Paz (the second one setting sail from Cape San Lucas a short while later), the first of the two land expeditions got under way, consisting mostly of soldiers and muleteers under the command of Captain Fernando Rivera y Moncada. When Fr. Serra received word that this latter group had arrived at Velicatá, some distance beyond the most northerly Jesuit mission, he sent word to Fr. Crespí to leave his mission of Purísima Concepción, where he had been stationed but a brief time, and to join the Captain at Velicatá. Crespí did so, and on March 22 reached the camp, where he found Rivera y Moncada impatient to continue the march northward. Meanwhile the second expedition set out from Loreto, under the personal command of Governor Portolá, on March 6, and took the same route for Velicatá.

Fr. Serra had planned to accompany this second expedition, but he did not manage to do so, because he had aggravated an earlier infection on his legs during his recent journey to La Paz for the sailing of the *San Carlos*. He therefore waited a few weeks at Loreto to give his legs a chance to heal, and then made the trip north on muleback, with the aid of some companions. He visited Fr. Palóu's mission (San Javier) en route, and after a sad farewell turned over to him the Presidency of the peninsula missions, retaining for himself the superiorship of those to be founded in the north. Proceeding from mission to mission, he eventually caught up with Portolá, and on May 13 Serra and Portolá, with their soldiers and Indian helpers, rode into Velicatá, which had been vacated by Rivera y Moncada and Crespí nearly two months earlier.

Fr. Serra saw that the land at Velicatá was good, and that the nearby Indians were capable of being Christianized (in fact the Jesuits had earlier noted this condition, and had intended to found a mission at this place of "Guiricatá," as it is spelled in the Jesuit reports), so he decided to found a mission there, dedicating it to San Fernando, King of Castile and Leon. This mission, the first to be founded by Fr. Serra, the first to be founded in the new lands to the north of the existing missions of Baja California, and the first to be founded under the direct command of the king to colonize Alta California, was established on May 14, 1769, with the usual solemn High Mass and the singing of the "Veni Creator Spiritus" to give it a spiritual tone, and with the customary fusillade of gunfire from the soldiers to supply the want of more formal music. Fr. Miguel de la Concepción Campa y Cos was appointed the first missionary of the new mission at Velicatá.

Meanwhile, on that same day, far away to the north, Fr. Crespí and Captain Rivera y Moncada, with his soldiers, muleteers, and the domestic animals they were leading, rode into San Diego, having been fifty-two days on the trail from Velicatá, and accomplishing the journey, says Crespí, "not without some misadventures on the way."

Crespí was one of the two diarists for this part of the expedition, the other being José Cañizares, whose official rank was that of *pilotín* (under-pilot, or assistant pilot). The two diaries agree with each other quite closely, except that the pilot's latitude readings, despite his presumably greater knowledge of such matters, are generally less accurate than Crespí's.

This was the first of seven diaries that Fr. Crespí kept of his travels in Baja California, Alta California, and on board ship to Alaska and British Columbia. It is typical of all the rest. Crespí was observant, careful, honest, and accurate. He described the land, the trees, the flowers, the small streams and arroyos, and above all the Indians. He never forgot that he was a missionary, not a mere explorer for the king, and he passed up no opportunity to tell the natives about God, or to record in the diary the tribes and places that seemed to him appropriate for future missions.

On Sunday, May 14, 1769, Crespí and Rivera y Moncada, "to our great happiness and joy, reached our long wished for, famous harbor of San Diego." Crespí was so happy, in fact, that he wrote the words "San Diego" in large letters on an extra line in his diary.

The two ships that had left from the south had already arrived and were visible in the harbor. So too was smoke arising from camp fires on the shore. Rivera's men gave a salute, "and at once the camp and the ships returned it with their own ordnance," says Crespí. It was a joyful reunion, and soon all the men were exchanging experiences. It was quickly apparent that the land party, which had suffered no loss of personnel at all, had fared better than those on either ship. The earlier one, the *San Carlos*, had taken three months to make the voyage, during which time several had died of scurvy, while nearly all the rest were sick with it; even the *San Antonio* (also known as *El Príncipe*), which had sailed a month later from Cape San Lucas, and had made a quicker trip than the *San Carlos*, arriving at San Diego before it, nevertheless came in with many of its crew and passengers sick or disabled. Fr. Crespí says that "we four fathers who had met at this harbor spent our time attending the sick men, of whom there were a great many." The four padres were himself and three who had come on the ships; and in this way they spent about five weeks waiting for the arrival of the Governor.

At last, at the end of June, Sergeant José Francisco Ortega and one other soldier put in an appearance at San Diego, as a sort of advance party for the Governor. Captain Rivera, anxious for his men to have something to do, at once dispatched ten of them to go and meet the Governor's party, which they did, escorting Portolá and Serra into camp at San Diego with as much ceremony as the frontier conditions would permit. It was another joyful reunion. Portolá and Serra had made better time from Velicatá than had Rivera and Crespí, partly because the road had been opened for them, and partly because they were not so burdened by the number of beef cattle that Rivera's party had brought up with them.

The first two weeks of July were spent in modifying their plans for the discovery of Monterey. The original plan had been for both ships to sail there, but with nearly all the crews of both ships dead or incapacitated, this was out of the question. Instead, Portolá gave orders for the *San Antonio* to sail back to San Lucas to make a report to Gálvez and to obtain more supplies, while the *San Carlos* was to remain in the harbor until such time as there were enough sailors recovered from scurvy to sail it to Monterey. Meanwhile the Governor himself prepared orders for a company of sixty-three persons to undertake a land journey to Monterey, leaving behind all the sick sailors, the blacksmiths, cooks, and others who had come on the ships, and also Fr. Serra and the two other Franciscans (Fr. Juan Vizcaíno and Fr. Fernando Parrón) to begin the mission of San Diego, to minister to the sick, and to preach to the Indians while awaiting water transportation to Monterey.

The Portolá Expedition left San Diego for Monterey on July 14, 1769, two days before Fr. Serra founded the mission of San Diego de Alcalá, his second mission, and the first to be established in the present state of California. The expedition consisted of Portolá, who had a personal servant (or "batman" as he would be termed in the British army); Captain Rivera y Moncada, who also had a batman; the engineer Miguel Costansó, who, like Crespí, kept a daily journal of the expedition; Lieutenant Pedro Fages and six of his Catalonian Volunteers; Sergeant Ortega and twenty-six of his *"soldados de cuera"* (a word sometimes, though not quite accurately, translated as "leather-jackets"); two Franciscans, Crespí and Francisco Gómez; seven muleteers to attend to the pack animals; and fifteen Christianized Indians from Baja California.

As stated above, both Crespí and Costansó kept diaries of this famous expedition, but of the two Crespí's is the more interesting, even in the abbreviated version of it that appears in Palóu's *Noticias.* He saw beauty in the trees and flowers, hope for the salvation of souls in the naked Indians, and a great future for a land so fertile and verdant. He was California's first booster, and some of his descriptions of the beautiful valleys make those of John C. Frémont, California's other great explorer, three-quarters of a century later, seem pale by comparison.

The expedition set forth from San Diego about four in the afternoon of July 14, and proceeded northwesterly along the coast. Leaving San Diego Bay area proper, they came a day later to a point where

we found ourselves upon pretty large tablelands, very grassy and with very good soil, all of it friable.... We saw seven antelopes together, running over these tablelands, and we noticed hares and rabbits running about at every moment. On going about a league and a half, we came to a most handsome little valley or hollow, which, when seen on the way down off the mesa, looked like nothing so much as a cornfield, because of its greenness.

This was the Soledad Valley, near Sorrento, a valley filled at that time with wild pumpkins and Castilian roses.

These wild roses fascinated Fr. Crespí. On July 16, at Batequitas (also spelled Batequitos and Batiquitos) Lagoon, near Leucadia between Del Mar and Carlsbad, he came across some springs where some of these roses were growing. He writes, "I looked at both springs, and plucked a sprig of roses there, with six very fragrant open roses, and about a dozen buds ready to open; there are a great many such patches of roses." Crespí was a good explorer, a good man with the astrolabe, a good diarist, and a good missionary. But he was also a man who loved flowers, and indeed loved all of God's gifts to mankind.

The expedition moved up the coast through San Diego County, turning inland to Orange County at present-day San Juan Capistrano, though they had already bestowed that honored name on the valley where later the mission of San Luis Rey was to be built. In general the names bestowed by Fr. Crespí have not survived. He invariably gave to some small rancheria or temporary native village the name of the saint of the day, while the soldiers preferred to bestow names on more permanent features of the land — springs, rivulets, hills, and arroyos — often choosing the name from some incident of the day's march, such as the capture of a deer or antelope, which might give the name of Berrendo to a spring, or the killing of a seagull, which might result in a campsite being named La Gaviota, or the fact that an Indian was making a canoe, which resulted in Carpintería.

Passing through Orange County, where they saw and named the Santa Ana River, one of the few names that has survived, they came to the vicinity of La Habra on July 29, and so passed into Los Angeles County, reaching the area of the Puente Hills on July 30. Camp was probably made near the present-day community of La Puente, on or near San Jose Creek. The next day, July 31, they

A spring of water still flows at the site of the first baptism performed in Alta California, by Fr. Gómez, companion of Fr. Crespí on the Portolá Expedition. Because of the difficulty of access to the site, now on the property of Camp Pendleton, another plaque, with slightly different wording, has been erected at the Civic Center of the city of San Clemente (lower photo). *All photographs used in illustrating this essay are courtesy of the author.*

46

proceeded west-northwest, along the general line of Valley Boulevard, passing to the south of El Monte, towards "a little low range sighted to the west." This low range is no doubt the area where the campus of California State University, Los Angeles now exists. Camp that evening was made somewhere in the vicinity of Wilmar or South San Gabriel. Neither Crespí nor Constansó is very clear as to the location of this campsite, merely stating that after crossing a "muddy stream" (perhaps the Rio Hondo) they halted "in an open clear spot in the same valley" not far from "the little low range."

The next day, August 1, Tuesday, was a day of rest for the expedition. Fathers Crespí and Gómez both said Mass for the men, who also received Communion that day, participation in both Mass and Communion, as well as the recitation of certain prayers, being requirements for the gaining of the great indulgence of the Porciúncula which began at noon that day.

The Porciúncula was (and still is) a plenary indulgence of the Catholic Church, and some explanation of its origins may not be out of place here. During the early manhood of the future St. Francis of Assisi, there existed a small rural chapel on the plain about three-quarters of a mile below the town of Assisi, which the local villagers called St. Mary of the Angels (in Spanish it would be Santa María de los Angeles). This ancient chapel belonged to the Benedictine monks of a nearby abbey, but it had been abandoned by them some time before, and had been allowed to fall into ruin. This desolate spot seemed to the young Francis an ideal place in which to retire from the world, and he made it his place of retreat, constructing a primitive hut for himself, and later setting about the restoration of the little chapel. This was in 1207. In 1210, by which time Francis had gathered a few followers, and had completed the reconstruction of the chapel, the Benedictines gave him title to the chapel and to a small plot of land around it, which Francis called his "little portion" of land. The chapel subsequently took this name of Porziuncula (or in Spanish Porciúncula).

It was while he was living on this small piece of property next to the chapel that Francis received a divine revelation concerning a plenary indulgence that any Catholic could obtain by visiting,

47

while in a state of grace, the little chapel that he had restored to the honor of Our Lady of the Angels. Though the historicity of this indulgence has been questioned by recent scholars (largely because many later thirteenth century documents do not mention it), its popularity is unquestioned. First granted by Pope Honorius III in 1216, and for a while limited only to those who made the pilgrimage to Assisi (that is to say, to the "little portion" of land where the restored chapel was), it has subsequently been extended by other popes so as to make it applicable to visits to any Franciscan church, then to any parish church where Franciscans of the Third Order (laymen) might meet, and finally to any church so designated by the various bishops throughout the world. It has remained, however, primarily a Franciscan devotion, and of course was much favored by the two Franciscan missionary-explorers, Crespí and Gómez.

The time for gaining this annual indulgence had been established by the eighteenth century as the period of a day and a half, from noon of August 1 to midnight of August 2. It was for this reason that, as recounted by both diarists, "on August 1 we lay by at this place," though Costansó adds that some scouts were sent out to explore, and that some of the other men went off to hunt wild antelopes to replenish their meat supply. But the most notable event of the day, which both diarists record, was another in the series of earthquakes that had begun several days before and were to continue for quite a few more days. But by now Fr. Crespí had come to regard these tremors with all the indifference of a true Californian. He writes:

Last night around Vesper-time, as we were sitting about, we all felt a strong earthquake, and the ground shook heavily, though it was very short; since we first began to experience these quakes, at the [Santa Ana] river, they have been felt on every day's march and by now there have been some seven or eight of them .... Today [August 1], while lying by, we experienced another strong earthquake, lasting a little longer than a Hail Mary.

One gets the impression that good Fr. Crespí, though no doubt instinctively moved to prayer when occasions seemed to demand it, was here using the Hail Mary as a somewhat scientific method of measuring the duration of the quake, rather than as an appeal to the Almighty for deliverance from these terrors.

Next day, August 2, the expedition moved across the plain, following generally the route taken by Valley Boulevard, and so passing a little to the north of the State University campus. Crespí says:

We set out from here in the valley, following through the same plain on a due west course. On going about a league and a half, we came to the little low range we had sighted in this direction, and here took leave of the [San Gabriel] valley, and came into a hollow with level, very grassy soil; and beyond that, up and down over low, flat, grass-covered knolls; on going three hours, in which we must have made three leagues as well, we came to the water found by the Captain and his scouts yesterday. It is another river in another lush, green valley, nowise inferior to the last two [the Rio Hondo and the San Gabriel]. Indeed, I should say rather that this one wins out above all the others. The river is a little smaller than the last ones, its bed being about seven *varas* wide where we crossed it [a *vara* was about a yard], and it is not deep; it flows from the north-northwest out of the high mountains nearby. .... This river can be seen flowing down, its bed not deeply sunken below the surrounding ground, through a very green, lush, wide-spreading valley — an extent, north and south, of some leagues of level soil . . . so that it can truly be said to a most handsome garden . . . and in time to come there may be a very large and rich mission of Our Lady of the Angels of the Porciúncula, this being the day upon which we came to it, when this well-known Indulgence is gained in our Seraphic order; and so we have proclaimed it El Río y Valle de Nuestra Señora de los Angeles de la Porciúncula.

It is not a difficult matter to reconstruct the expedition's route into and across the great city of Los Angeles that now covers the "lush, green valley" that Crespí and his companions saw, and in fact has become so large that the expedition would not pass out of its present city limits until five days later. They first saw the river somewhere in the vicinity of the point where North Broadway crosses the Los Angeles River, and must have made camp somewhat east of this point. This location is documented by yet one more reference from Crespí's diary. "Towards the north-northeast there is a large dry creek with a very large bed, so that it plainly must carry heavy floods." This was the Arroyo Seco, even then living up to its name, which could only be to the "north-north-east" if camp were made near the main stream and a little below the junction of the two rivers.

More quakes were felt this day, during the afternoon and evening, but these failed to dampen Crespí's enthusiasm for the lovely spot where later was founded the pueblo of La Reina de los Angeles. He even had some nice things to say about the native Angelenos, who appeared to him to be peaceful and prosperous.

Upon our reaching here, six or eight heathen came over to the camp from a good-sized village situated in this inviting spot among some trees. They came to us as we were seated in the shade of a tree with our Captain, and they brought two or three large bowls or baskets half full of sage tea, and other kinds of grass-seeds that they use. They all came up carrying bows and arrows, but with the strings loosened. Their chief bore in his hands some strings of shell beads, and on coming to the camp they threw each of us three handfuls of the beads. Some of them came up smoking upon Indian pipes made of baked clay, and blew three mouthfuls of smoke at each of us. After this their chief gave us a speech, and they all sat down with us. The Captain and I gave them tobacco, and the Captain made them a present of our sort of beads, and accepted their sage tea, of which he gave us a little to drink, and it is a very delicious, refreshing sage drink.

Such were the first inhabitants of the future city of the Angels, as seen by Spaniards for the first time. Crespí's description conveys a picture of a tribe of people wealthy enough in their own minds to be able to shower gifts on these unknown visitors, as well as to be able to offer them refreshment. It is a really idyllic picture — the younger men offering refreshment, the chief bestowing largess on the travelers, while the older men calmly smoke their pipes and appear to show little fear of what these armed soldiers might do to harm them.

The next day, August 3, "we set out from the lush and inviting Porciúncula River and Valley; we crossed this full-flowing river..." (thereby proving that they had camped on the east side of it) and they proceeded westward across the Los Angeles basin. "After crossing the river we came into a great vineyard of wild

Crespí himself did not see these "bolcanes de brea," as he called them, relying on the account given him by Portolá's scouts for his description of them in his diary. Even so, he described them quite accurately, and they are not much changed today.

grapevines, and countless rose-patches with a great many open flowers, the soil being all dark and friable. We took a westerly course, over flat ground all covered with tall grasses; we had a clear view of the course of the river, with the trees and plain drawing toward the south." Their route was from the river to the approximate location of today's Civic Center, then west to about the location of MacArthur Park. On the way they passed the village home of the natives who had visited them the day before; and once more the travelers were offered food. But as they did not have containers for the dried seeds they were offered, they declined the gift, whereupon the natives, perhaps to show off their wealth, threw the gifts that had been declined into the air and onto the ground.

Camp was made that evening somewhere in the vicinity of La Brea Avenue and Venice Boulevard, at a place which they named the Spring of the Sycamores, from which flowed the present-day (but now practically dry) Ballona Creek. While crossing the basin the scouts reported having seen

some geysers of tar [*bolcanes de brea*], issuing from the ground like springs;

Primarily a memorial to Allan Hancock, this plaque in Hancock Park, on the north side of Wilshire Blvd. near Fairfax Ave., contains a brief reference to the original discovery by the Portolá Expedition.

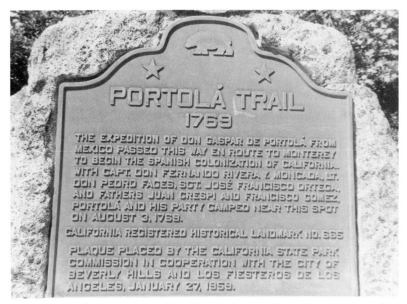

This plaque, State Registered Landmark No. 665, on the west side of La Cienega Blvd. and north of Olympic Blvd., in Beverly Hills, differs in its wording from the plaque in Elysian Park chiefly in the inclusion of the name of Sgt. Ortega. The August 3 campsite was about two miles southeast of this monument.

it boils up molten, and the water runs to one side and the tar to the other. The scouts reported that they had come across many of these springs, and had seen large swamps of them, enough, they said, to caulk many vessels. We were not so lucky ourselves as to see these tar geysers, much though we would have wished it; as it was some distance out of the way we were to take, the Governor did not want us to go past them. We christened them Los Bolcanes de Brea de la Porciúncula.

Most of these swamps and springs of tar have since dried up, but at least one group of them, the famous Brea Pits, are still bubbling away in Hancock Park, just a few feet away from Wilshire Boulevard along Miracle Mile, probably only a little changed from the days when Rivera's scouts first encountered them in 1769.

On August 4 the party continued across the plain, turning somewhat northwest, so as to bring them into the vicinity of the

Veterans Home at Sawtelle, where some springs of fresh water ran out of the hills, and where another village of natives was encountered. As before, these people also tried to give the visitors gifts — small round nuts with hard shells (walnuts?) and very sweet acorns. Crespí says that they also "made me a present of a good-sized string of their usual sort of beads, made of white sea shells; some of them are red, though not very bright-colored, and seem to be made of coral of very ordinary quality." Crespí named this place after San Rogerio, but the soldiers gave it the name of El Berrendo, because of capturing an antelope there. At the usual evening campfire, where the men gathered to report what they had seen that day, some scouts reported that they had gone as far as the ocean, which was only about five miles away. On hearing this, Portolá ordered the scouts to go back next day and investigate the possibility of continuing along the shore.

So on August 5, while most of the men remained in camp, some of the explorers went back to the beach to try to find a route below the high bluffs now called The Palisades. They returned about noon to report that after a short distance the cliffs came right down into the sea, and that a passage beyond them was almost impossible. On learning this, Portolá decided to try to cross the high hills in front of them (which they did not name at this time, but which are the Santa Monica Mountains of today). Proceeding up a canyon (Sepulveda Boulevard), "we went up to a large pass, over it, and down to a very large valley all burned off by the heathens; so that from the height it appeared to have all been fallowed." This very large valley was the San Fernando Valley of today. Crespí estimated its dimensions as "over two leagues in breadth, north to south; its length, east to west, may perhaps be six or seven leagues." These measurements are a fair approximation of the dimensions of the flat part of the valley, from Mission Hills south to Sherman Oaks, and from Burbank westward to beyond Canoga Park.

Descending into the valley, to which they gave two names, Santa Catalina de Bononia (St. Catherine of Bologna), and Los Encinos, they once more found friendly Indians to greet them. Their village was close to a "very large pool of fresh water," where

PORTOLÁ TRAIL
1769
ON AN INDIAN TRAIL
THROUGH THIS CANYON,
DON GASPAR DE PORTOLÁ,
LEADING THE FIRST OVERLAND
EXPEDITION INTO CALIFORNIA,
PASSED ALONG THIS WAY
AUGUST 5, 1769.

PRESENTED TO THE CITY OF LOS ANGELES BY
LOS ANGELES PARLOR NO. 124
NATIVE DAUGHTERS OF THE GOLDEN WEST
APRIL 7, 1946

This beautiful piece of marble is placed at the intersection of Sepulveda Blvd. and Moraga Drive in Bel Air. The coat of arms at the top is that of the Kingdom of Spain during the reign of Charles III.

The so-called "Serra Spring" on the campus of University High School in West Los Angeles. There is no direct evidence that Fr. Serra ever came here. If any priest came in 1769 or 1770 it would have been Fr. Crespí. The springs used to supply Santa Monica with its drinking water.

the expedition stopped for a Sunday's rest in the shade of the many huge *encinos*, evergreen oak trees. This large pool of warm water (about 80° F) is still there, in the community of Encino, and is now part of a State Historical Monument, incorporating the area of the pool itself as well as some adobes and other structures which were built later by early settlers in this delightful spot.

Monday morning, August 7, the expedition turned to the north and traversed the Valley of the Oaks, following the general line of today's Balboa Boulevard, led by friendly Indians toward the historic San Fernando Pass. The natives of the valley begged the travelers to stay, and Crespí reports that he delighted them with a promise to return, a promise he did actually keep. Surmounting the pass by approximately the same route as that now taken by Highway 14 towards Newhall, Portolá and his men reached the Santa Clara River on the 8th. This was one of the names bestowed

The "pool of fresh water," just off Ventura Blvd. in Encino, where the Portolá Expedition rested on Sunday, August 6, 1769. The water is warm, nearly 80°. The whole area, including the springs and adjacent buildings, is now a State Historical Monument.

by Crespí that has survived; but as usual he gave the name originally to a rancheria of Indians whom they encountered a few days later, on the eve of the feast day of the great saint, Clara of Assisi, August 12. The name was later extended to the river beside which this small village stood, and still later to the entire Santa Clara River valley of today.

The expedition now proceeded by easy stages through present-day Ventura County, then up the coast through Santa Barbara County, past Point Concepción, following the coast line all the way, and continuing on past San Luis Obispo, and turning inland only when the Santa Lucia Mountains interposed their barrier across the route along the sea coast, where Highway 1 now winds along the cliffs between Piedras Blancas and Carmel. But the expedition had no engineers to blast a pathway along the cliffs, so they proceeded to cross the Santa Lucias to the Salinas Valley, camping on the way near present-day Jolon. Descending the long Salinas Valley, they reached the point where it came out onto Monterey Bay. This was to have been the end of the trail. It was Sunday, October 1.

The company assembled at a point where they could view the land. There to the left was surely the Point of Pines mentioned by all the earlier explorers, including Vizcaíno, who had landed at Monterey in 1602, and who had described the anchorage as being sheltered from all winds. Where then was the snug harbor that Vizcaíno described? Surely that wide, open roadstead that lay before them was no harbor. Were they mistaken in their latitudes? Hardly, since both Crespí and Costansó had frequently taken the latitude, Crespí with an astrolabe and Costansó with an octant (an instrument similar to a sextant), and had come to within a few minutes of each other's figures. Even so, was there perhaps another Point of Pines not too far away? Was this one really the point that Vizcaíno saw? Was the real harbor of Monterey still just ahead of them, or possibly even behind them?

On October 2 Portolá determined to find out, and he set Captain Rivera to the task. But after a day's searching with his best scouts and guides, Rivera had to admit defeat. They had found no harbor, though they did see Carmel Bay to the south of the point. They had gone as far south as they could, but they had been forced back by the rugged Santa Lucias, just as the whole party had been forced to move inland from the southern end of the same range some two weeks earlier. Still they had found no harbor.

A council was held, and Portolá, though he knew that the final decision rested with himself as commander, did the honor to invite the two padres to attend. Portolá minced no words: he told his officers and the two padres that seventeen men were on the sick list; that food was running short; that it was now beginning to get cold at night. Perhaps the winter was setting in. Furthermore, the task of caring for their mounts, and guarding them at night was proving a wearisome task for the few able-bodied men. The commander asked each member of the council to cast a secret ballot, to decide what course should be taken.

Surprisingly, all members voted to continue the search. In this

The famous Beale Cut in the San Fernando Pass. This cut, fifty feet deep, was made by General Edward F. Beale in 1859 to make an easier passage for vehicles. The Portolá Expedition went over the top of this pass on August 8, 1769. The modern highway is about a quarter of a mile west of the historic route.

Two markers along the Portolá Trail in Ventura County. The upper one (SRL NO. 624) is in Waring Park in Piru; the lower (SRL NO. 727) is in Recreation Center Park, on Harvard Blvd., in Santa Paula.

This plaque, erected in duplicate on the north and south lanes of Highway 101 near the city of Carpinteria, is the most northerly of those marking the Portolá Trail through the southern counties of California. Additional plaques (State Registered Landmarks) exist in northern California, particularly in San Mateo County.

they were constantly supported by the hope and expectation of the arrival of a third ship, the *San José*, which they knew had been despatched from Loreto on June 16 with supplies for the new settlement at Monterey. They expected its arrival daily. They might perhaps not have voted so unanimously to remain in this unknown land if they had been aware that the supply ship, the *San José*, had foundered somewhere in its voyage, and was never to be heard from again.

The decision once made, they proceeded to implement it, and spent the next three days toiling up the coast, always seeking a harbor that was under the lee of a point of pines, but never finding anything that answered that description. On October 31, however, they did come to the end of the northward trail, in the city of Pacifica, about ten miles south of the city limits of San Francisco of today.

The expedition had been slowly moving up the coast, following the general line of Highway 1, and on the night of the 30th, to escape the wind-driven rain, camp was made in a little canyon that descended the slope of San Pedro Mountain, inland from the high cliff that today is called the Devil's Slide. Next day, October 31, the whole expedition, led by their scouts, climbed up to the summit of the mountain, and from there saw Point Reyes off in the distance, a sight that completely dashed their hopes of finding Monterey so far north. Crespí describes what they saw as follows:

> From the height of the hills we had a clear view of the six or seven white farallones, which seem to lie in a line on the southwest of a very large harbor; and on that side of this harbor is a very long point of land, middling high and from afar seeming bare . . . . There are three white bluffs seen far off, at one of which appears some sort of cove with shelter.

The Farallones are, of course, clearly identifiable, and the "very long point of land" can only be Point Reyes. In fact Costansó, who also describes it as "a point of land which extended a long distance into the sea," is very emphatic that this is Point Reyes, even though previous cartographers had placed this promontory a full degree farther north than his latitude showed. But if they had reached a point where they could see Point Reyes, and were in latitude 37° and about 35', it was obvious that they had passed Monterey, which they knew to be only three or four minutes north of latitude 37°. Bewildered and confused by the evidence of their senses, the party descended and made camp near San Pedro Creek, "a short distance from the beach," says Costansó, in the Pedro Valley area of the city of Pacifica, perhaps only a few feet away from a street that today honors the name of the great explorer and diarist, "Crespí Drive."

While Portolá and his men mulled over the situation, some of the men went off to hunt game in the hills to the east, and on the second day came back to camp to report that over the hills (formerly called Sweeney Ridge, but recently re-named Portolá Ridge), there was an "immense arm of the sea or estuary," according to Costansó, "which extended inland as far as they could see, to the southeast." This report, verified by the return of Sergeant Ortega and his scouts on November 3, was the first discovery of the true San Francisco Bay. It is clear that since Ortega and his party left on November 1 at Portolá's orders to "examine the land for a certain distance," and try to find out what he could about a route to the distant Point Reyes, the honor of the original discovery of San Francisco Bay should go to Sergeant Ortega, even though some of the hunters returned to the camp a day earlier carrying the news of its existence.

While Ortega's party were making their way across Portolá Ridge to the vicinity of San Bruno, and then, it appears, down the peninsula to somewhere near Palo Alto — which was about as far as he could get in the brief time allotted to him by Portolá — Fr. Crespí remained with the others in camp, discussing among other things the sailing directions given by the pilot Cabrera Bueno, which were not believed to be highly reliable, and the likelihood that they had reached what they called "the harbor of San Francisco," meaning the open roadstead that lay before them, as far north as Point Reyes. The Golden Gate had not yet been seen by any of the party, nor, until the return of the hunters and later of Ortega, had the true San Francisco Bay been seen. Nevertheless, both Costansó and Crespí were sure they had reached "the harbor of St. Francis." Crespí says: "From the markings given by the history [of Vizcaíno's voyages] and by Cabrera, this cannot be anything other than the harbor of San Francisco; and the point which must be Point Reyes ends at the tip in a sort of large island, though, as Cabrera shows, it is all part of the mainland." Costansó, in referring to the seashore westward of their camp in Pedro Valley, calls it "the beach of San Francisco," and when, the next day, they set out to seek "the harbor of San Francisco," he refers to a canyon where they spent the night as "la cañada de San Francisco."

Their route was eastward from Pacifica, over Portolá Ridge to San Andreas Lake, and then southeastward down Crystal Springs Valley to the San Francisquito Creek, which runs between Palo Alto and Menlo Park, where camp was made on the night of

November 6, traditionally located in the shade of the huge redwood, the *"palo alto"* that gave its name to the city. Portolá's policy seemed to be that the newly discovered estuary, as they termed it, on their left, must have an outlet to the sea, and they believed that this outlet was either just under Point Reyes, where Cabrera Bueno claimed it to be, or possibly was the nearer "cover with shelter" close to the "white bluffs" that Crespí noticed — presumably near Bolinas Bay. Portolá may have believed it was strategically important for Spain to have exact knowledge about the entrance to the great estuary on their left flank, or he may simply have yielded to the insistence of Rivera and Ortega who still believed that Monterey lay ahead of them; at any rate, on November 7, he made no protest when Rivera ordered Ortega to go on one more scouting expedition to see if he could discover the place where the estuary entered the ocean. Ortega and his men, spurred on by confused reports made by some of the natives about a ship with armed men in it — perhaps their missing supply vessel, the *San José*, they hoped — rounded the southern end of the bay and proceeded up the eastern shore to a point near San Lorenzo. Climbing a hill for a better view, Ortega could see that an enormous round estuary (San Pablo Bay) would prevent his party from ever reaching Point Reyes in the time allowed him. He returned on the night of the 10th, and sadly reported that he had not found the outlet of the great estuary; that the route to Point Reyes in that direction was blocked by yet another estuary which reached far inland; and that the rumors about a ship had proven false, or perhaps had simply been misunderstood from the beginning.

Another council was held, and this time the decision was to return to San Diego, Crespí and Gómez joining in the decision of the rest. So, on November 28, having returned from the San Francisquito Creek encampment by the same route as the one they had used going north, the expedition again reached the area of the Monterey peninsula, though again they failed to recognize it as the site of the "harbor of Monterey" they had come so far to find. For nearly two weeks the party remained in camp near the future site of Carmel, while exploring parties went out to reconnoiter a route on the seaward side of the Santa Lucia Mountains, but without success. Another council was called; it was first suggested that the party divide into two groups, one to proceed as rapidly as possible to San Diego and make a report, the other to remain for a while to see if the *San Jose* would come to relieve their hunger. But after further discussion it was decided to return to "the Channel," by which they meant Santa Barbara, but which in effect meant San Diego. They remained in camp for a few more days, however, while Fathers Crespí and Gómez celebrated Holy Mass and recited public prayers, at which all the men devoutly assisted despite the intense December cold, praying God for assistance in their near starvation, and asking the Holy Spirit to guide their councils aright.

On December 9 Portolá made up his mind to leave while there was still some food left. But first he ordered a large wooden cross to be set up on the beach, with a sign on it reading "Dig! At the foot you will find a writing." Then Costansó composed for him a long account of all that had taken place, naming areas they had visited, and the dates, and concluding with a statement that, "disappointed and despairing of finding (the harbor) after so many endeavors, labors, and hardships, and with no provisions except fourteen sacks of flour, the expedition set out today from this bay for San Diego .... At this Bay of Pines, December 9, 1769." Then he transcribed eight of his most important latitudes, from San Diego to Point Reyes; and finally he begged the commander of either the *San José* or the *El Príncipe*, should they read this message within the next few days, to return to San Diego by sailing close to the shore line, so that possibly the explorers might see them, and hopefully the ship might stop and land them some provisions. This long communication was placed in a bottle and buried at the foot of the cross which was erected "here at this point where we are," as Crespí says, meaning somewhere on the south side of the mouth of the Carmel Valley. Meanwhile another message was also written and attached to a cross that was set up right on the beach of what today we call the Bay of Monterey. This message was briefer, and informed anyone who should call at that place that the expedition had returned to San Diego for want of provisions.

These preparations for departure evidently consumed a considerable amount of time, and it was not until the morning of the 10th that they started the return trip, which took them by much the same route as that by which they had come. The remaining food was rationed out, and each man was told to guard his own allowance. On December 25 they feasted on fish which they received from Indians who had caught the fish near San Luis Obispo. In return the men gave the natives some of their few remaining glass beads. By January 15 the expedition was again in the San Fernando Valley, having entered it this time by the more direct route from Ventura by way of Calabasas. They again stopped at the pool of Los Encinos. On the 16th they went through the (unnamed) Cahuenga Pass into Hollywood. January 17 saw them on the San Gabriel River, and by the 24th they were in San Diego.

Their joy at finding their beloved Father Serra in good health was tempered by the disappointing news they themselves had to impart, that they had failed to find the port of Monterey. Moreover, there were other problems facing Portolá. Food was scarce, and the return of his party now put a severe strain on the available supplies. But the arrival of the *San José* (its sad fate not yet learned), or else the return of the *San Antonio*, was expected daily. On March 23 the *San Antonio* did actually appear in the harbor, and its food supplies were welcomed by the nearly starving men.

Portolá was now in a strong position to accomplish what he had been ordered to do, to found a mission at Monterey. He ordered the *San Antonio*, with a crew composed of some of the sailors who had recovered from the scurvy from the previous voyage, to sail for Monterey at once, with Fr. Serra and others aboard, while he himself, with Fr. Crespí and a smaller group of men — only thirty this time — made a second journey by land to the same place that they had encamped the previous fall, at the Point of Pines.

The route of this second expedition was much the same as that of the first. They stopped again at the Río de la Porciúncula; and it was about here that Crespí took the trouble to note in his diary that the plain that is watered by the three rivers which today we call the San Gabriel, the Rio Hondo, and the Los Angeles River could, without very much labor, form a great irrigation district for the production of crops from the fertile soil.

Their route from the crossing of the river into the San Fernando Valley is not very clear. The text reads as follows (retaining in this instance the original spelling and capitalization of Crespí's manuscript):

Pasamos adelante, y â poco subimos unas Lomas por el mismo rumbo del Norueste, y como â las dos leguas de andar desde este Rio, â la una de la tarde llegamos a un corto Arroyto de alguna agua solo para la Gente, al pie de un Portuzuelo del Valle de Sta. Catharina de Bononia.

This may be translated as: "We went onward, and shortly afterwards we climbed some low hills, taking the same direction towards the northwest, and after marching about two leagues from the river, about one o'clock in the afternoon we came to a small stream which had enough water for only the men, at the foot of a pass into the valley of St. Catherine of Bologna [the San Fernando Valley]." This passage in the diary recounts the expedition's journey from the Los Angeles River near the City Hall, by way of the present Hollywood Freeway, to the Cahuenga Pass. The "corto Arroyto" (small-sized arroyo) is no doubt the now dry canyon below the dam that forms Hollywood Lake, just to the east of the entrance to Cahuenga Pass. They went through the pass without naming it, and camped as before at Encino. Leaving this area they proceeded westward to the end of the valley, and left it by the Calabasas-Ventura route. From there they proceeded northwest, through the same counties as on the previous trip, finally arriving at the Point of Pines on May 24, 1770.

They found the cross still in place, but adorned with Indian feathers, and with a pile of votive offerings at its foot, evidence that the superstitious natives wanted to placate some powerful spirit which they thought this emblem represented. But Portolá and Crespí found no sign of the ship that had left San Diego a few days before their departure. However, now that they had more time to explore, and the fine spring weather put them into a better humor than had the previous winter's bitter cold, they observed that between the Point of Pines on the south and the headland some twenty miles to the north (at Santa Cruz) there was indeed a sort of open bay of relatively calm water. It was decided that this was after all the "bay of Monterey" described by Vizcaíno and by Cabrera Bueno, even if it was a bit wider and more open than these mariners' descriptions had led them to believe. This decision was confirmed a week later by the arrival of the *San Antonio,* which had no hesitation in sailing in close to the shore and anchoring under the lee of the Point of Pines. In fact, from the ship, the captain and Fr. Serra had had no difficulty in recognizing what must have been the great oak tree where Vizcaíno had ordered Mass to be celebrated in 1602, over a century and a half earlier.

On June 3, 1770, the presidio and mission at Monterey, the latter dedicated to San Carlos Borromeo, were solemnly inaugurated. This was Serra's third foundation, and like the other two it was accomplished with all possible ceremony. The two priests, Serra and Crespí, in their colorful vestments, the officers in their most lavish uniforms, and the soldiers firing round after round of musketry, reinforced by salvos from the guns on the *San Antonio* lying in the harbor, must have presented an astonishing spectacle to the terrified natives who watched the performance from the safety of the nearby hills. Mass was celebrated with as much solemnity as possible, and afterwards the civil acts of taking possession of the land in the name of the King of Spain — such acts as uprooting plants, disturbing large stones, and similar symbolic acts of legal possession — were all performed and then carefully recorded in an official report.

Portolá selected two young men from his small cadre of officers and men — barely enough to defend the presidio, he felt, if the natives should prove hostile — and ordered them to proceed as rapidly as possible to Mexico City, carrying the good news that Monterey had been rediscovered and identified, and that a presidio and a mission had been established. California had been saved for the Spanish crown, and soldiers were there to defend it from the alleged encroachments of the Russian Bear. Shortly after dispatching this message, Portolá himself set sail on the *San Antonio,* turning over the command of Alta California to his lieutenant, Pedro Fages. Portolá had well served the king in defending Alta California against its potential invaders, and he was entitled to receive his reward in person. He left for Mexico on July 9, 1770, and he did not again set foot in California.

Serra and Crespí, no longer teacher and pupil, but now colleagues working together for the salvation of the souls of the Indians of the vicinity, as well as caring for the spiritual needs of the officers and soldiers of the presidio, worked hard to get some structures built which could serve as a chapel for the men and also to attract the Indians to come and listen to instruction in the Christian faith. But by the time a year had elapsed, it became evident to the Father President that the area of the presidio itself was not a suitable place for a mission to the natives. The soil was not fertile, and the presence of the soldiery intimidated the Indians and, according to the later evidence of Governor Rivera's day-books (though the padres themselves make no mention of it), gave some encouragement to the Indian women's tendency towards prostitution. Furthermore, the requirements of the Spaniards took time away from what Serra considered to be of supreme importance, preaching to the aborigines. So during the fall of 1771 he moved the mission operations to the Carmel Valley, about four-and-a-half miles away from the dangers and distractions provided by the soldiers at Monterey, and by Christmas of 1771 the new establishment was ready. Fr. Crespí became its first resident priest, and Fr. Serra made it his official headquarters for the remainder of his life.

Not much is known of Fr. Crespí's daily life at Carmel mission. His name appears in the baptismal register as early as January 1771 (when it was still at Monterey), and statistics of the mission show that a fair number of Indian converts were made during these early years, though the local population was not very great. When not occupied with his labors as a missionary, Crespí rewrote and polished up his diaries, at the Father President's specific request, since he alone of all the Franciscans had made the trip by land from Loreto to San Francisco Bay. He was absent from his mission of San Carlos at Carmel for at least three periods of time, twice in 1772 and again in 1774, on the occasion of expeditions which he accompanied, but in general, except for a brief period in 1772 when he was stationed at San Diego, he considered Carmel to be his home.

The two expeditions which Fr. Crespí accompanied were the
occasions for yet more diaries from the pen of this indefatigable
traveler. In March 1772, Governor Fages (who had taken over as
Governor in 1770 when Portolá left) wanted to explore the eastern
shore of San Francisco Bay, to see whether a land route could be
found that would go to Point Reyes, inside of which the Spaniards
still, though erroneously, believed was to be found the real Bay of
San Francisco described by Rodríguez Cermeño in 1595 and by
Sebastián Vizcaíno in 1603. The bay had been "seen confusedly"
by the exploring party of 1769; and although an outlet to the sea,
which today we call the Golden Gate, had been discovered by
Fages' own scouts, and seen by himself from the eastern shore of
the Bay in November of 1770, he still wanted more information
about the upper end of "the estuary," as they called it, before
deciding where would be the best place for a mission. Fr. Crespí
was requested to go along with Fages as chaplain, and also to keep a
diary.

The party of sixteen men left on March 20, Fages himself in the
lead. The expedition went over the (present-day) San Juan Grade,
past Hollister, Gilroy, San Jose, Alvarado, San Lorenzo,
Alameda, Oakland, Richmond, Pinole, Martinez, Antioch, Dan-
ville, Pleasanton, and over the ridge to Mission San Jose, returning
by way of Gilroy and Mission San Juan Bautista to Monterey.
Crespí's diary is, as usual, full of interesting details. He noted the
fertile soil, the tracks of deer and bears, the running streams, the
mallows and other herbs that grew so lavishly in the spring sun-
shine. He gave specific names to places he thought suitable for
future missions. He noted that some of the Indians they met used
stuffed birds as decoys in their capture of doves and other fowl.
Coming to a point just above Richmond, and observing several
whales disporting in the "large round bay" (San Pablo Bay), he
commented that the harbor was presumably deep, and that "there
can shelter in this bay, I shall not say vessels, but tall ships of high
port, whole fleets of them."

Crespí and Fages returned to Monterey on Sunday, April 5.
Crespí now wished to devote his whole life to the Indians of the
locality, as he had done for the Pames in the Sierra Gorda, but the

poor state of his health did not seem to allow it. Even when he was at Monterey during 1770 and 1771, he had been continually plagued by coughs and colds, watering of the eyes, and migraine headaches. He believed that only a drier climate would help him; and when Serra offered to send him to the founding of Mission San Buenaventura, he at first accepted. But in the end he could not bring himself to leave Fr. Serra, and in any event he did not think the climate at the new mission would help him much. While on the northern trip with Fages he had somewhat recovered his health, but shortly after his return he had suffered a relapse. Serra was much distressed, and sought other means to relieve his friend's sufferings.

On April 13, 1772, an unexpected opportunity came. Because of the failure of the supply ships that year to reach California on schedule, the garrison at San Diego was very short of food. Fages, on learning of this, ordered a pack-train of supplies to be sent down. Serra suggested that Crespí go along as chaplain, and upon arrival take up the missionary duties of Fr. Francisco Dumetz, who had gone down to Baja California to try to obtain some sheep and cattle for the people at San Diego and at San Gabriel. Crespí went to San Diego and remained there until the fall. He was soon regretting the change, however, even though his health did seem to improve; homesick for the Monterey peninsula and above all lonely for the companionship of his friend, he humbly asked Serra to send him back. He returned to Carmel on September 22 of the same year, and aside from some short journeys on official business, and one long voyage to Alaska, he remained there until the last year of his life.

Crespí was a good explorer, indefatigable, uncomplaining, able to endure hardship, hunger, thirst, whatever might be encountered on the trail. Unfortunately he was not quite so heroic on board a ship, and it was a great hardship for him to keep a daily diary when he was so seasick he could hardly stand. Nevertheless, he did it. In June 1774 Serra requested Crespí and one other Franciscan, Fray Tomás de la Peña y Saravia, to accompany the expedition that was shortly to set out in the frigate *Santiago*, captained by Juan Pérez. The purpose of the voyage was to explore the coast as far north as the 60th degree of latitude, if possible, and then to turn southward along the coast, to land parties, to explore, to take possession of the country in as many places as possible, and to report on the existence of any Russian outposts they might see. Though no sailor, as he well remembered from his voyage across the Atlantic, Fr. Crespí, now fifty-three years of age, and worn out by the thousands of miles of hard travel up and down California, obeyed his superior and agreed to go on this voyage. He was told he need not keep a diary of the days at sea, but only of the landings and of explorations by land; but he decided to keep a day-by-day account anyway, which was just as well, as the northern weather proved too rough for them even to make one landing.

Departing on June 11, 1774, the frigate sailed slowly northward towards British Columbia and Alaska, aiming for the 60th parallel, which would be in the vicinity of today's Seward at the head of the Gulf of Alaska. While still out on the open ocean, on July 15, Pérez called his officers together and pointed out to them that the continuing fogs and contrary winds would probably prevent them from reaching their goal of the 60th parallel before running out of fresh water. The officers agreed that it would be best to turn towards the coast, and try to take on water, rather than continue to head north in a perhaps vain attempt to reach 60° before trying to land. They accordingly did so, and land was first sighted on the 18th, this land being Graham Island, the large north island of the Queen Charlotte group (in British Columbia), located approximately between the 53rd and 54th parallels. On the 20th, while still seeking a suitable landing place on Graham Island, a native canoe came out to visit the *Santiago*, but the timid natives refused to climb the ladder that the men threw over the side for them. On the 21st Pérez did manage to sail part way across (present-day) Dixon Entrance, but the strong currents of this "bay, pocket, strait, or gulf," they did not know which, kept him from achieving his objective, which seems to have been to anchor in the lee of Point Muzon, the southernmost point of Prince of Wales Archipelago, Alaska. Because they returned from this unsuccessful attempt long before noon, they could not "shoot the sun" to determine their most northerly point before putting back towards

Graham Island. Upon arrival at the latter place, they found themselves becalmed about a league from shore, somewhere near the northwestern tip of that triangular-shaped island. Soon a number of canoes, twenty-one in all, surrounded the ship. Crespí busied himself taking notes; he observed the various articles of native dress; he noted that many women were in the canoes with the men, and in fact one canoe was entirely manned by women, who "were rowing and steering as well as the most dextrous sailor."

These natives came out into the open sea in this way for the sake of barter, and they did a brisk business with the sailors, who traded knives, cloth, and beads for native beaver skins, quilts, furs, wooden trays, hand-carved spoons, and other artifacts, all of very fine workmanship. Crespí devotes approximately twelve pages of his diary to a description of these Indians, though he had to observe them mostly as they paddled their canoes around the ship, for of the hundreds present only two natives were bold enough to accept the Spaniards' invitation to come aboard.

Pérez made one more attempt on the 22nd to swing north, and, according to his pilots, did reach 55° at noon that day, though it appears from modern maps that their instrument calculations must have been off by half a degree, and that they were really about 30' south of that latitude. Dixon Entrance, that forty-mile-wide strait between Graham Island, Canada and Dall Island, now part of Alaska, seems therefore to have been the Spaniards' farthest northing on this memorable voyage of exploration, reached on July 21 or 22, 1774. The next day Pérez decided to turn southward down the coast, to try to make landings in accordance with his orders, and to explore the coastline for future Spanish ships. But in all of these he was continually frustrated by fog, strong offshore breezes, rock-bound coastlines, and other factors. Finally, on August 9, probably in Nootka Sound on Vancouver Island, he made one more attempt to land. Natives came out in canoes as usual and seemed friendly. A large wooden cross was brought out on deck, to be erected on the land as a sign of possession by Spain, and a launch was being readied, when a stiff breeze arose, causing the ship to drag anchor. Rather than run the risk of shipwreck, Pérez ordered the anchor cable to be cut and the ship to put about and head for the open sea. This was the last attempt to make a formal landing, and on August 27 the ship was once again in the harbor of Monterey.

This officially ended Crespí's career as an explorer and diarist for the Spanish realm. For the remaining seven years of his life Fr. Crespí was a quiet but zealous missionary at Carmel, content to live under obedience to his beloved teacher and friend, Junípero Serra. But in almost the last year of his life, in 1781, the sixty-year-old friar asked permission to make a journey to San Francisco, for the purpose of visiting once more the peninsula country he had not seen since 1769, and more particularly for a long visit with his beloved friend of school days, Fr. Palóu, whom he had not seen since 1779, and then but briefly, when the latter had come down to Carmel. Fr. Serra approved this request for a leave of absence, the first, it appears, that Crespí had taken for over fifteen years. Crespí therefore accompanied Serra on his next official journey to San Francisco, arriving there on October 26, and of course being heartily welcomed by the good Francisco Palóu. This was the last occasion when the three friends, Serra, Crespí, and Palóu, were to be united, for even in death they are not now together — Serra and Crespí are at Carmel, while Palóu is buried far away in Mexico City. They remained there at Mission Dolores for a happy period of about two weeks, when Serra and Crespí left to return by way of Santa Clara on November 9, remaining there for the laying of a cornerstone for a new church on November 19.

Shortly after their return to Carmel, Fr. Crespí came down with some sort of bronchial trouble, aggravated by swelling of the legs. There was no physician at Monterey at the time, and though Fr. Serra and the other friars there did their best to aid him with what little medical knowledge they had, he grew steadily worse all through the Christmas season. On New Year's Eve he was given the sacrament of the Final Anointing by Fr. Serra himself, and a few hours later, at about six o'clock in the morning of New Year's Day, 1782, his gentle soul went to its Maker and his weary body was afterwards laid in its resting place in the sanctuary of the church at Carmel.

So lived, and so died, a great eighteenth-century Spaniard —

missionary, explorer, diarist — in all three categories his fame deserves to live forever. As a missionary he was perhaps over-shadowed by his own superior, Junípero Serra; as an explorer he was certainly no match for the justly more famous Francisco Garcés, a Franciscan like himself, and a contemporary, and also a good man for the task of keeping a daily journal; but as a diarist Juan Crespí is supreme. Five thousand miles of land and sea explo-ration, mile after weary mile, were faithfully, accurately, and inter-estingly recorded by this humble friar, despite conditions of hun-ger, cold, rain, seasickness, monotony, boredom, thirst, and all the other trials that afflicted, but could not dampen, his ardent spirit. Had he done nothing else, had he not baptized, or preached, or converted souls to Christianity, had he not left behind him a legacy of kindly deeds among his Indian charges and his fellow Franciscans alike, he would still be remembered for a few outstanding features of his life: it was Crespí, not Serra, who was the first Franciscan missionary to enter Alta California by land and to arrive at San Diego; it was Crespí, not Serra, who made the first (and second) land journey to Monterey with Por-tolá; and it was Crespí, not Serra, who bestowed most of the first Christian names upon the land of California, including among them the name of the future city of Los Angeles.

Gaspar de Portolá: Disenchanted Conquistador of Spanish Upper California

BY DONALD A. NUTTALL

DURING THE YEAR 1969 Californians celebrated the bicentennial of the origin of their state's modern period — the birth of Spanish Upper California. Those familiar with that historic event know that delivery came only after a prolonged period of severe labor pains; for over two years the Spanish midwives of the colonizing expedition experienced extended voyages over unfriendly seas, lengthy marches over unfamiliar and difficult terrain, and agonizingly long vigils for overdue supply vessels. And through it all they had as their constant companions the twin scourges of hunger and disease. Credit for the enterprise's ultimate success despite such adversity has been generously distributed, and this is as it should be, for all of its participants displayed extraordinary courage and shared the common sacrifice. It generally is conceded, however, that a major factor in the preservation of Spain's precarious hold on Upper California during that crisis period was the capable and courageous leadership of the expedition's military-commander — Captain Gaspar de Portolá.

Recognition of Portolá's contribution as Upper California colonizer rests upon a broad and solid base. A grateful Spain promptly promoted him to the rank of lieutenant colonel. Historians invariably have lauded him both as a man and as a leader. Modern California has honored his name in a variety of ways. Portolá himself proudly noted his California achievements in subsequent service records and petitions to the crown.

When named commander of the Upper California colonizing expedition by Visitor General José de Gálvez in 1768, Portolá was a veteran of almost thirty-five years in the royal service. In the course of thirty years of European duty he had been wounded while campaigning in Italy during the War of the Austrian Succession, and he had also participated in Spain's abortive invasion of Portugal during the Seven Years War. He had come to New Spain as a captain in the Regiment of Dragoons of Spain in 1764, and since late 1767 had been in Lower California, where he had carried out the expulsion of the Jesuit Order and was serving as governor. Following his return from Upper California, Portolá would serve the crown for an additional sixteen years, half of them as governor of Puebla. Portolá's Upper California duty was, therefore, but a brief episode in a distinguished fifty-year military career. Evidence indicates, however, that it very probably was the most distasteful period of his life.

Father Francisco Palóu tells us that Portolá volunteered to lead the Upper California expedition, and this may well be true. Gálvez doubtless impressed the veteran soldier with the importance and urgency of saving the northern lands from the grasping Russian Bear. Portolá, moreover, probably welcomed the new assignment. Difficulties inherent in such an undertaking could be anticipated, but, on the other hand, he would be free of both "this miserable peninsula," as he once called Lower California, and of its governorship, an office he had found most onerous. Time and circumstance, however, would reveal that Portolá had struck an extremely bad bargain, and by the time I have completed my account of his experiences as leader of the Upper California enterprise I feel that you will agree with my view that we are dealing with a most disenchanted *conquistador.*

Various difficulties both delayed the expedition's departure and disrupted Gálvez's original plans for coordination of its sea and land branches. Portolá, nonetheless, could not have foreseen the problems which lay before him when he departed from Loreto on March 9, 1769, and began the first leg of his long journey — to Mission Santa María, the northernmost of the peninsular chain, about 400 miles distant. The trip was made with relative ease, for as he later wrote: "We were fortunate enough to be able to sleep under roofs and make the march with some comfort." Portolá, however, was not as comfortable in mind as in body, for his conscience was troubled by expropriations of supplies he was forced to make at the missions visited en route. Displaying considerable contrition, he later commented that:

In consideration of the great deserts into which I was going, and of the Russian danger with which I foresaw we were going to contend, I was obliged to seize everything I saw as I passed through those poor missions, leaving them, to my regret, as scantily provided for as I knew the three southern ones had been left in consequence of the orders given by the visitor for dispatching the packetboats *San Carlos* and *San Antonio* to the port of Monterey.

On May 11 Portolá broke camp at Mission Santa María and began the 300 mile march to San Diego, and before long his concern for the Lower California missions was replaced by more immediate problems. Although he followed a trail recently blazed by the expedition's first land party under Captain Fernando Rivera y Moncada, the terrain was still unfamiliar and often difficult to traverse. Moreover, Portolá's food supply soon ran low and had to be supplemented by hunting and fishing, which often brought scant or no reward. Consequently, many Christian Indians in the party died and others deserted. Lack of water also caused frequent suffering among both men and animals.

In late June, Portolá's ordeal ended, when, as he later wrote: "Overcoming these and other innumerable hardships, natural results of such unhappy fortunes, we arrived at the port of San Diego."

Portolá doubtless anticipated that the worst part of his undertaking would be behind him when he reached San Diego, for it was, as he later observed, "the spot at which the expeditionaries by land and sea were to meet in accordance with the visitor-general's instructions to recount the great events which had happened to us and the discoveries incident to our journeys." And had Gálvez's plans been on schedule, Portolá would have found the mission and presidio in San Diego well on their way to completion and preparations for founding the Monterey settlements already made.

Portolá, however, suffered the first major discouragement of his Upper California experience when he viewed conditions in San Diego. The packetboats *San Carlos* and *San Antonio,* which comprised the expedition's sea-branch, both had undergone prolonged voyages to the port, and by the time of their arrivals in April the crews, as well as the Catalan Volunteers carried by the *San Carlos,* were largely incapacitated by scurvy. Consequently, Captains Vicente Vila and Juan Pérez had been able to do no more than erect a crude settlement ashore, where Doctor Pedro Prat, the expedition's physician, could minister to the ill. After his arrival with his land party on May 14, Captain Rivera y Moncada had moved the camp to a more desirable site but otherwise had confined his efforts to giving what aid he could to the stricken. Portolá, therefore, found neither mission nor presidio in San Diego but rather a general hospital filled to capacity and a cemetery already possessing thirty-four occupants. And the planned advance to Monterey Bay had, of course, been impossible.

Portolá resolutely resolved to make the best of a poor situation. The *San Antonio,* manned by a meager crew, promptly was dispatched southward to the port of San Blas with news of the expedition's plight and requests for additional seamen and supplies. Since the members of the land parties were reasonably healthy and available provisions adequate, if not abundant, for the trip, Portolá then made preparations for a march to Monterey Bay, the expedition's primary objective. An early departure was considered imperative, for winter snows in the mountains might soon cut off the route, and time was of the essence if the race with the Russians to Monterey Bay was to be won.

Leaving a few soldiers in San Diego to protect the Spaniards remaining in the land settlement and on the *San Carlos,* Portolá began his journey to Monterey Bay on July 14. His party was comprised of sixty-some men, or, as he later described them, "skeletons, who had been spared by scurvy, hunger and thirst."

Portolá had no reason to believe that the location and identification of Monterey Bay would be particularly difficult tasks. He carried with him two written guides: Admiral José González Cabrera

Gaspar de Portolá: Disenchanted Conquistador

Bueno's *Navegación Especulativa y Práctica*, a navigator's handbook, and Miguel Venegas' *Noticia de la California*, which contains Torquemada's account of Sebastián Vizcaíno's California voyage of 1602–3. The party also possessed instruments with which to measure latitudes. Portolá planned to hug the coast as much as possible; this would permit him to take maximum advantage of the written guides and would also facilitate contact with the returning *San Antonio* or other possible supply ship arrivals.

During the next few weeks, the Spaniards traveled slowly northward over unfamiliar and often hostile terrain, which frequently forced them to abandon the coast. Crossing the Santa Lucia Range was a particularly trying experience. They struggled, wrote Portolá, "against the greatest hardships and difficulties; for, aside from the fact that there was in all that ungracious country . . . no object to greet either the hand or the eye save rocks, brushwood, and rugged mountains . . ., we were also without food and did not know where we were." On September 30, seventy-eight days after leaving San Diego, the Spaniards completed their descent of the Salinas Valley and encamped within earshot of the ocean. They were then confident that their march was over, for all their calculations indicated that Monterey Bay lay before them.

The most incredible circumstance of the entire Upper California undertaking then transpired. "For," as Portolá later lamented, "although the signs whereby we were to recognize the port were the same as those set down by General Sebastián Vizcaíno in his log, the fact is that, without being able to give the reason, we were all under hallucination, and none dared assert openly that the port was indeed Monterey."

Monterey Bay was, in fact, in full view of the Spaniards. Moreover, they recognized the Point of Pines, Point Año Nuevo, and other landmarks described by Vizcaíno and Cabrera Bueno. Yet, amazingly, they could not recognize the bay as such. Many reasons have been put forth in efforts to explain the Spanish confusion. Most frequently, the somewhat exaggerated descriptions of the bay's excellence as a harbor by Vizcaíno and Cabrera Bueno have been cited. Hubert Howe Bancroft, however, probably hit closer to the truth when he wrote:

Monterey had been much talked and written about during the past century and a half in connection with the fables of the Northern Mystery, and . . . its importance as a harbor had been constantly growing in the minds of Spanish officials and missionaries. It was not the *piloto's* comparatively modest descriptions as much as the grand popular ideal which supported the expectations of the governor and his companions, and of which the reality fell so short.

Regardless of its cause, the Spanish perplexity was a reality, and Portolá, on October 4, held a council of his officers to consider a future course of action. Several difficulties then confronted the expedition: eleven soldiers were suffering from scurvy, eight of whom were incapacitated; provisions were running low; and winter was approaching. It was unanimously decided, however, to continue northward in search of the elusive bay.

After three days of rest, the Spaniards turned their backs on their objective and resumed their march. Progress was slow, for scurvy continued to spread among the soldiers, and several had to be carried on litters. Six were given the last rites at various times but fortunately none died.

Spanish morale reached its lowest point on October 28. The party was then well above the reported latitude of Monterey Bay, but it was nowhere to be found. Its food supply was dangerously low, making rationing necessary. A form of diarrhea had afflicted all of its members, including Portolá. And heavy rains had begun to fall. The expedition's plight was such that Miguel Costansó, its cosmographer and engineer, feared it had reached its end. Miraculously, however, those suffering from diarrhea and scurvy soon began to recover, and the party was able to continue.

On October 30 the Spaniards reached a point from which they viewed and recognized Point Reyes, the Farallon Islands, and other landmarks of Sebastián Cermeño's Bay of San Francisco (present Drake's Bay). Three days later they made their historic discovery of present San Francisco Bay. After spending about a week exploring the Contra Costa region, the Spaniards realized that Monterey Bay had been bypassed. They therefore determined to return to the Point of Pines and make a more extensive search for that port.

On November 28 the expedition encamped near the Carmel River, and shortly afterward Captain Rivera y Moncada led a party southward to seek the bay which lay just to the north. His efforts, of course, proved fruitless.

Portolá, on December 7, convened another council of his officers to consider the expedition's plight. Proposals that all or a portion of the party remain in the area and await the arrival of a ship were rejected, since supplies were critically low and mountain snows might soon cut off all possibility of retreat. "In this confusion and distress," Portolá subsequently reported, "not under compulsion from the Russians, but from keen hunger which was wearing us out, we decided to return to San Diego, for the purpose of regaining our strength by means of the provisions which we judged would soon arrive on the *San Antonio*."

Delayed for three days by torrential rains, the Spaniards began their return to San Diego on December 10. With some minor modifications, they generally retraced the route which had brought them northward. Difficulties continued to be their lot: they suffered from cold in the Santa Lucias, were misguided and lost in the Santa Monica range by two elderly Indians, and several were again afflicted with diarrhea. The most serious problem, however, was exhaustion of the meat supply during the latter part of the trip, a circumstance which compelled Portolá to resort to a measure so distasteful that he had reserved it as a desperate and last extremity. He later described it most graphically:

In order that we might not die meanwhile [he wrote], I ordered that at the end of each day's march, one of the weakest of the old mules which carried our baggage and ourselves, should be killed. The flesh we roasted or half-fried in a fire made in a hole in the ground. The mule being thus prepared without a grain of salt or other seasoning — for we had none — we shut our eyes and fell to on that scally mule (what misery!) like hungry lions. We ate twelve in as many days, obtaining from them perforce all our sustenance, all our appetite, all our delectation.

"Smelling frightfully of mules," in Portolá's words, the unhappy Spaniards reached San Diego on January 24, 1770. One bit of good news greeted their arrival: Father Junípero Serra had formally founded Mission San Diego de Alcalá on July 16, 1769, which thus marks the generally recognized birthdate of Spanish Upper California. It was overshadowed, however, by the gloom of all other reports: on August 15 the Indians had attacked the Spanish settlement, killing Father Serra's boy servant and wounding Father Juan Vizcaíno and several soldiers; the scurvy had continued to take its toll, leaving only about twenty survivors to welcome Portolá's return; and, most critically, no supply vessel had reached the port.

Portolá, under the circumstances, certainly would have been justified in abandoning the entire enterprise and returning southward, for the more than eighty men under his command were then confronted with the distinct possibility of starvation. The conscientious veteran was reluctant to concede failure, however. He therefore formulated a plan which might still bring success and, at the same time, minimize the chances of disaster.

An inventory revealed that the food supply would last approximately three months. On February 12 Captain Rivera y Moncada with twenty-five men departed for Lower California, thus lessening the number drawing on the meager supplies. The remaining Spaniards were to stay in San Diego until March 19 (the day of San José, patron saint of the expedition) to await the arrival of the *San Antonio*. Should the *San Antonio* reach the port by that date, a second march to Monterey would be made, paralleled by the ship, which, it was believed, would facilitate the location and identification of the bay. Should it fail to do so, the rest of the expedition would begin its southward retreat on March 20. Barely enough food would remain for the trip if extreme economy was meanwhile practiced.

Portolá later described the Spanish ordeal which followed:

We remained in San Diego [he wrote] . . . waiting for the *San Antonio*, subsisting . . . on geese and fish and the other food which the Indians brought us in exchange for clothing. Some of the soldiers were left with hardly enough clothing to cover their backs, having given up the rest to avoid perishing from want.

Even California's avifauna conspired to add to the misery of the foreign intruders, for as Portolá continued:

84

We had planted a small quantity of corn in the best soil, but although it grew well, the birds ate the best of it while it was yet soft, leaving us disappointed and bereft of the hope we had cherished of eating the grain which our hands had sown.

As the designated day of departure approached, Portolá agreed to Father Serra's suggestion that a *novena* of daily prayers to San José be held, but March 19 arrived with no vessel in sight, and final preparations for leaving were made. That afternoon, however, the *San Antonio* was spotted off the coast, and although Captain Pérez continued northward towards Monterey as his orders called for, circumstances prompted him to return to San Diego a few days later. Abandonment of Upper California had been averted.

Portolá promptly began preparations for the combined land-sea expedition to Monterey Bay. On April 16 the *San Antonio* lifted anchor and set sail for that destination. Portolá began his northward march the following day.

Portolá's land party reached Monterey Bay on May 13. Immediately recognizing the port on this occasion, the Spaniards encamped in the Carmel region and awaited the *San Antonio*. The ship arrived and dropped anchor in the harbor on May 31.

On June 3 the assembled Spaniards celebrated the formal ceremonies required to claim the territory for Spain and to found Mission San Carlos Borromeo. Portolá later expressed disgust at having been required to perform the former, when he wrote:

I was not ignorant of the fact that the king of Spain had for centuries been owner and legitimate lord of those lands, but . . . as article eight of the visitor-general's instructions gave me to understand to the contrary, I repeated the formalities of taking legal possession which was therein ordered.

"In fulfillment of other orders," he continued with a touch of irony, "I proceeded to erect a fort to occupy and defend the port from the atrocities of the Russians who were about to invade us, as was to be inferred from the terms of the instructions." The fort referred to was a single palisade enclosing both presidio and mission. Designed by Costansó, it was constructed by the soldiers, under the supervision of Lieutenant Pedro Fages of the Catalan

Volunteers, who was to remain in Upper California as military-commandant of the new establishments.

Portolá impatiently awaited the time when he could take leave of California. His original orders had called for him to return to Loreto by land, so that he might seek out mission sites en route, but he meanwhile had requested and received permission to travel directly to New Spain proper. With work on the Monterey settlement having progressed sufficiently, he departed on the *San Antonio* on July 9.

The *San Antonio*'s voyage to San Blas was rapid, and it dropped anchor in that port on August 1. The brevity of the trip obviously pleased Portolá, for he later reported that, "I soon embarked for San Blas . . ., where happily I shortly arrived, for on the return voyage one travels as fast as Sancho Panza would have liked."

In his Panzanian haste, however, Portolá was guilty of his only reprehensible act in Upper California. He had promised Captain Vila that the *San Antonio* would stop in San Diego on its return voyage, so that the *San Carlos* might be given sufficient seamen to permit its sailing to San Blas. Stranded in San Diego for fifteen months, the *San Carlos* was threatened with ruin. Reportedly, because the winds were not favorable, however, the *San Antonio* bypassed the port, and only by acquiring a makeshift crew from Captain Rivera y Moncada was Vila able to make his return some time later.

Portolá was not only anxious to abandon the child he had fathered but was also critical of its character and skeptical of its chances for survival:

You must be weary . . . of listening to all the plagues I encountered on my journey [he shortly wrote], but believe me also when I say that the unhappy Spaniards whom I left in those new establishments are at present enduring the same discomforts. I reported them all to the viceroy and the visitor-general in official and confidential letters; without reserve I explained to them that it will be impossible to send aid to Monterey by sea, and still more so by land, unless it was proposed to sacrifice thousands of men and huge sums of money.

While overly pessimistic with regard to Upper California's

future, Portolá was correct in his assessment of another matter. "Even if Monterey is at last fairly well fortified," he wrote, "and California should through an extravagant desire be coveted by the Russians, there are still many other ports which, being undefended by troops and fortifications, could not oppose them, and where they may freely establish themselves if they desire." Fort Ross proved Portolá to be an able prophet.

Portolá remained in the royal service for sixteen years after his return from Upper California. Rejoining the Regiment of Dragoons of Spain, he promptly requested promotion to the rank of lieutenant colonel, which was granted him in January 1771. In March 1773, Portolá departed for Spain, having received a two-year leave of absence so that he might resolve a legal case which involved him there. After his return to New Spain he was appointed governor of Puebla, and he assumed office in February 1777. His promotion to colonel was forthcoming in July of that same year. Portolá apparently enjoyed a relatively tranquil governorship. The only Puebla disturbance which may have approached his California experience was the *Vida Comun* controversy; the result of governmental efforts to impose a more austere life upon the worldly nuns of the city, it placed Portolá, an elderly bachelor, in the midst of a highly irate group of women. In August 1781, Portolá requested that he be relieved of his office and be given a similar position in Veracruz, Campeche or Caracas. For some unexplained reason, his petition was denied, and it was not until June 1784 that he was permitted to resign. Returning to Spain, he was appointed colonel of the Regiment of Dragoons of Numancia on September 7, 1785. And on February 7, 1786, he was named Teniente de Rey de la Plaza y Castillos de la Ciudad to Lérida. Already in failing health when he assumed the latter position, Portolá, at approximately sixty-eight years of age, died on October 10, 1786.

Don Gaspar de Portolá's fifty-two years of distinguished service to the Spanish crown would be little noted today were it not for his contribution to California's development from March 1769 to July 1770. Indeed, there are few who would be familiar with his name but for his accomplishments of that brief sixteen-month period.

Modern California, however, is fully cognizant of his significance to the area, and it has recognized him in many ways: festivals have been held in his honor; a city, a state park, and numerous streets bear his name, all destined to be frequent victims of mispronunciation; the recent celebration of California's bicentennial was, in a very real sense, a recognition of his achievement.

California historians have likewise been generous in their treatment of Portolá. Characterizations such as "good professional soldier," "dutiful soldier," "steadfast soldier," "gallant captain," and "an easy going, popular man, but brave and honest withal," are invariably found. His "wise and courageous leadership" has been cited. Even Father Omer Engelbert, who is not particularly known for his generosity toward the military of Spanish California, referred to Portolá as an "admirable man." Perhaps most eulogistic was Nellie V. Sanchez when she wrote:

In the history of California he must always be a prominent figure, as the first of her governors, the leader of the first party of settlers over the long trail from Velicatá, and the discoverer of San Francisco Bay.... He was a brave, capable, humane, and conscientious soldier, worthy in every respect of all the honor that California can give him.

The purpose of all such honors and statements is, of course, to congratulate Portolá on a job well done. But one can almost hear a discouraged and tired voice, muted by two hundred years of time passed, replying: "Many thanks, my friends, but in my mind it simply is well that the job indeed is done."

Junípero Serra and His Approach to the Indians

BY FRANCIS F. GUEST, O.F.M.

THE CALIFORNIA MISSIONS, as religious and educational institutions, have been but partially explained. There are pastoral policies and practices of the missionaries which still remain a source of perplexity. The social and cultural presuppositions on which the approach of the friars to the Indians were largely based have never been adequately treated. The intellectual background of the padres and its possible influence in shaping and directing their missionary methods has been almost totally ignored. The religious culture of Junípero Serra and his followers has never been thoroughly researched. Because of the development of anthropology, abundant information on the intellectual, religious, and cultural heritage of the California Indians has been accumulated, whereas that of the Franciscan missionaries has been insufficiently investigated. The result has been a concatenation of logical inferences which, apparently sound, actually leads to confusion. But if the phenomena on which these conclusions rest are examined carefully in the light of the intellectual, religious, and cultural antecedents of the Spanish Fernandinos, they will be found to admit quite readily of a clear and satisfactory explanation.

Let us begin with certain assumptions about aborigines and aboriginal life that were widely held both in Spain and New Spain in Serra's day.

First of all, to understand the approach that Junípero Serra and his missionaries took to the California Indians, it is important to remember that the eighteenth century was one in which European scholars had no scientific means of measuring intelligence. Hence it was not unusual for one nation in Europe to be considered brighter than another, at least in some respects, or for people of the upper classes to be looked upon as more intelligent than those of the lower ones. The Spanish Benedictine theologian, Benito Fey-jóo, defended the Germans, who had in his day in Spain the reputation of being slow of comprehension. *Philosophes* of the French Enlightenment thought that, with the proper education, the deficient intelligence of the common people would improve. The English poet James Thomson drew a clear contrast between "the godlike minds of the enlightened few" and the limitations of "the fond, sequacious herd." William Cowper, more widely read in his day than Thomson, said of the poor that, "inured to drudgery and distress," they act "without aim, think little, and feel less." In view of these admittedly unscientific opinions on the native endowment of the various races and levels of society in early modern Europe, it is not surprising to find that many Spaniards, although by no means all, regarded the Indians of the Americas, or at least the commoners among them, as limited in their mental capacity. In the sixteenth century Francisco de Vitoria and Bartolomé de Las Casas, both Dominicans, and Toribio de Motolinía, a Franciscan, maintained that what the Indians lacked was not intelligence but education. Others disagreed. At the first provincial council of the Society of Jesus in Mexico City in 1577 the Indians were described as a timorous people of poor intelligence. Viceroy Luis de Velasco, in a letter to the king in 1554, spoke of the intellectual capacity of the Indians as poor. Many missionaries underestimated the ability of the Indians to learn. Unfavorable impressions of the reasoning power of the Indians were carried on into later centuries. Alonso de la Peña Montenegro, bishop of Quito from 1653 to 1687, published in 1668 a manual of pastoral theology for pastors of Indian parishes in Peru. In various passages of this widely used volume, the bishop describes Peruvian Indians as uncultured, barbarous, thickheaded, simple, forgetful, obtuse, dull-witted, and the like. Furthermore, a jurist, Gaspar de Villaroel, explains that Indians in colonial Spanish America were categorized, in Spanish law, as *personas miserables*, a legal term which comprised, besides Indians,

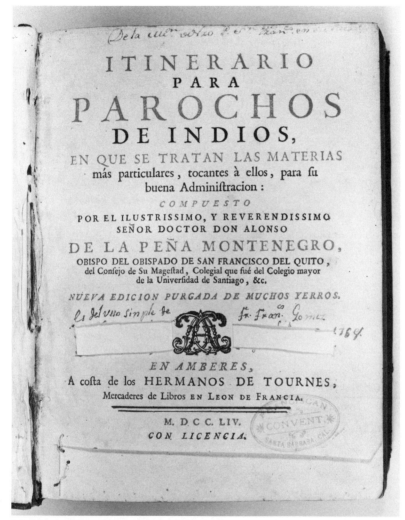

Title page of a volume on pastoral theology written by Bishop Alonso de la Peña Montenegro for pastors of Indian parishes in Peru. It became popular among missionaries in California. Photo by William B. Dewey. *Courtesy Santa Barbara Mission Archive-Library.*

the poor, the orphans, the blind, the lame, and the leprous—in a word, the unfortunate and disadvantaged, those in need of protection and aid, especially legal assistance in cases of litigation. Bishops were authorized by law to transfer the cases of such people from a civil to an ecclesiastical court, if necessary, and they were under an obligation to aid needy plaintiffs and defendants with alms. Indians were bracketed as *personas miserables* because of their poverty, timidity, continual labor, personal services, simplicity, ignorance, and weakness of understanding. Presumably, Villaroel, in this passage, was speaking of Indian commoners.

Juan de Palafox y Mendoza, bishop of Puebla (1600–59), was a fervent admirer of the Indians and stoutly defended them with respect both to their learning ability and their virtue. Benito Feyjóo took up the cudgels in behalf of the Indians in the same essay in which he came to the rescue of the Germans. The Spanish jurist, Juan de Solórzano Pereira (1575–1655), wrote, "We have an obligation to teach them [the Indians] and to ease the weight of the burden they bear. The reason for the limited progress they make lies more in our own laziness or malice than in their ignorance or dullness of mind." In this context, however, Solórzano was speaking of Indians of more advanced culture. Those who lived in the wilderness after the manner of animals he considered deficient in intelligence. Manuel Pérez, a priest who wrote a book for pastors on the administration of the sacraments to Indians, was doubtful about the intellectual endowment of Indians. Sometimes he found these people sharp-witted and clever, sometimes not.

The *Noticia de la California*, written by Miguel Venegas, S.J., but edited by Andrés Marcos Burriel, S.J., and other scholars in the service of the Spanish government, fills four pages with numerous synonyms, all of which emphasize the spiritual deficiencies of the Indians of Lower California. The text portrays them as poor in culture, lacking in talent, weak in powers of soul and body. "The movements of their will are in proportion to the scarcity of light in their understanding." Luis Sales, O.P., in his *Observations on California, 1772–1790*, complained about the stupidity of the Indians, their lack of reflection, their intellectual poverty, the dimness of their mental powers.

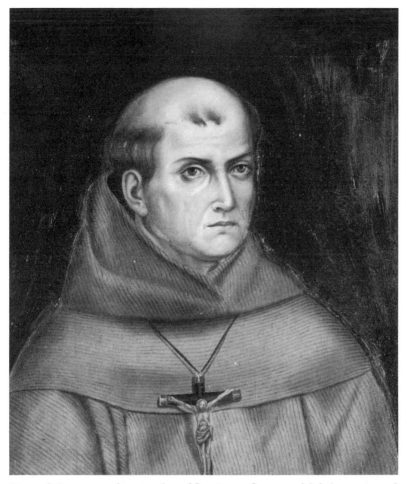

One of the reputed portraits of Junípero Serra, which is a copy of another. *Courtesy SBMAL.*

Junípero Serra, in his letters, is lavish in his praise of the California Indians. He describes them as gentle, peaceful, cordial, courteous, charming, tractable, interesting, gifted, mild, affectionate, submissive, amenable, and well fitted to receive the Gospel. He declared that he could not find words to express how attractive they were. "They have stolen my heart away," he said. According to Serra, others extolled the Indians, too. He wrote to Viceroy Antonio María de Bucareli y Ursúa, "I am most anxious for the spiritual conquest of this territory and of its poor gentiles in whose praise all sing so highly."

In keeping with this long list of laudatory epithets, one would normally expect Serra to commend the Indians for their intelligence and, in one passage, he does. Using material he had gotten from diaries written by two friars who had accompanied Juan Pérez on a voyage up the coast of the North Pacific to fifty-five degrees north latitude, he described Indians who had rowed out in canoes to visit the Spanish ship: "They came — men, women and children of all ages—with such a display of cleverness in everything they did . . . a people clever, sociable, and friendly." In another letter, however, he presents the intellectual qualifications of the Indians in a different light. Explaining how difficult it was for Indian wives to follow their soldier-husbands wherever military obedience might send them, he wrote, "And, surely, the slow intelligences of these poor people will fasten on the thought that many of our men came to provide themselves with women, and take them, if they can, to their own country."

In two paragraphs of his Refutation of Charges, a 130-page defense of the mission system written in June 1801, Father Fermín Francisco de Lasuén, second Father President of the California missions (1785–1803), describes the intelligence of the Indians in favorable terms. Pointing out that some Spaniards had taught Indians to play cards, Lasuén said, "By this time some of our neophytes, and even some pagans, have become so adept at cards that they win from their teachers." And a few lines further on, the Father President observed that the Indians did not lack intelligence.

In the answers the Spanish missionaries wrote to the questionnaire sent them by the Spanish government, 1813–15, the dullness of the Indians is mentioned three times and their intellectual limitations once. But at Mission San Luis Obispo Fathers Antonio Rodríguez and Luis Antonio Martínez offered testimony of a different character. The text says, "I have taught some of the Christians how to read. They manifest application and are sufficiently bright and diligent."

Generally speaking, one does not find in the writings of the Spanish Fernandinos the strongly worded complaints about Indian stupidity featured in the pages of Venegas's *Noticia de la California* and Sales's *Observations on California*. And the intelligence of the Indians is described as often in creditable as in uncreditable terms.

Secondly, the Spanish missionaries of the sixteenth century in New Spain commonly thought that the Indians they were attempting to evangelize resembled children. In the seventeenth century Juan de Solórzano Pereira wrote that, because of their childlike mentality, barbaric and uncivilized races, including the Indians of the American wilderness, should be treated as if they were children. The *Noticia de la California*, referred to above, said, "In a word, these unfortunate people can be equated with children who have not quite succeeded in entirely developing the use of their reason." Several passages in the correspondence of Serra, Lasuén, and other friars show that the Spanish Fernandinos looked upon their Indian converts as children in a mission family in which the padres themselves occupied the place of fathers. In fact, the way the neophytes in the Califomia missions were taught to recite their summary of Christian doctrine, reeling it off by rote every day twice a day for a lifetime, implies that, in general at least, they were thought not to have the maturity and intelligence characteristic of educated European adults. On the contrary, they were presumed to need the same care and attention that children customarily received in Spain. In 1813 Father Ramón Olbés, at Mission Santa Barbara, wrote, "The missionary fathers supervise planting and harvesting at the proper seasons for the Indians are not capable of doing this alone for in such undertakings they are like children." In 1814, at Mission San Carlos, Father Juan Amorós wrote, "Therefore in these matters [the proper care of a garden] they [the Indians] behave like children of eight or nine years who as yet have not acquired a constant or steady disposition." In 1815 Father José Señán said that the Indians "are but children habituated to live like little birds that do not plough nor sow nor possess barns."

As is commonly known, Spanish law made the missionaries the legal guardians of their Indian converts. In virtue of their conversion and baptism, the neophytes became the wards of the friars. The padres had the same responsibilities toward their missionized Indians as Spanish parents were thought to have, in the Spanish theology of the eighteenth century, toward their children. Except for cases of criminal violence, when the arm of the Spanish government intervened, "the management, control, punishment, and education of baptized Indians" pertained exclusively to the missionary Fathers.

On one occasion when the present author was explaining all this to a priest who had served as a foreign missionary in a distant land for twenty years, the missionary smiled and said, "That is the way the people in my mission seemed to me. They seemed like children." Three other missionaries who were questioned independently of one another and who had labored in the same general area for a like number of years said the same thing. Modern anthropologists have an explanation for this phenomenon. Anyone is like a child in matters that are foreign to his culture. Confronted with planting, harvesting, gardening, and Spanish technology, the Indians, mystified, seemed to the padres to be like children. On the other hand, the unfamiliarity of the missionaries with certain aspects of forest lore probably made them seem like children, in their turn, in the eyes of the Indians. At any rate, the friars who toiled in the missions of Hispanic California two hundred years ago were not anthropologists. Hence, in view of this testimony given here and above, and of much more that could easily be assembled, one should not find it extraordinary that the padres were accustomed to look upon their Indian converts, not as adults, but as adult children.

With respect to the concept of American Indians as adult children, Father Jerome Theisen, a Benedictine priest and an authority on the history of Catholic ecclesiology, says that, following the Reformation, Catholic theologians manifested particular concern for the many peoples whom the age of discovery had revealed to them. "They suggested various ways in which peoples outside the visible church could nevertheless be united to the church and thereby achieve salvation, *e.g.*, by proposing that many belong to the soul of the church and not to its body; by supposing that adults must really be regarded as infants, morally speaking; by postulating an explicit or implicit desire for the church."

It is true that the Franciscan missionaries of Alta California regarded the Indians, both Christian and non-Christian, as adult children. But when one views this principle in the light of the European background sketched briefly above and in the light of the efforts made by Catholic theologians in early modern Europe to ensure the salvation of centuries of unbaptized American Indians, one finds it easier to understand.

Thirdly, the Franciscan missionaries of Alta California, in dealing with both Christian and non-Christian Indians, had frequent recourse to the theological principle of inculpable ignorance. The friars argued that, although the Indians had the obligation in the objective order to accept Christianity and observe the precepts of the natural moral law, nevertheless, in the subjective order—the order of the mind, the order of conscience— they were excused from many sins because of inculpable ignorance or because, when they performed a given immoral act, they did not advert to its culpability.

In 1795, when some recently converted Indians at Mission San Buenaventura became involved in the murder of some other Indians, Father Lasuén pleaded that the guilty should have all the clemency the case might allow, pointing out that "although it is a shocking one, it is the work of those who little realize its gravity." In 1817, when parties of one Indian faction at Mission San Jose murdered parties of another, Father Narciso Durán wrote of "these unfortunate people who have no realization of what they have done." With respect to the California Indians in general, Lasuén observed in his Refutation of Charges that death was their customary way of avenging injuries.

Now then, let us apply to mission organization in Alta California these fundamental presuppositions of the friars regarding the intelligence of the Indians, their status as adult children, and their inculpability in the moral order. And let us also apply some of the elementary principles of the moral theology of the eighteenth century which were universally accepted by Spanish Franciscan scholastics of that period.

It will be observed, first of all, that Serra and his missionaries segregated their Indian converts from their native villages in the wilderness and kept them in residence at the mission to which they were attached. Why did they do this? First, it was required by the Laws of the Indies. Secondly, the gravest obligation the missionaries had, as priests, with respect to their neophytes was to give them religious instruction. And thirdly, the missionaries, in their relationship with their Indian converts, were burdened, not only with the duties of pastors, but also with the responsibilities of parents. As legal guardians, the friars were looked upon as responsible before God for the religious education of their neophytes, just as Spanish parents were for the proper upbringing of their children. The Indians, for their part, were accustomed in their culture to have no set hours for breakfast, lunch, or supper, but to spend the greater part of each day in an interminable search for food. Hence they could not reasonably be expected to show up regularly every day twice a day for the recitation of their summary of Christian doctrine at the mission. It would have been quite normal, then, for the friars to keep baptized Indians in residence at the mission and summon them to regular meals and regular religious services each day by means of the community bells. Missionaries who were notably remiss in fulfilling their obligation to provide religious training for their neophytes were thought to have sinned grievously.

A second reason why the missionaries segregated their Indian converts from their non-Christian relatives and friends in the back country and kept them in residence at the mission was, as Father Francisco Palóu tells us, that they found it necessary to correct their faults and thought it could be done more effectually this way than by allowing them to follow their native way of life in their natural habitat. "And if parents are obliged under pain of grave sin to teach their children Christian doctrine and the law of God, much greater, without doubt, is the obligation they have to see that they put it into practice, that is, that they live a Christian life." The faults that needed correction included theft of property from those who lived outside the tribal unit; divorce and remarriage; indulgence in promiscuity and, in some tribelets, in homosexuality; the practice of abortion; and the tradition of taking human life in punishment for personal injuries.

Thirdly, the missionaries allowed their neophytes to make a visit of five or six weeks to their native villages every year but did not want them to associate freely and for a prolonged period of time with non-Christian Indians in the wilderness among whom they would inevitably encounter bad example and the occasion of sin and, in consequence, run a grave risk of a fall from grace. Lasuén, in a letter he wrote to Fray José Gasol, Guardian of the College of San Fernando, on June 16, 1802, explains clearly and in detail the reasons why he did not want Indian converts to be free to come and go at the missions as they pleased and to live in non-Christian villages in the wilderness for extensive periods of time. In this letter he does not use technical theological jargon, to be sure, but, to anyone who is acquainted with the moral theology of that period, it is evident that the theory of the occasion of sin underlies the text from beginning to end. To appreciate the value of this fact, one must read the entire letter of three and a half pages. It is impossible to quote it all here. The same principles that forbade neophytes to associate for too long a time with non-Christians in the forest applied with equal force to spiritual dangers that might be encountered in presidios or towns. In his Refutation of Charges Lasuén wrote as follows: "If in some missions, or in all of them, certain Indian men and women are sometimes denied permission to associate with certain individual people *de razón*, it is for precisely the same reasons as those for which every good father of a family in every civilized nation should forbid his children to go with bad companions."

At this point a brief word of explanation on what was meant by an occasion of sin is necessary. An occasion of sin meant any person, place, or thing which involved spiritual danger for a given individual. It is evident from the list of objectionable habits and customs given above that, for the neophytes, an extended residence in their native villages was an occasion of sin. However, the occasion of sin they encountered by visiting their parents and relatives for a brief period of five or six weeks every year was regarded as necessary. For a number of reasons, it was unavoidable. First of all, the neophytes were obliged by the fourth commandment to honor and love their parents. It was looked upon as seriously wrong for sons and daughters not to visit their parents for a long time. Secondly, the non-Christians in the forest kept inviting the neophytes for a visit. If there was no response, or if the non-Christians were told as an excuse that the missionaries did not want to give permission, they reacted by hesitating to become converts. And, finally, as Lasuén observed, "the majority of our neophytes are so attached to the mountains that if there were an unqualified prohibition against going there, there would be danger of a riot." With respect to a necessary or unavoidable occasion of sin such as has here been described, the necessity involved was not the necessity of sinning but the necessity of remaining in a physical situation that was or could be a proximate occasion of sin. In this case, spiritual means were taken to diminish the danger and render the proximate occasion of sin more remote, *e.g.*, prayer, counsel, the mutual assistance of Christians, prudence, caution. On the other hand, if a given Indian entered the proximate occasion of sin freely and voluntarily and remained there, as fugitive Indians did, the theological implication of this act was that he was willing to commit the sins to which he was exposed. And this in itself was regarded as sinful by the missionaries. This was what their theological manuals told them.

Now then, let us explain the fourth reason why the missionaries wished to keep their neophytes at the missions. Indian converts had a perfectly normal tendency to tire of the novelty of mission life after a while and go back to the ways of their forebears in the forest. Even if, at the missions, there had been no workshifts, no physical punishments, and no deaths from white men's diseases, the neophytes would have been inclined to drift back to aboriginal ways anyhow. Residence at the missions was irksome for the Indians for cultural reasons that the padres, not being anthropologists, did not understand. It kept the converts, who were children of the forest, from living in their natural habitat the way their ancestors had for thousands of years. The missionaries were aware of this attraction the forest had for the Indians but, unable to decipher the meaning of it, kept trying to wean them away from it. For the padres, the presence of their neophytes in non-Christian villages for a prolonged period of time meant primarily one thing: it meant that they had freely and voluntarily entered a proximate occasion of sin and were remaining there as fugitives from the mission. It is doubtful if the neophytes had a very clear understanding of all this theology about the occasion of sin. But the friars did. And they knew very well that they were responsible for the moral conduct of their converts. For the friars, the missionized Indians who had become fugitives in the forest were like adult children who had run away from home and had become involved in serious spiritual danger. And since the missionaries, as the legal guardians of their neophytes, were responsible before God for their moral and religious training, they sought to induce or even, if necessary, to force them to return to the mission, just as Spanish parents would normally have sought to recover control over their wayward children. On July 20, 1775, Junípero Serra wrote to Fernando de Rivera y Moncada, commander of the presidios in Alta California, as follows: "Now, my dearest Sir, I state to you that these wayward sheep [fugitive neophytes] are my burden, and I am responsible for them not at the treasury in Mexico but at a much higher tribunal than that, and so you should not be surprised if I should be a little importunate in the matter." Other quotations on this theme, based on the same theological principle and conveying the same message, are easily available in Serra's correspondence.

Before proceeding any further, let us make three observations that are worth bearing in mind relative to this question of the occasion of sin: Serra lived in an age when Spanish Catholics had a profound consciousness of sin that is seldom to be found any more in western culture, as his fiery sermons and self-flagellation in the pulpits of central Mexico bear witness; furthermore, the theological manuals of the missionaries, with their heavy emphasis on reprehensible actions forbidden under pain of grave sin, are regarded today as rather sternly negative in character; and, finally, it should be borne in mind that, with respect to theological opinions and the theory of probabilism, the great majority of Spanish Franciscans in the eighteenth century were inclined in the direction of probabilism, a theory which required its adherents, in cases where there was a doubt, to follow the opinion that was commonly considered more rather than less probable. All this implies that the friars, generally speaking, felt inclined to take the safer, more reliable course of action in a given case.

Fifthly, Indian converts who had fled to the wilderness to live there for a while in response to their cultural or other inclinations were looked upon by friars as adult children who had been guilty of disobedience to their legal guardians. Hence, depending on the amount of time they had remained absent from the mission, fugitive neophytes were liable to punishment for the same reason that a boy in Spain would have been for going with bad companions or otherwise exposing himself to grave spiritual danger. For parents, says a theological manual commonly used by the friars, "correction consists in that they should scold their children and punish them for their excesses when they do not live in a Christian manner and are disobedient or, notwithstanding their admonitions, are incorrigible." A second source, speaking of the duties of parents with respect to badly behaved children, says: "They should rebuke them for their excesses and punish them seriously and perseveringly until they mend their ways, for otherwise they become responsible for their sins; and God will punish them unto the third and fourth generation, as Sacred Scripture threatens." A third source asks whether or not parents should punish their adult children, and the answer is in the affirmative. The parents should thrash them well on their backs, and the children should accept the punishment with patience, for it is for their own greater good. But Father Lasuén writes in his Refutation of Charges, "As regards fugitives from the missions, even those who have been absent for a long time, and even those who have committed misdemeanors during their absence (provided they present themselves voluntarily), they are pardoned."

Sixthly, the friars had a very important reason for returning to the missions neophytes who had fled to the forest. The missionaries were taught by their manual of pastoral theology that if their converts committed moral faults that were intrinsically wrong (*e.g.*, concubinage, incest, sexual perversion, murder), and if their correction and improvement were then neglected and the vices tolerated, those who were responsible for them, namely, their legal guardians, would incur the same guilt the offenders had in falling into such defects. Even in the face of defamation, loss of property, or death itself, the missionaries were obliged to teach the faith and eradicate these forms of corruption. As priests, the missionaries were not required to pursue fugitive neophytes for great distances into the wilderness and bring them back to the mission. But as parents, they were. The two obligations, taken together, constituted a considerable threat to the ordinary padre's peace of mind.

Finally, as Francisco Palóu explains, the friars could civilize their Indian converts only by keeping them at the mission. In the minds of the Fernandinos, the Christianization of the neophytes necessarily included Hispanicizing them, teaching them to live an urbanized way of life, the beginning of which was mission life.

Why, then, did the missionaries go into the forest themselves to bring fugitive neophytes back to the mission, or ask other missionized Indians to induce them to return, or even send soldiers after the runaways to compel them forcibly to take up once more their Hispanicized way of life? Because they thought they had to; because they thought they were under a grave moral obligation to do so.

This line of historical argumentation, in the mind of the present author, has at least two merits. First of all, like Cinderella's storied slipper, it fits. And secondly, it seems to be the only thing that does. Nothing else really makes much sense. How did two missionaries and half a dozen soldiers imprison two thousand Indians at a given mission and then force them to remain there?

As for the Indian converts, did not the missionaries, in their catechetical instructions, explain to them why they should not associate freely and for prolonged periods of time with non-Christian Indians in the forest? In given cases it probably took the friars some time to make their point but, normally speaking, it is not one they would have neglected. And if the fugitive Indians knew that

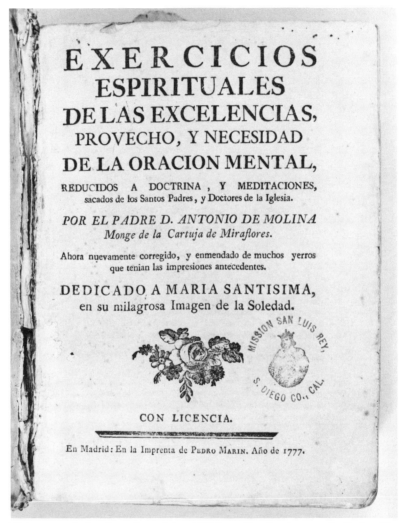

Title page of a book on the spiritual life by a Carthusian monk, Father D. Antonio de Molina, which was much in use among the Franciscan missionaries. Photo by William B. Dewey. *Courtesy SBMAL.*

the missionaries had their best interests at heart, what would have been their attitude toward the priest, neophytes, or soldiers who came into the forest to take them back to the mission? As converts to Christianity, what would they have thought? Finally, if the Indians at the mission understood what the obligation of the missionaries was in their regard, then they knew that the obligation would always be there, that, if they fled to the forest, someone — a priest, a group of neophytes, or a squad of soldiers — would show up some day in search of them. They knew the missionaries would never give up in their efforts to return fugitive neophytes to their mission. They would never give up because they could not.

The Indians were regarded by the missionaries as adult children, to be sure. But the longer these converts remained in residence at a mission, and the more they learned about Christian doctrine, especially Christian morality, the less able they were to take advantage of the saving principle of inculpable ignorance. The more they learned about what Christian virtues required of them, the more deliberate their lapses became and the greater their guilt. Hence the anxiety of the friars about Indian converts who fled to the wilderness to live. In 1814 Fathers Juan Bautista Sancho and Pedro Cabot wrote as follows about the Indians of Mission San Antonio: "Behold how these poor Indians, fathers of families, if not entirely, at least in part, are held excused before both God and man." The friars were ever ready to apply to the Indians the principle of inculpable ignorance but, on the other hand, they were keenly conscious of their responsibilities as substitute parents. So they took no chances. Studiously and perseveringly, they kept up the effort to return fugitive neophytes to the missions to which they belonged.

In the correspondence of the missionaries, it is interesting to trace the references to the converted Indians as children. Writing to Teodoro de Croix, Commandant General of the Internal Provinces, on August 22, 1778, Serra said: "In reference to the care we take of our converts—let me tell you, Sir, they are our children; for none except us has engendered them in Christ. The result is we look upon them as a father looks upon his family. We shower all our love and care upon them." On January 7, 1780, Serra wrote to Governor Felipe de Neve as follows: "That spiritual fathers should punish their sons, the Indians, with blows appears to be as old as the conquest of these kingdoms; so general, in fact, that the saints do not seem to be any exception to the rule." And he added, ". . . we have engendered them all in Christ . . . and I feel sure that everyone knows that we love them."

In a volume of doctrinal instructions intended for preachers and catechists, Father Manuel Denche, a priest of the Trinitarian Order, wrote as follows:

Therefore children should conduct themselves, in the presence of their parents, with much humility and modesty, and speak to them, when in their company, with words full of submissiveness and esteem. To foster this due veneration, it is very proper for the children to kiss their parents' hands often, as at the beginning of the day when they arise, when they finish eating, when they leave the house with their parents' permission and when they return to it. And if they make these demonstrations of respect while on their knees, they will please God very much.

In connection with this doctrine, it is worth noting that Captain George Vancouver, describing the return of Father Vicente de Santa María to Mission San Buenaventura after a brief absence, says:

Although it was yet very early in the morning, the happy tidings [of the priest's return] had reached the mission, from whence these children of nature had issued, each pressing through the crowd, unmindful of the feeble or the young, to kiss the hand of their paternal guardian, and to receive his benediction. His blessings being dispensed, the little multitude dispersed in various directions.

Apparently, Father Santa María was venerated, not only as a priest, but also as a "paternal guardian."

The selection from Lasuén on this same theme is worth repeating. He says, "If in some missions, or in all of them, certain Indian men and women are sometimes denied permission to associate with certain individual people *de razón*, it is for precisely the same reasons as those for which every good father of a family in every civilized nation should forbid his children to go with bad companions."

Toward 1801 a missionary at Mission San Francisco de Asís wrote to Lasuén that "in an average school a person would receive more punishment for not knowing his lesson than he would receive here for living in concubinage." By concubinage the missionaries meant that some of the Indian converts tended to continue at the missions the custom of divorce and remarriage they had inherited from their tribal life in the forest.

On June 2, 1816, Governor Pablo Vicente de Solá issued a manifesto on the whipping of Indians at the missions. Having conducted a careful and thorough investigation of the practice, the governor found that the friars were not guilty of cruelty, that the punishment they generally administered to neophyte offenders consisted of twelve to fifteen strokes with a whip made of two strands of rope, that the faults for which the Indians were punished were most often theft and concubinage, and that the whipping the transgressors received was "more adapted to children of six years than to men, most of whom accepted it without an exclamation of pain."

Finally, to understand the friars properly, we must bear in mind that, so far as they were concerned, the primary reason for the colonization of Alta California by the Spanish government was the evangelization of the Indians. This was what King Charles III himself had written in a letter received by Viceroy Bucareli early in 1773. This was what Viceroy Bucareli had explained to Fernando de Rivera y Moncada and Junípero Serra in letters he sent them. Hence this was undoubtedly what Serra and his followers believed, whatever else Charles's royal ministers had had in mind in promoting the sacred expeditions. In consequence, the friars most probably expected the Spanish governors to cooperate accordingly in their support of the missions.

Now then, because the freedom of Indian converts was so rigidly restricted by the Franciscan missionaries, many authorities in the field of California history have long been accustomed to describe the condition of the neophytes at the missions as one of virtual slavery. In recent years in some academic circles the qualifying adjective, once so time-honored, even shopworn, has been much neglected. It is difficult to escape the feeling that if earlier researchers, like Father Zephyrin Engelhardt, for example, had devoted more attention to the theology of the missionaries, this widely accepted inference on the status of the Indians at the missions might have been expressed in somewhat different terms.

With respect to the concept of the enslavement of the Indian converts by the Spanish padres at the missions, Sherburne Friend Cook writes as follows:

The term slavery has been uncritically applied to the mission social system. It should be pointed out that there was no implication of personal ownership whatever. Furthermore, in theory always, and in practice usually, the fruit of Indian labor was devoted to the welfare and improvement of the Indian himself. Any selfish enrichment of the mission was incidental and contrary to the tenets of the Church. The system was much closer to socialism or communism, in the Marxian sense, than slavery.

Thaddeus Francis Horgan and Raphael Brown look upon the missions of Spanish America, not as institutions in which Indians were enslaved, not as concentration camps, and not as socialistic enterprises, but as communes. Horgan writes as follows: "The prosperous Jesuit reductions of Paraguay and the Franciscan missions that trained thousands of Indians in South America and California in religion, crafts, and government were paternalistic communal societies."

In these paternalistic communes of which Horgan and Brown speak, the approach of the Spanish Franciscans to the California Indians was characterized by *españolismo*, which was an almost universal characteristic among Spaniards during the Age of Absolutism. Españolismo, in this context, means "a complacent self-satisfaction with everything Spanish, accompanied with a disdain for everything foreign." At this juncture, it will be worth our while to quote a significant paragraph on European missionaries during the age of discovery and exploration:

But let us not judge the missionaries too quickly or too harshly. Children of their time, they were born into and nurtured by a European culture that was incorrigibly chauvinistic, that saw itself as the culture, the norm by which other cultures should be judged. People who did not belong to this culture were barbarians to whom one could do no better service than that of lifting them out of their abysmal ignorance. A similar way of thinking, it must be admitted, existed in ancient Israel, in Greece, in Rome, in India, in China, and in most parts of the world where civilization has been highly developed. In this respect Europe is not unique.

To appreciate more fully these principles and patterns of thought, both cultural and theological, to which the Franciscan missionaries clung with such tenacity, it will be helpful to treat their relationship with certain political, economic, and military policies of the Spanish government.

First of all, it will be important to recall that King Charles III followed a policy of regalism with respect to the Catholic Church in Spain and Spanish America. This means that he thought the Church should be brought more firmly and securely under the control of the state. An enlightened monarch and a reformist, Charles wanted to modernize Spain, to bring his country into the mainstream of enlightened progress in Europe, a project for which he needed the cooperation of the clergy.

Secondly, the Catholic Church in Spain in the late eighteenth century was divided much as it is today. Traditionalists and scholastics looked to the theology and religious precedents of the Counter-Reformation for guidance, whereas enlightened Catholics either rejected scholasticism altogether or were critical of it and were open to much of the science and philosophy of the Enlightenment. The king and his royal ministers encouraged and favored the enlightened Catholics.

Thirdly, most of the mendicant orders, including the Franciscan, were traditionalist and scholastic in their theology and tended to keep their distance from the philosophy, if not the science, of the Enlightenment. Prominent in Spanish university circles and popular as preachers and confessors, these friars, with their enormous prestige and influence among the people, posed a problem for the king and his ministers. To bend these religious more completely to the royal will, the government determined to strengthen its control over them, to weaken their economic and social position, and gradually to diminish their numbers. In many respects,

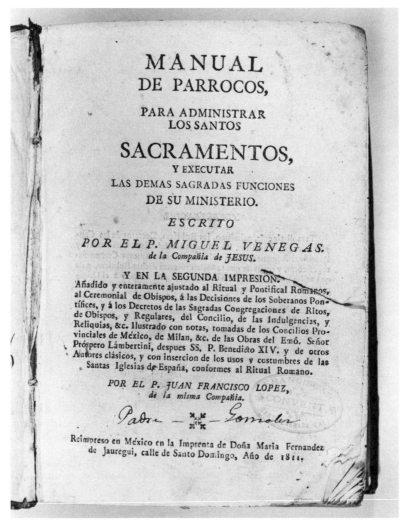

MANUAL
DE PARROCOS,

PARA ADMINISTRAR
LOS SANTOS

SACRAMENTOS,
Y EXECUTAR

LAS DEMAS SAGRADAS FUNCIONES
DE SU MINISTERIO.

ESCRITO

POR EL P. MIGUEL VENEGAS.
de la Compañía de JESUS.

Y EN LA SEGUNDA IMPRESION.
Añadido y enteramente ajustado al Ritual y Pontifical Romanos,
al Ceremonial de Obispos, á las Decisiones de los Soberanos Pon-
tífices, y á los Decretos de las Sagradas Congregaciones de Ritos,
de Obispos, y Regulares, del Concilio, de las Indulgencias, y
Reliquias, &c. Ilustrado con notas, tomadas de los Concilios Pro-
vinciales de México, de Milan, &c. de las Obras del Emô. Señor
Próspero Lámbertini, despues SS. P. Benedicto XIV. y de otros
Autores clásicos, y con insercion de los usos y costumbres de las
Santas Iglesias de España, conformes al Ritual Romano.

POR EL P. JUAN FRANCISCO LOPEZ,
de la misma Compañía.

Reimpreso en México en la Imprenta de Doña Maria Fernandez
de Jauregui, calle de Santo Domingo, Año de 1811.

Title page of a treatise on the administration of the Sacraments, authored by a Jesuit priest, Miguel Venegas, and revised by Juan Francisco López, S.J., in 1811. This copy belonged to Padre Francisco González, who served in California 1797–1805, before loss of eyesight forced his return to Mexico. Photo by William B. Dewey. *Courtesy SBMAL.*

enlightened Catholics were critical of the mendicant orders.

Fourthly, the prodigious amount of ecclesiastical property that had accumulated piece by piece over several centuries in Spain was a roadblock in the royal path of economic reform. Held in mortmain, this property could not be disposed of by sale or gift. It had to remain with the church. And because of its immense economic power, it constituted, when taken together, a sort of state within a state, as church historians of today frankly acknowledge.

Fifthly, enlightened Catholics, both in Spain and in Spanish America, advocated the principle of a poor church. Relative to this concept, Pedro Rodríguez, the Count of Campomanes, had some interesting and forward-looking ideas. For him, the ideal church was one which would possess no temporal goods at all, in common or otherwise, would be completely liberated from all material concerns, would be totally independent of the crown in the performance of all spiritual duties but totally dependent on the crown in all temporal matters. In the mind of Campomanes, the church should confine itself to prayer, penance, exhortation, and correction, after the manner of the early church of Christian antiquity. Edgar Allison Peers writes, "It is commonly said by historians that in the middle of the eighteenth century the Church owned about one-third of the land in the country [of Spain]. One can quite believe that the generalization, though unsupported by figures, was at least approximately true." Recent historians treat this theme with greater caution. William J. Callahan says, "It is not yet possible to establish the total wealth of the church [in eighteenth-century Spain] with accuracy." During the reign of Charles III this question of ecclesiastical holdings, already sensitive, was soon to become, first a burning issue, then an explosive one.

Sixthly, the latter half of the eighteenth century was a period in which the Spanish government in New Spain was experimenting with different ways of improving the missions on the frontier. José de Escandón, in colonizing Nuevo Santander, introduced the idea of Christianizing and civilizing the Indians by integrating them with Hispanic families who were intended to serve as object lessons in the Spanish way of life. The plan for the development of the California missions originally embodied this principle. Hispanic families and missionized Indians were to form mixed nuclei of future centers of urbanization. Land was to be distributed both to settlers and to Indians. Ultimately each mission, as it developed, was to be erected into a formally established Spanish town in accordance with the requirements of the Laws of the Indies. But the plan did not succeed. For one thing, Hispanic families did not come to settle at the missions. And, for another, Serra and his companions sometimes tended to discourage close social relationships between their Indian converts on the one hand and, on the other, the inhabitants of the presidios, a policy based in part on the doctrine of the occasion of sin. Governor Felipe de Neve (1777–82), when he first came to Alta California, determined to discontinue the building of missions altogether and use towns instead as a means of Christianizing and civilizing the Indians, a principle probably borrowed from precedents established by José de Escandón. Later he changed his mind. But his concept, when viewed from the standpoint of the plans originally made for the development of the California missions, does not seem so strange as it otherwise might.

Before coming to Alta California, Neve had participated actively in the expulsion of the Jesuits from northern New Spain in 1767. He believed the allegations that had been made against the Jesuits—that they were ambitious, power-hungry, anxious to acquire wealth and influence. And he tended to be critical of the mendicant orders just as he had been of the Jesuits. In his eyes, the Dominicans and Franciscans were headed in the same direction the Society of Jesus had taken. In 1774, before he became governor of California, he wrote an important letter to the viceroy, accusing the friars of wanting to be "entirely independent of the royal officials so that they could accumulate all the cattle and crops produced on the missions as their own, in addition to their stipends." And he argued that the viceroy should give control of all mission crops, cattle, and hides to the governor.

This letter was but a foreshadowing of the legislation on the missions which Neve incorporated into his *Reglamento* of 1781. In this document he declared that no mission should have any temporalities. This meant no grain fields, no livestock, no workshops—

nothing except the church and the priest's residence. He further stipulated that Indian converts were to be free to come and go at the missions as they chose. And, except for the four missions nearest the presidios, there was to be but one missionary at each mission. In drawing up this legislation, Neve did not consult the friars. It is not difficult to see why.

Neve explained in his correspondence the reason why he did not want the traditional type of mission to continue in California. He pointed out that, since the shoreline of the province was so long and so straight, it was too difficult to defend. In a word, the missions could easily have been looted by any invading force that might attack the coast in strength. This was true. The Spanish army did not have the manpower, the firepower, or the mobility to protect the missions under such circumstances.

More extended reflection on the pertinent clauses in the Reglamento seems to suggest, however, that Neve, in endeavoring to discontinue the traditional type of mission in California, had more in mind than military defense against possible enemy attack on the coast. Either that or the royal ministers who directed his operations did.

First of all, the principle that there should be only one missionary at each mission enabled the Fernandinos to save manpower and extend their chain of missions into the San Joaquin Valley, thus expanding Spain's power and influence.

Secondly, with respect to the principle that converted Indians be allowed to come and go at the missions as they pleased, one will recall that this policy was followed, in limited measure, by José de Escandón in Nuevo Santander. And one will recall further that José Rafael Rodríguez Gallardo, Inspector General of Sonora and Sinaloa in 1750, wrote in praise of French missions in Canada in his report to his superiors in Mexico City. He pointed out that French laymen lived among the Indians and intermarried with them. He explained that where there was close association between the French and Indians, there was no discord between the two, a fact which contrasted painfully with the readiness of missionized Indians in Sonora to revolt against Spanish rule. In 1775 the Yuma Indians at Mission San Diego had rebelled unsuccessfully against Spanish authority. Leaving the Indian converts free to come and go at the missions would normally do much to avoid such outbreaks in the future. Free to live in the forest as they wished, or anywhere else for that matter, the neophytes would have been liberated from all control by the friars. There would have been no more enforced recitation of the summary of Christian doctrine, no more work shifts, no more physical punishments, and the like. In French Canada, largely because the Indians there were more nomadic and warlike, the missionaries had had to modify the Spanish type of mission, although they had been influenced by it. In New France there was no law which required that Indian converts reside at a mission. Indian neophytes were not looked upon as minors subject to missionaries as to legal guardians. Instead the French government adopted the policy of accepting all Catholic Indians as equals of the French. One sees in Neve's legislation a possible French influence that invites further investigation. It follows, of course, that the less inclined converted Indians were to rebel against Spanish authority, the stronger Spain's hold on the California coast would be.

In Neve's legislation on the missions, the more elementary principle regarding the freedom of the Indian converts to dwell wherever they wished led logically to the corollary that, at the missions, there should be no temporalities. With no resident Indians, or with none whose presence could easily be relied upon, how could a given mission plant and harvest crops, care for herds of livestock, or staff and maintain workshops? But the absence of temporalities at the missions was not only necessary for the freedom of the Indians, it also had important consequences both for church and state, missions and missionaries in Alta California.

First of all, the missions, without temporalities, could never have developed their enormous economic wealth. By 1803, the year in which Lasuén died, there were eighteen missions whose economic power greatly overshadowed that of both the presidios and the towns taken together. From 1791 onward, the presidios drew their supplies of maize, wheat, and beans from within California, mostly from the missions. In a word, the military government of Alta California was heavily dependent on the missions

114

Front and back of a prayer board used at Mission San Antonio. Spanish and Latin texts are used along with translations into the local Indian language, Salinan, a testament to the mission fathers in trying to preserve distinctive cultural elements among the neophytes. *Courtesy The Smithsonian Institution, Washington, D.C.*

which, like ecclesiastical estates in Spain, clearly constituted a state within a state. Neve was a regalist. If he foresaw this situation threatening to develop, he would normally have taken steps to avoid it. Actually, if the California missions had developed in accordance with Viceroy Bucareli's original plan, with land distributed both to Indian and Hispanic families, and with the growth of urbanization as a result, the Franciscan friars, as the legal guardians of the Indians, would not have been in a position to exercise such extraordinary economic power. Viceroy Bucareli, when he wrote his instruction in 1773, does not seem to have intended the missions to become a state within a state or to have foreseen that they would. Since the concept of private ownership of land and of entering into competition in business with others was foreign to the Indian mentality, it was much easier for the neophytes to adjust to mission life, where farming, ranching, and the like were done in common, than to develop holdings of their own in a spirit of private enterprise, a point the Spanish government seems not to have appreciated at its true value.

Secondly, if the missions had been deprived of their temporalities, the missionaries would have been unable to draw upon them for commodities of any kind, particularly marketable goods like hides and tallow which could be used to develop economic wealth more rapidly. The friars, without mission temporalities, would have been entirely dependent on their annual salaries for their livelihood—for food, for clothing, for medicines, for books, tobacco, chocolate, Mass wine, and the like. And they would have been greatly impeded in their efforts to build, equip, and adorn impressive churches for the edification of their neophytes. In a word, the relationship between the church and the state in California would have been reversed. Instead of the governor and his presidial forces depending heavily on the missions, the missionaries would have been compelled to rely upon the military government in many important respects. The ultimate outcome of Neve's legislation on the missions would seem to parallel, in California, the regalist policies of Charles III with respect to the church in Spain.

Thirdly, if Neve's legislation on the missions had been carried out, what would most probably have happened to the temporalities of the nine missions that had been established and developed under Serra's leadership? Before hazarding a reply to this question, let us recall that Neve, when he first came to Monterey, wished to discontinue the building of missions altogether and, after the manner of José de Escandón, make use of towns for the further evangelization of the Indians. The policy he ultimately decided upon involved but a limited modification of this concept.

If his laws had been implemented, the agricultural development of Alta California would undoubtedly have been promoted. Presumably, however, it would have been in the hands of the laity rather than of the clergy. The military government would eventually have been in a position to draw its supplies of maize, wheat, and beans from within California, to be sure, but from the fields of townsmen and rancheros, not from mission farms. The Indians would have been Christianized and civilized partly by contact with the missionaries in their distant outposts in the wilderness, and partly through association with the inhabitants of the presidios, towns, and ranchos.

To some, the hypothesis here briefly outlined might seem of dubious value, but when visualized against the background of Bourbon reform, it becomes more convincing. Alejandro Filgueira Alvado says, "With the arrival of the Enlightenment and its philosophical ideas, there will appear some bold efforts, idealistic in character, to improve the situation and education of the aborigines."

In those parts of Spanish America which were occupied by Indians of more advanced culture, the higher the social status of the Indian, the more he tended to collaborate with the Spanish government both in the evangelization of the native peoples and in their Hispanicization. The ordinary Indian, however, was reluctant to learn Spanish because of the unfortunate treatment he had received from so many of the conquerors and colonists. The Indians in the more urbanized areas of the empire commonly understood and spoke Spanish but, among themselves, preferred their mother tongue because they loved it. Some Indians, reacting against the foreigners who had subjugated them, made it a point of honor not to speak Spanish. In 1771 the establishment of a new government was proposed for Spanish America "so that the Indians might put aside the horror with which they were filled by the name Spaniard."

The Bourbon reform, conscious of the negative attitude of the Indians in New Spain and Peru towards things Spanish, was preoccupied with the political necessity of assimilating them more fully into the empire, into a society that could genuinely be called

Spanish. In 1770 King Charles III issued a drastically important decree on the importance of the Indians learning Spanish.

The Spanish missions in Alta California were begun early in the course of the Bourbon reform, and it was inevitable that, sooner or later, they would feel the effects of it.

Some European authors, whether well informed or not, expressed sympathy for the Indians of Spanish America. Writing from the Enlightenment viewpoint, Montesquieu, Voltaire, Diderot, and Condorcet were critical of Spanish Indian policy. In 1779, the year in which Governor Neve finished writing his Reglamento, Bernardo Ward's *Proyecto económico* was published. The author, an Irishman who had held high office in Spain, advocated an approach to the Indians that was markedly different from that of Junípero Serra. It will be remembered that the Spanish missionaries followed a program that involved, for converted Indians, an abrupt and drastic change from their native way of life to the Spanish way of life, including subjection to Spanish civil and military government. Ward thought the progress the Indians of the forest made in the direction of Spanish culture and embodiment into Spanish society should be slower and more gradual. The Spanish, he thought, should trade with the Indians first, as the French and English did, leave them independent of the machinery of government, respect their native way of life, treat them with kindness, and encourage them to work. Ultimately, he thought, the Indians would settle down and become useful subjects of the king. The similarity between Ward's ideas and those of José de Escandón in Nuevo Santander is noteworthy. There is a resemblance, too, between Ward's ideas and those of Governor Neve, who recommended that there be as little interference as possible with the life led by the Indians in their native villages, that Indians were to be civilized by example and led gradually to become vassals of the crown, and that force was not to be employed in Christianizing them. "It is probable that these ideas were in the air at the time rather than having their origin in any one book." In their approach to the Indians, the difference between Neve and Serra seems to have been, in large measure, the difference between the thought patterns of the Spanish Enlightenment and those of the pre-Enlightenment scholastics and traditionalists among the clergy.

Governor Neve, in his relationship with the California Indians, reflected Enlightenment ideals. As Serra himself testifies, Neve was opposed to the whipping of delinquent Indians by the missionaries, an application of his principle that, in the Christianization of the Indians, no force be employed. And Edwin Beilharz, Neve's biographer, says of him:

He [Neve] condemned no Indian to death, and commuted the sentences of even the worst offenders. He deplored the loss of Indian lives during police actions, as in the pursuit of runaways from the missions, and he curtailed such pursuits. He prohibited any mistreatment of the natives, and punished soldiers who dared to disobey his stringent orders, bringing in the offended Indians to give them the satisfaction of witnessing the punishment. One of his practices was picturesque: he made it a rule to give a present to every Indian he met on his tours—this at his own personal expense.

A paragraph written by the Count de La Pérouse on Felipe de Neve emphasizes the governor's humanity, his opposition to restraints and punishments imposed on the Indians, his advocacy of greater liberty for them in their relationship both with missions and presidios, and his view that Neve was a "Christian philosopher." The French navigator ascribed to Neve an appreciation of the ideals of the Enlightenment.

The influence of the Spanish Enlightenment was manifested further in the plans made in 1795 for the establishment of the Villa de Branciforte. The citizens of the town were supposed to consist of retired soldiers from among the Catalonian Volunteers together with headmen from neighboring Indian villages. Alternating with the houses built for the soldiers were to be places for the Indians to make their dwellings. This visionary project reminds one of "the bold efforts, idealistic in character," advocated by the Spanish under the influence of the Enlightenment "to improve the situation and education of the aborigines."

Now then, it will be helpful at this point to recall that the College of San Fernando, led by its guardian, Father Francisco Pangua, opposed the clauses on the missions in Neve's Reglamento. According to the constitutions of the college, no priest could be required by obedience to serve as a missionary among the Indians. And, according to Spanish law, there was nothing that the guardian himself, or Governor Neve, or even the viceroy, could do about it. It became evident, then, that the Spanish government, if it wanted more Fernandinos to come as missionaries to Alta California, would have to yield on this point about mission organization. And yield it did, for the moment. But it did not give up, as Lasuén's letters abundantly testify.

Lasuén, in a letter dated January 21, 1797, to Father Antonio Nogueyra, Guardian of the College of San Fernando, explained that five new missions were soon to be founded in Alta California. He added, however, that, according to instructions which Governor Diego de Borica had received from government authorities in Mexico City, the rancherías were to be evangelized but the converted Indians were to remain in their own homes in the forest. It was probable, Lasuén went on, that soldiers might be altogether removed from missions already established and no mention had been made of any increase of troops who might serve at the five new missions. "In that case," said Lasuén,

I would make bold at any hour to sign any document to the effect that they may lose everything, or run the risk of doing so. The majority of our neophytes have not yet acquired much love for our way of life; and they see and meet their pagan relatives in the forest, fat and robust and enjoying complete liberty. They will go with them, then, when they no longer have any fear and respect for the force, such as it is, which restrains them.

To be appreciated, the letter should be read in its entirety.

To understand Lasuén more fully, however, it is important to read carefully the letter he wrote on June 16, 1802, to Father José Gasol, Guardian of the College of San Fernando. Here he explains that he had received from Father Guardian, on June 3, an order to send to the college "detailed information regarding the question which has often been raised of instructing and baptizing the Indians in their rancherías, and permitting them to continue there after they have been baptized."

Lasuén was strongly opposed to the plan which provided that converted and baptized Indians be left free to come and go at the missions as they pleased and make their home in their native villages in the wilderness. His reasons were two: first, there was danger to the faith of the Indian converts, and secondly, there was danger to their morals.

The non-Christian Indians in their natural habitat, said Lasuén, were accustomed to their abominable fiestas, the memory of which was invoked at all hours. Under these circumstances, how could Indians who had been recently converted, instructed, and baptized pay proper attention to what had been taught them in their catechism lessons and to the obligations they had contracted in virtue of the sacrament of baptism? The same principle would logically hold for missionized Indians who associated freely and for prolonged periods of time with their non-Christian relatives and friends in the forest.

To emphasize moral dangers involved for neophytes who indulged in overly extended visits to rancherías in the forest, Lasuén pointed to the deplorable experience he had had at Mission San Diego, where some groups of neophytes had to remain in the wilderness while others lived at the mission because the farms of the padres could produce enough food for only limited numbers of people at a time. It will be remembered that the second Father President had served as head missionary at San Diego from 1777 to 1785. Recalling these eight years among the Diegueños, he wrote, in an emotional passage, as follows:

Oh, my revered Father! What anxieties! What Disappointments! What vigilance! What anguish of mind! What labors day and night for the missionaries! What liberties! What excesses! What irregularities! What ignorance! What disorders! How Christian civilization and pagan barbarity can give way to one another in the same neophyte!

In writing his letters, Lasuén, as a general rule, is calm, self-possessed, cautious, thoughtful, and tactful. The above passage is unquestionably the most turbulent in all his correspondence. His agitated feelings are profound and sincere.

In the two letters treated in this context Lasuén's message is

121

abundantly clear. If converted Indians were free to come and go at the missions as they pleased, the temptations against faith and morals that they encountered in the wilderness would be too much for them to resist, and the missionaries, in their efforts to Christianize their charges, would make little or no genuine progress. In theological language, the proximate occasion of sin in which the Indian converts lived would inevitably lead them to spiritual disaster.

With respect to the political and economic implications of Neve's legislation on the missions, it should be pointed out that the most basic principle the governor advocated was that Indian converts be free to come and go at the missions as they chose. This was seminal. This was the fountainhead from which all the rest flowed. Once this concept had been elevated to the level of policy and then successfully implemented, the other reforms at the missions would logically follow.

Now then, before going any further, let us emphasize the political as well as spiritual importance of the principle whereby missionaries became the legal guardians of their neophytes, administering their property for them, educating them in the doctrine and practice of Christianity, summoning them to religious services, meals, work shifts, recreation, and the like. By Spanish law, Indians were exempt from inquisitorial prosecution and procedure during the seventeenth and eighteenth centuries. The missionaries, as priests, were not required to pursue fugitive Indians for great distances into the wilderness for the purpose of bringing them back to the mission but, as parents, they were. If Spain was going to build up an empire into which Christianized Indians were to be embodied as subjects of the crown, the concept of the missionaries as parents of converted Indians who lived as adult children at the missions had a politically significant role to play.

But Governor Neve, in his legislation on the missions, seems to have abandoned this age-old concept and to have substituted for it an entirely different principle. And if the missionaries based their primary objections to Neve's innovations on the doctrine of the occasion of sin, how did the governor morally justify his clauses on the missions, how did the Commandant General of the Internal

Provinces and the king himself approve of them, and how could the Spanish government require Governor Borica, by order, to carry out the legislation? The answer to these questions is not difficult to explain.

Gerónimo de Ripalda, S.J. (1536–1618), a professor of theology, published at Toledo, in the last year of his life, a catechism entitled *Catesismo y exposicion breve de la Doctrina Cristiana*, a small volume that went through hundreds of editions and was still used for children in Spanish schools in the early twentieth century. In this book there is a treatment of the occasion of sin which, though brief and succinct, covers a lot of ground. It reads as follows:

> Question. What remedy is there against the occasions of sin?
> Answer. The best remedy is to flee from them.
> Question. And when this cannot be done?
> Answer. Anticipate and overcome them by means of prayer, counsel, and caution.

Well-educated Catholic gentlemen like Borica and Neve who were unaware of the nature and application of fundamental moral principles like inculpable ignorance and the avoidance of the occasion of sin would have been like American students to whom names like Benjamin Franklin, George Washington, and Thomas Jefferson had no meaning. For Borica and Neve, leaving the baptized Indians free to come and go at the missions as they pleased would normally have been a necessary occasion of sin to be overcome in accordance with moral principles that all well-educated Catholic people of the time clearly understood.

For the Franciscan missionaries, however, as is evident from Lasuén's correspondence quoted above, there was nothing necessary about such an occasion of sin at all. For them, what was necessary was to keep the Indian converts in safety and security at the missions. On this point the friars firmly rejected innovations and resisted change. They were standpatters.

After 1802 one hears no more of this controversy between the Franciscan missionaries of Hispanic California and the Spanish government. From 1793 onward Spain was involved, first in the wars of the French Revolution, then in those of Napoleon Bona-

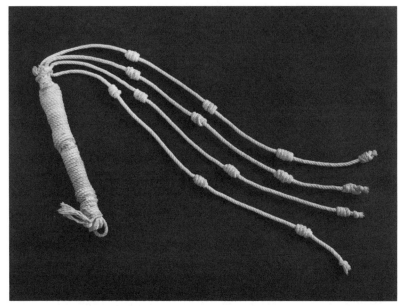

A typical *disciplina* which was used by the Franciscan friars in their quest for spiritual perfection. Serra himself used the discipline regularly. Photo by William B. Dewey. *Courtesy SBMAL.*

parte, and by this time, harassed by an impoverished treasury and the threat of European conflict, she had more important things to think about than the reform of the Franciscan missions on the California frontier.

The critical comments of Neve and Borica on the treatment of Indian converts by the Franciscan missionaries of Hispanic California are well known. On one occasion Neve wrote, "The unhappy treatment which they [the Franciscans] give the Indians with whose care they are charged renders the Indians' fate worse than that of slaves." On another occasion he described the educational discipline to which the neophytes were subjected by the missionaries as *algo rígida*, somewhat rigorous, rough, hard. In this context he stopped just short of saying it was brutal. In 1798 Governor Borica wrote to Viceroy Miguel José de Azanza as follows: "Generally speaking, the treatment given the Indians is very

124

harsh. At San Francisco it even reached the point of cruelty, as is evident from the documents I sent Your Excellency on July 1 of last year."

Governor José Joaquín de Arrillaga (1800–14) said that if a stranger should travel through Lower and Upper California and observe the manner in which the Indians were treated, he would consider it cruel and tyrannical. But if he would probe beneath the surface of things and study the subject more thoroughly, he would change his mind. Governor Pablo Vicente de Solá (1815–22), after investigating thoroughly in all the missions the physical punishments administered to Indian offenders, exonerated the padres of all charges of cruelty or even excess.

Father Lasuén, having studied carefully the reports sent in to him by his missionaries, wrote, in June of 1801, a long and detailed defense of the entire system of mission administration. In one passage he said, "It remains for me to describe the very gentle way in which customarily we treat these Indians." And he added that, although there were many individual differences among the friars, he had never come upon anyone who could be called hard-hearted, still less one who could be called cruel. He even appealed to the testimony of the Indians themselves, insisting that "the more the pagans understand the kind of treatment we give their Christian relatives, the more pleased they become with the missions."

The testimony of foreign visitors to Alta California will help us to see our object of study in somewhat clearer perspective.

The Count of La Pérouse, who visited Monterey and Carmel in 1786, two years after Serra's death, spoke of the behavior of the missionaries as wise and pious, repeated himself in describing the friars as religious, charitable, and austere, and praised their gentleness and charity, virtues which he thought tempered the austerity with which they lived. "The affairs of the afterlife," he wrote, "could not be in better hands." As is well known, the French navigator, although he extolled the missionaries, found fault with the missions, which he compared to the slave plantations of the French West Indies. A devotee of the French Enlightenment, he thought the Indians should be allowed more freedom in the way they lived. It is worthy of remark that La Pérouse was perceptive enough to draw a distinction between the character of the missions, which he found wanting, and the character of the missionaries, which he greatly admired.

Captain George Vancouver, in the three visits he made to the coast of Alta California from 1792 to 1794, commended the missionaries much as La Pérouse had. To him, they were these excellent men, kind, worthy, and benevolent. The authority they exercised over the Indians was mild and charitable. And they seemed entirely devoted to the benevolent office of rendering the Indians a better and a happier people.

Dr. Georg Heinrich von Langsdorff, a surgeon and naturalist of the Rezánov expedition, which was welcomed at San Francisco in 1806, wrote as follows: "All these missions have a great number of cattle and abundance of other productions necessary to the support of man, and the monks conduct themselves in general with so much prudence, kindness, and paternal care, towards their converts, that peace, happiness, and obedience universally prevail among them."

The Russian ship *Rurik*, under the command of Lieutenant Otto von Kotzebue, visited the presidio and mission of San Francisco in 1816. In the journal of the expedition Adelbert von Chamisso, the ship's botanist, a former subject of the French crown and a former Catholic, criticized the missionaries for not being skilled in the arts and trades in which the Indians were being schooled, for not having learned well the various Indian languages spoken at the mission, for not paying the Indians wages for their work, for not imparting to them the concept of property, for not allowing Indian converts to return to the forest to live, and for looking upon Indian languages and culture with contempt. And yet he wrote, "We do not deny the mildness, the paternal anxiety of the missionaries, of which we have several times been witnesses."

In assembling these passages, one does not wish to "prove" that the missionaries had the virtues ascribed to them by navigators or by chroniclers. The intent here is to draw a comparison and contrast between the statements of these witnesses and the criticisms of Neve and Borica. Both sets of testimony need to be examined in context. They should not be read and judged singly and in isolation from each other or from the intellectual, religious, and cultural background in which they were made. The point here is that, when one reads the negative observations and complaints of Neve and Borica in the light of Spain's program for the development of Alta California and of the accounts written by foreign visitors to the presidios and missions along the coast, one feels inclined to interpret them much differently than if one lifted them out of the pages in which they are to be found and treated them in and of and by themselves as if they were independent of everything else.

In addition to all this, one must remember that the California missions developed at a time when humanitarian sentiment, nurtured by the European Enlightenment, was growing apace. The Spanish Cortes decreed, on September 8, 1813, that the Indian, along with all other men, could not be punished by whipping. On July 4, 1833, Father Francisco García Diego y Moreno forbade the missionaries of his jurisdiction in California to employ this form of punishment on recalcitrant neophytes. In his view at this time, whipping had outlived whatever usefulness it may once have had and was contrary to the basic principles of pedagogy.

It took time, however, for these ideas on educational discipline to develop. During the governorship of Felipe de Neve, Junípero Serra found it necessary to defend the custom of whipping neophytes for their misdeeds, although he recommended leniency in this regard. It is interesting to observe that, on the question of whipping schoolboys in England, opinions varied during the period of Serra's administration in Alta California (1769–84). Samuel Johnson (1709–84), the great man of letters, was a contemporary of Serra and held some rather conservative views on the subject. In the school attended by Johnson it was customary for a boy who was to be whipped to lean over a three-legged flogging-horse with his stomach on top of the horse. While other boys held the arms of the student who was to be punished, the schoolmaster whipped his posterior. Once, when a schoolmaster spoke of the abolition of flogging in the schools, Johnson said, "Sir, I am afraid that what they gain at one end they will lose at the other." And when he was asked how he had acquired such an accurate knowledge of Latin, Johnson replied, "My master whipped me very well. Without that, Sir, I should have done nothing." The point to be made here is that belief in the efficacy of whipping as a form of punishment was not, in Serra's time, a necessary indication that one was a savage. The most representative author of England's Augustan Age, Dr. Johnson has been described by literary historians as a Christian humanist and a moralist. "Few men have left finer examples of the art of living than Samuel Johnson."

The Catholic Church no longer conducts missions among aboriginal peoples as the Franciscans did in Alta California two hundred years ago. The church requires that, when aborigines are evangelized, Catholicism is to be integrated with their aboriginal culture, which is to remain as undisturbed as possible. The reason for this is that, as is recognized now, such people have a right in the moral order to maintain their culture intact. Ironically, the legislation on the missions in Neve's Reglamento was closer to the missionary ideals of the contemporary church than the methods of Serra and his successors were.

If the California missions had been established, not by Spanish friars coming up from the south, but by Japanese Buddhists coming down from the north, the ordinary historical investigator would normally be inclined to devote a generous portion of his time to a close study of the religious thought and observances of the Japanese people, especially those of the Buddhists. He would do this because he would be afraid that, if he did not, he might make mistakes, perhaps very serious ones, in interpreting the data, the multitudes of external phenomena, he had gathered on the buildings, the journeys, the missionary methods, and the evangelical activities of the Japanese. And all the present author has done is study the intellectual, religious, and cultural background of the Spanish missionaries just as he would have if their antecedents had been eastern instead of western. After all, one cannot reasonably write a book, or even an article, about a Buddhist monastery unless one knows enough about Buddhism, its history, its development, its beliefs, practices, traditions, and spirituality. The same principle applies, with equal force, to the Catholicism of the Spanish padres.

Because the missions and missionaries of Hispanic California have been understood but partially, the friars have been described and categorized in different ways by different people. To the present author, the dominant characteristic of the Fernandinos was a profoundly religious idealism, dedicated, persevering, and absolutely unyielding. True Spaniards, the padres did not excel at compromise. If anybody on the coast of the north Pacific ever tilted at windmills after the manner of Cervantes' famous hero, it was the Franciscan friars in their efforts to Christianize and Hispanicize the California Indians. Sitting on a mule instead of on Rosinante, clad in a grey habit instead of in armor, wearing a broad-brimmed, flat-crowned hat instead of a helmet, and brandishing a crucifix instead of a lance, the padres pursued fugitive Indians all over the thousand hills between San Diego and San Francisco. Undoubtedly, the Indians knew more about why the friars kept after them than the friars did about why the Indians had fled from the missions. The chase went on year after year until the missions were secularized. And the missionaries undertook the enterprise, not primarily as priests, but primarily as parents, casting, as they swung into the saddle, the gigantic shadow of Don Quixote de la Mancha on the farthest frontier of the Spanish empire.

Rafael González, a Hispanic soldier born in Santa Barbara, testifies as follows: "Already before 1820 and many times thereafter I took part in campaigns in search of Christian Indians who had fled from the missions which belonged to the jurisdiction of this presidio [Santa Barbara]. On no occasion did the Indians use weapons against us." If the Chumash Indians from San Buenaventura to San Luis Obispo did not know, at least in a general way, why they were being brought back to the mission to which they belonged, it is difficult to understand why they failed to resist the presidial forces.

The Confirmation Controversy of 1779, Serra vs. Neve: A Rationale

BY WILLIAM E. EVANS

WHEN FRAY JUNÍPERO SERRA arrived in Baja California in 1768, he discovered, among the papers left behind by the Jesuits, a copy of a bull by Pope Benedict XIV, which had authorized the Jesuit missionaries to administer the sacrament of confirmation. Serra then petitioned for himself or some other missionary the privilege of giving confirmation. The matter was referred up through the chain of command, and eventually to Pope Clement XIV, who granted the faculty to the Father Prefect of the missions on July 10, 1774. Also granted was the authority to pass this privilege on to one missionary from each of the four missionary schools in New Spain.

The faculty of confirmation which had been granted to the Father Prefect and the four missionaries was limited to a period of ten years from the date of concession. As far as Spain was concerned, this privilege was contingent upon approval of the King of Spain and the Supreme Council of the Indies. The document was approved by all parties, passing on to the Royal Audiencia and Viceroy Antonio María Bucareli y Ursúa, who sanctioned the use of the faculty in September, 1776, approximately eight years after Serra had found the bull authorizing the Jesuits to administer this sacrament in Baja California.

By this time Fray Juan Domingo Arricivita of Querétaro College had taken the position as Father Prefect. On October 17, 1776, he appointed Serra as the one missionary from San Fernando College to administer confirmation. On June 17, 1778, the document appointing Serra and copies of the papal brief arrived in San Francisco, and were subsequently sent to Serra at San Carlos. He received the documents four years after the date of concession.

Remember, this privilege had been granted for a period of only ten years, so Serra had to accomplish his task in the six years remaining. And this is exactly what he proceeded to do, until 1779, when he was forced to sharply curtail his confirmation program in Alta California because the governor, Felipe de Neve, challenged Serra's right to administer this sacrament.

Serra assured the governor that all the formal amenities had been strictly observed, showing him a congratulatory letter from Viceroy Bucareli and the patent for confirmation. As far as Neve was concerned, this was insufficient evidence. He wanted to see the original brief, which had been approved by the Royal Council. Serra replied that he had been exercising this power for an entire year before the governor had seen fit to suspend his privilege. And so the story continues with a tale of petty bickering, all of which leaves one in the dark as to the possible causes.

Under the terms of the papal bulls "Inter Cetera," "Eximiae Devotionis Sinceritas," and "Universalis Ecclesiae Regimini," a system of royal patronage had been established which granted the king of Spain external control over the Church in Spanish America. No church building could be erected without the express approval of the king as General Patrono or the viceroy or governor as Vice-Patrono. They governed many aspects of ecclesiastical life in the Spanish colonies. Often the king's subordinates from the viceroy, right down to the presidial commander, claimed this supremacy over the local clerics. If we keep this in mind, we are better able to understand Neve's position. From this, one could possibly conclude that Neve was, after all, simply exercising what he thought was his bureaucratic prerogative. Certainly, that is the way he wanted it to appear for the record. But we are forced to ask why he persisted in assuming this particular posture at this particular time.

When Neve first took office in California, his immediate superior was Viceroy Antonio María de Bucareli y Ursúa. Bucareli's instructions were quite clear. Neve was to follow the policy that had been established by Visitor General José de Gálvez in 1769, and the Echeveste Reglamento of 1774, except where this policy was superseded or modified by Bucareli himself.

In 1776 Bucareli advised Neve of a change in the chain of command. The provinces of Nueva Viscaya, Coahuila, Sinaloa, Sonora, Texas, New Mexico, and the Californias had been taken from the viceroy's jurisdiction. Teodoro de Croix, nephew of the Marquis Carlos Francisco de Croix, was to assume the position of commandant general of these separated provinces, which were to become known collectively as the Interior Provinces.

It would appear that most of the controversy in Alta California during the Neve administration finds its genesis in the pro-temporal attitude of Don Teodoro de Croix, Caballero of the Teutonic Order and the newly appointed commandant general of the Interior Provinces. He became Neve's immediate superior in 1777. As soon as the military jurisdiction over California had been transferred to Croix, Neve began issuing orders calculated to completely incapacitate the Franciscan mission system in California.

After the Echeveste Reglamento had been in effect for about fifteen months, King Carlos III ordered another set of regulations drawn up which was to contain provisions for colonizing California. On August 15, 1777, Croix forwarded the order to Neve with instructions to report what changes were needed. Neve finished framing a whole new set of regulations on June 1, 1779. Superseding the Echeveste Reglamento, the new plan was entitled "Regulation And Instruction For The Presidios Of The Peninsula Of California, The Erection Of New Missions, The Encouragement Of Colonization And The Extension Of The Establishment Of Monterey."

It is quite obvious that the new regulation not only provided for colonization, but also established a new policy for the government of the missions in California. While Serra had worked with the civil authorities to put together the Echeveste Reglamento, none of the clerics had been consulted by Neve regarding that portion of the new regulation which applied to mission administration.

It seems strange that the task of designing a new form of government and complicated plans for colonization should be left to a minor provincial official, such as Neve. Why was he given this responsibility? The fact is that Croix trusted Neve. Croix felt that Neve could carry out specific acts which would implement the commandant general's secular policy. Also, at the time, Croix's major concern was with bolstering the defenses of the northern frontier. For this reason, he was forced to rely on those whom he could trust to handle specific detail in terms of prevailing policy.

Upon taking office, Croix's immediate attention was drawn to the northern frontier because of the growing problem of marauding Indian tribes, especially the Apache. When Croix found time to consider problems in California, "he approved anything that the governor [Neve] actually got done." He was so pleased with the set of regulations drawn up by Neve that he did not wait for the king's approval. The reglamento went into effect, provisionally, in January 1781, but the measure did not receive the king's sanction until October 24, 1781.

Croix's enthusiasm notwithstanding, it must be understood that Croix was giving his apparently unqualified support to the implementation of his very own policy. Croix's preoccupation with the Indian problem along the northern frontier resulted in Neve's being permitted and even encouraged to exercise his initiative, but Croix set the policy. Neve did not make policy in California.

Probably, a brief résumé of Neve's New World career would be helpful at this point. Shortly after his arrival in 1766, Neve precipitated a small riot at Valladolid, when he attempted to draft local married men forcibly into the army. When he and his men were attacked by the citizenry at Pátzcuaro, he was forced to discontinue his recruiting mission. He was simply following orders. He was rather unsuccessful, but he undoubtedly did all that he could to carry out his orders. Neve was a good soldier and always attempted to accomplish his assigned task, even if it meant creating marked civil unrest.

Later, in 1767, Neve took part in the Jesuit expulsion. Although the Jesuits had been expelled from Spain in March 1767, the order for the expulsion of the Society did not reach the Marquis Carlos Francisco de Croix until May 30, 1767. The preparation was kept secret, and the Jesuits were arrested at dawn on June 25, 1767. Their properties were ordered confiscated on July 18, 1767. Neve was sent out to seize the Jesuit property in Zacatecas, and he was able to accomplish this without incident. In other parts of the country, however, there was violent resistance on the part of the people to this "shocking exhibition of despotic violence." Again, Neve was a good soldier and carried out his mission with dispatch.

In 1774 Viceroy Bucareli named Neve governor of the two Californias, but Neve was in poor health, and shortly after his arrival at Monterey, tendered his resignation, requesting that he be returned to Spain. He complained of a "weakened head" that would not allow him to dispose of the routine work. This may, in fact, explain some of the hair-splitting and petty bickering Neve exhibited in his dealings with Serra. His request for retirement was denied, but, in lieu thereof, he received a raise in pay and a promotion.

Shortly after Don Teodoro de Croix became Neve's immediate superior, the governor stopped the flow of supplies to the missions. This took place on October 7, 1778. Eventually Serra reported the matter to his superior in Mexico, who appealed to Viceroy Martín de Mayorga. Mayorga was sympathetic, but there was actually little he could do. He wrote a letter to Croix, "suggesting that so small an expense as that involved would be well repaid by having the missionaries cheerful." Croix did not agree and said so in his reply to Mayorga. Eventually the matter was settled through compromise by the Minister of the Indies, José de Gálvez, on February 8, 1782. Neve could cut rations, but the missions would not be required to pay for the rations which already had been issued to them.

On October 21, 1779, Neve forbade the Franciscans to leave

California without special permission from himself. The matter was referred to Father Guardian Rafael Verger, in Mexico City, who could only appeal to the viceroy. Again Mayorga sent his recommendation for moderation to Croix.

When Neve insisted that Serra stop confirming, Croix commanded Serra to "surrender the Pantente and Original Instructions, through which the faculty of giving Confirmation was committed to you, to the governor of the peninsula." Croix further stated in a letter to Neve that he should "proceed with the use of his powers and take the original documents from his [Serra's] possession [presumably by force if neccssary] and send them in."

Mayorga intervened and, on December 24, 1780, Croix was forced to advise Serra to proceed with his confirmation program. Croix also sent a letter to Neve, informing him of the situation. This was dated December 23, 1780. On May 19, 1781, Neve acknowledged receipt of Croix's orders and notified Serra, but it was not until August 16, 1781, that Serra finally received written permission from Croix and Neve to continue confirming. This was *seven* years after Pope Clement XIV had granted the faculty to confirm, and *thirteen* years after Serra had discovered the papal bull authorizing the Jesuits to administer this sacrament in Baja California.

We could go on and on with this business. Neve attempted to limit the number of Franciscans to one at each mission. This decision was eventually set aside by royal edict.

Neve's set of regulations purposely omitted any provision for equipment or instructors in the new missions in California. This, too, was eventually overruled, and the subsequent missions of Santa Barbara and La Purísima Concepción were founded in the traditional manner in 1786 and 1787.

Neve insisted that the neophytes elect two *alcaldes* and two *regidores* in each mission, but the friars of both Alta and Baja California felt that the Indians were not yet ready for even limited self-government.

Neve's harassment of the missions kept up until September 4, 1782, when he received word, near the Colorado River, that he had been promoted to the position of inspector general of the Interior

Provinces. When Croix was appointed viceroy of Peru, Neve was named his successor. Neve became commandant general of the Interior Provinces on February 15, 1783, but, alas, he was to die the very next year in 1784.

In ten years Felipe de Neve managed to rise from sergeant major in the Spanish army to the position of commandant general of the Interior Provinces, serving as Teodoro de Croix's successor. He was definitely a successful politician. Edwin A. Beilharz, in his biography of Felipe de Neve, based on his doctoral dissertation, makes the following appraisal:

The significant fact about Felipe de Neve is that he was a good bureaucrat. He was competent, intelligent, and loyal. He was not merely obedient; he possessed the rarer talent of being able to anticipate the desires of his superiors. He read his instructions carefully, absorbed their general purport, and proceeded to carry them into detailed execution without waiting for specific directions.

Possibly the most important controversy between church and state during the Neve period concerned Serra's right to administer the sacrament of confirmation in California. It would be misleading, however, to depict this conflict as a singular display by a prideful politician in an otherwise fairly congenial atmosphere. Let us not forget that from 1777 to 1782 Neve effectively championed secular authority in every way possible, that his administration followed the policy set by Croix, and that the much discussed Neve Reglamento was, in fact, part of the commandant general's design for relieving the frontier missions of temporal control over the Indian.

Neve was a career-minded politician who anticipated commands. He worked diligently and planned those specific acts which were most likely to implement superior policy. He was a political puppet who danced when, and sometimes even before, the maestro pulled the strings. In California he did what he was told to do: namely, attempt to impede the development of the Franciscan mission system so that the missions could be declared parishes and pueblos.

To be brief, the Fernandinos were fighting for their very existence. Secularization of the missions at that time would have put an end to effective proselytizing in California. Any attempt to analyze an isolated incident in this bitter struggle without reference to the total controversy is inconceivable.

Los Angeles, California: The Question of the City's Original Spanish Name

BY THEODORE E. TREUTLEIN

ON A TUESDAY, the fourth of September 1781, Lieutenant José Darío Argüello, on the orders of Felipe de Neve, governor of the Californias, led a party of settlers to a site on the banks of the Porciúncula River, and founded a pueblo with the title, *La Reyna de los Angeles* (The Queen of the Angels).

The background to the pueblo's founding had been Governor Neve's careful examination, a physical survey, from San Diego to San Francisco, early in the year 1777 to determine the water capability and soil conditions in upper California. In the Los Angeles region Neve wrote approvingly of the Santa Ana, San Gabriel, and Porciúncula rivers, and north, of the Guadalupe. His conclusion was to recommend the founding of two pueblos, one on the Guadalupe, which became San Joseph (San Jose), the other on the Porciúncula, which became Los Angeles.

When Neve's plans ultimately reached Don Teodoro de Croix, the governor and commandant general of the Interior Provinces, the latter gave his approval in a dispatch dated September 3, 1778. By that date San Jose had already been founded, and Croix gave specific permission for the establishment of the pueblo "en el Río de la Porciúncula."

Although Governor Neve had initiated the idea of founding the pueblos (as well as other establishments), Commandant Croix's position required him to write of the projects as his own. Croix now instructed Captain Fernando de Rivera y Moncada to recruit colonists for the Río Porciúncula pueblo. In his order to Rivera, dated at Arispe, Sonora, December 27, 1779, we find the first use of the original Spanish name for Los Angeles.

Croix's words are of historic importance because they do define the city's title and also make clear his primary role in the higher echelon of Spanish administration. Croix wrote:

With the due aims of defense, conservation and development of the Province of Californias [*sic*], toward which the service of God and King is especially directed, I have resolved upon occupation of the Channel of Santa Barbara with a Presidio of this name, and three Missions; the erection of a Pueblo with the title of *la Reyna de los Angeles* on the River of *la Porciúncula*, and His Majesty has approved the [pueblo] named San Joseph which I ordered founded on the margins of the river of Guadalupe....

In almost the same language Commandant Croix then informed Viceroy Martín de Mayorga (the successor to Viceroy Antonio Bucareli who had died in April 1779) of his decision about the Channel establishments and of his order to found a pueblo with the title of *la Reyna de los Angeles* on the river Porciúncula.

On the 10th of February 1780, Commandant Croix also wrote to Governor Neve, stating in part, ". . . I have ordered the founding of a pueblo with the título de la Reyna de los Angeles sobre el Río de la Porciúncula" (title of the Queen of Angels on the River of Porciúncula).

After the pueblo had been founded, Commandant Croix wrote to Minister of the Indies, José de Gálvez, February 28, 1782:

The Governor of the Peninsula of California [*sic*] Don Phelipe de Neve informed me on November 19, of last year verifying that on the preceding September 4 there was founded "el nuevo Pueblo de la Reyna de los Angeles al margen del Río de la Porciúncula" with some of the settlers recruited by the deceased Captain Don Fernando de Rivera....

Minister Gálvez then wrote to Commandant Croix on October 29, 1782 telling him that the king had been informed of the establishment of the "nuevo Pueblo de la Reyna de los Angeles al marjen del Río de la Porciúncula en la Peninsula de Californias."

A romanticized sculpture of Governor Felipe de Neve, who ordered the founding of the Pueblo of Los Angeles. The statue, erected in 1931 to commemorate the 150th anniversary of the founding of the pueblo, is still located in the main plaza of El Pueblo de Los Angeles Historic Park. *Courtesy SBMAL.*

The fact that The Queen of the Angels title was provided the King of Spain by the Minister of the Indies, Gálvez, would seem to confirm that this name for the pueblo was the accepted one. It should also be noted that when Croix referred to the Río Porciúncula he was indicating the site of the pueblo; the river's name is not a part of the pueblo's title.

Later in the year 1782 Governor Neve was named inspector general of the Interior Provinces (September 4, 1782). In his instructions to his successor, Don Pedro Fages, in article 9, Neve expressed the view that very special attention be given to support the new pueblos, and he referred to "the pueblo of Nuestra Señora de los Angeles." This may be the only usage in the founding days of the form, *Nuestra Señora de los Angeles*, but the official form, as noted, had already been established.

However, generations of writers on California history have apparently disregarded the documentation and have compounded the name for the pueblo or have modified its name. The examples of misuse are very numerous and very easy to come by. Some special examples have been selected for this paper.

In the *Annual Publication* of Historical Society of Southern California, 1931, one finds a feature article by Thomas W. Temple II, "Se Fundaron un Pueblo de Españoles." In this article there is reference to the city's Spanish name, as follows: "Governor Neve's Reglamento of 1 June, 1779 approved the founding of two pueblos, one provisionally established [*i.e.*, San Joseph, or San José], the other to be known as Nuestra Señora de los Angeles, on the Porciúncula River."

Actually, the Reglamento states in the Fourteenth Title, "Political Government and Instructions for Settlement," Paragraph 1, "...the Pueblo of S. Joseph is already founded and settled, and the building of another is determined upon, for which settlers and their families must come from the Province of Sonora and Sinaloa...."

In other words, unless the reader is very careful in interpreting Mr. Temple's wording he would form the impression that the famous Neve Reglamento provided the name of the new pueblo, which it definitely does not do. What makes the wording in the

A splendid illustration of how historical error continues to be perpetrated by well-meaning parties is this plaque which was erected on the mall of the new Los Angeles County Administration and Courts Buildings. Note that the plaque commemorates "... THE FOUNDING OF EL PUEBLO DE NUESTRA SEÑORA LA REINA DE LOS ANGELS DE PORCICUNCULA ..." This same gross error is also carved on the cross which greets each visitor who comes to Olvera Street in El Pueblo de Los Angeles Historic Park! So much for plaques. Let the reader beware! *Courtesy SBMAL.*

Temple article especially ironic and curious is that many of the documents reproduced in the extremely useful commemorative edition use the form, *La Reina de los Angeles*. Space will not permit citing all of these documents. However, it is worthy of special note that settlers were recruited in Sonora with the designation that they would be settled in the Pueblo de la Reina de los Angeles.

Also in the review of settlers to determine those "who enjoy wages and draw rations," made by Lieutenant Josef Francisco de

Ortega (December 2, 1781), the title of the piece is Pueblo de la Reyna de los Angeles.

The census made on November 19, 1781, reads: "Padron del vecindario, el qe. tiene el pueblo de la Reyna de los Angeles fundado el 4 de Ste. del 1781, al margen del Río de Porciúncula...."

The confirmation of titles to pueblo lands ordered in August 1786 by Governor Pedro Fages refers to the Pueblo de la Reyna de los Angeles, as does the Act of Obedience, September 1786 by José Argüello.

There is also reference in the commemorative volume to a *Plano de el Pueblo de la Reyna de los Angeles, y tierras de Labor* [undated].

Considerably later, in another era, there is record of a litigation: "Transcript of the Proceedings in case No. 422. City of Los Angeles Claimants vs. The United States, Defendant, for the Place named 'Pueblo Sands'." In the first paragraph there is stated:

For the foundation of the Pueblo of la Reina de los Angeles in the neighborhood of the River of Porciuncula, and upon the land selected for this purpose; ... Samuel D. King, Surveyor Genl. Cal. His seal affixed April 20, 1852. Filed in his office, October 26, 1852. Geo. Fisher, Secty.

Returning to the theme of the apparent disregard of the documentary evidence by writers on the history of the beginnings of Los Angeles, one notes that Henry Raup Wagner in an early publication used the title: "The Earliest Documents of El Pueblo de Nuestra Señora La Reina de los Angeles" (1931).

Zoeth Skinner Eldredge, *The Beginnings of San Francisco* (2 vols.; San Francisco, 1912), I, 91, third footnote, goes a step farther than Wagner and asserts:

Portolá crossed the Los Angeles river on the 2d of August, 1769, the day of the Feast of Porciúncula and named it in honor of the day Río de Nuestra Señora de los Angeles de Porciúncula. It is to this incident the city of Los Angeles owes its name which is in full Nuestra Señora La Reina de los Angeles de Porciúncula — Our Lady the Queen of the Angels of Porciúncula.

In writing this, Eldredge provided a clue to the cause for confusion which has surrounded the original Spanish name of the city;

THE ROUTE OF THE SETTLERS OF THE CITY OF LOS ANGELES

ON FEBRUARY 2, 1781, A COMPANY OF SETTLERS RECRUITED IN THE STATES OF SONORA AND SINALOA, MEXICO, BEGAN A HISTORIC JOURNEY FROM LOS ALAMOS, SONORA. THESE WERE *Los Pobladores*, WHOSE MISSION WAS THE FOUNDING OF EL PUEBLO DE NUESTRA SEÑORA LA REINA DE LOS ANGELES DE PORCIUNCULA AS PLANNED BY GOVERNOR FELIPE DE NEVE. THEY MARCHED DOWN THE RIO MAYO TO SANTA BARBARA BAY, CROSSED THE GULF OF CALIFORNIA TO LORETO, LOWER CALIFORNIA, SAILED NORTHWARD IN THE GULF TO SAN LUIS GONZAGA BAY, THEN WENT INLAND TO THE MISSION SAN FERNANDO DE VELLICATA. IN MAY THEY STARTED THE LONG OVERLAND JOURNEY NORTHWARD WHICH ENDED AUGUST 18, 1781, AT MISSION SAN GABRIEL. ON SEPTEMBER 4, 1781, THE 11 FAMILIES--44 MEN, WOMEN AND CHILDREN IN ALL--MOVED TO THE SITE ON THE RIO PORCIUNCULA WHICH IS NOW THE CITY OF LOS ANGELES.

A close-up of plaque on the mall of the Los Angeles County Administration and Courts Building. Note error in city's name. *Courtesy of the editor.*

namely, he confused the official title (of which he was perhaps not aware), La Reina de los Angeles, with a religious festival which was celebrated by members of the Portolá expedition. It is very important to recognize that a pueblo was a civil, not a religious or a military community. No evidence exists that a priest was even present when the pueblo was founded.

The most recent example of this confusion, in this writer's knowledge and estimation, is found in the otherwise excellent article entitled "The Man Who Named Los Angeles," by Raymund F. Wood wherein is quoted from Father Juan Crespí's diary (1769):

This river [the Porciúncula] can be seen flowing down, its bed not deeply sunken below the surrounding ground, through a very green, lush, wide-spreading valley — an extent, north and south, of some leagues of level soil . . . so that it can truly be said to a most handsome garden [*sic*] . . . and in time to come there may be a very large and rich mission of Our Lady of the Angels of the Porciúncula, this being the day upon which we came to it, when this well-known Indulgence is gained [*i.e.*, noon of August 1 to midnight of August 2] in our Seraphic order; and so we have proclaimed it El Río y Valle de Nuestra Señora de los Angeles de la Porciúncula.

In note 13 of the Wood article we find: "The addition of the words 'la Reina' into the title of the city, even though these words are not to be found in the original name given by Crespí to the river, has aroused considerable argument." Mr. Wood then goes on to cite the use of the words, La Reina, in the instructions to Rivera, December 27, 1779.

There truly should be no argument and the discrepancy noted by Mr. Wood has an obvious reason. The religious festival of August 2, 1769, provided the historical background for the name selected by Commandant Croix, *La Reina de los Angeles* (The Queen of the Angels), which is the original Spanish title for the pueblo, but the religious festival did not establish the title for the pueblo itself.

Francisco Garcés:
Explorer of Southern
California

BY RAYMUND F. WOOD

THE CITIZENS OF KERN COUNTY, California, have long recognized the merits of the Franciscan explorer-priest Francisco Garcés; for not only does there exist in Bakersfield, the county seat, an important street intersection named Garcés Circle, and a fine private school named Garcés High School, but there is even a heroic sized statue of Father Garcés close by two of the main thoroughfares of the city. It would not be unreasonable, then, for some uninformed person to assume that this Garcés, whoever he was, must have been some local luminary, perhaps an early missionary or a founding father of the city; but presumably local to Bakersfield, since only in Bakersfield and in nearby Arvin does he seem to be honored. Indeed, save for a bronze plaque in the garden of Mission San Gabriel, honoring him and the other victims of the Yuma Massacre of 1781, and a monument (State Registered Landmark 618) in San Bernardino County, commemorating the passage over the mountains not only of Garcés but also of Jedediah Smith, who followed part of the Garcés route in 1826, the name of Garcés is almost unknown south of the Tehachapis.

This is perhaps unfortunate, for the accomplishments of Father Garcés were acted out on a far vaster stage than the single county of Kern would provide, and indeed his travels encompass not only the western half of the state of Arizona, but also the counties of Riverside, San Bernardino, Imperial, and Los Angeles, with a brief excursion into Tulare County as well.

Southern California's Spanish Heritage

Garcés was one of the two padres who made the preliminary journey with Anza, in February and March of 1777, from the Altar Valley in Sonora, by way of Tubac in (modern) Arizona, and across the sand dunes of the Colorado Desert, to Mission San Gabriel in California, the first white men to establish the feasibility of such a route. The immediate result of this particular expedition was, as is well known, the famous Anza Expedition of 1775–76 to San Francisco Bay, when many colonists, including women and children, were safely brought across the deserts from Sonora to Alta California. Garcés went along on this second expedition also, though he stayed with it only as far as the Colorado River. But even this brief outline of his accomplishments up to the year 1775 is enough to indicate that the name of Francisco Garcés should be better known in all of southern California.

Francisco Tomás Hermenegildo Garcés, to give him his full name, was born in the Villa (or country estate) of Morata del Conde, in the Kingdom of Aragon, in Spain, April 12, 1738. He was educated by his father's brother, the local parish priest, who instructed him so well that at the age of fifteen he was permitted to enter the Franciscan Order as a novice, and to continue his studies in literature, sciences, philosophy, and theology with the Franciscans for another ten years. He was ordained a priest at the age of twenty-five.

He applied for missionary work in "the Indies," as America was then usually called, and was accepted, along with some other Spaniards, for training in Holy Cross College at Querétaro, Mexico. He remained at Querétaro for nearly five years, from 1763 to early in 1768, when he was finally judged by his superiors mature enough (though he was still only thirty) and sufficiently trained to undertake the perils of a long sea and land journey, and then to begin the conversion of the heathens in that difficult missionary district, the Californias.

The ship carrying a group of missionaries sailed from San Blas on January 20, 1768, and after a voyage of several months reached Guaymas. Garcés was then assigned to the already existing mission of San Xavier del Bac, originally a Jesuit foundation, near modern-day Tucson, but at that time the farthest outpost of civili-

The Santa Fe Railroad named many of its stations after local or historical personages. *All photographs used in illustrating this essay are courtesy of the author.*

zation. Father Garcés reached his new post June 30, 1768.

From this home mission of Bac, Garcés made, during the years 1768 to 1776, five separate *entradas* or journeys of discovery (since from his point of view they were "entrances") into the mysterious lands that lay to the west.

The first *entrada*, 1768, took him north and northwest to the Gila River, where he established friendly relationships with the tribes along the Gila, from present-day Phoenix right down to Yuma.

On the second entrada, 1770, he again went as far as the junction of the Gila and the Colorado, to visit some sick Indians who had been stricken with measles.

On the third entrada, 1771, he again went down the Gila, visited his Yuman friends, and then went all the way down the Colorado until it ran out into the Gulf. In two months he travelled nearly a thousand miles among these friendly Indians.

The fourth entrada took him to Mission San Gabriel in California, with Anza's first expedition of 1774, as mentioned earlier. Anza took with him from his military headquarters at Tubac, a few miles south of San Xavier del Bac, two Franciscan missionaries, Father Garcés and Father Juan Díaz, an Indian guide, twenty soldiers, and several muleteers. The object of this preliminary expedition was to test the feasibility of a land route between the "old" establishments of the Altar Valley in Sonora and the "new" missions and pueblos being founded in Alta California, specifically those of Monterey and San Francisco. They left Tubac on January 8, 1774, and arrived, after incredible difficulties in the sand dunes between the Colorado River and the Salton Sea, at San Gabriel on March 22, after travelling about 700 miles. It may be well to note that on this journey through unknown country (that portion of it between Yuma and Mt. San Jacinto being crossed by white men for the first time), when Anza was for splitting the party up and sending half the soldiers and pack animals back to the Colorado — presumably in the belief that it was better that only half the expedition should perish in the wilderness than that all of them should die — it was Garcés who objected to the plan and it was Anza who yielded on this point. Garcés was not a man to give up merely because the going got a bit rough at times.

Francisco Garcés did not continue with Anza beyond San Gabriel, but instead returned at once to the Colorado, as Anza — acting under orders from the viceroy, Bucareli — directed him, to maintain peace and friendly relations with the Yuman tribes. One of these chieftains, a man named Palma, the Spaniards were particularly anxious to placate, and they constantly sought his favor with many gifts all during this period. Garcés therefore returned alone, accompanied only by some Indians, across the desert to Yuma. There he remained as a guest of Palma, strengthening the bonds of friendship between Palma and the Spaniards by his own kindliness, until Anza and Father Díaz came back from Monterey, on May 14. Anza, Díaz, and the soldiers then went directly on to Tubac, the military headquarters, reaching that place on May 26. But Father Garcés had not yet had his fill of exploring for that year. He therefore decided to return to his own mission of San Xavier by way of the Gila Valley. But at a point near present-day Gila

Bend, he turned north, towards Bill Williams River, to visit the wild tribes that lived north and northeast of the Yumans, and did not return to Bac until July 10, 1774, traversing this harsh desert in summer, entirely alone. This ended his fourth entrada.

He remained at or near San Xavier del Bac from July 1774 to October 1775, preaching the Gospel, establishing friendly relations with the pagan tribes round about, and constantly doing for himself, and by himself, all that was necessary merely to exist at this remote outpost on the perimeter of Spain's far-flung empire.

It might well be asked at this point what manner of man was this, whose energy was so great, whose love for the Indians was so strong, and whose interest in exploring and in seeking sites for future missions so keen that it kept him so constantly on the move? He was still young; in 1775, when he began his fifth entrada, which was to last for eleven months, and to cover a distance of 2,000 miles, he was still only thirty-seven years of age. He has been described as a well nigh perfect physical specimen, tall, well-formed, of iron frame, and absolutely fearless.

On October 21, 1775, at Tubac in Arizona he began his fifth entrada, the longest and most famous of all. It began simply enough. Garcés, along with two other padres, Father Tomás Eixarch, who had been with him for a while at Bac, and Father Pedro Font, an excellent diarist, were requested to report to the headquarters of Lieutenant Colonel Juan Bautista de Anza at Tubac for the purpose of accompanying the expedition of soldiers and colonists he was to lead all the way to San Francisco. But Garcés and Eixarch were given specific instructions not to proceed beyond the Colorado. There they were to stay until Anza returned for them; in the meanwhile they were to "look over the country and treat with the near-by Indian nations, determining if they were disposed and ready for religious instruction and for becoming subjects of our Sovereign," as Garcés states in the introduction to his diary (Galvin's translation). In accordance with this instruction, Garcés and Eixarch remained at Yuma, where Chief Palma very kindly built a hut for them, while only Father Font went with Anza's expedition across the Colorado, and on to San Gabriel, Monterey, and ultimately to San Francisco.

Francisco Garcés, however, was not the man to sit idly in a hut, among comparatively peaceful and converted Indians, when there was exploring to be done. No sooner had Anza's expedition of 240 soldiers, colonists, wives, children, servants, Indian guides, nearly 700 horses, and over 300 cattle, finally left the long-suffering Yuman Indians in peace, and were out of sight across the Colorado, than Garcés was off again, accompanied by a young man, a civilized Indian named Sebastián. This time he went southwest, fixing each day's position with fair accuracy by the use of a quadrant which Father Font had loaned him as a farewell gesture, though he modestly admits that because of his lack of skill in using it some of his reckonings may not be exact.

He spent most of December 1776 in pursuit of his superior's instructions to "explore the region," crossing the Colorado only a day or so after the main expedition had got across, and actually catching up with the slowly moving colonists at Laguna de Santa Olaya, where they were resting for a few days. We have no precise record, other than the Font and Garcés diaries, as to what Anza said when this indefatigable explorer, to whom he had said farewell at Yuma some days before, came riding into his camp. Garcés merely relates that he "met the señor comandante, Padre Font, and all the expedition." Father Font, on the other hand, was in a good position to observe his fellow Franciscan in action, and in *his* diary he wrote quite a bit about Father Garcés. He noted that Garcés was very energetic in trying to convert the natives who had assembled to witness the extraordinary expedition that was slowly passing through their country. Father Garcés had made, or rather had painted on a piece of canvas, a picture of the Blessed Virgin holding the Christ-child in her arms, the other side of the canvas being a representation of a man burning in the flames of hell. This picture he used with great success in conveying the elements of Christianity to the pagan Indians who were hanging about the encampment. Father Font noted this, and he wrote down some rather acrid remarks about his fellow religious. "Padre Garcés," he wrote,

is so well fitted to get along with the Indians and to go among them that he appears to be but an Indian himself. He sits with them in the circle, or

152

at night around the fire, with his legs crossed, and there he will sit musing two or three hours or more, oblivious to everything else, talking with them with much serenity and deliberation. And although the foods of the Indians are as nasty and dirty as these outlandish people themselves, the father eats them with great gusto and says that they are good for the stomach and very fine. In short God has created him, as I see it, solely for the purpose of seeking out these unhappy, ignorant, and rustic people.

Father Garcés, unaware of the impression he had created on the rather acidulous Pedro Font, left the expedition on December 9, and spent the rest of the month exploring the lower Colorado, going from one Indian *rancheria* to the next, carefully noting the position of each with the quadrant; and *his* diary, far from making snide remarks about his fellow Franciscans, has nothing but praise for the generosity of Father Font in making this instrument available to him. He returned to Yuma on January 3, 1776.

On February 14 he was off again, this time northward, to visit new tribes. On February 28 he reached the tribe of the Mojaves — or Jamajabs, as he calls them — about where the city of Needles is today. These Jamajabs, who were to become his firm friends, he describes as fine physical specimens, whose men were warlike, and whose women were modest and prolific. He speaks in one place of a gathering of 2,000 people who came out to greet him.

From the Mojaves he learned that it was possible, though not easy, to pass from the Colorado River to the newly established missions on the coast — San Gabriel and San Luis Obispo — because some of their young men occasionally made the trip. He had long kept in mind that it was the desire of the viceroy, indeed one of his principal concerns, to establish an easy route between Sonora and Monterey, and even, if it were possible, between Santa Fe and Monterey. Remembering his own bitter experience in trying to get across the Colorado Desert with Anza less than two years before, Garcés wondered if there might be a route through the Mojave country, westward from Needles, which might be better than the route, westward from Yuma, that led through the nation of the unfriendly Cajueches, to say nothing of the sand dunes which had given Anza and himself so much trouble in 1774. Since the Mojaves claimed to know of a route to the west, and offered to accompany him and guide him, he took the opportunity at once, and on March 1 he set out, going northwest a little until he reached, by his own calculation with the quadrant, the 35th parallel, which is the point where the state of Nevada line strikes the Colorado River today.

He continued northwest and west for the next several days, his route taking him a little south of present-day Highway 66; but his Mojave guides undoubtedly took him along a trail they themselves knew about. Coues believes that Garcés was following the route that later became known as the Government Road, between Fort Mojave and Camp Cady, established east of Barstow. This route followed the old watering holes of Piute Springs, Rock Springs, and Cedar Springs, and through a pass at the northern end of the Providence Mountains. It is more probable, however, that Garcés' Indian guides were leading him by a series of watering holes somewhat south of this line, and that consequently he went around the south end of the Providence Mountains, through Foshay Pass, rather than through Cedar Canyon.

On March 9, 1776, occurred the event for which the name of Francisco Garcés will always be remembered. In his own words he states: "I encountered an arroyo of saltish water that I named the Arroyo de los Mártires." This was at the southwestern corner of the huge sink today called Soda Lake, and the stream of saltish water flowing into it was the terminus of the Mojave River, no part of which had ever before been seen by a white man. Garcés of course did not yet know the significance of his discovery of this great river of the desert, or even know that he was the first white man to see it.

For the next two weeks he did not leave for long the Mojave River bed, but followed its course, almost due westward to the site of today's Barstow, meeting with many tribes of Indians on the route. He was astonished by the marks of respect which these poverty-stricken people paid to him, probably the first white man they had ever seen. They tossed over him small sea shells, treasures which they prized above all else, much as women toss flowers to conquering heroes as they ride along in triumphal procession. Such was the reception accorded to Garcés, in his old torn and bedraggled grey habit, by a people who in their nakedness had even less of this world's goods than he.

Somewhere in the vicinity of Harvard, just east of Daggett, on March 12, Garcés and his Indian guides were forced, by cold and hunger, to kill one of their animals for food. They remained there for three days, as they had no way of preserving the meat, or even of carrying it with them. So they made camp for three days, drinking the good water of the Mojave River and renewing their strength. On the 18th, about where the community of Lenwood is today, Garcés observed, by the use of the quadrant, that his course along the river bed was taking a bend to the south, and that he was getting below 35 degrees of latitude, whereas he wanted to continue on to the west, hoping to strike Mission San Luis Obispo which he knew to be not far from the 35th parallel. He says: "I entreated the Indians that they should take me towards the west; but they simply responded that they knew of no other road" than the route they were taking along the bed of the Mojave to its source, and then over the San Bernardino Mountains to the plain where the mission of San Gabriel had been built. So Garcés had to go along with them, turning sharply to the south at about Helendale, and even turning to the southeast after passing the site of present-day Victorville. He certainly did not cross the mountains by the Cajon Pass. To do so his guides would have had to leave the life-giving water of the river and strike off across the dry, open country to the southwest. Moreover, his diary on March 19 and 20 specifically states that as he approached the mountains he went southeast and even east. He probably crossed the San Bernardino range at the head of Devil Canyon or Cable Canyon, on March 22. He described the view from the summit — "I could clearly see the sea, the Santa Ana River, and the whole valley of Saint Joseph," by which he meant what today we call the San Bernardino Valley.

On March 24 he reached Mission San Gabriel, after passing through the area where afterwards were established the many communities which today lie between San Bernardino and San Gabriel—Fontana, Ontario, Covina, El Monte, and so on. He remained at San Gabriel for two weeks, during which time he applied in vain to the corporal in charge for an escort and for more

Plaque at Monument Park above Cajon Pass honoring Father Garcés.

rations. The corporal claimed he had no authority to grant the request, so Garcés was forced to write to the highest military authority in California, the comandante, Captain Fernando Xavier Rivera y Moncada, who happened to be in San Diego at the time, having gone there, with Lieutenant Colonel Anza, to help put down a rebellion of the Indians in which Father Luis Jayme of San Diego had been murdered. Father Garcés did receive a reply from Comandante Rivera, but it too was negative. "Impossible," said the captain. However, a few days later the comandante himself arrived back at San Gabriel, and Garcés, unwilling to take no for an answer, sought an audience with him. He pointed out to Captain Rivera that the letter which he, Garcés, had just received was full of inconsistencies. The matter was not an impossibility, he insisted, since Anza's expedition, which had encamped near San Gabriel while Anza joined forces with Rivera y Moncada to settle the San Diego uprising, had plenty of spare horses. He also pointed out that, since the comandante himself was about to go

156

north to Monterey again, Garcés could tag along, at least as far as San Luis Obispo, and so a separate escort would not be needed. But the captain was as slippery as Garcés was earnest. Seeing that he could no longer allege that it was "impossible" to do as Garcés requested, he now changed his tune and said that he had no orders from the viceroy, and therefore he could do nothing about it.

Garcés was by this time quite disgusted with the vacillating policy of the military comandante. He was shrewd enough to see that Rivera y Moncada was not pleased that Garcés had opened up a new route from Yuma to San Gabriel, by way of the Mojave villages; and he was also sensitive enough to realize that the captain would prefer to make his journey back to Monterey without the company of this overly energetic Franciscan.

Accordingly he begged some supplies for himself and for his still faithful Mojaves and for Sebastián, supplies which he obtained from his Franciscan brothers at San Gabriel, and on April 9, astride a horse which Rivera had grudgingly allowed him to take from stock belonging to the expedition (presumably to replace the one they had been forced to kill on the desert east of Barstow), Garcés once more set forth. This time he stayed away from the regular "Camino Real," the trail that ran from San Diego to Monterey, because the route through present-day Ventura County was infested with hostile Indians, and Garcés had no military escort to protect him. He had with him, besides Sebastián and the Mojaves, only two guides from San Gabriel, and these two Indians left him at the end of the first day.

Guided by these two, however, he skirted the foothills of the San Gabriel range, crossing the Arroyo Seco, and probably passing through the present-day cities of Pasadena, Glendale, and Burbank, or possibly keeping closer to the hills, in which case his route would have taken him through Altadena, La Canada, La Crescenta, Tujunga, and Sunland. In either event he was probably well north of the Río de Nuestra Señora de Los Angeles de Porciúncula where, five years later, a small pueblo would be founded. At any rate, on April 11 he made camp at a spot somewhat to the south of the future Mission San Fernando, which was not established until 1797, nearly a quarter of a century later. Here he

157

remained a day or so because, as he had the humility to admit in his diary, he made the mistake of leaving a small book (his breviary, perhaps?) at San Gabriel. So he sent one of his Indians all the way back to get it. When the Indian returned with the precious book he again set forth, following the route out of the valley now taken by both the railroad and Interstate 5 (old Highway 99). His precise route through the mountains is difficult to determine, but he probably went through Newhall and Saugus, striking the Santa Clara River about where Castaic Junction is today. From here he went northward, and may have passed by Lake Hughes. Coues believes he was a little farther to the west. Garcés mentions a "laguna," and the next day "he completed the passage of the sierra." The laguna may never be definitely identified, but the sierra is probably the Liebre Mountain or Ridge, whose highest point is the old Sandberg's, on the original "Ridge Route." He next says that after crossing a valley he came to another, larger sierra, which he called San Marcos, but which today we call the Tehachapi. This he also crossed, probably passing somewhat to the east of the present-day Tejon Pass, between Gorman and Lebec.

At any rate, by whatever route he passed over the mountains, he at length came out on the north side, and must have been able to look out over the tremendous extent of flat valley that spread out before his eyes—the Great Valley of California, nearly 450 miles long and from 30 to 40 miles wide, probably the largest absolutely flat valley in the world, with a fall in its principal rivers of only about two feet per mile. Garcés, however, made no comment on what he saw. His only concern was for the possibilities of converting the Indian tribes, and at this point he gives a lengthy description of the manners and customs of the next tribe he meets, the Cuabajays, probably a Shoshonean tribe, to whom he earnestly preached the rudiments of Christianity.

Encouraged by his success with these Indians, Garcés set out again, and on April 27, by which time it was no doubt getting quite warm on the floor of the valley, he reached the vicinity of today's Greenfield. Here his faithful Mojaves refused to go any farther, and even the partly civilized Indian, Sebastián, who had accompanied him all the way from Arizona, refused to go any farther among these completely unknown tribes. But nothing could stop Garcés himself. Leaving his companions in camp, while he went off "for four or five days," he traveled with only one Indian, a member of the next tribe to the north, the Noches, not clearly identified but presumably one of the Yokuts peoples, since they were not friendly with their neighhors, the Shoshonean Cuabajays. Proceeding north and somewhat northeast, probably passing near the community of Edison, Garcés reached the river that was later to be called the Kern just below the point where it tumbles out of its narrow canyon in the Sierra Nevada and comes to rest on the broad bosom of the great valley. This river he named the San Felipe, and it appeared later on Father Font's map as the Río de San Phelipe. Garcés descended this stream a few miles, towards modern Bakersfield, seeking a place to cross it. At last, at a point where there were Indian rancherias on either side of the river, and a crossing could easily be made during most of the year, when the water was low, he decided to cross over and he asked some nearby Indians to help him. But unfortunately the water was high and he could not swim. The Indians agreed to help him, and tried to persuade him to undress. He, with the modesty of his religious training, refused to remove anything but his habit, retaining, as he says, his shirt and underwear. At any rate, the Indians, who were good swimmers, managed to pull him across, two taking his arms and two his legs, while some others transported his garments and his personal effects in *coritas*, baskets that were closely woven and then made completely waterproof by an application of pitch which they obtained from the petroleum seepages that abounded in this oil rich country. For, though Garcés did not know it, the country he was entering was to become part of the fabulously wealthy oil fields of Kern County. The spot where he crossed, incidentally, has been marked as an historical monument.

"Disengaging myself as best I could from the Indians," he writes, who would have him stay with them forever if they could so persuade this charming missionary, Garcés proceeded northward, and on May 2 reached Posey Creek, still in Kern County, and on May 3 reached the region of White Creek, in Tulare County, where he performed the first authenticated religious ceremony in the San Joaquin Valley, the baptism of a young boy who was dying. Garcés remained a few days in this area, visiting several rancherias of Indians and speaking to them about God. On May 5 he prepared to take his departure. He realized now that he was within striking distance of Mission San Luis Obispo, which the Indians told him was only four days' journey to the west. They also told him that seven days to the northwest was a great river, larger than the San Felipe (the Kern), and that he ought to go to see it. This was, of course, the San Joaquin River, principal stream of the great San Joaquin Valley. Garcés would like to have visited it, as well as to have gone westward to San Luis, but he simply did not have the means to do so, as he laments in his diary. He no longer had any gifts for the Indians, and he had left his companions south of the Kern with a promise to return "in four or five days." He had already been gone eight days. So, reluctantly, he returned, going by way of some villages on the upper White River, then south to Posey Creek, and finally to the Kern (San Felipe) which he reached on May 7, about three miles above the place where earlier he had been ferried across. By this time, he was very worried about his companions, particularly about his good friend Sebastián, who evidently, from what he could learn from the nearby Indians, had come to the Kern River in search of him. He hurried to the point where he had left his companions, and found them at last, though two of the Mojaves had gone back to their own country, but two others, recent arrivals from the Mojave country, had consented to take their place. Garcés comments that this fact indicates that there was already a fairly constant flow of commerce and travel along this trail that led from the Colorado to the coast.

On May 14 Garcés began to ascend the Tehachapi range. The Mojave guides were totally unfamiliar with this route out of the valley, though today it is the principal route taken by both railroad and highway. They normally went south, over the Tejon Pass to San Gabriel, and then over the San Bernardino Mountains. It is all the more to the credit of Father Garcés, therefore, that he insisted on going due eastward, rather than south, despite the fact that even the aborigines did not know of a route in that direction, and also that he could no longer depend on the use of his compass. He had lost the needle of the compass when his horse stumbled while crossing a plain infested with pocket-gophers, south of the Kern River. He reached the crest of the Tehachapis on May 17, and then crossed the Mojave Desert, reaching the future site of Barstow and the "Río de los Mártires," the Mojave River, on the 19th.

Garcés then retraced his earlier route, this time descending the Mojave River to its sink in Soda Lake, and continuing on until he reached the Colorado at the end of May, amid the great rejoicings of the entire Mojave nation.

Upon his arrival at the principal rancherias of the Mojaves, Garcés found letters awaiting him, one from Anza, and one from his old companion, Father Eixarch, requesting or obliging him to return at once to Yuma. However, the letters had been written earlier in the month, and they stated that Garcés should return to the Yuma territory "within three days." Since it was now much more than three days since the letters had been received by the Mojaves, Garcés chose to ignore these instructions—indeed, it would have been foolish of him to have complied, since he would have found, upon his late arrival at Yuma, that Anza, Father Eixarch, and all the rest of the party had already departed for Tubac long before.

Instead, he diligently inquired of some visiting Hualapai Indians about the route to Moqui (the land of the Hopi Indians of today), and he was overjoyed when these Hualapais informed him that they knew the route to Moqui and would take him there if he wished to go.

At this point an incident favored Garcés' plans, and confirmed his decision to go across to the Moqui, rather than down to Yuma. The incident was as follows: some hot-headed Mojaves recognized the Hualapais as belonging to a tribe that in earlier times had killed some relatives of theirs, and despite a recently concluded peace treaty they tried to attack them. Garcés came to the aid of the Hualapais, and to show his good will he offered to accompany them, as a sort of hostage, through the Mojave country, if in return they would agree to guide him all the way to Moqui. The Mojaves did not dare attack them as long as the beloved Garcés was among them, and the grateful Hualapais agreed to guide him, by way of the land of their cousins, the Havasupais, all the way to Moqui, the land of the Hopis.

On June 5, 1776, Francisco Garcés crossed the Colorado River into the present state of Arizona, and began an entirely new journey of exploration, as significant in its way as the one he had just completed in California. One major difference, however, is that from this point on he was entirely alone, save for those Indians whom he could persuade to guide and accompany him from one rancheria to the next. Sebastián had developed a kind of heart ailment, and was not in shape for further travel; while the Mojaves who had shared his journey up the Mojave River, across the San Bernardino Mountains, then past San Gabriel, by way of the Tejon Pass, to the valley of the Tulares and back across the Mojave Desert, in the heat of summer, now declined to travel any farther with this mad explorer, who insisted on going across the still more barren Arizona desert in June and July to visit the Moqui Indians—just to prove it could be done! Even for a Mojave this was a bit too much. Let the Hualapais aid him if they would!

Garcés began well enough, guided by a few friendly Hualapais, and in ten days reached Peach Springs, which he named the Pozos (wells) de San Basilio. Here he left the route of the present-day Santa Fe Railroad, which he had been pioneering since he struck it near today's Truxton, and turned northeast towards the country of the Havasu Indians, cousins of the Hualapais, the People of the Blue Water, who lived then, as they do today, at the bottom of Cataract Canyon—today the only people in the United States who have never been visited by a four-wheeled vehicle, and whose post office, Supai, Arizona, is the only post office in the continental United States served only by mule back and helicopter.

Garcés descended into the "horrible abyss" of Cataract Canyon, part of the terrifying descent being by means of a rickety ladder, a descent which Lieutenant Ives, of the later Railroad Survey party of 1858, did not succeed in negotiating. Garcés spent the next five days among the hospitable Havasupai, enjoying fresh meat, both deer and beef, corn, vegetables, and "mezcal" (the agave, or century plant)—all of which the Havasu Indians raised on their irrigated lands in Cataract Canyon, just as they still do today. Garcés, the first white man to visit the People of the Blue Water, made many notes on their way of life; he noted that they used hoes and hatchets which they obtained from the Moqui; and he noted that their women were light colored, because, as he says, "this canyon is so deep that it is ten o'clock in the day when the sun begins to shine," even in mid-summer. On June 25 he bade farewell to these hospitable people, and set out again on his lonely journey to Oraibe, the chief town of the Moqui (Hopi), a people that his fellow Franciscan, Father Silvestre Vélez de Escalante, from Zuñi, had tried in vain to convert.

His journey took him along the regular Indian trail from the Havasu territory to the Moqui, the same trail that Cardenás, one of Coronado's men, had taken, but in the reverse direction, in 1540, when he first discovered the Grand Canyon. But Garcés, standing on the brink of the South Rim of the Grand Canyon on June 26, 1776, probably did not know that another explorer had stood there 36 years earlier. At any rate, Garcés was the first white man to see this "profound canyon," as he called it, for over 200 years, and he was the first to discover it from the west. Like all subsequent travellers to the South Rim, he was duly impressed by the stupendous view, but he did not linger. Passing rapidly along the trail, guided by a handful of Havasu Indians, he passed by "Desert View," went across the "Painted Desert," and on July 2 reached the hilltop town of Oraibe, chief city of the Hopi Indians.

Garcés had been particularly anxious to reach Oraibe, for a reason not yet explained in these pages. The previous year, Father Escalante had reached Oraibe from Zuñi, in western New Mexico, and had tried in vain to preach to the flint-hearted Moqui, just as many earlier generations of missionaries had tried to do. But the point was that there was frequent communication between Oraibe and Zuñi, and of course between Zuñi and Santa Fe, the capital of all the settlements in the valley of the Río Grande, the New Mexico of today. Therefore, if Garcés could reach Oraibe he would have proved his major point. It was possible for white men to go from New Mexico to California, or from California to New Mexico.

Garcés found the Moqui as obdurate as ever, and but for his

Statue of Father Garcés on Yuma Hill, California, dedicated in 1928 at St. Thomas Indian Mission, site of Mission La Purísima Concepción, near the junction of the Gila and Colorado rivers where Garcés was martyred in 1781.

Plaque on the Garcés statue on Yuma Hill.

The Hopi Indian hilltop town of Oraibe, little changed from the time of Father Garcés.

friendly Havasus he would not have found even a place to lay his weary head. No Moqui would open his door for the Franciscan, and he was forced to spend the night, as he had done so often along the trail, under the stars, stretched out under a blanket in the street, guarded from further insult by his faithful Havasus.

On July 3 there arrived by chance three Indians from Zuñi and they recognized Father Garcés as being of the same friendly type as their own Father Escalante (who at that moment was on his way to Utah on an exploring expedition of his own). They cordially invited Father Garcés to go back with them to Zuñi.

Garcés was strongly tempted to go. He wanted very much to prove that one person could travel all the way from San Luis Obispo or Monterey to Zuñi in New Mexico. But his innate sense of practicality got the better or him. He saw that he could get to Zuñi easily enough, with these three Zuñi Indians to guide him. But how would he get back again? With no Havasus to act as his bodyguards he might receive rough treatment from the Moqui upon his return; and how would he get back to Cataract Canyon? He could hardly expect these friendly guides to sit around at

166

Oraibe awaiting his return; they were anxious to get back to their own land.

Besides, he had already proved his point. He knew that Father Escalante had been here at Oraibe the year before; and here *he* was at Oraibe, having come all the way from San Gabriel, by way of the Tulare Valley! He had proved his point; it was possible for Spaniards to travel from California to New Mexico, even in the heat of summer. He had fulfilled the wish of the viceroy; he had opened up a line of communication between these two outposts of the Spanish empire. There was no need to go farther east.

Still, to make sure that the governor of New Mexico, in Santa Fe, should be officially informed, Garcés wrote a letter, dating it at Oraibe, July 4, 1776, and addressing it to the acting Reverend Superior at Zuñi, and asking him to forward the letter to the governor at Santa Fe.

Totally unaware of the historical implications of the letter that the padre handed to them — as indeed Garcés himself was equally unaware of the significant events occurring that same day on the Atlantic seaboard — the three Zuñi Indians departed eastward for their homes, while Garcés once more turned his steps towards the west. Perhaps he felt like Alexander, sorrowful that there were no further lands to explore. His homeward journey was largely a reverse of the trip east. He again stayed most of a week with the Havasu, urged thereto by their prodigal hospitality, but eventually, on July 15, he left Cataract Canyon; but this time he insisted on being taken out by a longer but less formidable route. He was not going to ascend that ladder, or follow the headspinning trail that wound up the face of the cliff, if he could help it!

Ten days later he was on the Colorado, where the Mojaves "ran to embrace him, leaped for joy, and knew not how to express their delight," as he notes in his diary. After a sad farewell to his few Havasu friends who had accompanied him so far, and "to whom he was indebted for so many favors," and also a farewell to his firm friends the Mojaves, he departed for Yuma on July 26, reaching that point, after visiting many different tribes and villages along the way, and crossing and recrossing the Colorado several times, on August 27. His Yuma friends, members of Palma's tribe, received him joyfully, having believed him dead, for he had been gone eight months. Also the Pimas, who lived on the Gila, rejoiced to see him when he passed through their country a few days later; in fact they put on quite a celebration and, much to Garcés' disgust, the men got embarrassingly drunk and slobbered all over the good padre in their enthusiasm to welcome him back to his own country.

Finally, on September 17, 1776, Father Francisco Garcés arrived safely at his home mission of San Xavier del Bac, having been gone approximately eleven months since the previous October 26, and having travelled, by his own reckoning, exactly 698½ leagues, or approximately 2,000 miles, during the last 1,200 of which he had not seen the face of a single white man, though he estimates that he encountered, just along the banks of the Gila and Colorado Rivers alone, close to 25,000 Indians. He probably met over 100,000 Indians during his year of wandering from one rancheria to another. Only the Moqui were unfriendly to this exuberant Spaniard; only the community of Oraibe resisted the charm and earnestness of this great missionary.

Because he was of such a character that he could pass freely among savage tribes, even among those who had heard bad things of the Spaniards, and who hid their young women when they heard a rumor that Spanish soldiers might be coming their way; because he worked so hard to make treaties of peace among the Indians, not only with the Spaniards but among themselves also; and because he himself was so warm and friendly that he was greeted as a long lost brother whenever he returned to a tribe he had once visited — because of all this it is sad to relate that five years later Padre Francisco Garcés was murdered, or assassinated, or martyred, depending on your point of view, by a group of hotheaded young rebels from the Yuman tribes.

Father Garcés was not idle during the five years of life remaining to him. The last part of 1776 was spent in writing up his diary into proper form for submission to the viceroy, and in helping Father Font, who also wrote up his diary, to construct a detailed map of the entire southwest. This was completed at Tubutama, in Sonora, in January 1777, and duly submitted, along with a report

Plaque commemorating the 1781 Yuma Massacre victims at Mission San Gabriel.

to his superiors; and Garcés was then free to return to his missionary duties at Bac. Meanwhile, however, events were occurring which would culminate in the Yuma Massacre of 1781, in which not only Garcés would lose his life, but three other priests and some fifty other Spaniards as well.

The reason for this Yuma Massacre, as it is called in history, seems to stem from the incompetence of a certain Teodoro de Croix, nephew of a former viceroy of New Spain, and now made commandant general of the frontier provinces, a position that made him independent of the viceroy, Bucareli. He has been described as a hard working, well meaning, but rather stupid man. His stupidity, in the present case, lay in his parsimonious attitude towards the missions along the Colorado which he was specifically ordered to establish by no less a person than his Royal Majesty; and one result of the interest that the king took in the reports was this specific order to establish missions among the Yumans, something that Father Garcés had been hoping for, and his friend Palma had been clamoring for, for a long time. Nevertheless, Croix and his subaltern Don Pedro Tueros, the military governor of Sonora, wasted nearly the whole of 1778 in administrative delays, and then detailed the minimum number of soldiers possible for an escort. And the paymaster of the province, instead of providing the lavish gifts which Palma, on an earlier visit to Mexico City had been led to expect, doled out to Father Garcés and to his one Franciscan companion, Father Díaz, only the barest necessities of travel, and no gifts for the Yumans at all. The first attempt to found missions on the Colorado in 1779, therefore met with little success, despite the personal efforts of Father Garcés, and despite the fact that a third missionary was later sent along, Father Juan Barreneche.

Then, in March 1780, Croix had a brilliant idea. Instead of just founding missions he decided to establish colonies on the Colorado as well, two of them in fact, which should be joint missions and pueblos — something that no one in New Spain had ever successfully tried before, and which, because of the necessary division of authority — civil, military, and religious — was doomed to failure from the start. However, Croix insisted, and he spent half a year rounding up ten soldiers and about ten colonists for each settlement, all of whom were to be accompanied by their wives and children, and in the fall of 1780 he sent them on their way, still without the promised gifts for the Yumans.

During the winter and spring of 1780–81 two of these colony-missions were established, one, Purísima Concepción, on the hill where Fort Yuma subsequently stood (and where St. Thomas Indian Mission now stands), and the other, San Pedro y San Pablo de Bicuñer, about eight miles upstream, just below the spot where Laguna Dam was later built. An additional priest, Father Matías Moreno, was also sent along, so that there were two missionaries at each colony, whose duties were to be divided between converting the Indians and ministering to the spiritual needs of the families of the colonists and soldiers.

Troubles arose from the start. Palma had been led to believe that his people would have the padres all to themselves, and that they would receive from the king of Spain horses, tools, implements, blankets, and the like. Instead, there were sent among them a horde of colonists, with armed soldiers to back them up, who appropriated the best lands along the river, and allowed their cattle to graze at will in the Indians' cornfields.

Then, in June 1781, to make matters worse, along came Captain Rivera y Moncada, Garcés' old adversary at San Gabriel some five years before, with an even larger gang of colonists, recruits for the California pueblos, escorted by yet more soldiers. Most of these people did move right on to California, but the captain himself stayed, with about a dozen men, at a camp directly opposite the Gila from Yuma, where his animals did still further damage to the fields of the Indians. A group of "angry young men" of Palma's tribe, and of some other tribes over whom he had little or no control, decided to take things into their own hands and, rebelling from his authority, organized the massacre of all Spaniards along the river, planning to attack the three separate colonies at almost the same time.

They attacked first at Yuma, on July 17, while Father Garcés was saying Mass. They slew the two soldiers on guard, but did not slay the priests. Evidently it was the high regard they had for Father Garcés that saved his life at this time, for in the almost simultaneous attack on the other settlement they spared no one, and both padres were slain along with most of the soldiers and settlers. On the 18th the savages returned from their slaughter of Rivera and his men across the Gila, and killed the remainder of the unarmed colonists who had been working in the fields, while capturing most of the women and children and holding them as hostages.

On July 19 Palma tried to appeal to his unruly subjects to cease any further slaughter and burning of buildings, and to spare the lives of the remaining two Franciscans. For a moment it seemed that they would do so, but at the instigation of a certain Nifora (Apache) Indian, not even one of their own people but what today we would call an "outside agitator," who called out "If these two are left alive, all is lost!," Father Barreneche and Father Garcés were likewise beaten to death with clubs.

So perished, in a period of three days of slaughter, some notable names in Spanish-American history; Captain Rivera y Moncada, who for all his faults deserved a better fate; at least a dozen of the soldiers who were with him; about forty other soldiers and settlers who had come up from Sonora to Yuma at the bidding of the commandant general; and four Franciscan missionaries, one of them the much beloved Francisco Garcés, the intrepid explorer, discoverer of the Mojave River, the man who, by his extraordinary, yearlong journey from Arizona to San Gabriel, and from there to Tulare County, and from the Tehachapis to Oraibe by way of the Grand Canyon, did more than any other explorer to unite these distant outposts of the Spanish empire. Like the intransigent old captain who was slain along with him in the Yuma Massacre, he was deserving of a better fate.

Alta California's
Four Fortresses

BY RICHARD S. WHITEHEAD

SPAIN'S PLAN FOR CLAIMING and colonizing Upper California involved establishing a chain of missions to convert and civilize the heathen Indians under the care and guidance of Franciscan priests. The padres and their charges, in turn, were to be protected from attack by England, France and Russia as well as from other hostile Indians by four presidios, conveniently spaced to protect the missionary settlements. The dictionary translates the word "presidio" as "a garrison of soldiers, a fortress garrisoned by soldiers, a place destined for punishing criminals by hard labor, house of correction, penitentiary." Considering that under attack, occupants of a fortress are forcibly confined within its defensive walls, the double meaning is understandable. A Spanish-speaking person, however, might have some apprehensions about working or living in a presidio. In this article we are concerned only with the four presidios that protected Spanish settlements in Alta California from their enemies.

Actually there were five California presidios. Prior to August 29, 1804, Baja and Alta California were one Spanish province under one governor, the first being Don Gaspar de Portolá who, in 1769, led the expedition to explore the California coastline and rediscover the port of Monterey. Portolá's initial headquarters were at the presidio at Loreto, capital city of the Californias, located on the east coast of the peninsula about 250 miles northwest of Cape San Lucas, the southerly tip of Baja California. Existence of this presidio explains why, in 1783, Diego Gonzáles, commandant at the Monterey Presidio, received a directive to order five branding irons for the horses and mules of the presidios as follows:

Place	Brand	Founding Date
Loreto	$\mathcal{J}^A$	October 1697
San Diego	2^A	July 16, 1769
Monterey	$A\!\!\!\!3$	June 3, 1770
San Francisco	$\mathcal{L}^A$	July 28, 1776
Santa Barbara	$A\!\!\!\!5$	April 21, 1782

The A above the number is presumed to be the feminine noun ending of the word *compania*, each presidio garrison being designated Company 1 through 5, corresponding to the chronological sequence of each presidio's founding.

Reliable documentary data for the presidios is generally much scarcer than for the missions. One might conclude that this is due to the fact that the priests were well educated and erudite while the soldiers were inclined to be more common individuals lacking education and even, in many cases, illiterate. Since the military has always had a reputation for its high volume of paperwork, this conclusion is faulty, but it does appear that much of the information we need is still hidden in the archives. There seems to be more information available for an authentic reconstruction of the Santa Barbara Presidio than for any of the other presidios, perhaps because more time and effort has been put into the research by the Santa Barbara Trust for Historic Preservation, the organization that is rebuilding that presidio.

One category of data which provides some information is the early plans of the San Francisco, Monterey and Santa Barbara presidios, together with limited descriptions of the buildings. A major breakthrough in this area only occurred early in 1982. Fr. Harry Morrison, a priest at St. Joseph's Catholic Church in Pinole, situated north of Berkeley, California, is also an avid history researcher who in his spare time delves into the archives of the Bancroft Library at Berkeley. Going through the papers of

Edward Vischer (1808–78), a talented artist who painted the California missions, he discovered a set of drawings of all four Alta California presidios, dated 1820, Plates IV, VII, X and XI. Accompanying the plans was a request dated October 19, 1878, and signed by General Mariano G. Vallejo suggesting that the presidios were no less important than the missions, and that Vischer also paint them for posterity, using as a basis the 1820 plans. Knowing of the interest and activity toward reconstructing the Santa Barbara Presidio, Fr. Morrison contacted the author of this article. Since both Vischer and Vallejo died soon after, the presidios were never painted at that time.

Who made the drawings, when and why, are questions so far unanswered. Since all four are dated the same year, it would seem logical that they resulted from an order, probably by the governor, who was also military commander. In 1820 Pablo Solá was governor. In 1818 he visited all four presidios and nineteen missions and reported his observations to the viceroy of New Spain (Mexico) by letter dated April 3, 1819. No mention is made in this letter of plans of the presidios, but it is possible Solá ordered them drawn on this trip. It is also possible, since those sent Vischer are all on the same kind of blue-lined paper, that Vallejo had one of his staff make copies of the originals to send to Vischer, and the originals remain undiscovered to date.

In addition to revealing the layout and state of the presidios after a period of some thirty to fifty years after their founding, during which earthquakes, fires and enemy attack occurred, the discovery of these drawings provided the first known plan of the San Diego Presidio. For nearly twenty years, archeologists had been probing the mounds on Presidio Hill above Old Town in San Diego and excavating the foundations of the Presidio Chapel without benefit of a plan to tell them what to look for. Comparing the 1820 plans with those of earlier dates and supplementing these data with various reports, the combined data provide us with some interesting sidelights on the history of these civil and military installations.

One must keep in mind that the presidios were not just forts, but fortified settlements, intended to house a garrison of soldiers

Plate I
LEGEND

Escala que demuestra las habitaciones que tiene el Presidio de San Francisco.

No. 1. Guardia de Prevension, tiene de largo 6¼ varas, de ancho 4½ y 3½ de alto.

  2. Cuartel: de largo 16 varas, 3½ de alto, 2 de largo y 4½ de ancho.

  3. y 4. Calabosos de 2 varas de alto, 2 de largo y 1½ de ancho.

  5. Almacen de ropa, 18 varas largo, 4½ alto y 6 ancho.

  6. Ydem de viveres, 18 varas largo, 4½ alto y 6 ancho.

  7. y 8. Casas del Comandante, 37½ varas largo, 6 de ancho y 4½ de alto.

  10. Yglesia 19 varas de largo, 8 de acho y 4½ de alto.

  11. Casa mata, 4 varas en cuadro y 2½ de alto.

  9. Casa del Sargento.

Habitaciones de la Tropa desde a hasta k.

(Es copia sacada del original)

[Above north facade] Tiene este lienso 116 varas. Mira al Norte

[Beside west facade] Tiene este lienza 120 varas. Mira al Poniente

TRANSLATION

Scaled drawing showing the rooms of the Presidio of San Francisco.

No. 1. Guard room, being 17.2 feet long, 12.4 feet wide and 9.6 feet high.

  2. Soldiers' barracks: 44 feet long, 9.6 feet high and 12.4 feet wide.

  3. and 4. Jail cells 5.5 feet high, 5.5 feet long and 4.1 feet wide.

  5. Clothing warehouse, 49.5 feet long, 12.4 feet high and 16.5 feet wide.

  6. Provisions warehouse, same dimensions as clothing warehouse.

  7. and 8. Commandant's dwelling, 103.1 feet long, 16.5 feet wide and 12.4 feet high.

  10. Church, 52.2 feet long, 22 feet wide, 12.4 feet high.

  11. Casemate, 11 feet square and 6.9 feet high.

  9. Sergeant's quarters. From a to k, houses of the soldiers.

A copy taken from the original

Above north facade — This facade is 319 feet [long]. Looking to the north

Beside west facade — This facade is 330 feet [long]. Looking to the west

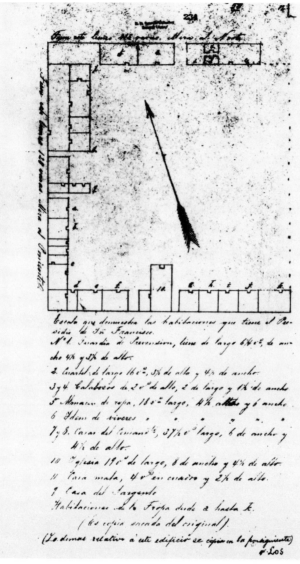

Plate I. The San Francisco Presidio. The drawing is a part of a letter dated March 4, 1792 at San Francisco from Hermenegildo Sal, acting commandant, to Governor Antonio Romeu. California Archives 6, State Papers, XI: 234. *Courtesy Bancroft Library, University of California, Berkeley.*

Southern California's Spanish Heritage

Plate II
LEGEND

Plan del Presidio que se propone para alojar la Compañia de Cavalleria del Puerto de San Francisco en la nueba California.

A. Puerta Principal
B. Cuerpo de Guardia
C. Calabozo
D. dos Almacenes para Sentenos y Viveres
E. Quarta para el Hato
F. Ydem para la sal
G. Casa del Abilitado
H. Idem del Capellan
I. Oficina para utencilios de Yglesia
J. Sacristia
K. Yglesia
L. Casa del Comandante
M. Ydem para Oficiales
N. 21 casas para la Tropa
O. Cozinas y corrales de Ydem
P. Carpinteria
Q. Herreria
R. Enfermería para Marinos
S. Callejones de los Rebellines
T. dos Rebellines
U. Casa del Sargento
X. Cozina para los Solteros
Y. Quartel
Z. dos Corrales para Cavalleria y Ganado

Monterey 27 de Junio de 1795
Diego de Borica

TRANSLATION

Plan of the Presidio that is proposed to house the Cavalry Company of the Port of San Francisco in New California.

A. Main gate
B. Guardroom
C. Jail
D. Two warehouses for grains and provisions
E. Quarters for the cattle
F. The same for salt
G. House of the paymaster
H. The same for the chaplain
I. Workroom for the utensils of the church
J. Sacristy
K. Church
L. House of the commandant
M. The same for other officers
N. Twenty-one houses for the soldiers
O. Kitchens and corrals for the same
P. Carpenter's shop
Q. Blacksmith shop
R. Infirmary for seamen
S. Passageway to the bastions
T. Two bastions
U. House of the sergeant
X. Kitchens for the single soldiers
Y. Quarters for single soldiers
Z. Two corrals for horses and cattle

Monterey, June 27, 1795
Diego Borica

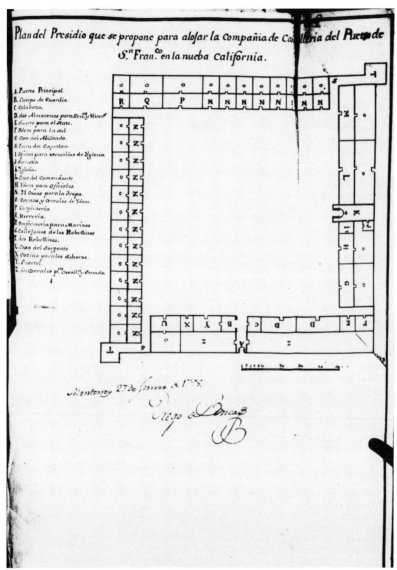

Plate II. The San Francisco Presidio. This plan is incorporated in a report by Hermenegildo Sal, dated Monterey, June 26, 1795, to Governor Diego de Borica which gives construction costs of the presidio from July 26, 1776 to November 1781. Provincias Internas, 216:217 (Tomo 216, Californias). *Courtesy Archivo General de la Nacion, Madrid; copy in Bancroft Library.*

179

Plate III

LEGEND

Plan que manifiesta el nuevo proyecto del Precidio de San Francisco para alojar las tropas de su Guarnicion.

Explicacion
1. Puerta principal
2. Cuerpo de Guardia
3. Calaboso
4. Quarteles
5. Almacenes
6. Casas para los Sargentos
7. Casas de los Oficiales
8. Almacen de Ropas
9. Casas para los Soldados Casados
10. Casa del Capellan
11. Yglesia
12. Corrales de los casas y Quarteles
13. Ydem para Ganado y Cavallada
14. Cerca y Baluartes para la defenza del Precidio

Nota
Por ser la escala de este Plano mui reducida, no se expresan en el las puertas y ventanas de las casas.

Precidio de San Francisco 24 de Julio de 1796

Escala de cincuenta varas

Albert de Córdova

TRANSLATION

Plan that shows the new design of the Presidio of San Francisco for housing the troops of the Garrison.

Explanation
1. Main gate
2. Guardroom
3. Jail
4. Quarters for single soldiers
5. Warehouses
6. Houses for the sergeants
7. Houses for other officials
8. Clothing warehouse
9. Houses for married soldiers
10. House of the chaplain
11. Church
12. Corrals for the houses and quarters
13. Same for cattle and horses
14. Enclosure and bastions for the defense of the presidio

Note:
Because the scale of this plan is very small, the doors and windows of the houses have not been shown.

Presidio of San Francisco July 24, 1796

Scale of 50 varas

Albert Cordova

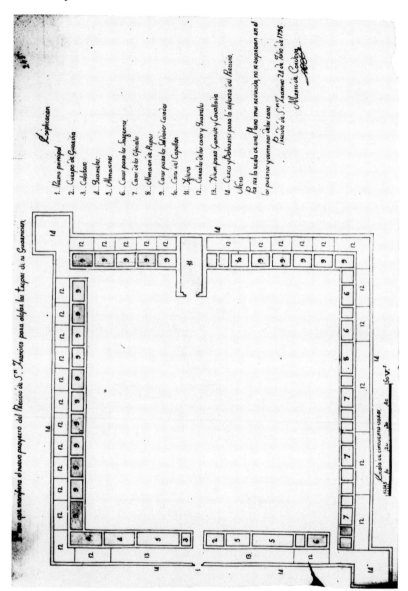

Plate III. The San Francisco Presidio. Plan by Alberto de Córdova, July 24, 1796. *Provincias Internas,* 215:245. *Courtesy Archivo General de la Nacion, Madrid; copy in Bancroft Library.*

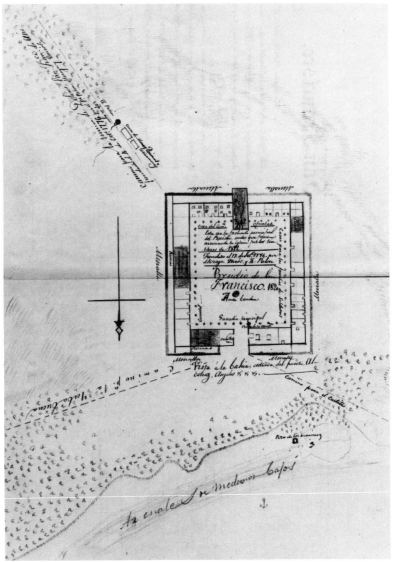

Plate IV. An 1820 map of the San Francisco Presidio found in the Edward Vischer Papers. *Courtesy Bancroft Library.*

with their families and with such amenities as were available to distant outposts during that period. Each presidio was located far enough back from the shoreline, generally 2,000 to 4,000 feet distant, that an enemy ship could not inflict much damage with cannonball ranges of that period. For protection of the harbor, each presidio had a fort, or *castillo*, a level esplanade of wood planking on which were emplaced several cannon behind an embankment of dirt or adobe and stone. This so-called battery was located on a hill overlooking the harbor and, in theory, prevented ships from attacking the presidio. Had a foreign power wished to invade the territory, however, they could easily have landed at a distance from the harbor and laid siege to the presidio.

All four presidios consisted of a quadrangle of buildings grouped around a parade ground and surrounded by a defense wall. In each case, the main gate faced toward the ocean and in some cases, the church was on the opposite side of the parade ground from the main gate. At San Diego, and probably in all of the initial or palisade construction, the defense wall also served as the back wall of the presidio buildings, thus saving the time and cost of building another wall. This design was also followed in the presidios, forming a cordon of earlier forts generally following the southerly boundary of the United States and protecting the northerly boundary of Mexico against the Apaches and other hostile Indians. In case of attack, the defending soldiers climbed on top of the roof of the buildings and fired over the defense wall, using it as a parapet.

The design that replaced it by the 1780s is illustrated by the Santa Barbara layout, Plate IX, in which the buildings are separate from the defense wall, providing a rear garden area for the houses and corrals for the horses. In the presidios of the Southwest where there were no corrals as part of the presidio and the horses were grazed outside the defensive wall, it was found that the fort could be immobilized when the Indians swooped down on the grazing herds, killed the handful of guards and stole the horses.

According to de Mofras, a visitor to the presidios in 1844, it was standard practice to construct a dry moat twelve feet wide and six feet deep around the outside of the defense wall. Excavated dirt

183

Plate V
TRANSLATION OF LEGEND

Plan of the Royal Presidio of San Carlos of Monterey
Interpetation

A. Present church
B. New church
C. Sacristy
D. Quarters for the Leatherjacket troops
E. Quarters for the Volunteer troops
F. Guardroom
G. Presidio warehouse
H. King's warehouse
Y. Mission warehouse
J. Officer's dwelling
K. Dwelling of the reverend missionaries
L. Blacksmith shop and forge
M. Carpenter shop
N. Pack-train drivers' dwelling
O. Surgeon's dwelling
P. Infirmary
Q. Dwelling for visiting heathen
R. Hospital for new Christians
S. Dwelling for heathen women
T. Chicken yard
V. Pigpen
X. Common kitchen
I. Storage room for farm implements
Z. Privy
Vr. Embrasures

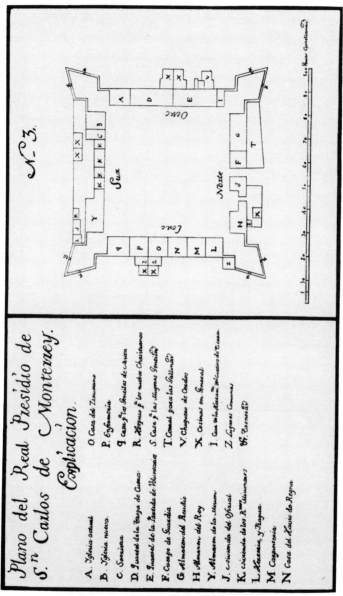

Plate V. The Monterey Presidio, c. 1771, prepared by Miguel Costansó, reproduced from Irving B. Richman, *California Under Spain and Mexico, 1835–47* (Reprint ed.; New York, 1965), p. 338.

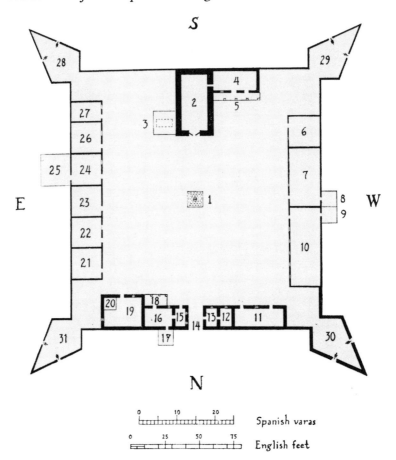

Location of various quarters in the Monterey Presidio: 1) central cross on pedestal; 2) church; 3) belltower; 4) missionaries' quarters, former church and sacristy; 5) porch; 6) dispensary or pharmacy — originally the first chapel; 7) Catalonian Volunteers' quarters; 8) Volunteers' kitchen; 9) Leatherjacket troops' kitchen; 10) quarters of the Leatherjacket soldiers; 11) government stores; 12) jail; 13) guardhouse; 14) main gate; 15) commandant's store or commissary; 16) commandant's quarters; 17) commandant's kitchen; 18) porch; 19) storehouse; 20) bin for grain; 21) postriders (mails) and smithy; 22) carpenter shop; 23) storage for muleteers' pack gear; 24) servants' quarters; 25) kitchen; 26) Indians' quarters; 27) storage for field implements; 28–31) ravelins with cannon in place.

Plate VI. The Monterey Presidio in 1773. Drawing by Alan K. Brown. Reproduced from the *Southern California Quarterly,* 49 (September 1969): 329.

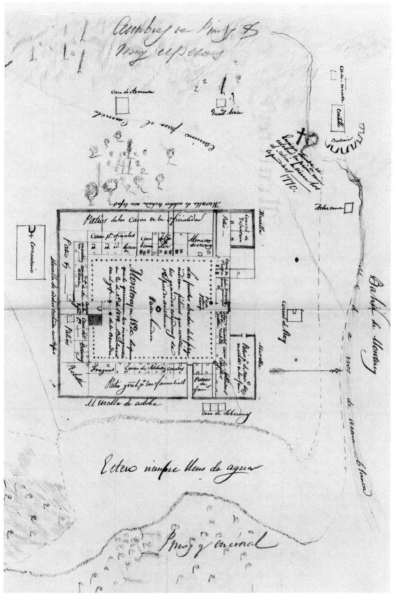

Plate VII. The Monterey Presidio in 1820, found in the Vischer Papers. *Courtesy Bancroft Library.*

Plate VIII

TRANSLATION OF LEGEND

Of the thirteen houses shown on the fourth front of the quadrangle, the walls are finished — three-quarters (of a vara) thick, and three varas high without the ridge of the roofs, which are to be the same as the other (houses) for the soldiers, and also the corresponding woodwork has been put into seven of them, and the little that is lacking for the rest is being brought, and more than four thousand tiles are made for their roofs. [Note: a vara = 33 in. or 2.75 ft.]

All of the outer wall shown in this plan is ready to be built, and it will be started beginning with the month of November, at which time the quadrangle will be completed.

The front walls of the first front are standing; they are one and a half adobe (bricks) thick, mortared, because of the poor quality of the soil for adobes.

1. Main gate with an opening of 4 varas.
2. A storehouse for supplies, 20 varas in length and 5½ in width, its roof of beams, finished boards, and good quality tile.
3. Two of the same, of the same size, for provisions and other effects, the roof of beams, wattles, and tile as above.
4. Thirteen houses for families — 8 varas in length and 5 in width — the roofs of rafters, wattles and good tile.
5. Private gate with an opening of 3 varas, roofed like the houses.
6. Church, 20 varas in length, and 7½ in height, lined with mortar and whitewashed — its roof of beams and finished boards and good tile, and adorned with painting.
7. Sacristy, 5 varas in length and 4 in width — its roof like the church.
8. Living-room of the second lieutenant, 8 varas in length, 5 in width — its roof of rafters, wattles, and good tile.
9. Two bedrooms for the above — 5 varas in the clear — the roof like the living-room.
10. Bedroom of the Comandante — 5 varas in the clear, its roof of beams, finished boards, and good tile.
11. House for the sentry.
12. A living-room for the Comandante, 11 varas in length and 5 in width, its roof of beams, finished boards, and good tile.
13. Entrance-hall of the above — 4 varas in the clear — 4 in height (sic)
14. Office for writing, 5½ varas in length, 5 in width

) whitewashed on the inside,) 3½ varas in height.)

15. Living-room and bedroom of the chaplain, 11 varas in length for both rooms, and 5 in width, the roofs of rafters, wattles, and good tile.
16. Five houses for families — 8 varas in length, 5 in width — their roofs like that of the chaplain.
17. Fifteen houses on the fourth front for families — 9 varas in length and 5 in width — their roof like those before-mentioned.
18. House of the sergeant, 15 varas in length, 5½ in width — its roof as above.
19. Barracks for the soldiers — 20 varas in length, 5½ in width — its roof as above.
20. Guardhouse — 12 varas, and two small cells of 4 varas.
21. Kitchen and pantry of the second lieutenant, 6 varas in length and 4 in width, its roof as above.
22. Two yards for the second lieutenant's house — one of 14 varas and the other of 7.
23. Kitchen and pantry of the Comandante, 6 varas in length and 4 in width, roofed as above.
24. Two yards for the Comandante — one of 25 varas in length and 14 in width, and the other 14 in length and 8 in width.
25. Yard of the chaplain's house, 14 varas in length and 11 in width.
26. Bastion facing the west, of 6 varas.
27. The same, facing the east, of 6 varas.
28. Gates to two corrals for stock — 60 varas in length and 14 in width.
29. Gates or passageways to enter the bastions — 2½ varas in width.

Royal Presidio of Santa Barbara, September 16, 1783.
Pedro Fages
[Note: prepared by Felipe de Goycoechea, but signed by Fages.]

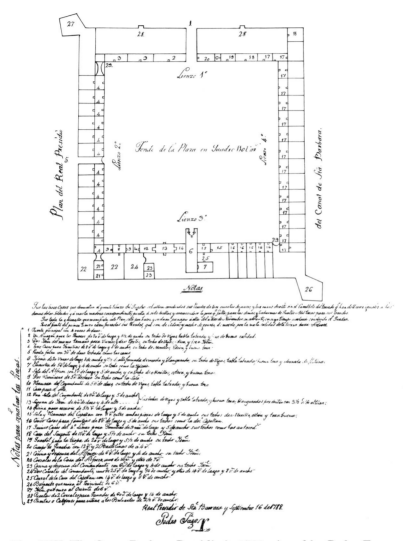

Plate VIII. The Santa Barbara Presidio in 1788, signed by Pedro Fages, though the original was drawn and signed by Felipe de Goycoechea, the second commandant. *Courtesy Bancroft Library*.

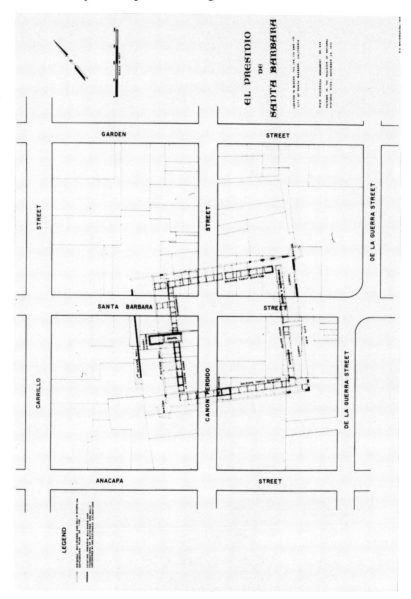

Plate IX. The Santa Barbara Presidio superimposed on the present street and lot system. Drawing by Richard S. Whitehead.

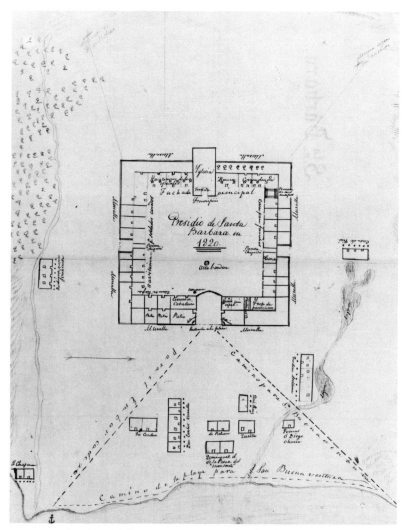

Plate X. The Santa Barbara Presidio in 1820, found in the Vischer Papers. *Courtesy Bancroft Library.*

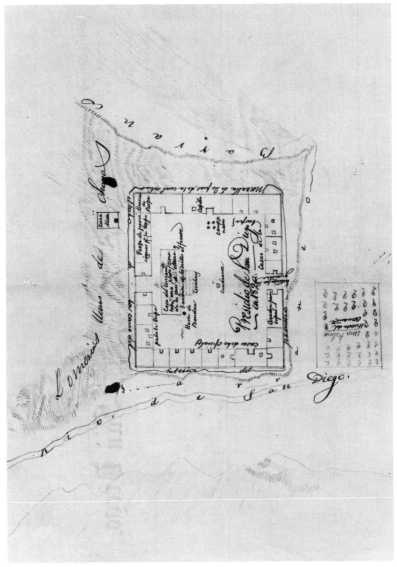

Plate XI. The San Diego Presidio in 1820, found in the Vischer Papers. *Courtesy Bancroft Library.*

formed an embankment along the outside of the ditch. Attacking Indians were first exposed to fire from the top of the defense wall as they surmounted the embankment, then had to scale the ten-foot-high defense wall. If they were successful in climbing over the wall, they found themselves trapped in the back garden, exposed to fire from the rear windows and doors of the buildings. This design thus augmented the presidio defenses.

The earliest plan of the San Francisco Presidio (Plate I) is contained in a letter dated March 4, 1792, from Acting Commandant Hermenegildo Sal to Governor Antonio Romeu. Sal gives the dimensions of the guardroom, barracks, jail cells, dry goods and provisions warehouses, commander's house, church, casemate and sergeant's house, and shows the length of the north side as 319 feet and of the west side, 330 feet. Sal describes the deteriorated state of the structures, walls out of plumb, some walls wider at the top than at the bottom, stone walls cemented with mud, roofs of grass and reed, poor adobe and a shortage of timber. The plan shows that the entire east side of the quadrangle is completely gone, leaving the troops defenseless against an attack from that direction, although another document states that there was a post fence along that side. Sal states that the buildings shown on the plan represent the third construction since the founding sixteen years before, and attributes the bad state of the buildings to lack of intelligent workmen and supervision.

Plate II is a translated copy of a plan dated June 27, 1795, and signed by Governor Borica but prepared by Sal who submitted to the governor a detailed list of materials prepared by the stonemason Manuel Ruiz with the cost estimates by Sal. Construction in accord with this plan was never accomplished, but Sal's warnings apparently led to the assignment of Engineer Captain Alberto de Córdova to Alta California to make recommendations for improving its defenses. Plate III is a translated copy of Córdova's plan for the San Francisco Presidio, but again it was not carried out, perhaps because Córdova himself considered all the California presidios pretty much ineffective because of the fact that an enemy could land at a good many undefended points along the shoreline. He recommended instead a greatly enlarged cavalry corps with mobility to repulse an attack anywhere along the coast, supplemented by mobile batteries on ships cruising along the coast. Perhaps because Córdova's primary project while in California was to plan and found Branciforte, named after the viceroy and later to become the city of Santa Cruz, his recommendations were not acted upon.

Plate IV is the plan of the San Francisco Presidio found in the Vischer papers and dated 1820. This plan is quite similar to the 1792 plan prepared by Alférez Sal. It is also comparable to the plan for the Santa Barbara Presidio which could be considered the typical layout for all presidios after it was decided to separate the buildings from the surrounding defense wall.

Like the other three presidios, Monterey Presidio started out as a palisade structure, poles set close together in a trench and tied together with willows and reeds, called wattle construction, and the whole plastered with mud. Roofs were flat, covered with leaves and branches, grass and sod and then plastered with mud. Obviously such construction left much to be desired when winter came and the wet mud dripped down on the occupants, and adobe buildings were built as soon as the garrison could spend the time on them.

In 1967 the late Fr. Maynard Geiger, O.F.M., archivist at the Santa Barbara Mission Archive-Library, translated and edited for publication in the *Southern California Quarterly* an article entitled "A Description of California's Principal Presidio, Monterey, in 1773." The article contains a translation of a report written by Captain Pedro Fages, commandant of that presidio but later governor of California. Dated September 29, 1773, a little over two years after the presidio was founded, it describes the construction and design of the presidio. Details are given of the length, width and height of various buildings as well as the materials of construction and the uses of the various buildings. To illustrate the article, Fr. Maynard had historian Alan K. Brown make a drawing of the presidio utilizing measurements given in the report. In all probability, Dr. Brown was guided by a drawing of the Monterey Presidio attributed to Engineer Miguel Costansó made at Monterey prior to his departure for Mexico, July 9, 1770, never to return to

California although he later wrote a report on California's defenses. Costansó's drawing, merely a proposal, is shown in Plate V and Brown's drawing is reproduced in Plate VI which indicates that some of Costansó's features were not constructed.

A letter dated August 10, 1778, from then Governor Felipe de Neve to the commanding general at Arispe, Mexico, Teodoro de Croix, states that on July 3, 1778, the defense wall and bastions were completed, all constructed of stone. The wall was 1,476 feet in circumference (approximately 369 feet on each side), 11 feet in height and 44 inches wide. It enclosed ten adobe houses, each having a frontage of nineteen feet and a depth of twenty-two feet, and the guardroom and soldiers' quarters with a frontage of 93 feet, a depth of 16½ feet and double wall of adobe, were under construction. These were the permanent structures to replace the temporary palisade buildings described in the 1773 article. Plate Vll shows the 1820 plan preserved in the Vischer papers.

The first two years of the life of the Santa Barbara Presidio were under the command of Lieutenant José Francisco Ortega who was replaced by Lieutenant Felipe Antonio de Goycoechea in January 1784. Although the record indicates that Ortega sent a plan of the Santa Barbara Presidio to the governor, no plan of such an early date has so far surfaced. It might have been a plan of Ortega's palisade construction or of a proposal for permanent construction. In any event, the earliest plan, representing permanent construction, is dated September 16, 1788, and is signed by Felipe de Goycoechea. An identical plan, with the same notations and date, but with a few additional measurements and signed by then Governor Pedro Fages, is reproduced in Plate VIII. Surveyed locations of buildings and structures in relation to city streets, based on archeological findings, are depicted in Plate IX.

Utilizing deeds giving measurements tied to "the old church," the foundations of the presidio chapel were first uncovered in 1967. Since then, the foundations of buildings and structures in sixteen different locations in all four sides of the quadrangle have been uncovered and surveyed. One of the soldiers' family quarters in the southwest facade, now known as El Cuartel, survived the two hundred intervening years, although renovated, and another building reconstructed on the foundations of one of the quarters for non-commissioned officers remains and is known as the Caneda Adobe. These, together with land totaling three quarters of the land within the boundaries of the original presidio are now publicly owned by the State Department of Parks and Recreation or by the city of Santa Barbara in streets and the Federal government in the Post Office property, plus land purchased by the non-profit Santa Barbara Trust for Historic Preservation. The trust is concessionaire for the State with responsibility for operating the Royal Presidio of Santa Barbara State Historic Park and reconstructing the presidio buildings. The Padre's Quarters, consisting of two rooms, plus an adjoining non-commissioned officers' quarters have been completely reconstructed on the original foundation and the presidio chapel, a structure twenty feet high to the eaves and over 100 feet long is currently (1982) under construction.

The reconstruction is as completely authentic as possible within the requirements of the City Building Code. In preparation for this reconstruction, the Trust for Historic Preservation researched and published in 1980 two reports written in the 1930s by Fred C. Hageman and Russell C. Ewing for the National Park Service, and edited by the author of this article. This book, entitled *An Archaeological and Restoration Study of Mission La Purísima Concepción*, describes the history of that mission, its original construction as revealed by the archeological excavations of the 1930s, its reconstruction by the Civilian Conservation Corps during the Great Depression, and its present status. It is the most complete and detailed source of information available on mission-period construction. Features of the Padre's Quarters and Chapel of the Santa Barbara Presidio not readily duplicated from archeological excavations were reconstructed using the original techniques and materials of construction discovered at Mission Purísima. Adobe blocks were handmade, timbers were adzed and joined with rawhide, floor and roof tile were handmade by an Indian tribe and hardware forged by a Mexican blacksmith.

It is the intent of the Santa Barbara Trust for Historic Preservation to reconstruct the entire Santa Barbara Presidio in accord with the 1788 plan updated by changes made up to 1800 as recorded in archival documents. This will take years of work and considerable sums of money, but when completed, it will be the only reconstructed presidio of the eighteenth century in the West, and the only representation of the civil and military government institutions of the Mission period.

The earthquake of 1812 caused a considerable amount of damage to the Santa Barbara Presidio buildings, resulting in changes in the uses of structures reflected in the plan shown in Plate X, which is the 1820 plan found in the Vischer papers. This latter plan is useful not only in showing the earthquake damage and changes resulting therefrom, but also in verifying the location and use of structures shown in the 1788 plan.

Since 1965, the foundations of the chapel of the San Diego Presidio have been excavated archaeologically by students of San Diego State University with cooperation from the San Diego Historical Society and the city of San Diego. Although no plan of the presidio was available until discovery of the 1820 plan in the Vischer papers in February 1982, the entire foundations of the presidio's most important building, the chapel, have been excavated along with the foundations of some adjacent structures. To what extent the 1820 plan shown in Plate XI will assist those involved in the excavation program depends on the future of the program. Because the presidio is in a city park devoted to recreational uses, the agreement by which the State University undertook its archaeological program required backfilling and resodding after the excavation was completed, which has been done. It is hoped that at the very least, enough probing can be done to verify the accuracy of the 1820 plan and identify some of the mounds that outline the remains of presidio structures.

It cannot be emphasized too strongly that what remains undiscovered about the four California presidios, as well as the Loreto presidio, probably far exceeds what has already been discovered, both in documentary and archaeological evidence. Virtually no work has been done to research the documents directly relating to the presidios in the Archivo General de Indias in Seville, Spain, and very little on documents in the Archivo General de la Nación in Mexico City. Work is under way on a book on the Santa Barbara

Presidio using as the primary source the California Archives at the Bancroft Library, Berkeley, California, and the archaeological work at the Santa Barbara Presidio. Much of value would result from just a compilation of all the documentary information in the California Archives on the other three presidios permitting comparisons and filling in gaps in the knowledge of that period relating to the presidios. It is hoped this article will stimulate such research.

The Building of Mission San Gabriel: 1771–1828

BY MAYNARD J. GEIGER, O.F.M.

THAT IT TOOK OVER FIFTY YEARS to build completely Mission San Gabriel, one of the most flourishing of the California missions, may come as a surprise to many. From this it does not follow, of course, that buildings were constructed every year during the mission's development. There were definitely some years when no building activity took place at all and this we learn from the statements of the padres in residence. It must be recalled, likewise, that the mission occupied two different sites and that repairs had to be made after two disastrous earthquakes.

The site that had been chosen for the establishment of the original mission was along the banks of the Santa Ana River in present Orange County. The missionaries chosen to establish the mission, Fathers Pedro Benito Cambón and Angel Somera, did not consider the site an apt one and continued traveling northwest until they reached the southern limits of the present San Gabriel Valley where they founded California's fourth mission on September 8, 1771. The location of this original mission site is indicated by a marker at San Gabriel Boulevard and Lincoln Avenue close to the Rio Hondo. There the mission remained for four years and eight months when the site was changed to its present location.

At the original site the padres had built the following structures: a chapel, 12 × 4 *varas*, all of tule; a house, 12 × 4 varas with walls of palisade and mud covered with jacal; a storeroom, 10 × 4 varas

199

of palisade with an earthen roof; two rooms of palisade with earthen roofs, 6 × 3¹/₂ varas; a *monjerio* or sleeping quarters for young girls, 6 × 3¹/₂ varas; a room of tule for gear, dimensions not given; a room for young boys, of palisade with earthen roof, dimensions not given; and a smaller room for carpenter's tools. All the above-mentioned buildings, except the one for boys, had doors with their corresponding locks. There were two corrals built of palisade for cattle and sheep. From this description given as late as November 20, 1783, by Fathers Antonio Cruzado and Miguel Sánchez, it is clear that not a single adobe or tile had been manufactured at the original site and from this it might be inferred that the site was only provisional to start with.

Then in May 1775, state the same padres, the mission site was moved northward to a distance of a league along the Camino Real, namely the present site. "The location is very good. It has an oak grove quite close which is very advantageous for obtaining timber and firewood, and is within sight of a great plain where the soil is not of the best quality for in part it is very sandy and rocky, but with the irrigation ditch which is very serviceable, the land will fructify."

When the missionaries left the original site they did not bother to tear down the old, primitive buildings. This is indicated by Father Pedro Font, O.F.M., chronicler and chaplain of the Anza expedition, who passed by there on January 7, 1776, on his way to San Diego. "After going a league [from the second site] we passed the site of the old [original] mission, where the huts were still standing."

Font was sanguine about the locale of the new site and its prospects. He called it "a site of the most beautiful qualities, with plentiful water and very fine lands." Again he wrote: "This mission has such fine advantages for crops and such good pastures for cattle and horses that nothing better could be desired." He described the abundant, available timber for building and firewood and stated that the aqueduct leading from the river was adequate. It ran before the house of the missionaries and the small huts of the Christian Indians. According to him the buildings were largely constructed of logs and tule though some were of adobe, all of which, however, he considered "very insecure and exposed to fire."

He stated that the mission buildings consisted of a

very long shed, all of one room with three divisions, which serves as a habitation for the fathers and for a granary and everything. Somewhat apart from this building there is a rectangular shed which serves as a church, and near this another which is a guardhouse . . . and finally some little huts of tule which are the houses of the Indians, between which and the house of the fathers the acequia [aqueduct] runs.

Shortly after Font wrote this description of Mission San Gabriel into his diary on January 5, 1776, Father Antonio Paterna, the resident missionary, composed the first annual report of the mission that survives. He states that at the new site there had been built a wing, 50 × 6 varas and 3¼ varas in height, whose walls were of adobe a little more than a *vara* in thickness. This wing contained three rooms, one of which was 25 varas long and which was used for the storage of seeds; the second, 4 varas in length, was used for the storage of articles; the third, 21 varas long, constituted the living quarters of the missionaries. This then, was the "very long shed" described by Font. The chapel, 18 × 6 varas, was covered with tule. About 100 varas distant from the mission there was a corral for cattle, 50 varas square. Immediate to the mission was another corral for sheep, 16 varas long. At a distance of about half a league, there was a corral for colts, measurements not given.

The report for 1788, signed only on April 10, 1779, reveals that the roof of the church had been removed and replaced with beams of pine overlaid with earth. A room, 7 varas long, a second, 6½, a third, 6, and a fourth, 4 varas long, all 5 varas in width, were built of adobe and covered with earthen roofs. The report for December 31, 1779, declares that a granary, 56 × 5½ varas constructed of adobe with roof of earth, had been built. No building activity is reported for the years 1781 or 1782.

Fortunately, on November 20, 1783, Fathers Cruzado and Sánchez composed a report which covers all the building operations undertaken since 1775. A new church of adobe construction, its walls two adobes in thickness, had been built. It had a ceiling of

This original 1832 painting (36½ by 27½ inches) is in the Santa Barbara Mission Archive Library. It shows the Sierra Madre range of mountains with snow-capped San Antonio or Mt. Baldy, a Corpus Christi procession in progress, a padre speaking with a visitor, a number of Indians, and several animals in the foreground. The painting was executed by Ferdinand Deppes. *Courtesy SBMAL.*

pine beams and a cane layer of oak covered with an earthen roof
and this was overlaid with tule. The church had its door to the
front and had six windows. It measured 36 × 7 varas. A sacristy, 5
varas square, had walls and roof like the church. Its door led to the
patio and it had one window. The cemetery was at the south side of
the church. Then there was a storeroom, 50 × 5½ varas, with its
loft where *frijoles* were stored. Built of adobe its roof was of *jacal*. It
had its door and lock.

A second storeroom, 25 × 6 varas, of adobe with earthen roof
covered with jacal, had doors and locks. A third storeroom measured 7 × 6, while another room, its use not mentioned, 20 × 6
varas, of adobe, had an earthen roof with an overlay of jacal. There
was a kitchen, 6 × 5; a *sala*, 7½ × 6, three more rooms, 6 varas
square, and a room for guests, dimensions not given. All of these
latter structures were built of adobe with earthen roofs and over
that, jacal. The sala and other rooms had a corridor running along
them. The above-mentioned rooms formed a quadrangle of 50
varas and contained a large door which led to the fields. The sala
had two doors, one of which led to the patio, the other to the outside. The hospice room had its own door, windows and lock.

Beyond this quadrangle, a second one had been begun which
the padres stated "will be finished shortly." This consisted of two
rooms for the sick, 10 × 2 varas, which were of adobe with a roof of
jacal. Another room, the monjerio for the girls, 7 × 5 varas, was
likewise built of adobe and had an earthen roof. Another room of
the same construction, for boys, measured 9 × 5 varas. Three
more rooms of the same construction, two of which were 5 varas
square, the other 5 × 4, were used as tanneries and a hennery. The
padres mentioned that the last mentioned rooms were next to a
storeroom and the guardhouse with an adobe wall "built this year."
All this constituted the second quadrangle. There were besides
three corrals, a vineyard and garden, all enclosed.

There are no extant reports for the years 1784–5. Those for the
years 1786–8, mention no building activity. That for the year 1789,
states that the missionaries had finished covering the roofs of
the quadrangle with tiles. Moreover, three additional rooms of
adobe were built and roofed with tile, one 16 × 5, the other two,

8 × 5. By the end of 1790, another storeroom of adobe and tile, 23 × 6 varas, had been built.

The reports from 1792 to 1796 inclusive mention no building operations. This is rather strange for the Father President, Fermín Francisco de Lasuén, disclosed in his general biennial report of March 11, 1795, that the padres had begun to build a new church, the present one. He stated that it was built of stone and mortar and that the walls had already been raised to one half of their intended height. Engelhardt states, without giving his source, that the cornerstone had been laid about 1790 or 1791. On February 6, 1797, Lasuén says that the church was still under construction and on February 20, 1799, informs us that the church had been roofed except for the portion over the choir. Furthermore, in his report of February 25, 1801, he revealed that the vaulted roof of the church was finished but that the ceiling had sustained cracks with the result that the roof would probably have to be replaced with beams. However, on February 21, 1803, the president states that the cracks in the ceiling had been repaired and that the interior of the church had been whitewashed. Finally, Lasuén's successor, Fray Estevan Tapis, announced on February 21, 1805, that the church had been blessed but that in consequence of an earthquake, new cracks appeared in the vaulted roof and that in the judgment of the master mason it would have to be replaced with timber and tiles after the rainy season.

On December 31, 1804, the resident padres' annual report reveals continued building. Ten rooms were constructed to serve as granary, weavery, carpenter shop, pantry, storeroom and missionaries' dwelling. These measured 125 × 13 varas. They were roofed with pine timber and tile. The corridors were likewise tiled and the pillars of the same were constructed of brick and mortar. By the end of 1805 nine more rooms were added to be used as granaries and other purposes. They measured 135 × 6½ varas. Built of adobe, they had plastered walls and tile roofs and brick floors. Along the whole length there ran a corridor with pillars of brick laid in mortar.

In 1807 the padres began to build houses for the Indians. Thirty such houses of adobe roofed with tile appeared, their doors and window frames of pine. Each house measured 6 × 5 varas. During 1808, forty-seven additional such houses were added in the same manner. Likewise the vaulted roof of the church was taken down because it threatened to collapse and this was replaced by a flat roof of brick and mortar. In 1809 or 1810, according to Engelhardt, a wing, 70 × 6 varas, comprising six rooms, was added to existing buildings. All were of adobe and roofed with tile. This long structure faced a corridor and completed the inner court or patio. Another building, 30 × 6 varas, contained four tanks for tanning hides. In 1811 two granaries, one 62 × 8, the other, 42 × 7 varas, the first roofed with tile, the second with tule, were constructed.

In the earthquake of December 12, 1812, a portion of the church was badly damaged. Many cracks appeared in the tower so that the top with its weather vane finally fell down. A crack also appeared in the sacristy while the padres' quarters and the work rooms were so badly damaged that they threatened to collapse. Two more granaries, each 42 × 7 varas with tile roofs, were built. In 1813 a granary with a loft was erected, 55 × 7 and 7 varas in height with walls of adobe 1½ adobes in thickness. This was roofed with tile and joined to the granary built in the preceding year. Both granaries served as a temporary church. The report states that the old portion threatened to collapse and would have to be renovated.

The mission hospital was finished in 1814. It had four comfortable apartments and measured 112 × 12 varas. In 1815, to enclose the hospital's patio, a room was constructed, 100 × 6 varas, and a chapel for the sick, 37 × 5¼ varas, was added. The walls of the chapel and the large room were of adobe and roofed with tile. Two other buildings of adobe with tile roof were constructed in 1816, the one serving as a mill which measured 18¾ × 9¼ varas, the other a smithy, 18¾ × 7 varas. A water basin was built for the fountain together with two drainage sewers in 1817. One of these was of stone and was in the center of the patio of the girls' quarters. This was surrounded by adobes and measured 67 × 50 varas.

In 1819 a hennery was built and on the second story a dovecot. Two mills were commenced in 1820, one powered by water for grinding wheat, the other for making oil. Both were developing well by the end of the year. In 1821 two adobe rooms were built for preserving seeds, 66 × 7, and 57 × 7 varas in measurement. In 1823 a building was erected for housing a machine for cutting wood. Likewise a forge was built. In 1825 the mill for grinding corn was finished as well as the one for sawing wood. Both were driven by water power. The report for 1826 states that "this year nothing was done except to repair existing buildings." In 1827 the report tells us that "we are bringing to a close the repair of the church," and finally, in 1828, that "the repair of the church has been completed." Reports continue up till the end of 1832, just two years before secularization, but there is no mention of building operations. It should be recalled that meanwhile the padres of Mission San Gabriel had built a long building at Rancho San Bernardino in 1827 and the church of Our Lady of the Angels in Los Angeles which was dedicated on December 8, 1822.

While these details given in the annual reports and elsewhere serve to show what building was done through most of the years of the mission's development, the padres left us no floor plans at any time — a regretful lacuna — nor in their descriptions did they for the most part make it clear just how the mission compound appeared in a given year. Already at the end of 1782 the resident missionaries stated that a second quadrangle had been nearly completed. But considerable activity in building took place after that which might suggest even a third quadrangle but no statement to that effect was ever made. The plat of the mission drawn by a United States Government surveyor in 1858 when the mission and some of its land were adjudicated to the Church would seem to indicate only two quadrangles with exposed ruins though a third cannot be absolutely ruled out.

The painting of Mission San Gabriel by Ferdinand Deppe in 1832 shows the mission before secularization with the church and one complete quadrangle attached to it directly to the west, roofed with tiles and its front corridor intact. Farther to the west are three long rows of houses which are evidently the houses built for the Indians in 1807 and 1808. The aqueduct runs between them and the quadrangle of the mission. What I believe happened was that at various times older and decayed or partially destroyed buildings were removed and then replaced without destroying the original mission pattern of structure, this especially after earthquakes or other deterioration from natural causes. Today there remain the church, a portion of the front wing of the quadrangle, floor remains of a colonnade, vats and a small building in the former patio. With the high rise buildings going up in nearby Los Angeles in record time today, Mission San Gabriel appears to be a midget. But the more than fifty years of heroic work even to build that made of it a stupendous structure compared with the Indian huts that had preceeded it for uncounted centuries.

Adobe Interiors
in Spanish California

BY WILLIAM M. MASON

THIS ARTICLE ATTEMPTS TO GIVE an overview of California home interiors between 1790 and 1822. Influences and origins will also be discussed, as well as sources of supply for home furnishings.

A variety of sources are used in this assessment of California home interiors. Selections from the literature have been made, consisting largely of travelers' accounts of their experiences in California. Wills, lists of supplies sold or on hand in stores, lists of holdings by one or another person in legal proceedings, criminal actions, or other relevant lists are included. Ships' manifests and cargo lists are also helpful in deciding just what Californians wished to import from overseas and from other Mexican provinces or states.

Californians' reminiscences are also valuable in assessing what was to be found in a home. The on-the-spot observations by foreigners are sometimes confusing if they are not correlated with the explanations of just what the odd or puzzling objects occasionally found might be. These reminiscences are too often far from complete, or sometimes presuppose some definite knowledge on the part of the reader, or are vague as to time and place. When one realizes that there is a process of evolution involved in assessing home interiors, time factors become more critical. One would like to know, for example, when Californians decided that foreign bedsteads were important to own. Sometime between 1807 and 1835 beds became a significant home appurtenance, and if we can believe foreign observers, a mark of status. This represents an

209

interesting shift in tastes, for prior to this time it would appear that the interior of a home was much less significant than the exterior of the person. Clothes were always an outstanding hallmark of a Californian's self-esteem, but when the possession of a bed from overseas, that is a four-poster complete with tester and curtains, became a status symbol, it bid fair to rival the finery any man or woman might wear.

Another important source, especially for Monterey and Santa Barbara, are the mission account books, which list such things as tile, plaster, and carpentry work done for private persons outside the mission itself. We learn, for example, that benches, tables, and chairs were made for soldiers and civilians living near the mission, and that cots or beds were also produced from time to time. While these records are lamentably far from complete for all the missions, they do suggest that mission and presidio carpenters were employed in making the necessary furniture for the soldiers and settlers in California. Lists of supplies from Mexico shipped through San Blas are another source for the presence (or lack) of construction materials sent to California. While such items as table service, mirrors, and griddles (*comales*) are found, almost no furniture was shipped, suggesting that such would be of local manufacture.

After 1800, smuggling seems to have been more important. As early as 1806 we find that the sea-otter fur trade was responsible for many goods being illegally brought into California. Such ships as the *Tamana* and the *Mercury* were busily engaged at this time in selling a variety of goods, though but little furniture, in Alta California. In Baja California, however, the *Mercury* was able to sell no less than fifteen beds in 1807. Perhaps there was a scarcity of either wood or carpenters in Baja California, which would account for the need to purchase beds from foreigners. Also, as the purchasers were missionaries, differences in tastes between Dominicans and Franciscans may be a factor. Only four beds were unloaded in Alta California, and these were probably dumped on one man as a package compensation for some assistance rendered to the ship. Bartolo Tapia, who had acted as agent-collector for the *Mercury*, was the recipient of the four beds, at a point near Los Angeles.

For the most part, there are three major periods spanning the sale of foreign furnishings in California, the formative, 1769–90; colonial, 1790–1822; and the Mexican era, 1822–46. This essay will concern itself only with the first two periods, the Spanish era. The period up to about 1800 is largely devoid of foreign goods. Between 1800 and 1821, foreign goods were smuggled into California and such clandestine commerce was tolerated by the governors, especially after 1810, when goods from Mexico were hard or impossible to obtain. Between 1822 and 1846 foreign goods were imported in increasingly larger quantities. By 1835 foreign goods had begun to supplant items of domestic manufacture in the way of household goods as well as some others. It is probably that the taste for foreign materials in California was an acquired one, which took about a decade to become significantly important for the importation of furniture.

PART I: 1769–90

Alta California was the final expansion of Spain's northern Mexican frontier. This expansion, beginning in 1769, was largely left up to a combined occupation comprised of soldiers and priests. The soldiers were eventually stationed in four presidios, or forts, established along the coast, while the missionary fathers occupied a chain of missions, today celebrated in song and story by present-day Californians. There were also three civil establishments, called pueblos, which were founded to supply the support to the presidial soldiers. Eventually, a strip of coast from San Diego to San Francisco Bay, which varied from thirty to fifty miles in width, was occupied.

By the end of the Spanish regime in Mexico, and in the very early years of Mexican independence, twenty-one missions had been founded, along with the four forts and three towns. With Mexican independence in 1822, Spain lost California; the last mission was founded in the year following. During the Spanish era the province's population of settlers and soldiers grew slowly. There were about 1,000 colonists by 1790, which increased to about 3,000 in 1820. Even on the eve of the American conquest in 1846 there were but 7,500 non-Indians in California. The Indian population converted to Christianity numbered about 20,000 in the heyday of the missions, with about 250,000 Indians in what is now California prior to the conquest by Spain. In spite of the ravages of epidemics during the Spanish and Mexican regimes, there were probably still at least 100,000 Indians left in California by 1846, the majority of whom still lived outside the sphere of Mexican control.

Neither the Russian settlement at Fort Ross nor the Indian home interiors will be considered here. Instead, the focus is on those non-Indian homes within the Hispano-Mexican region of settlement. (Non-Indian is used here as distinct from the California Indians.) Indian settlers from Mexico, however, are included. The home of a Yaqui Indian of Los Angeles in 1792 is therefore part of the evidence for the early period.

It would be a false assumption to presume that the descendants of California's first soldier-colonists were brought up to be accustomed to small, sparsely-furnished, one-room dwellings, such as those provided at the presidios and for mission guard detachments. Accustomed as they were to small spaces with little furniture, it is well to consider other possibilities. For example, what sort of housing was common in the regions from which the majority of these colonists came? Where, then, did the California colonists come from?

We are reasonably sure about the origins of the first colonists. At least seventy percent of the adults were natives of northwest Mexico. Even those who were from other parts of Mexico had usually lived in northwest Mexico for some time prior to coming to California. Northwest Mexico today embraces the states of Sinaloa, Sonora, and Baja California Sur. Very few of California's settlers came from Spain. Only four or five survivors of the Catalonian detachment of twenty-five soldiers married native Indian women and decided to stay in California, in addition to another six or seven other Spaniards. As to other European settlers, there were two or three in California, including a Belgian and an Italian. All total, there probably were less than twenty European Spaniards in California at any one time during the colonial period. After 1800, there were some Spanish officers in the presidios as well as an occa-

While a leaky shingled roof has permitted the rains to badly pit the hardpacked earth floor, the furnishings seem to be typical of a modest Californian home of the 1830s. Note truns, benches, and homemade table, in addition to objects hung on the walls (c. 1880s). The bedsteads and chair are typical of items which would be imported after the liberalization of trade in the 1820s. *Courtesy Los Angeles County Museum of Natural History* (hereinafter cited LACMNH).

sional settler, but for the most part Spaniards' imprint on Alta California was hardly distinctive.

As to the sort of housing to be found in California *circa* 1790 or 1800, one finds some similarities to what was found in Sinaloa, Sonora, or Baja California. The two-room adobe house was typical in Sonora around 1767. A chest for clothing, a bench or log for seats, clay pots and plates, and an oxhide bed, which could serve as a table during the day, were the rule. The houses of the wealthy miners and merchants were larger and better furnished.

In Sinaloa, a surviving description of a house and its furnishings in 1708, probably reflects what might have been found in California eighty years later. At Mazatlán, the following was inventoried in a militiaman's home: a water jar with its wooden rack, four *equipales* (cane and leather chairs), a wooden table and bench, a chest for clothing, and an old bed. An old hut adjacent to the living quarters was used as a kitchen. A detached kitchen was a common feature of Californian homes as well. The use of equipales, though perhaps less common than in Sinaloa, was a trait shared in California also. While Californians stored water in earthen pots, also, it is not known whether a wood rack was a feature commonly used for storage purposes.

In Baja California, especially in the northern coastal part of the peninsula, descriptions seem to tally closely with the Alta Californian pattern of houses. Important descriptions of beds in the southern part of Baja California are provided by an 1828 visitor who reported: "The beds were cattle hides stretched on a frame. There was no other mattress." At the town of Santiago, the same traveler recorded: "The furniture consists of one poor looking table, a few chairs made of reed cane, and some frames covered with stretched hides, which are used for beds." Simón Avilés, an old soldier of Baja California, in his reminiscence about his life in the peninsula, had this to say about the typical home interior of the early period:

We lived in great unhappiness, in little, low houses with palm or earth roofs, very tiny and with cowhide doors for lack of boards; the entire furnishings of the house consisted of a bad cot or a wattle bed, a rough table

A fair example of the type of adobe homes made c. 1795–1805 at Santa Barbara of materials purchased from the nearby mission. About 800 tiles would be necessary to roof a building this size. Although this little structure has had at least two additions, the original building is still quite discernible (c. 1894). *Courtesy LACMNH.*

and chairs made out of sticks crossed over two little adobe posts; at that time there wasn't even one man in the country, with the exception of Don Manuel Ozio, who could be called rich or moderately well off.

Avilés added a bit more to Baja California life. "Generally in the cold season we warmed ourselves with fire; for that reason wood was never lacking in the house and was left in the middle of the rooms we lived in." He said that the above conditions prevailed from Cabo San Lucas to San Diego, in other words, all of Baja California. Avilés had served in northern and southern Baja California, so he was able to generalize. He also added, "the fathers and the comandants enjoyed more comforts, but not many."

The type of houses in southern Baja California, Sonora, and Sinaloa, was transplanted to Alta California. Some adaptations were made over the years, especially in the northern part of California. The climate was different; the temperature was colder than

215

Typical of early roofing in California, with crosssbeams overlaid with willow poles and topped with reeds or sedges covered over with earth. Photo from the *Historic American Building Survey*.

in northwest Mexico, and the rainfall was greater. Also, the rains came in winter, not summer, as in the northwest of Mexico and Mexico generally. Still, even in northern California, a few degrees colder and substantially wetter than southern California, the colonists were slow to change their housing to meet the climate change. Not until the 1830s, with foreign influences to help such modification, did chimneys and fireplaces become a feature of Monterey homes. Southern Californians, less challenged in a climate somewhat warmer, were even slower to adopt this innovation, though by the 1840s there were a few houses with chimneys.

PART II: 1790–1822

The adobe age in California began about a decade or so after the first permanent occupation in 1769. As late as 1777, Governor Felipe de Neve complained that there were almost no adobe buildings in all of California. None of the presidios, as yet, had such construction, even in their outer walls. Only at San Diego, grumbled Neve, was there so much as an adobe house. At this time there were about 400 soldiers, settlers, and their families in the province. About half this number had arrived within the two years prior to Neve's complaint.

After 1777, within a few years the province could claim a few more adobe structures and others under construction. By 1787, adobe presidios began to take the place of the palisade defenses and wattle-and-daub huts within the presidio compounds. The missions, of course, were well along in adobe construction, for the most part, but at the four presidios, all were still in process. Los Angeles had twenty-five adobe houses and an adobe wall surrounding the houses on the plaza as a defensive measure. By 1790, adobe buildings in California had become more common. At San Jose there were as yet no adobes, because the citizens were not ready to risk building in a location exposed to damage from flood. The town was finally moved during the 1790s to a more secure location, and the citizens soon began building adobe homes.

The presidios were much the same pattern in California. They were rectangular forts, enclosed adobe walls with cubicles within for living quarters, storage, and guard rooms. In the center of each was a plaza or parade ground, with a large door, or gate, at the only entrance. Just exactly what life was like within the presidios is not precisely known. There was not a great deal of space, even for the officers. As an example, Commandant Hermenegildo Sal had two rooms for himself and his family, the larger one thirty feet long, which was seen by Captain George Vancouver in 1792 when he visited Sal in the San Francisco Presidio. Soldiers were obliged to make do with less space. One or two soldiers occupied rooms within the presidio, which were 15 by 24 feet, in the case of Santa Barbara's presidio, and roughly the same elsewhere. Sergeants had 16 by 45 feet, and the *alférez*, second in command, had five more linear feet. The average family used one cubicle measuring from 15 by 24 feet ranging to ones of 15 by 27. It is not likely that families had more space than one room until they were able to build their own houses outside the presidios, which in the cases of

217

Santa Barbara and Monterey seem to have been as early as 1795.

When families were living outside the presidio walls, it is probable that unmarried soldiers were permitted to occupy individual rooms in the presidio all to themselves. San Diego does not seem to have been as quick to expand outside the presidio as the other presidios. As late as 1802 or 1803 a house was finally permitted to be built in what is now Old Town in San Diego, at the foot of the presidio's hill.

In Los Angeles there were adobes in 1792 which compared to the above, such as that of Juan Álvarez at his death. His adobe house was five *varas* wide and ten varas long, or roughly 28 feet long and 14 feet wide, about the same size as the rooms in the presidios. He also had two kettles for cooking, two pans, a chocolate pot, a *comal*, two *metates*, an old box with molds, a point for a bar, a hammer, an old lance, a grindstone, a useless barrel (perhaps the term "useless" meant that it leaked), assorted clothing of the deceased, sacks of *agave* thread, chiles, and tallow. Aside from the kitchen utensils there is no mention of household items or furniture. It may be that whatever furniture there was could have been considered part of the dwelling or it is equally possible that there was none.

What furniture there was in the presidios was probably either made by the presidio carpenter, or by the soldiers themselves. The carpenter at San Diego made a *catre* (a cot, or bed) for the lieutenant there in 1781. He also made, during 1781–82, a bench, a bed headboard, lid for a chest, and two chairs for the presidio's blacksmith. Whether presidio carpenters were supposed to make cots for the soldiers as a matter of routine, or whether the soldiers paid him for the service, or made them themselves, is not certain. The will of Alférez Marino Carrillo mentions a mattress, two old sheets, two pillows with cases, a bedspread, and a tablecloth, but no bed or table. Perhaps beds were appurtenances of the presidio and were not individually owned. The only other household item in Carrillo's will was a box, with key, perhaps a storage box for clothing.

Travelers' accounts of Alta California are rare for the period prior to 1800. However, a few men did manage to visit Monterey

An example of the so-called mission furniture (c. 1820), such benches were crafted either by Indian neophyte carpenters or the craftsmen brought from Mexico to teach their arts to Californians, both Indian and non-Indian. Photo from the *Index of American Design*.

and San Francisco, despite Spain's reticence about allowing foreigners into the new province. The visits of Captain George Vancouver, commanding the HMS *Discovery* and HMS *Chatham*, provide us with some early views of the two northern presidios.

When Vancouver visited Lieutenant Hermenegildo Sal's home in 1792, he provided the following data: Sal's quarters consisted of two rooms, the larger one 30 feet long, 14 feet wide, and 12 feet high. The walls were whitewashed and the roof was of flags (leaves of marsh plants, which were broad, such as local cattails and rushes). The floor was dirt. Concerning furniture and other objects within the home, Vancouver says only, "a very sparing assortment of the most indispensible articles, of the rudest fashion, and of the meanest kind" were observable. One article of furniture he does describe. Lieutenant Sal's wife, Josefa Amézquita de Sal, was "seated cross-legged on a mat, placed on a small square

This type of bed (c. 1840) was probably the most common between 1790 and 1820. Few examples are extant, however. This bed consists of a hide stretched on a frame, with the short legs characteristic of such beds made prior to 1820. This one is on exhibit at Mission Santa Barbara, although it has been given much longer legs by the restorer. From the *Index of American Design*.

wooden platform raised three or four inches from the ground, nearly in front of the door. . . this being the mode observed by these ladies when they receive visitors." When Vancouver makes reference to the soldiers' quarters, he describes only the "thatched roofs of their low small houses."

Vancouver described the commander's quarters at Monterey as "much more extensive than those of San Francisco, as they consist of five or six spacious rooms with boarded floors," although here, as there, glass was lacking in the windows. There is no reference to any furniture, nor is there any comparison with San Francisco in that respect. A red-tiled roof at Monterey presidio is mentioned and was evidently superior to the modest thatch of San Francisco in Vancouver's mind.

At San Francisco and Monterey Vancouver's observations were

amplified by the account of Archibald Menzies, who attended a reception given the British naval visitors in San Francisco. He was somewhat interested in the manner the women at the reception greeted them. He noted that the women did not arise to greet guests, but remained seated, "squatted down on their heels upon a mat spread on a part of the floor that was a little elevated from the rest." The women were amused or surprised at two Hawaiian women in the Vancouver party, who when invited to sit with the Monterey women, sat with their legs stretched out in front instead of sitting on their heels. Later, at a dance held at Monterey, Menzies observed that the women "seated themselves on cushions placed on a Carpet spread out at one end of the room...."

In respect to buildings, he saw that, as lime was not available locally, it was made from shells and used in mortar or for whitewash. As for the houses he saw at the presidio, they were "only one story high and generally divided into two apartments, in one of which a small place near the Wall elevated about a foot higher than the rest of the floor on which a Mat is spread, & sometimes Cushions for the women to sit on...." While Menzies refers to the dearth of "culinary utensils," he also admired the silver table service given them for a picnic or two the English party had near Monterey, provided by a Spanish officer aboard ship at Monterey.

While at Santa Barbara enjoying Commander Felipe de Goycoechea's hospitality, Menzies observed with surprise that most of the plates and dishes were from England, common stoneware though they were. He also noted that Goycoechea valued them highly. At San Diego Menzies appreciatively recorded that the commandant's quarters was a "much neater dwelling" than they had seen to the north, but the soldiers' quarters "which are arranged contiguous to the wall round the square are wreched [*sic*] Hovels" and that the presidio in general was not so clean as that of Santa Barbara.

The brief account of Captain Francois Peron, who was at Monterey briefly on Captain Ebenezer Dorr's ship in 1796, gives a few more aspects of that presidio. His party on entering the presidio compound saw the interior of one building, where "the sight of a camp bed showed us we were in the guard room." As for Monterey

This is reputedly one of the chairs made by Russian-trained Kodiak Indians from the Aleutian Islands, c. 1815. Given the fine craftsmanship, it could be so, in consideration of foreign visitors' comments about such furniture made by the Kodiaks. From the *Index of American Design*.

generally, Peron recounts that "the houses and cabins are constructed without taste, the furniture coarse, the utensils imperfect,—an absolute lack of the conveniences of life."

The shipping manifests, which record what was shipped from California's supply port of San Blas, do not include furniture, aside from equipales. However, they do list dishes, pots, pans, and other kitchenware. At the presidios, even as early as 1782, such articles are listed in an *arancel*, or price-list, which usually meant the maximum which could be charged for an article. In this list one finds clay pans, wooden spoons, glazed griddles (*comales vidriados*), copper and clay pots, plates, both crude and Puebla, and Puebla cups. Other kitchen utensils which were shipped from San Blas include such things as *atole* (thin gruel or mush) strainers and handmills for beating chocolate.

The California missions had much in the way of household goods, according to their supply manifests. At Santa Barbara, for example, when the mission was founded in 1786 the supplies included knives, forks and spoons, metal plates, copper pots, a cauldron, chocolate pots, brass mugs, basins, frying pans, comales, box latches, door latches, door locks, an iron, plates from Puebla, cups, bowls, and trunks. Added in 1787 were some *goznes* (snipe hinges) for both doors and windows. These goznes were a common item, and reappear from time to time in later Santa Barbara manifests, as well as at other missions.

Monterey accounts in 1802 list some items sold to soldiers, such as candle holders and snuffers, a metate, coverlets from Acatzingo (a textile-producing region near Puebla), and bed blankets. There was also the sale of the deceased Hermenegildo Sal's wardrobe (*armario*) in 1802 to Gabriel Moraga. In 1804 copper pots, Puebla plates, Guadalajara plates, a copper kettle, Guadalajara mugs, and some equipales (leather and wicker chairs) were listed. In 1806 there was mention of repairs to the broken glass of the windows of the "government house," suggesting that glass had at least been added to the presidio's windows; in Vancouver's time there had been none. The broken windows were repaired with paper, probably oiled paper mentioned in another account. Repairs to María Antonia Carrillo's cot (catre) included a screw and a barb or nail (*pua*). There are also repairs for a wall cupboard and a lantern, as well as a glass lamp. The presence of these articles between 1802 and 1806 adds to our scant knowledge of what was available in California at that time.

Monterey was able to acquire goods from Mission San Carlos, much in the way that soldiers of Santa Barbara bought materials from Mission Santa Barbara. A fairly good list is extant for Santa Barbara, however, and it is possible to consider what was available from most missions in California, based on what Santa Barbara supplied soldiers and civilians living around the presidio. Proximity, however was one consideration in favor of Santa Barbara's inhabitants. It is possible that the reason people in Los Angeles used less tile for roofing than in Santa Barbara was the cost of transport, plus the ready supply of *brea* (tar) from the nearby pits,

An example of early Californian cooking utensils, this beaten copper pot was probably sent up from San Blas prior to 1810. Copper and brassed utensils were not highly prized by the Californians, who preferred iron or tin. From the *Index of American Design*.

which explains why tar was commonly used in that pueblo, although there are cases of brea roofs in Monterey and San Jose as well.

Mission Santa Barbara sold tiles to the soldiers and settlers who wished to build houses outside the presidio walls. Such home construction began in the 1790s, shortly after the presidio was finished. By the early 1800s there were many houses outside the presidio. In addition to tiles, Mission Santa Barbara supplied carpenters, lime for plastering, doors, casual laborers, masons, windows, and in short, an entire house. The mission also supplied the furniture. For example, in 1801 Alférez Francisco Ruiz purchased two catres, or cots, from the mission, made of leather and wood, and later another of rawhide. He also purchased a bench two varas long, and a table of a *vara* and a half. The vara measured not quite a yard, perhaps three inches less. The mission built his

Chinese-made decorated trunks were a prized piece of furniture in early California homes. Often lined with camphorwood to discourage insects, they were usually raised on small platforms or benches off the dirt floors. Photo taken at the Mission Loreto Museum in 1984 by the author.

house, as well. Cots, chairs, washboards, tables, bed headboards, and coffins were made for the soldiers and sold to them by the mission as well, all manufactured at the mission. Items which had been brought from Mexico were also sold to Santa Barbara inhabitants, such as metates, *manos*, goznes, chamberpots, bedspreads, candle holders, chocolate pots, chocolate mills, plates, bowls, and cups. They also sold *asadores*, or meat spits, but whether these were made at the mission by the blacksmith, or whether they were imported, is not certain.

During the first decade of the nineteenth century a fairly regular commercial intercourse with foreigners gradually developed in California, sparked by the sea otter trade. Though quite illegal, the trade flourished intermittently between 1803 and 1821 due to the disruption of Spanish rule resulting from the Napoleonic struggle in Europe. Though it tapered off in the last few years

before 1821, it remained brisk, albeit illegal and occasionally inter-
dicted by Spanish authority. Sea otter pelts, highly prized by Chinese merchants, were much in demand. However, China did not
care for most articles of foreign manufacture; consequently it was
hard to induce Chinese to trade for anything except specie or furs.
The fur trade was by far the more profitable of the two, since it was
much cheaper to barter or purchase furs on the Pacific Northwest
coast and transport them to China than it was to pay hard cash for
such articles as silks and other costly fabrics, teas, and items of
Chinese manufacture. The markup on furs was three to five times
the original purchase price, sometimes even higher. As a result,
trans-Pacific maritime trade developed by the beginning of the
nineteenth century; though much of the trade involved items of
European and eastern American manufacture, the trade could,
and sometimes did, function with Chinese items alone.

While Spanish authorities were opposed to this trade as contrary to their restrictive mercantilist policies, their colonials, and
even those in command, were hardly anxious to halt smuggling
and clandestine trade. Californians, on the far frontier of the
Spanish empire, practically abandoned and neglected, seized on
the opportunity not only out of necessity but also desire. The Californians were able to secure goods more cheaply through this
trade, and in some cases even items otherwise unobtainable
through San Blas could be had from foreign ships. Smugglers,
however, prefer to travel light. It is probable that the relative
absence of furniture in ships' manifests and the small number of
such pieces traded was in part due to the preference of the foreign
traders to purvey smaller pieces. Another factor would seem to be
the preferences of Californians themselves.

The absence of furniture as an important trade item as compared with cloth and clothing was probably as much due to the
market as it was to the convenience to the smuggler. It should be
remembered that furniture was not a common article in the trade
with San Blas, and whatever furniture available had been made in
the province. The sole significant materials in this era which could
conceivably have been considered large pieces of furniture were
four beds unloaded on Bartolo Tapia for services rendered to the

ship *Mercury* traders, along with other hard-to-sell items, and the probable use made of empty gin cases for shelves and boxes sold to Californians in 1806–7. A variety of knives, dishes, glasses, mugs, forks and spoons, bowls, and similar tableware were readily traded for sea otter furs with both the missionaries and the military. Civilians, too, out of proportion to their numbers, were involved in the illicit trade as they had access to sea otter furs and could trade with supplies for the ships as well.

A good example of the trade is included in the account book of the *Mercury*, 1806–7. To missionaries, soldiers, and settlers the following variety of household goods were sold: tumblers, frying pans, tureens, plates, knives, gin cases, wash bowls, mugs, pitchers, chafing dishes, bottle stands, waiters, trunks, blankets, spoons, muffin tins, kettles, glass candlesticks, candles, chair webbing, mirrors, and the four beds mentioned above, were traded to southern Californians during the ship's visit. While there is a less clear picture of the cargo of the *Tamana*, another ship trading at this same time, the goods mentioned are interesting because they are almost entirely Chinese in origin. This vessel was built in Hawaii and acquired its Chinese cargo there. Aside from dishes, there was little in the way of household articles traded though it had a considerable quantity of Chinese fabrics in its cargo. The ship's articles for barter indicate that the trade with California was a Pacific enterprise, and items from the Atlantic seaboard were not vital to the sea otter trade.

The *Mercury* was later seized as a smuggler by a Spanish warship based in Peru, and a manifest of what was aboard was made in 1813, shortly after it was taken in June. Over 1,500 plates, platters, cups, saucers, pitchers and bowls were aboard. There were also fifteen frying pans, twenty-four English blankets, and fourteen muskets.

Other items included an English cot, a Chinese cot with frame and a Chinese cushion, which were probably for ship use. The 563 otter pelts and 947 tails aboard indicate that some articles had already been traded ashore.

In 1822 another ship, the *Eagle*, was seized at Santa Barbara as a smuggler. Though trade was now legal, the *Eagle* was taken

Dishes and tableware were frequently imported from Puebla via San Blas. Occasionally examples of English and Chinese dishes were found in California, as well as Pueblaware. Photo taken at Mission Carmel Museum in 1986 by the author.

because of a criminal act against another ship. Aside from much cloth, there were four bottle-racks with twelve bottles in each, nineteen tea sets of ordinary china, plus two more which were not complete sets, eight and one-half dozen brass spoons, five dozen plates, twelve serving bowls, five small serving bowls, eight salt cellars, and twenty platters. One interesting item in the manifest was window glass. The ship carried two boxes of 200 small window-panes, a rare article in California even in the missions as late as 1822.

Until the 1820s, the introduction of foreign goods paralleled the sort of goods which might be expected to be found in the supplies sent from Mexico. The presidios usually had such materials on hand for sale, though at higher prices than the smugglers charged. An inventory at San Diego's storehouse in 1810 lists several articles for household use: door latches, locks, chest and trunk latches, copper candle holders, chocolate mills, napkins, mirrors; chocolate cups made of gourd, in three sizes; crystal flasks, copper pots, bottles, atole sieves, copper kettles, Guadalajara earthenware mugs, metates, assorted common pottery, and, of course, much cloth and clothing and other items not for household use.

The missions continued to be a source of supply for the inhabitants of the presidios and pueblos, especially after 1810, when economic difficulties for California came with the wars for independence in central Mexico and the virtual cessation of supply ships from San Blas. Not only were the supplies cut off, but also the military payroll ended, a considerable factor in California's economy. Over half of the adult males of Spanish California were in the army, and the payroll was still more critical when it is considered that retired soldiers were also dependent to a considerable extent on their pensions.

The governors of California obliged the missions to supply the army with whatever it could, keeping accounts of what was expended, though as it developed these accounts went unpaid. Food, clothing, and incidentals were manufactured by the missions and sold in this manner to the presidios. The pueblos subsisted well enough on their own food supplies, though they were dependent on smuggled goods and the missions for their other necessities.

At Santa Barbara, where the records were fairly complete, some household goods are found. Fewer evidences of houses constructed with mission materials and labor are found, perhaps in part because there was no longer money to pay for them, and in part because enough houses had been built during the period 1800–10 to satisfy the need. Officers continued to order furniture, from time to time. José de la Guerra had two chairs made, plus a large table and drawers, a stand, and a backed bench. Doors, windows, and some building materials were ordered, candles, metates, a comal or two, blankets, and beds were supplied by the mission, both to private persons and to the soldiers. A cadet, in

Chocolate was usually prepared as a drink and heated, then poured from this copper receptacle. Smaller cups were used for drinking the chocolate, a favorite beverage of the Mexicans. From the *Index of American Design.*

addition to a cot, also had some fine headboards made for his bed. A trickle of mission-made goods no doubt continued into the pueblos, but there is scant record of such transactions let alone an inventory.

While supplies were still being shipped from San Blas they would have, from time to time, items from the Philippines and China as San Blas had some contact with the Philippine trade. In fact, some goods were actually shipped from the Philippines to California on at least one occasion. In 1783 supplies expressly for the missions of California were shipped from Manila by Father Benito Cambón, who had already seen service in California and was involved in obtaining supplies and vestments for Mission Dolores in San Francisco. Among many other items he sent expressly for the church, Cambón also sent goods which could have been sold by the mission, thus finding their way into California households. For example, he sent trays of painted wood, lanterns of tin and glass, Chinese toys, wax tapers and candles, fiber and rattan mats, copper flatirons, platters, red tea boxes, red and blue chocolate cups, a parlor clock, plates, bottle cases, and a hand mill, similar to the Mexican metate. The above had no specific use by Mission Dolores, though most other pieces did.

A few goods still came irregularly from San Blas during the Mexican struggle for independence from Spain, among them some copper pots were sent in 1817, probably for storing medicines which were sent in the same ship. Early in 1821 some metates and several loads of pottery, both from the San Blas–Tepic region arrived, and in the same shipment some money was credited for California Indian baskets sent earlier. A case of crystal was also sent at the same time. In 1818 some vinegar cruets and more glassware arrived from Mexico. Because the San Blas trade was irregular at best, foreign imports replaced domestic ones after 1810.

In 1806 Dr. George H. von Langsdorff visited San Francisco and made a few pertinent comments about the commandant's quarters. He dismissed Captain Argüello's habitation as "small and mean." He did remark that the walls were whitewashed, and that the rooms were "very scantily furnished." Half the floor space in the room for receiving guests had straw matting, von Langsdorff recorded, but he was surprised to see fine silver table service in such ordinary surroundings, "considering the humble nature of the rest of the furniture." It would seem that life for San Francisco's commandants had not changed greatly since Vancouver's visit fourteen years before.

Camille de Roquefeuil, a French visitor to San Francisco in 1817, observed that Commandant Gabriel Moraga lived in three large rooms, and that "a certain unstudied neatness reigned which excluded anything which could shock a European." He criticized Vancouver's assessment of San Francisco, saying that life was more comfortable there than Vancouver had depicted it. It must be added, however, that Roquefeuil visited San Francisco more than twenty years after Vancouver. Roquefeuil was less impressed with the housekeeping of schoolteacher Gómez and his wife. During the time of his visit he observed Señora Gómez sitting on a small stool, teaching little girls to read and sew. In addition, Luis

Argüello's quarters were "like that of Don Gabriel but a little better furnished and especially a little better cared for." Roquefeuil also found "very well made tables and benches" fashioned by a Kodiak prisoner, which were "the only objects suggesting the idea of ordinary industry." He suggests, by this statement, that the other Californian furniture he saw had a rather rustic appearance.

When Roquefeuil visited the Indians' quarters in San Francisco, he noticed some articles used in their homes, such as a "plaque" (no doubt a comal) for making "griddle cakes" (*tortillas*), wooden buckets and pots, plus "some baskets so closely woven that they hold water." A small oven and a "bed of wickerwork, covered with a cowhide" completed his assessment. Similar items were also probably found in the homes of non-Indians as well.

Roquefeuil saw some benches in the officers' quarters at San Francisco while the room was temporarily serving as a chapel. The presidio chapel had recently burned, and the room was so designated while the chapel was being repaired. It would seem that the benches were furniture from the officers' quarters, rather than that of the chapel.

During the late 1870s Hubert H. Bancroft had his researchers interview several persons who had lived in California prior to the American conquest. They gave several interesting versions of many historic events and encounters, and some of these old inhabitants offered some insights on the material culture of early California. They provide several that foreign observers did not know or record.

One such reminiscence was by José del Carmen Lugo, who was born in Los Angeles in 1813, son of Antonio María Lugo, later a wealthy *ranchero*. Lugo's father owned a rancho near Los Angeles, just south of the pueblo's boundary. The summary of a rancho dwelling by Lugo probably does not antedate 1818 or 1820, as he probably did not remember much before then. He explains that the typical home was of poles and thatched with tule. There were not more than two rooms, one a sleeping room, the other a living room. The sleeping room might be partitioned if the family was large. Many of the houses had doors made of sticks (probably the frame) and backed with horsehide or bullhide. The doors had no

232

The *equipales* imported during the 1790s and early 1800s were probably made in western Mexico, from what is now Nayarit and Jalisco. They may have been of somewhat different shape, but of basically the same material. Photo taken in Ensenada in 1987 by the author.

latch or key, as there was nothing worthwhile to steal if the family was absent. If everyone were to be absent for some days, they took the only thing of value, which was their clothing, carried in a trunk, and perhaps they might have brought along a bed or cot.

There were some *rancheros* and *vecinos* of the pueblo who had cots made of *alamo* or *alamillo* (cottonwood or quaking aspen), covered with a hide, which formed the bed. The sheets, blankets, bedspread, and pillows were used, according to each family's resources.

Lugo also described a type of bed, which he calls a *cacaiste grande*, or large wicker-work affair, the size of a cot, made with sticks and covered with a hide. (His term cacaiste is probably a variant of *cacaste*, a word used for the wicker carrying-baskets used in Mexico to transport small animals and birds.) Those who had no bed slept on a hide. Lugo also notes that these types of furnishings were from the earliest years he could remember and that with the development of trade, more variety in furniture came.

In the early times families of relative wealth tended to have some essential furniture, such as a table, bench, or stool. Some families used whale vertebrae as seats, others had what Lugo describes as *cacaistes chicos*, evidently equipales, which were chairs of cane, sticks, or any other wood, and leather. These latter chairs were the most common, according to Lugo. Another sort of seat was what Lugo calls a *poyete* (probably a variant of *payate*, or shelf) of adobe, on either side of the door, less than three feet from the ground. If the house were plastered and whitewashed, these seats would be also. If the house were devoid of plaster, the poyetes would be also.

Kitchens in some households had small ovens of adobe on which the *ollas* (clay cooking pots) were placed for cooking. In other kitchens there were only rocks with the fire underneath the ollas placed on the rocks.

Those who had plates used them at meals, though few families had them. Most ate off clay *cajetes* (unfired clay dishes or bowls) which looked like an ordinary plate. Only a very few had knives, forks, and spoons of metal. Most used forks and spoons made of horn, or in Lugo's own words, "changed their spoon with every bite" through the use of tortillas to scoop up their food. They used their everyday work knives also as eating utensils.

Meals were customarily eaten in the kitchen by the fire. Those who had tables ate much as people of Los Angeles did in the 1870s, but Lugo again reminds us that very few did so when he was a child. He also adds that the style of living was much the same in the pueblo as in the ranchos.

A similar reminiscence from northern California substantiates what Lugo had to say. Estevan de la Torre, who came to California as a ten-year-old around 1801 with his uncle, José de la Guerra, says that on the ranchos of the poor the houses were small, made of poles which were covered with mud, not whitewashed, and roofed with tule. The usual household furniture consisted of a bed or couch made of willow sticks covered with leather, two poles at the ends and with four forked sticks firmly planted in the ground. The bed itself was made of wood or straw with pillows, blankets, and sheets. There were also cots of leather with four feet, or legs (de la Torre uses *pies*, or feet), which were a sort of stretcher with a hide nailed or tied below with crisscrossed leather thongs. Seats were made from logs worked with an axe or hatchet. Some had benches

Manos and *metates* were imported from San Blas to California and were apparently made in Nayarit or Jalisco. Because they frequently broke, two manos were brought with each metate. In some cases these items were of California Indian manufacture. *Courtesy LACMNH.*

made from whale backbone, that is, individual pieces of the vertebrae were used.

These poor people ate in the kitchen (as Lugo also said), carrying their seats with them. They would place their tortillas on their thighs and their plates of meat, beans, or whatever in hand, using the tortillas in place of spoons, fingers for forks, and teeth for knives. While de la Torre does not clarify who these poor were, Lugo states that they were the majority of the population. It is probable that only army officers and missionaries prior to 1820 had anything more elaborate than that described above.

Other recorded narratives help fill in some details of the early picture of California home interiors. José Fernández, who came to California as a youth in 1817, gives the height of the average adobe dwelling as twelve feet, and adds that the doors were low and the windows small. Some homes were fortunate enough to have glass for their windows, but the poor, instead of glass, placed a piece of oiled paper in their windows, which, if not transparent, was at least translucent. Cured hides were used for *catres* (cots), and Fernández "could assure that the hide beds were much cooler than those of canvas," which were much in style during the 1870s.

Combined with what has been gleaned from archival sources, the above information presents a clearer picture of the average California home interior between 1790 and 1820 than one might expect from the meager amount of information available. The typical home had emerged from almost nothing in the way of furnishings to simple tables, chairs, benches, and a few other accessories. Throughout the period, from 1790 to 1822, there were some three or four references to whale vertebrae being used as seats, which suggests they were either used with some frequency, or the novelty of their use was certainly a conversation piece. There would appear to be a lack of interest on the part of Californians about acquiring imported furniture prior to 1820, with the possible exception of a few missionaries and an occasional army officer.

On the other hand, there was no lack of interest on the part of Californians about acquiring cloth and clothing. Dishes, trays, lacquerware, candle holders, and other similar accessories found a ready market, probably because Californians had been accustomed to importing such pieces through legitimate trade channels for years. But furniture was not an avidly sought commodity until after 1820. Probably two reasons account for the later rise of interest in furniture: one, advanced earlier, was that when trade with foreigners was illegal, smugglers carried only that which was relatively light and small, such as dishes and cloth. The other, if correct, is offered as a conjecture. During the 1820s, foreigners, frequently merchants, settled among the Californians and replicated a comparatively lavish life-style compared to their prior experience. Mayhap influenced by the new arrivals' mode of living, Californians began to acquire a taste for foreign imports, which included household articles, such as furniture. Leaders in setting the new trend were probably the army officers and the missionaries. Rancheros, however, were not far behind them; in fact, by the 1830s they overtook both groups. But that is another subject to be explored in depth.

California Ranchos: Their Hispanic Heritage

BY IRIS H.W. ENGSTRAND

NO PHASE OF CALIFORNIA'S HISTORY has produced more far-reaching consequences than the granting of large private land holdings to individuals during the Spanish and Mexican eras. In time, the private rancho became as much an integral part of the society and culture of Hispanic California as any of the other settlements. By 1846 more than eight hundred rancho grants had been made and the legal entanglements regarding these lands continued well into the American period. But this large number of grants contrasted sharply with the slow beginnings of civilian settlement.

Although today California lies within the mainstream of human occupation, this was not the case during the first half century of European penetration when our state was a remote outpost of the Spanish empire. Despite continued efforts to attract colonists, the Spanish government found few takers to participate in its liberal land granting policies. Even though the first private rancho, a small tract near Mission San Carlos in Monterey, was awarded by Governor Fernando de Rivera in 1775 to Manuel Butrón, no other grants were made until the fall of 1784.

The three earliest ranchos in California were enormous in area and made up a good portion of the region surrounding the original pueblo of Los Angeles. These 1784 grants were made to soldiers of the San Diego Presidio by Governor Pedro Fages just three years after the founding of Los Angeles in 1781. To José María Verdugo was granted Rancho San Rafael, also called Rancho La Zanja, whose lands were adjacent to the northern border of the pueblo. Some 36,000 acres in extent (and thus the smallest of the three), it included a major part of the present cities of Glendale and Burbank. Rancho San Pedro was twice as large. Granted to Juan José Domínguez, it encompassed more than sixteen Spanish square leagues — well over 75,000 acres in the area of San Pedro, Palos Verdes, Carson and Dominguez Hills. The most immense tract — some 33 square leagues or more than 158,000 acres extending from the San Gabriel River to the Santa Ana River and from the Pacific Ocean to the San Gabriel–San Diego Mission Road — was granted to Manuel Nieto. When this rancho was divided among Nieto's heirs in 1804, it was regranted by the Mexican government as five separate ranchos including present-day Westminster, Bolsa Chica, Garden Grove, Santa Fe Springs, Downey, Norwalk and most of Long Beach.

Other early private land grants near Los Angeles included Rancho Los Feliz, 6,647 acres along the west side of the Los Angeles River on the northern border of the pueblo awarded to Vicente Feliz in 1802 and Rancho Topanga Malibu Sequit, 13,315 acres granted to José Bartólome Tapia in 1804. It bordered the Pacific Ocean at today's Malibu and extended far into the mountains. Rancho San Antonio, containing nearly 30,000 acres on both sides of the Los Angeles River immediately south of the pueblo, was granted to Antonio María Lugo in 1810.

The procedures for granting land in California during the Spanish and later Mexican periods were based upon the legal heritage of Castile as modified by the discovery of America and the opening up of new lands for colonization and settlement. The three rancho grants awarded in 1784 by Governor Pedro Fages to Verdugo, Domínguez, and Nieto did not follow the precise legal formalities as normally required during the colonial period, but were nevertheless based upon a legal tradition that had evolved since the days of the Christian reconquest. Unlike other countries of Western Europe, Spain had a history of land granting activities resulting from the capture of Spanish territories lost to the Moslems during the Middle Ages. Military, religious and civilian traditions of this and the previous period of Roman domination provide a back-

238

ground for understanding the occupation of lands involving Spaniards and Indians in the New World. The broad legal heritage of the ranchos is perhaps less well known than the history of individual grants.

Since the first expedition of Columbus was authorized and financed by Queen Isabella, the ruling monarch of Castile, any benefits derived therefrom were to accrue to that kingdom rather than to Aragon. Shortly after Columbus returned from his first voyage, Isabella chose a member of the Council of Castile to take charge of all matters relating to the newly discovered lands. After 1508 he was assisted by other members of the Council and, with the death of King Ferdinand in 1516, a separate council emerged. Charles V, grandson of Ferdinand and Isabella, succeeded to the Spanish throne and established the Council of the Indies with full administrative and judicial authority in America on August 1, 1524.

Legislation concerning the Indies, therefore, maintained the spirit and intent of the laws of Castile. The principles inherent in these laws were influenced by customs and traditions of the Iberian peninsula and by laws concerning the use of land and town founding introduced by the Romans, by far the most influential of the early conquerors of Spain. By the third century of the Christian era, Roman law dominated within the peninsula and became the norm for establishing settlements. "From the moment of the conquest, Romans appropriated all of the royal domain and frequently part of the common lands; and in some instances they appropriated the whole territory of the conquered . . ." The inhabitants held these lands as tenants of the state and were obliged to pay property taxes. Even though they were Roman citizens they could not own the land which they occupied; it was held as a fief from the state. Lands within the colony were eventually subdivided into small tracts called *sortes*, from which comes the Spanish word *suertes* for farm lands. The lots, together with houses, were apportioned to colonists according to rank.

Another class of Roman settlements resulted from the establishment of protective frontier garrisons. There was a gradual development of civilian towns from these military centers or *presidia*.

239

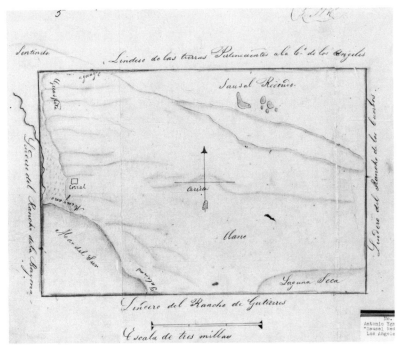

One of the traditions which carried over into the Mexican period was the Spanish use of these crude maps to describe a given rancho grant. The one depicted here is the Sausal Redondo, granted to Antonio Ygnacio Abila. The Spanish called these *diseños. Courtesy Bancroft Library, University of California, Berkeley.*

The soldiers married persons from the countryside, cultivated the soil, and became permanent settlers. Retired veterans were given lands in payment for services or as pensions. This exact system, utilized effectively by Christian Spaniards during the seven centuries of the Reconquest, was transferred almost intact to the New World. The period of Roman dominance gave Spain a legal heritage specifically adaptable to a colonial land use situation and a tradition of legalism that has endured until the present day.

The basic legislation for the New World was gathered together under orders of Carlos II as the *Recopilación de leyes de los reynos de las Indias* or Laws of the Indies. It was not a special code issued for the

240

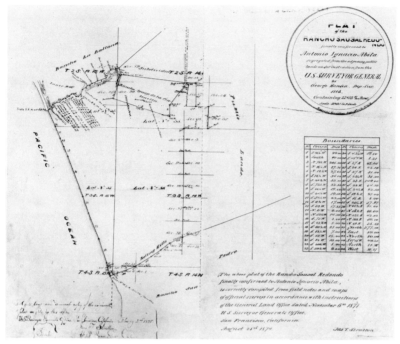

The original plat map of Rancho Sausal Redondo in the Los Angeles County Recorder's Office consists of two separate sheets. In order to photograph the map for publication, the two pages were trimmed and pasted together to present the appearance of a single map. To accommodate this arrangement, two endorsements had to be omitted. On the left-hand portion of the map in the lower right-hand corner, the following was deleted: "Approved March 22, 1875 // S.S. Burdett // Commissioner of the General Land Office." On the right-hand portion, lower bottom, James T. Stratton's title, "U.S. Surv. Gen. Calif.," was removed along with this endorsement: "A full true and correct copy of original (patent & Map) recorded May 27, 1875 at 3 mins. past 1 PM for D. Freeman, Esq. [signed] J.W. Gillette, County Recorder." A comparison of this survey with the *diseño* provides a graphic illustration of the fundamental difference between Spanish and American land measurement requirements.

241

Indies but a compilation of all laws and regulations promulgated by the Spanish crown for its American provinces from the time of discovery through 1680. The compilation contained nine books of royal decrees covering ecclesiastical, military, and civil administration in America. Book II, Title I, Laws 1 and 2 provided that only the laws actually set forth in the *Recopilación* would apply in the Indies, although in matters for which no provisions were made, the laws of the Kingdom of Castile were to be observed. These latter laws were principally contained in *Las Siete Partidas*, the code of Alfonso X "The Wise" sanctioned in 1348 and the *Nueva Recopilación de los leyes de España* of 1567. New laws promulgated in Castile could not be enforced in the Indies unless they were specially authorized by the Council of the Indies.

Throughout the entire period of Spanish control in the Indies, few changes were made in the laws concerning land use. Despite dynastic changes and individual differences of ruling monarchs, early legislation dealing with the American provinces continued to follow the traditions of Castile. Primitive customs of the Indians, like those of persons living in the provinces outside of Castile, were to be respected if they were not in contradiction to the crown's supreme interest. Perhaps the most comprehensive body of law concerning Indian rights is found in Spain's Laws of the Indies.

Even though many Indians in California were under the administration of Franciscan missionaries by 1784, laws protecting their welfare were often utilized by the priests. Most of these laws showed a paternalistic "preoccupation with the well-being of the indigenous population" and detailed the relationship between the new settlers and the natives. The mission fathers were knowledgeable about the laws and were quick to cite them. For example, several laws in Book IV provided that towns had to be established without prejudice to any Indian pueblo or private person and that settlers had to "establish their settlement without taking what belongs to the Indians and without doing them more harm than what is necessary for the defense of the settlers."

In Book IV, Title 12 there are several other laws concerning Indians that protect their rights to and possession of cultivated lands, pastures, and "all that belongs to them, both individually and as communities, [including] the waters and irrigated lands, and the lands through which they have built irrigation canals, or any other improvement...." Indians in California had no agriculture prior to the arrival of the missionaries but natives in other areas such as New Mexico did have irrigated lands and were protected in their use of them.

Specifically, when settlers arrived in a new area, property for the grazing of livestock had to be located far enough from the towns and cultivated fields of the Indians so as not to cause them damage. Farms for cattle and horses were to be a league and a half from Indian villages and farms for sheep and goats at a distance of half a league. In contrast to the later American period in which ideas of riparian water rights prevailed, the basic laws of Book IV, Title 17, provided that "the pastures, woods, and waters be common in the Indies" and that the "woods, pastures, and waters of the settlements and the woods contained in grants that have been made . . . in the Indies be common to the Spaniards and Indians." Laws 9 and 14 of Title 3 provided that even though Indians were relocated in settlements, they were not to be denied lands and cultivated areas that they held before, but if it became necessary to take land, water or pastures from them, they were to be compensated in another area.

The laws concerning the founding of towns or pueblos were extremely detailed and had to be followed, albeit with difficulty, in the establishment of San Jose and Los Angeles in 1777 and 1781. These royal ordinances were issued in 1573 by Philip II and were incorporated into the Laws of the Indies in Book IV, Titles 5 and 7. They controlled almost every aspect of municipal organization such as choice of site, design, construction, assignment of lands, governmental administration, and the subservience of local to the central government.

Requirements for townsites included a healthful environment, a clear atmosphere, pure air, weather without extremes of either heat or cold, a location near a navigable river but not too close to the sea where there might be a danger of pirates. Land had to be suitable for farming and ranching; there had to be mountains and hills with an abundant supply of stone and wood for building materials and an adequate source of water for drinking and irrigation. Lands, lots and waters were to be given to settlers in the name of the crown, according to the resources of the land without prejudice to third parties. Other laws stipulated the number of settlers required, the time in which they had to take formal possession (three months), and that settlers of one city could not abandon their residences in order to move to another place.

The Laws of the Indies were designed primarily for the attainment of political stability and royal control while the process of conversion and civilization of Indians was carried out. With the town residents forbidden to alienate their land, committed to a program of agricultural and industrial development, and subject to a uniform system of government, the king could reasonably expect that those parts of his dominions newly populated would rest safely under his control. Even in California, an area far removed from the centers of administration in Mexico City and the Commandancy General of the Interior Provinces in Sonora, the military governors, the missionaries, and the civilians followed the basic laws in effect. The town settlers, however, were few in number and progressed slowly in agricultural pursuits.

Beginning in the early days of the conquest, certain persons applied for and received lands outside of settled areas in order to raise livestock and cultivate fields. These large grants, which were to be made without prejudice to missions, Indian pueblos, or Spanish towns, were variously called *haciendas, estancias* or, in California, *ranchos*. They were generally made to persons of means or to retired soldiers as a reward for services. The first grants were made on the Island of Hispaniola and the procedure was continued throughout the Americas. An important royal instruction was issued on October 15, 1754, giving the viceroys and presidents of the *audiencias* in New Spain the right to name persons delegated for the granting of lands in the provinces.

The first step in obtaining a rancho grant was the submission of a petition containing the name, religion, residence, occupation, family size and available livestock of the applicant. The petition also included a description of the vacant lands and a *diseño* or map of the property. Descriptions were often vague since the land was essentially unoccupied and the need for accurate measurement not great. Boundaries generally were those of rivers, hills, other grants, Indian settlements, groves of trees, piles of stones, or even an aging skull. The next step was to present the petition to the appropriate granting authority which could be the governor, intendant, commandant general, audiencia, viceroy, or special subdelegate for that purpose. Sometimes the procedure was simplified, as in California in 1784 when Governor Pedro Fages approved the first three large grants of Los Nietos, San Pedro and San Rafael. Nevertheless, the opinion of attorney general Pedro Galindo Navarro rendered to Commandant General Jacobo Ugarte y Loyola in 1785 indicated that the petitioners had complied with the Laws of the Indies and assured the protection of Indian and other rights.

The land to be granted was visited by a commissioner to see that all qualifications had been met. After securing the necessary approval, the grant was issued either as a separate document or as a marginal note on the petition with the signature of the granting official. The grantee had to remain on the land at least four years in order to receive title in fee simple. In California, the lands granted did not infringe upon settled villages of Indians but did have to consider the extensive and nearly contiguous mission holdings which could not be prejudiced. Manuel Nieto's original grant overlapped the property of Mission San Gabriel (established 1771) and was reduced from some three hundred thousand acres to one hundred sixty-seven thousand acres. José María Verdugo of Rancho San Rafael became involved in disputes with both Mission San Gabriel and Mission San Fernando (established 1797) over grazing lands. More accurate boundary lines were finally drawn.

Even though considerable land was available for ranchos in the interior, the majority of persons living in California during the Spanish period settled around the presidios or lived in the pueblos. Only about twenty-five private rancho grants were issued, most of which were located along the coast from present day Orange County to the San Francisco Bay area. With the Mexican War for Independence and the expulsion of peninsular Spaniards from the administrative hierarchy, certain changes took place. The secularization of the missions after 1835 opened up extensive lands for colonization. Foreign traders, primarily fur trappers and merchants, began to enter California during the period from 1830 to 1846 and apply for land grants. The policies of the Mexican government simplified the acquisition of land by newcomers.

After several upheavals in the governmental structure of Mexico following independence, a federal constitution for the Republic was adopted in 1824 and two significant land laws were passed. The first and most important was the colonization law of August 18, 1824, which not only made it possible but encouraged foreigners to establish themselves in Mexican territory. The amount of land available to one person included one square league of irrigable land, four of non-irrigable land, and six of grazing land — or a total of eleven square leagues (48,000 acres). The next decree relating to land was adopted November 21, 1828, and authorized the governors to grant vacant lands to *empresarios*, families, or private persons, whether Mexican or foreign, who solicited them for inhabitance and cultivation. The conditions for receiving the land grants were much the same as during the Spanish period and involved a petition, description, diseño and proof of occupation. Each new colonist, after having cultivated or occupied the land, was ordered to prove the same before the municipal authority so that the necessary record could be made and forwarded in a quarterly report to the supreme government.

At present, American inhabitants of California tend to look back at the rancho period as a time when much land was available and there were few rules and regulations governing procedures for obtaining a large grant. This attitude was common from the very beginning of American occupation following the end of the Mexican War and the Gold Rush of 1849. The Spanish and Mexican land grant system inherited from its parent Hispanic-Roman civilization did not fit easily into Anglo-American concepts of 640-acre sections laid out in a neat gridiron pattern. The conditions of life in California prior to American sovereignty did not require clear-cut boundaries and the documents proving legal title were sufficient for those times. All of the original grantees, or their descendants, of the 1784 ranchos suffered through interminable litigation to establish their claims under the precise demands of the Land Act of 1851. The Domínguez family of Rancho San Pedro had the best record of survival but many Hispanic families paid heavily to lawyers and suffered losses of property. In other areas families such as the Bixbys and Irvines were able to purchase large portions of these ranchos and become founders of a new generation of landed entrepreneurs. Other changes also took place as a result of the continuous flow of immigrants into southern California and the inevitable adjustments in the occupation of land.

Today, two hundred years later, we have a better understanding of our Hispanic roots, more complete information about our Anglo-American heritage, and should be able to base future decisions about lands and waters on broader knowledge and an unbiased look at the issues at hand.

The Story of
California's First Libraries

BY MAYNARD J. GEIGER, O.F.M.

LIBRARIES AND LIBRARY SCIENCE in California are less than two hundred years old. Not until 1969 will we be able to say that we are removed two hundred years from the Stone Age, that preliterate era of aboriginal pictographs in painted caves. Not until the coming to California of western civilization and its implements of mission and presidio in 1769 did books and manuscripts accumulate with the subsequent formation of our first formal libraries.

The reader should not be surprised when it is stated that California's first libraries were located in the twenty-one missions which were established between San Diego and Sonoma during the period 1769–1823. In the course of time private collections of books also appeared in the libraries of Vallejo, Hartnell and other intellectually curious personages of our early era. In all cases these libraries remained private. The public library concept as we know it today is an American contribution to our mode of daily living. Before 1848 California life was chiefly agricultural and pastoral and what interest there was in books manifested itself chiefly among the padres and some of the better educated laymen who settled in the province as the colony developed.

However small these libraries were and however limited their scope, it must be emphasized that they were genuine libraries. They were called such by those who fashioned and used them. They were augmented as time went on and were preserved with loving care. The books were highly valued by their readers who waited long to obtain them from Mexico or Spain. The books were

249

located on shelves or in cabinets often under lock and key and in one case at least they were catalogued. The number and type of books were considered important enough to be noted in a mission's annual report. When the missions were secularized, an itemized list of all the books and their value constituted a section in the formal inventory. Besides the books contained in the formal library of the mission, there were books which each padre had for his own use as long as he served in the missions.

When the mission president, Fray Junípero Serra, was debating points of law with the governor, Felipe de Neve, the friar felt keenly the need of a copy of the *Recopilación de Leyes de las Indias* or *Codification of Spanish Laws for the Indies,* so that in the contest the arms of the padre would be equal to those of the governor. Thus began the Battle of the Books in those long ago days of early California.

When Fray Juan Crespí was dying at Carmel late in December 1781, and the nearest doctor was residing in San Francisco, Serra and Noriega took down from the library shelves their *Forilegio Medicinal* to see if they could find some remedy to alleviate his sufferings. When Fray Antonio Jayme planted grain and vegetable fields in what is now the rich Salinas Valley at Mission Soledad, he studied his *Agricultura General* by Alonso Herrera printed in Spain in 1797. When the padres of Mission Santa Barbara planned their new stone church in 1815, they had recourse to a famous book of architecture, *Los Diez Libros de Arquitectura de Marco Vitruvio,* a Spanish translation of the Latin published in Madrid in 1787, being available. Vitruvius himself was a contemporary of the classical age of Augustus, B.C., whose manuscript was found during the Renaissance and which went through many editions in Europe. The Santa Barbara padres used his designs for the façade and the interior decorations of their church. In so doing they were transmitting western culture to the Pacific shores through their libraries.

After 1787 at any mission a padre, after a dull and perhaps disappointing day where progress was slow and the natives perhaps uncooperative, could reach for a copy of Palóu's *Relación histórica* or *Life of Serra* to draw strength and inspiration therefrom to continue

A view of the restored library at Mission San Carlos Borromeo, Carmel. *Courtesy Norman Neuerburg.*

his own labors despite disappointments, setbacks and the *ennui* of the passing weeks and months. The mission libraries were indeed functional and practical.

Because San Diego was the first mission to be founded, it rightfully claims to have housed the first — although very modest — library in California. However, its existence has been neither continuous nor permanent. That frontier establishment with its entire contents was destroyed in the insurrection of 1775 and had to start all over again literally from the bare ground. Even so, despite the fact that in 1848 Colonel Jonathan D. Stevenson during his occupancy of the buildings that year stated that the library was very large, but by 1852 nearly the whole collection had vanished.

Meanwhile, Mission San Carlos had been founded at Monterey-Carmel with a handful of necessary books on the inventory.

Mission Santa Barbara has an extensive collection of old and rare books which date back to the arrival of the Franciscans in Alta California in 1768. On the far right, seated at the table, is the distinguished California mission historian, Father Maynard Geiger, O.F.M. *Courtesy SBMAL.*

It has continued to endure since 1770 down to the present day always under ecclesiastical management, at first under the Franciscans, then later under diocesan administration. Although in the course of the years some of the volumes were dispersed, most have been retrieved in modern times. Should a person visit Mission Carmel today he can see a special room displayed containing almost the total library which was at the headquarters of all the Alta California mission chain and which had been catalogued about the turn of the nineteenth century. To the mind of this writer this restored library room and all its appurtenances constitute one of the most truly precious restorations of our Spanish colonial era.

The library of Mission Santa Barbara began in 1786, the mission being the tenth in the order of founding. It is the oldest library in the State of California that still remains in the hands of its originators, the Franciscans, for it is the only mission in which the founders have continued to live uninterrupted until the present time. It has grown from a few needful volumes to about 65,000 because in the course of time Mission Santa Barbara has become an educational institution, principally a professional school of theology. It also evolved into a significant archive after 1833 when this mission became the center of authority for the Fernandino missionaries. This documentation originated in 1768, the year before the founding of missions in Upper California. It has grown with the years until it contains about 5,000 documents besides a large body of mission material in print and photograph. The archives as well as the library have been a center of study for historians for almost a hundred years starting with the researches made by the collaborators of Hubert Howe Bancroft. It is the prayerful hope and desire of the Franciscan Fathers to build at Mission Santa Barbara a semipublic library and archive to afford access to the rich yet unmined materials to qualified researchers, readers, and students. [That hope was realized in 1972.–ED.]

Now these early libraries and archives did not just happen to come into existence. On the contrary, they were planned in detail and fostered with care. The one hundred and twenty-eight Franciscan missionaries who came to California through the College of San Fernando in Mexico City between the years 1769–1833, as well as the ten Zacatecans who arrived in 1833, each brought along — with the approval of his superiors — the books of his choice. It is well to recall that the land was a frontier: there were no printing presses, no bookstores, no department outlets for many years and California was referred to both by padre and soldier as *"este último rincón del mundo"* (this last corner of the earth). Hence the books the padres brought with them were understandably necessary or useful ones, professional in nature and utilitarian in purpose.

Neither the individual Franciscan nor the Order of St. Francis as such can own anything whether it be the building in which the friars reside or the material things they use. All property which is allowed for the friars' use is held in the name of the Holy See. Moreover, according to the Franciscan concept of canonical poverty, use of material things is limited by their need. Still in the matter of books a generous flexibility was and is permitted. However, each missionary was responsible for the books he used and was limited in the manner of their use. That is why one will find inscribed on the inside cover or title page of a book in temporary possession of a missionary of the Order, the Latin phrase: "Ad usum N.N.," or the Spanish statement: "Del simple uso de tal y tal," or some similar wording.

When a future Franciscan missionary left his friary in Spain, he was allowed to take along with him certain books of his preference and these together with himself, baggage and other items were transported to the port of embarcation at government expense, and from there across the sea, once again overland to Mexico City and from there to the port of San Blas and by ship again to California. If a missionary returned to Mexico City after ten years of service, he brought back his books with him, or if he died in California, the books were sent back to San Fernando College. This explains why not all the books brought to California remained there. However, in 1808, Fray Estevan Tapis, President of the Missions, requested and obtained from the governing body of San Fernando College, permission that books of missionaries who died in California be retained here rather than be sent back to the capital of the viceroyalty.

Besides the volumes that individual missionaries brought with them, the Franciscan superiors sent books yearly both by overland and ship routes, especially books that were requested. Occasionally a book was donated to a mission by a prominent visitor. At the time of secularization of the mission establishments in 1834, inventories had to be drawn up in detail containing precise statements concerning each item, movable and immovable, at each mission together with an appraisal of its monetary worth. Among such books was the *Life of Serra* by Fray Francisco Palóu (the *Relación histórica*) printed in Mexico City in 1787. At Santa Barbara its worth was noted at one peso; at Carmel, two pesos! Today it is a collector's item and sells for as high as $350.00.

The Story of California's First Libraries

Here is the list of books at Mission Santa Barbara taken from the original inventory as signed by the resident padre, Antonio Jimeno, and the appointed commissioner, Anastasio Carrillo, signed on March 15, 1835. It is much shorter than most mission inventories of the period and in the opinion of this writer contained only the books of the common library and not the books of the individual missionary.

Concilio Tridentino	1 vol.	2 pesos, reales
Mística Ciudad de Dios	4	2
Barcía	8	25
Potesdad	1	11.4
Indice Expurgatorio	1	2
Villalobos	3	4
Biblia en Latin	1	4
Año Cristiano	12	20
Vida de Santo Domingo	1	1.4
Croiset	6	8
Parras	2	3
Filosofía del Corazón	2	3
Vida de Fr. Junípero de Serra	1	1
Misionero Parroquial	4	6
Molina de Oración	1	2
Fr. Luis de Granada	12	12
Sermón de Nuestra Señora de Guadalupe	1	1.4
Florilegio Medicinal	1	2
Madonna Pouquet	1	1
Diccionario Geográfico de América	5	10
Diccionario Geográfico de Universal	3	8
Soto-Exposición de los Salmos de David	1	2.4
Berty	1	1
Villarruel	1	4
Homo Attritus	1	2
Diccionario Castellano	1	8
Duhamel Exposición Sacrae Scripturae	1	8
Montargón	5	6
Corella	1	1

Today Mission Santa Barbara has over 1,000 volumes bound in sheepskin which date from the mission period though not all of them were actually brought to California by the missionaries nor did they belong to the library of San Fernando College originally. Only those which are marked as belonging to the college, to a mission or to an individual missionary can be proven to be of the original collections of the missions.

One cannot fully understand the mission libraries of California without a knowledge of the motherhouse of the missions, San Fernando College, which supplied the personnel and material goods needed. Included were books shipped to the missions. This college was established in 1734, a daughter college of Santa Cruz de Querétaro (1683), precisely to train missionaries who were to convert Indians to Christianity. Its initial books came from the mother college and through the years the incipient college library was augmented by purchase and donation. In the year 1800 it contained close to 12,000 volumes and an extensive archive of original manuscripts. This writer considered himself fortunate during his Serra research in Mexico to discover in the Biblioteca Nacional in Mexico City, the complete catalogue of the college library that revealed the fact of its identity and many other interesting aspects. It disclosed, for instance, something about the history of the library and particularly its modus operandi.

Seldom can one inject humor into a discussion about libraries, but our unnamed friend, a Franciscan who was in charge of the library, painstakingly compiled the catalogue in 1800 and unintentionally provided us with a chuckle. Certainly he lacked a funny bone himself and had learned little from history — especially about libraries — for he pontificated in his introduction to the catalogue in the following vein: he had lived at the college for fourteen years and had seen the library reorganized in four different ways. Well, at least the library interest was alive, someone was bestirring himself, things were happening. But then he added: "Now at long last, beloved reader, has that longed-for time arrived when this library has been put in order forever." God bless his soul, for today neither the physical library exists nor do those orderly shelves of books beckon an anxious army of researchers for both the archives and books are scattered far and wide.

Besides this catalogue, this writer found in another archive in Mexico City — the Archivo General de la Nación — a *"Libro de Decretos"* of the College of San Fernando, or the official book of records of the ruling body of the college. Many paragraphs contained significant references to the library between 1734 and 1858, how it was improved from time to time, how the collections were broadened, how the official inspections were made concerning it every three years. Thus it was learned that only in 1774 was a full-time librarian appointed, Fray Benito de la Sierra — who was relieved of certain duties of the college common to all friars in order that he might be a more efficient librarian.

The *Catálogo* stated that all books of the college were arranged in ten categories, each book marked on its spine with the letters B, S, D, H, F, T, P, M, A, and L, which were the first letters of the Spanish words corresponding to the categories: Bible, Patrology, Law, History, Philosophy, Theology, Homiletics, Morals, Ascetics, and General Literature. Law included canon and civil law and Franciscan legislation. History contained both profane and ecclesiastical subjects together with biography. Philosophy embraced medicine and mathematics. Homiletics comprised preaching, rhetoric and catechetics. General Literature represented belles lettres, education and varia. Even so, narrated the librarian, occasionally he found books that seemed to defy classification. But then, who has not?

Also explained was the system of enumeration. On the spine of the book, at the top, first came the letter indicating the category to which the volume pertained. Below that appeared a Roman numeral indicative of the shelf on which the book was to be found within its proper category. Underneath the Roman numeral was inscribed an Arabic figure designating the exact spot on the shelf occupied by that particular volume. If the Roman numeral were painted red instead of in black ink, the reader was immediately reminded that the work was of particular importance and could not be removed from the library without special permission from

257

the chief librarian or of the superior of the institution. If an asterisk was placed after the letter on the spine, it meant that the book belonged on the front shelf of its particular category, while one without such an asterisk would be found on the rear shelf.

Thus a book marked H, III, 107 — which was the analytic marking ascribed to Father Francisco Palóu's *Life of Serra* — meant that it was located in the section of history though it is truly a biography, that it stood on the third shelf in that section and that it was book number 107 thereon. Such a copy is in the Santa Barbara Mission Archives. Moreover it has burned on its edges: "S. Fernando." There is no indication who brought it to California. The Mission Archives also has a copy of the *Statutorum Generalium Compilatio pro Familia Cismontana Regularis Observantiae Seraphici P. N. Sancti Francisci* (Madrid, 1751) with "S. Fernando" burned into its upper edge and with the following inscriptions on its flyleaf: "Del uso simple del Pe. Fr. Jph. Ortes de Velasco" He was a contemporary of Serra. Below that is the following inscription in another hand: "Requiescat in pace. Es de la Librería de San Fernando." On its spine is the following enumeration: D, IV, 62. It belonged to the section of Law, was on the fourth shelf in that section, and was book 62 on that shelf. An asterisk follows the D. Moreover the D and IV are painted in red as is Palóu's *Life of Serra*. Both were consequently considered important books.

Thus volume by volume the entire library could be reassembled today in perfect order as it was in 1800 if all the books could be found and returned to their original owners. It is interesting to note that when San Carlos Mission, Carmel, was catalogued by 1803 under Fray Fermín Francisco de Lasuén, he followed the general system used at San Fernando College. Since all missionaries who came to California remained at the college for some time — one, two or three years — before actually embarking on their northward journey, the friars became thoroughly acquainted with the well-stocked library, its rules of procedure, its management, its methods of indexing and cataloguing.

Sometimes these books which the missionaries brought to California give a short history of their travels which indeed enhances their value. Thus, when Fray Pedro Benito Cambón, co-founder of Mission Dolores with Father Palóu, left his friary in Spain, he wrote in his neat hand on the flyleaf of volume I of *Dispertador Christiano* (Madrid, 1762) the following facts:

This volume entitled "Dispertador Christiano" together with all the works of the famous Barcía, were purchased by means of the alms which our Brother Syndic of the Convent of Our Father, St. Francis, known as the Royal Convent of Coruña, for the journey taken from my province to Cádiz. The Rev. Father Commissary, Fray Rafael Verger, who conducted the mission [to Mexico] in the year 1770 can testify to this fact.

Written at the Port of Santa Maria, June 4, 1769. Fray Pedro Benito Cambón, most unworthy son of the Province of Santiago [Galicia].

This statement opens up a whole field of speculation as to the book's travels. We are certain that it left from Coruña for Cádiz, traveled over the Atlantic, across Mexico to Lower California and then to Upper California where Cambón served at San Gabriel, San Carlos, San Antonio, San Francisco, after which he returned to Mexico, then went to the Philippines, and back to California, serving again at San Francisco, then at San Buenaventura until 1791 when he again returned to Mexico and finally to Spain. The book was left in California. It may have been a very, very traveled book for besides the lengthy inscription on the flyleaf, the padre put his name also on the title page as well as on the sheepskin cover. He wanted it known that the book was for *his* use.

When Fray Felipe Arroyo de la Cuesta left San Fernando College for the California missions, he brought along the *Teologia Moralis* by the Rev. Anaclete Reiffenstuel (Barcelona, 1736) . On the book's flyleaf he wrote: "Fray Juan Capistrano Hermogenes Uzquiza gave this book to Fray Felipe Arroyo de la Cuesta at San Fernando [College] in Mexico in 1807 when I left there for the conversion of the pagans in New Upper California." Arroyo de la Cuesta remained in California until 1840. The book has remained here ever since.

The music book, *Arte o Compendio General del Canto-Llano Figurado y Organo* by Francisco Marcos y Navas (Madrid — no year given), contains the statement: "This book is for the simple use of Fray Juan Bautista Sancho." Sancho was at Mission San Antonio from 1804 till 1830. The statement is crossed out and below it is found another in the hand of Fray Mariano Payeras who died at Purísima in 1823: "This book belongs to the library of San Fernando in Mexico."

The whole point in these inscriptions is that these books were the "property" of the Franciscans and were not ecclesiastical property so that when a diocese would supplant the missionary organization, the books were to remain in Franciscan hands. When Mission Santa Barbara itself became an apostolic college in 1854 — the daughter of San Fernando — the mother college evidently relinquished its rights to the books then in California which had originally come from San Fernando. Hence it was that Archbishop Alemany of San Francisco directed that any and all books bearing the marking of San Fernando College, extant in California and particularly in the Diocese of Monterey, which were still not in Franciscan custody, and explicitly those in private hands, were to be sent to the Apostolic College or ex-mission of Santa Barbara. There is no record at Mission Santa Barbara as to which books and how many were returned, but the fact that a significant number of books belonging to the early missionaries who did not labor at Santa Barbara are there today appears to indicate that at least some volumes from other areas were forwarded to that mission.

Today some of the missions have only small fractions of the larger collections known to have once existed there. Other missions have been more fortunate in that they have retained or retrieved many of their original books such as Mission Santa Clara founded in 1777. When the last Franciscan there handed over the establishment to his Jesuit successors in 1851, the library contained 244 volumes. These books are now at the University of Santa Clara on the grounds of the former mission. When Fray José María de Jesús González Rubio, the Zacatecan, took over Mission San José from the Fernandino, Fray Narciso Durán, in 1833, the former inventoried the books on the shelves as numbering 177. To these he added some 107 that he himself had brought with him from Mexico. Dr. J. N. Bowman, former state archivist of California, in a study made some years ago, calculated that the twenty-one missions in the year 1835 possessed approximately 3,185 volumes or a mathematical average of over 151 books per mission.

According to the original inventory of Mission San Carlos, Carmel, signed by Father José María del Real and José Joaquín Gómez, December 10, 1834, the mission library had 405 volumes. Among them were the sermons of Bossuet and Masillon, *Medicina Práctica, Recopilación de Leyes de las Indias, Crónica de los Colegios Apostólicos, Navegación Especulativa, Educación Popular,* the *Relación histórica* by Palóu, a *Diccionario Castellano,* Bibles and their commentaries, books on philosophy, Church law, asceticism, preaching and several volumes on mathematics.

When there was no longer a resident pastor at Mission Carmel, the books at some unspecified time were taken to the parochial rectory in Monterey. It was in the thirties of this century that Monsignor James E. Culleton found 174 volumes in Latin and Spanish there all dated before 1830, fifty-three of which bore the catalogue marks of the Library of San Fernando College, Mexico City. It was found that this library was started by Fray Junípero Serra himself (1770–84), twenty-five of the volumes bearing his handwriting and which contained the statement that they belonged to the "Library of the Mission of San Carlos de Monterey." Others denoted that they were presented by individuals. During Lasuén's tenure of office as president (1785–1803), the number of books, according to Culleton's estimate, rose to about 410.

It was a worm that gave a clue concerning the fact that the library had been catalogued in mission times. It had been hatched within one of the books and worked its way in a straight line through three others, died within the fourth book and left its ashes as a record of its travels. The four books were not of one set but were marked on their spines consecutively. The worm had done its work in the library which had catalogued them. It had also worked its way through a scrap of paper used as a bookmark bearing the date 1836, but did not reach another such bookmark having the date 1839. Once it was determined that the books belonged to the Mission Carmel, it was easy to determine which books were the oldest in the collection and which had gone astray.

A search was begun for the missing books since the markings on the spine indicated a uniformity of lettering and numbering. The catalogue marks were made with black India ink on a small square white lead field painted on the spine's upper section. This section contained a Roman numeral, the place of the book in the section by an Arabic number. The books were not catalogued according to categories as at San Fernando College. The highest numbers of the four sections into which the library was divided were I/79, II/119, III/113, and IV/84.

A search was begun throughout the area for the missing volumes. In course of time, sixty-seven were found in Santa Cruz, eight at Mission San Juan Bautista, others in Hollister and Watsonville, and in isolated places. One section in private hands yielded 117 volumes. By 1933 the total Carmel collection could count 458 volumes of which 143 bore the signature of the Mission San Carlos catalogue work. Among several of the books received were two which had been given to the mission by members of the La Pérouse expedition of 1786 while another was a gift of Governor Diego Borica. All had the catalogue markings. It was found that the oldest and catalogued section consisted of books between 1770 and 1803. All markings were the same so it was determined finally that the work was done during the administration of Lasuén between June 1798 and June 26, 1803. No cataloguing was done at Carmel after his death. The library room at Carmel today containing the original and retrieved books was arranged by Mr. Harry Downie, the restorer of Mission Carmel and its curator [now deceased].

As indicated earlier, most of the books in the mission libraries were professional books of the padres, the majority dealing with the various branches of theology. There were Bibles and books on the Bible, moral theology, preaching and ascetical life. There were also books on profane and sacred history, agriculture, music, medicine, geography, biography and architecture. Mission San José had a copy of *Don Quijote*, a *Summa* of St. Thomas, a *Medicina Práctica*, *Letters of St. Jerome*, *Reflections on the French Revolution*, and dictionaries in the Latin, Spanish and French languages. Yes, indeed, books were limited in number, heavy as far as reading fare goes, but they were practical, purposeful, professional. And they did constitute libraries, *viz.*, "collections of books for study and reading" — and they were the first in the land.

The Function of Prints
in the California Missions

BY NORMAN NEUERBURG

HISTORY IS MADE UP of an infinity of details. Some of these details may not seem of major importance in themselves and often have been ignored, but they can take on significance as they fill gaps in our understanding of the life of a given period. Thus it is with prints in Hispanic California. When one thinks of the devotional art of the California missions one thinks exclusively of paintings and statuary, yet an examination of the surviving records shows that engravings and other types of prints belong in the same category.

A fundamental characteristic of the printed picture is that it is not unique, that it can be reproduced as long as the image on the plate or block remains clear enough to be transferred to the page or sheet of paper. This aspect not only had economic consequences but also permitted the wide divulgation of an image. Although many printed pictures, especially those executed by famous artists, came to be collected for their aesthetic value, the overwhelming majority had a more humble function as illustrations, whether for decorative purposes or for didactic goals. Religious images fall into the latter category, and that is where most of the prints used in California belong.

Prints also have a special value to artists. They form a marvelous repertory of designs that can save the artist the trouble of preparing his own drawing from a model. Since the common production of prints began in the fifteenth century, artists, both major and minor, have used prints to suggest compositions, the pose of a figure, or details in a landscape, and the like. Prints were especially important in the New World. The prints used for both practical and didactic purposes were illustrations in books and independent impressions as well. In Mexico in the early decades after the Conquest few paintings had been imported from Spain and even fewer professional artists had arrived so prints became the major source of inspiration for the mural paintings that soon decorated the churches, monasteries, and upper class dwellings of the colony. Not only did illustrations in Bibles and other books serve as models for paintings such as those done on the underside of the choir at Tecamachalco by the Indian Juan Gersón in 1562, but decorated title pages suggested the frames for niches in the cloisters of the monasteries. A copy of the *Summa* of Saint Thomas Aquinas, originally from the Franciscan monastery at Zinacantepec and now at Mission San Gabriel, shows such a typical design.

In the late sixteenth and following centuries the sources for oil paintings were frequently independent engravings, often of famous paintings by contemporary European artists. In Spain we know that such masters as Velázquez and Zurbarán did not hesitate to base their work on prints, even of lesser masters. In Mexico some of the most important works of Cristóbal de Villalpando are free copies of paintings by Rubens which he knew from engravings. In 1775 Fr. Junípero Serra, on requesting a painting of Saint John Capistran, said they "should find a good engraving and have Paez paint it, or some other good artist." In time it took the place of a print used at the mission's founding along with other prints.

Since only a few prints, principally woodcuts, were made in Mexico itself in the sixteenth century, most of those used at first were from Flanders, with smaller numbers from Spain, Italy, France, and Germany. Although Mexican engravings became more numerous in the following centuries the imported prints never lost their importance.

The artists' use of prints as models was secondary to the importance of these inexpensive pictures as an aid to devotion among the general populace. A late eighteenth-century painting in the cathedral of Puebla shows a young Christ offering an image of the Immaculate Conception to a group of clerics. The image, in this

Engraved altar card, uninscribed but probably Venetian, eighteenth century. Collection of Mission San José. This same set of engravings for altar cards can be found at other missions as well. *Courtesy SBMAL.*

case, is an engraving of the bust of the Virgin, seemingly based on Manuel Tolsá's statue on the main altar of the cathedral. Such printed images were, in fact, extremely significant in the popularization of certain sanctuaries with miraculous images. Pilgrims to the sites usually purchased prints of the images to take home. Those who could not make the pilgrimage would obtain prints of these as well as their own favorite saints and hang them up, too. Sometimes they were just tacked to the wall; some were mounted on boards, while others might be framed, with or without glass. Although by far the largest number of prints used in Mexico were religious in their subject matter we do find genre paintings, especially those in the series of *mestizaje*, of the castes, which show landscape engravings, and there would have been portraits and maps, too, as we know was the case in California. One such painting shows a landscape print simply tacked to the wall while another has a neatly framed print of a landscape hung between two elegant mirrors of the type known as *cornucopias*.

Both for reasons of space occupied in shipping and for economy prints were especially practical in the frontier missions. How common they were and how they were used can be verified, for example, at a specific moment in history in the missions of New Mexico, according to the report of 1776 of Fray Atanasio Domínguez. He had been sent to report on conditions in that outlying area and sent back to the Franciscan headquarters in Mexico City a most detailed account of his findings. In his descriptions of the mission churches he mentions prints on the wall above the high altar in a half dozen sites. They were interspersed among paintings and other images, apparently always symmetrically arranged, as few as two or as many as fourteen. Most were middle-sized prints, often on their little boards. Four, however, were large, and in one case they are described as colored prints. Six at Sandía were in dreadful shape, while four old ones at Santa Ana were too dirty to be recognizable. Only at Abiquiú was the subject matter mentioned: a set of the Stations of the Cross hung along the walls of the nave. Except for a series of crosses in the cemetery of the parish church at Santa Fe these are the only Stations of the Cross mentioned in his report. Other prints would have served a devotional function in private homes as well.

In New Mexico prints were also very important in the development of the typical *santero retablos* of the first half of the nineteenth century. In fact, the breakdown of the supply lines in the early nineteenth century meant that there were not enough prints to supply the demand, and the *santeros* filled the gap. Once Currier and Ives prints and then French lithographs began to appear, the art of the santero ceased except in the most remote areas.

With this preface to set the scene we can now turn to California in the Spanish and Mexican periods. While collecting documentation on the works of art in the old missions I came across numerous references to prints in the documents of the period. The usual word for print is *estampa* in the general sense; one also finds *estampa de papel, imagen de papel,* and *cuadro en papel.* The word for engraving is *lámina,* but one also finds *cuadro de buril; cuadro de madera* appears to mean woodcut, while the words for lithograph are *lito-*

266

José de Ibarra, "Christ Child Offering a Print of the Immaculate Conception to a Group of Clerics," Cathedral, Puebla, Mexico. *Photograph by Mardith Schuetz Miller.*

grafía, cuadro de litografía, or *estampa de litografía.* I have yet to find the current word for print, *grabado. Iluminado* means the print is colored, presumably by hand. The references appear in the *memorias* or requests for supplies, the *facturas* or *cuentas* or invoices and bills for goods sent, or inventories made at various times during and at the end of mission days.

The earliest reference to prints sent to California that I have found is in a list of objects sent from Baja California to Fr. Junípero Serra which mentions a "small box with ten engravings and their frames of tortoise shell." This document, dated October 13, 1769, indicates that the objects were to go on the *San Antonio.* In 1788 there are invoices for shipments of 30 prints and three maps sent to each of five missions, while 229 prints and 10 maps of California were sent to Carmel; Santa Clara also got two maps of California at the same time. In 1791 three dozen prints were sent to San Luis Obispo and 1,000 to Mission San Diego. The presidios also made use of prints. In 1793 Santa Barbara Presidio requested 300 paper prints of various images while San Francisco received a dozen prints in 1796 of which three were colored, and Monterey requested 100 prints of various subjects in 1805.

In 1807 Mission San Buenaventura requested 400 prints, about a quarter of a *vara* in size (about 8¼ inches), to be divided as follows: 60 of the Christ of Esquípulas; 60 of the Immaculate Conception, Our Lady of Guadalupe, etc., 40 of Saint Joseph; 40 between Saint Anne and Saint Joachim; 30 of Saint Michael; 40 between Saint Gabriel and Saint Raphael; 30 of Saint Francis; 30 of Saint Bonaventure; 30 of Saint Anthony of Padua; and the remaining 40 to be divided among Saint Roch, Saint Apollonia, Saint Gertrude, Saint Sebastian, etc. These refer mostly to saints venerated in the mission church and certainly were intended for distribution to the Indians, perhaps as rewards for good conduct, such as the Sisters in parochial schools used to give Holy cards to good students. A similar destination was perhaps meant for the prints of Fr. Serra that Mission Dolores received in 1787 and the 30 that San Juan Capistrano got the following year. Some also may have ended up in the homes of the colonists.

The maps which we have mentioned were, of course, for the

quarters of the Fathers, and some of the prints ordered would also have been used there and in the church as the inventories tell us. Some were framed, often with glass, while others went unframed.

In some sources, as we have seen, the subjects were not specified, but in others they are clearly indicated. The use of prints in the church was usually a temporary substitute for hoped-for paintings, some of which did eventually arrive. This was especially true with the sets of the Via Crucis, the Way of the Cross, which, unlike in New Mexico, were to be found in all the mission churches in California. This is the subject matter most frequently documented, as a brief survey will show. San Diego mission had received a set as early as 1774. It was lost in the Indian revolt of 1775, and a second set was obtained in 1776. This same set was still in the church at the time of the 1834 inventory but has not come down to us. In 1771 San Gabriel also requested a set of prints; in 1798 a set of paintings arrived and the mission fathers apparently gave the prints to the newly founded San Fernando where a set of prints appears in an inventory of 1808. Mission Dolores got a fine set in 1782, but most of them were lost in a hurricane five years later. San Juan Capistrano requested a rather cheap set of prints in 1785 which arrived in 1787. There is a bill for a set of paintings sent in 1806, just in time for the dedication of the stone church; they survived the earthquake of 1812 and are now hanging in the Serra Church. The fate of the prints is not known, but perhaps they ended up in the hospital chapel of the mission.

Mission Santa Clara acquired a set of Roman prints in 1801; they were still there and framed and under glass fifty years later. In 1805 Carmel requested three sets, unframed, presumably for distribution as well as for the mission's own use, though in 1809 a set of paintings was sent from Mexico. In 1818 both La Purísima and Santa Inés received sets of prints, possibly identical ones. One print alone survives at Santa Inés, but the mission soon obtained a set of paintings. The inventory of Mission San José lists a set of framed prints, but we learn in a note that these were given to San Francisco Solano as San José had acquired a new set of French colored lithographs. The Monterey presidio had received a set of large prints in 1795. The inventory of the chapel of the presidio in

Santa Barbara made soon after statehood includes a set of small prints and very probably the other presidio chapels and pueblo chapels had prints for their Stations of the Cross.

The fourteen Stations of the Cross would have hung on the side walls of the nave of the church, seven on each side. We have some idea of where other prints were located from the annual reports and inventories. At Mission Dolores in 1782 there was a print of Our Lady of the Remedies with a hammered silver frame with glass on the main altar; it came through the hurricane of 1787 undamaged. Two prints, one of the Virgin of Montserrat and a small one of the Immaculate Conception, were hung above one of the side altars at Mission San Antonio.

Mission Carmel, the headquarters of the chain, had the largest number of prints recorded. In the church there were two small prints of the "Soul" of Mary Most Holy and of the Savior as well as nine medium or small prints of saints with wooden frames and glass along the side walls. In the sacristy there were framed prints of Saint Helen, Saint Clare, the Immaculate Conception (a large one given by the king), and a large woodcut representing the family tree of the Franciscan Order. In the padres' quarters there were an engraving of Our Lady of Guadalupe (another gift of the king), prints of the Virgin and Saint Joséph, of Pius VI, and of Saint Felix, a large woodcut with portraits of the Popes and Cardinals of the Franciscan Order, a similar one three *varas* high of the saints of the Order, another one two and a third varas of the Superiors General of the Order, a map of the world and a map of Spain. Most of these probably decorated the reception room of the *padre presidente*.

Mission Santa Cruz had numerous prints, many of them in the padres' quarters, and three maps mounted on linen. Santa Barbara had a set of seven engravings of the Seven Sacraments, 18 inches high and 15 wide, and a Roman print of the Institution of the Holy Sacrament, that is, a picture of the Last Supper, and a portrait of Ferdinand VII in a gilded frame with glass. Santa Inés also had a print under glass of this same monarch.

One class of prints that we have not mentioned because they are rarely so specifically defined in the records is that of altar cards. Altar cards are frequently mentioned in the documents, but only

Asistencia of Pala. Detail of an old photograph of the decoration surrounding the baptismal font in the chapel, showing a small print of the
7th or 9th Station of the Cross tacked to the wall. *CHS/TICOR Collection,
No. 6207, Doheny Library, University of Southern California.*

once have I found mention made of their being prints, because
almost all, if not all, of them were just that. A number of these still
exist, again largely ignored.

We have mentioned lithographs only once in this survey, the
lithographic Stations of the Cross at Mission San José which were
acquired some time in the mid or late 1830s. Around the same time
the mission also acquired and hung in the sacristy six colored
French lithographs of various scenes from Holy Scripture. In 1834
Santa Barbara had a lithograph a foot high and ten inches wide of
Saint Francis Xavier. The 1858 inventory of that mission mentions
a colored lithograph a foot high and a foot and a half wide of Christ
and the Woman Taken in Adultery, and a lithograph 14 inches high
and 10 wide of Saint Emigdius.

With this survey, incomplete as it is due to the lacunae in the

271

Eighteenth-century Spanish engraving of the Pietà, given to Sergeant Ortega by Padre Junípero Serra. On display at the Santa Barbara Mission Archive-Library. *Courtesy SBMAL.*

surviving documentation, we can draw some tentative conclusions. Certainly it would seem that prints were relatively abundant in the missions, abundant enough to distribute them to the neophytes. Prints, especially the Stations of the Cross, were used in the churches and prints were hung in the sacristy as well as in the padres' quarters. The reception room at Carmel must almost have seemed a print gallery. Presumably most of the prints were Spanish or Mexican, though there are references to Roman prints and French lithographs and the Station of the Cross at Santa Inés is Venetian. By this time Flanders had lost its importance as a center of printing, and probably few, if any, Flemish engravings found their way into California. One does not know the origin of the maps, unfortunately, though Spain is perhaps the most probable source. William Beechey mentions seeing maps dated 1772 at Mission San José.

So far we have looked at the background and the documentary evidence. What, then, about the actual surviving examples? Prints by their very nature are fragile, consumable, and biodegradable, and they have usually been ignored or treated as objects of little value. Some, of course, appear in books, but they are not abundant here. Missals often have a few engravings; frontispieces are found occasionally, and printers' ornaments on the top or bottom of pages are not rare, but the majority of the books in the mission libraries have nothing at all. One book that should be mentioned, however, is Palóu's *La Vida de Fray Junípero Serra*, published in Mexico in 1787. It contains as its one illustration an engraving of Fr. Serra preaching to Spaniards as well as Indians. It was possibly the source for another engraving, probably the one requested by two of the California missions. A relic associated with Fr. Serra is a small framed colored print of the Pietà displayed at Mission Santa Barbara. Small devotional books, of which Mission Santa Barbara has a small collection perhaps brought by Bishop García Diego, often have engraved or woodcut prints as frontispieces. Beyond these we have mentioned, very little in the way of prints seems to have survived. However, further search is likely to turn up some.

A photograph taken inside the chapel of the Asistencia of Pala in the 1890s shows what appears to be a tiny print above the niche

Pellegrino de Colle, engraving of the 10th Station of the Cross, after the painting of Giuseppe Angeli in the church of Santa Maria del Giglio in Venice, published by Wagner in Venice, 1778. *Collection of Mission Santa Inés, Kurt Baer photograph, courtesy of SBMAL.*

containing the baptismal font. On close examination it is possible to determine the subject; it is one of the Stations of the Cross. It could have come from a little prayer book or it could easily have been cut out of a whole sheet with little pictures of the Via Crucis on it. I have seen in the print collection of the National Library in Madrid just such a sheet with little pictures of the Via Crucis on it meant to be cut up. Unfortunately the little print at Pala disappeared long ago.

As was mentioned the tenth Station of the Via Crucis sent to Mission Santa Inés survives. It is an Italian engraving, printed in Venice in 1778. Like most Italian representations of the Via Crucis it is vertical in format, while the Spanish prefer a horizontal shape. In fact, the painted set which replaced it in the church is horizontal. More curious, however, is the fact that the painted set is based on another copy of the same engravings for its model, though extensive modifications were clearly necessary because of the change in format. This set, like most sets of the Stations, was mass-produced, and other replicas can be seen at Mission Soledad and San Juan Bautista. The date of acquisition is only known for the latter, and it is 1818, the same year the printed set arrived at Santa Inés. The originals which the engravings copy are in the church of Santa Maria del Giglio in Venice, Italy, and were painted around the middle of the eighteenth century.

It was quite typical that many Stations of the Cross were copied from or based on prints. There is a set of Stations of clearly Indian workmanship now at Mission San Gabriel which had originally been at San Fernando. There can be no doubt whatsoever that, rather than being original compositions, these paintings are based on other paintings or on engravings, most probably the latter. It was previously mentioned that in 1808 there was a set of prints of the Via Crucis at San Fernando, and it was suggested that they were those which had been requested by San Gabriel in 1771 and subsequently replaced by paintings. In that same year the Fathers there had requested a book entitled *Pintar sin Maestro, o algo semejante: How to Paint without a Teacher,* or something like that. It would seem logical that not only did the Indian artist or artists use the prints as their model, but that they may also have borrowed the book of instructions. That set of prints disappeared long ago, of course, but, as was pointed out at the beginning of this article, one of the advantages of prints is that they are *not* unique and one can still hope to find a copy of that set, somewhere.

While speaking of Stations of the Cross and Mission San Gabriel we should mention a set of lithographs which hung on the walls of the mission church until a few years ago. They were produced by the firm of the Widow Turgis in Paris and Toulouse. They are signed "Victor" in the stone, and he is known to have been active in the decade of the 1830s. The prints are labeled in French, Spanish, and English. Just when they came to the mission and why they replaced the painted set is not known, but they could have come as early as the years just before secularization.

An identical set used to hang in the church at Mission San Miguel, and other products of this lithographic studio have been found as Stations in Spain and Mexico as well as New Mexico. In fact, they must have dominated the market for Stations of the Cross in much of the Roman Catholic world until they were pushed out by the more showy chromolithographs which usually came from Germany. They can be found in different sizes, both vertical and horizontal, as well as oval, either in black or white or hand colored.

Proof that French lithographs had already arrived in California at the end of mission days is supplied by San José's acquisition of a set of French hand-colored lithographs some time between 1833 and 1840. They survived as late as 1905 when George Wharton James photographed them in a corridor of the Dominican convent behind the mission. A recent attempt to find them was unsuccessful. However, a second set of French lithographs, stored in the attic at Mission San Gabriel, is identical in size to those mentioned in San José's inventory and quite possibly are another set of the same, non-unique works.

It has been suggested that the Indian-painted Stations were based on unbound engravings. In a like manner book illustrations could have served as models for a variety of purposes. There must have been pattern books on which wall decoration was based, but handbooks of architecture also came. In 1803 Carmel received a

Victor, lithograph of the 11th Station of the Cross, published by the Widow Turgis, Toulouse and Paris, c. 1830. *Collection of Mission San Miguel, Kurt Baer photograph, courtesy of SBMAL.*

277

small book of *The Three Orders of Architecture*, and it is well-known that Santa Barbara still owns a copy of the 1787 Spanish edition of Vitruvius. A plate showing an Ionic temple front provided the model for the facade of the mission church, and another plate of details served to suggest two types of ornaments for the ceiling of the church.

This essay has been an attempt to suggest how an up-to-now ignored detail of the material culture of the California missions can contribute a few pieces to help complete the historical jigsaw puzzle that comprises the mission period of California. If nothing else, it may result in the discovery of other prints once used in the missions and save them from being discarded as being without importance.

Franciscan Colonization
at Santa Barbara

BY MARVIN W. MIKESELL

THE CRUDE MAPS OF THE NEW WORLD which appeared in the early part of the sixteenth century depicted California as an island. Contemporary legends placed it "on the right hand of the Indies" and held that it was inhabited by a fabulous tribe of Amazons who knew only one metal: gold! Inspired by these legends the Spanish made early but unsuccessful attempts to reach the "island" by land and sea. Actual contact with the California peninsula was delayed until 1533, when the Jiménez expedition reached the Bay of La Paz. Two years later a colony was established at the same location. But the hazards of crossing the Gulf, the distance from the mainland, and the unexpected barrenness of the country offered difficulties for centuries to come.

Nevertheless the Spanish maintained their faith in the "island." The discouraging truths that the area discovered was unproductive of hoped-for riches and that the strait to the East Indies had not been found were dismissed by a belief that both prizes lay farther to the north. It was in search of that "Strait of Anian" that Juan Rodrígues Cabrillo became involved in maritime exploration on the west coast of New Spain. Finally, in 1542 his expedition landed on the coast of Santa Barbara Channel.

After the departure of the first group of explorers many years elapsed before the Santa Barbara area was again visited. Then, in 1602, the Vizcaíno expedition entered the Channel. A spell of bad weather, however, prevented the crew from landing except at a few sheltered coves, and contact with the Indians was reduced to a minimum.

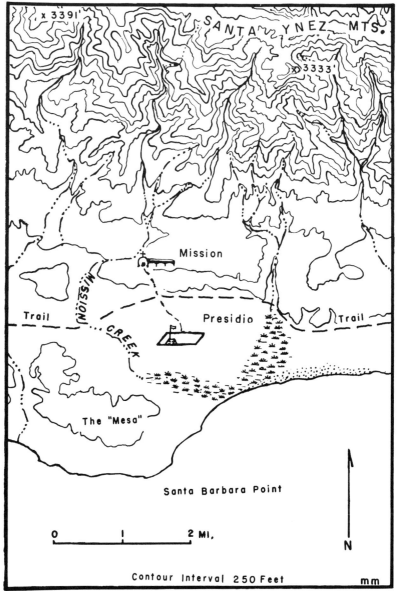

THE SANTA BARBARA PLAIN
Sketch map shows sites of the Mission, the Presidio,
and the immediate vicinity.

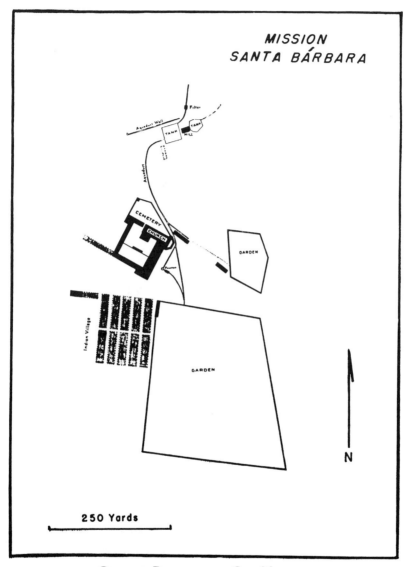

GROUND PLAN OF THE OLD MISSION
After Fr. Zephyrin Engelhardt, *Santa Barbara Mission*,
San Francisco, 1923, p. 85

Another long interval, extending over a century and a half, followed before the area was again mentioned by early chroniclers. It remained for land expeditions to fill in geographic details. Fr. Kino's overland expedition from Sonora destroyed the island myth in 1701. In the interval between 1769 and 1774 Alta California was surveyed by the Portolá and Anza expeditions. By the end of this period the densely populated Channel coast was regarded as one of the new territory's most promising regions. The colonization of the Santa Barbara area was only natural when fear of foreign encroachment spurred the Spanish to extend their settlements northward.

The selection of a site for colonization required careful analysis. Without a large and amenable Indian population a mission could scarcely be established, let alone succeed. Recognizing this fundamental requirement, the padres established the Santa Barbara mission within sight of a large Chumash village. The original plan was to erect a mission and a presidio at the same time, but political difficulties delayed the founding of the mission until 1786, four years after the establishment of the military post.

The presidio was located near the center of the plain now occupied by the city of Santa Barbara. Bancroft remarked that the site was on "the shore of a small bay affording tolerably secure anchorage." Actually, the site of the presidio was three quarters of a mile from the shore at an elevation of about fifty feet. The "bay" referred to was the slight indentation of the coast east of Loon Point. The mission was located in the foothills, about two miles from the coast and about a mile and a half from the presidio.

There are several explanations for the separation of the two units. The most important of these was the fact that the submissive attitude of the local Indians did not necessitate elaborate provisions for defense. There was little justification for a military post in the area, and as events turned out the colony would have been better served without it. The presidio complex was a relict of the generations of conflict in the "Southwest" and the *Gran Chichimeca* that preceded Spanish expansion into California. In the Santa Barbara area such an establishment was both useless and potentially harmful. By settling away from it, the padres hoped to minimize

The earliest known view of the Santa Barbara Presidio, though in decaying ruins. The chapel has recently been completely restored. Watercolor by J.M. Alden, 1855. *All photographs used in illustrating this essay are courtesy SBMAL.*

An early 1850s photograph of Mission Santa Barbara.

undesirable contacts between mission neophytes and military personnel.

The foothill site had practical advantages as well. A scant hundred yards away was the stream now known as Mission Creek. By damming this stream in its upper reaches and through the use of a system of aqueducts and two small reservoirs the mission was able to secure fresh water throughout the year.

In accordance with royal instructions the Santa Barbara mission was thus established in an area where there was "productive land, water and a large Indian population." The formal organization of the colony progressed along established lines. An initial financial stake was provided by the "Pious Fund." This was to be expended for clothing and various articles useful in attracting the Indians. Livestock, seeds and necessary implements and utensils were to be collected from the surplus of the other missions. The Franciscan Order was prepared to underwrite the first year of activity, but thereafter the colony would be on its own. It would have to satisfy local food demands and train natives in handicrafts. "Luxury items" could be purchased with funds derived from trade in hides and tallow or the harvests of local crops.

In theory, the colony rested upon a dual foundation. The presidio was responsible for protection, while the mission was responsible for the satisfaction of economic needs. In practice, the arrangement proved to be less harmonious. The military contribution was almost entirely negative, whereas the mission provided the very life-blood of the community. As the years passed the two units came to be at odds with each other. The custom of "peonage" whereby mission neophytes were bound out to the soldiers proved to be a particular source of difficulty, as the latter were often unable or unwilling to compensate the mission for the labor they received.

At the time of the founding of the mission, the presidio was already near completion. An imposing structure, it consisted of a large courtyard surrounded by adobe buildings. The latter were used for storage and as quarters for the military staff. A chapel fronted the courtyard on the east and there were heavy gates at the west and south. Enclosing the entire area was a solid adobe wall.

The completed unit may have been less fortified than its name implied, but it was still unduly elaborate. Again we are reminded of the conservatism of colonial planning: it was better policy to erect an expensive and impractical structure than to flout tradition.

Construction at the mission was delayed until 1787, but by the end of that year no less than eight buildings had been completed. The first units were constructed of poplar or sycamore poles, clay plaster and thatch; but later when an additional wing was added, walls were made of adobe, pine timbers were used for beams, and tile was employed for the roof. The characteristic "adobe-tile" style eventually became the mode for all buildings, but during much of the pioneer stage of colonization makeshift thatch structures existed alongside those with thick adobe walls.

For the first few years the Indians resident near the mission continued to live in their native villages, but eventually they were settled at the mission in rectangular adobe huts. This final touch of orderliness must have delighted the padres, but when epidemics of Occidental disease swept over the area at the beginning of the nineteenth century the compact arrangement clearly led to fatal results.

Since it was imperative that the mission achieve self-sufficiency as soon as possible, planting began early in 1786. The agricultural report of that year reveals that wheat and chick peas had been sown. In the following year corn and barley also were sown. The two-year harvest amounted to 918 bushels of grain. How far the padres were from the desired self-sufficiency at this time may be inferred from the fact that they were still importing grain from Mission San Luis Obispo and La Purísima in 1795. In later years grain yields fluctuated widely. In 1795 only 167 bushels were harvested, whereas in 1821 an impressive total of 12,820 bushels went into mission storage bins.

At first all crops were dry-farmed, but after the completion of the Mission Creek dam in 1806 some irrigation was practiced on the gentle slopes near the reservoir. The inadequacy of the water supply prevented large scale application of the practice. In his *Informe General* of 1787 Governor Fages remarked:

The dam constructed by the local Indians under the direction of the Franciscan missionaries still survives on Mission Creek, upstream from the mission complex.

The reservoir displays considerable engineering skills in its construction.

The remains of the aqueduct which delivered the water to the mission.

Without doubt it [the mission] will be suffering from lack of water sufficient for irrigating the fields which they desire, and even must begin, to
cultivate in spite of the lack of sufficient water. However, if well directed
there is hope of a middling sufficiency. In addition it [the mission] has in
its neighborhood some plots of land which are appreciable for the raising
of crops with the aid of rains alone.

Because livestock assigned to the mission were slow in arriving,
there were only 80 head of cattle, 27 sheep and 32 horses at the end
of 1787, but natural increase and additional imports raised the
total to 3,500 head of cattle, 11,500 sheep, and 800 horses by the
end of 1804. The increase was less than had been expected because
of "damage done by bears, leopards, wolves and coyotes." The
progress in animal husbandry proved to be a compensation for disappointing crop returns. As cattle and sheep were allowed to range
widely, the mission expanded the territory under its control. By
the end of the eighteenth century animals from the Santa Barbara

289

The water arrives at the mission.

mission were grazing in the Santa Ynez Valley and for a distance of over thirty miles along the coast.

The struggle of the padres to achieve self-sufficiency is best understood in light of the existing state of communications. Although better situated than some of the interior settlements, Santa Barbara enjoyed only intermittent contact with the "outside world." Popular routes of travel in the area gradually evolved from simple paths to cart or wagon roads and finally to stage lines, but during most of the colonial period the celebrated Camino Real was little more than a trail.

In the Santa Barbara area the trail probably avoided the beach east of the presidio, for it would have been difficult to reach the mission or the presidio from that direction. The 1871 sub-division map of "The Santa Barbara Pueblo Lands" represents Arroyo Pedregoso ("Mission Creek") as emptying into a marsh. Farther eastward the area formerly occupied by the race track would have been under water after rains. The practical all-weather route from the Carpenteria area to the mission would thus have been north of the Summerland hills and along the base of the mountains. In the hilly country between the Santa Barbara plain and the Goleta basin the trail probably followed the general trend of the modern highway. East of the Goleta area the best route would have been in the narrow belt of terraces between the dissected foothills and the poorly drained bottom lands.

The practicality of a route along the base of the foothills seems to have been recognized by the early exploring parties, for in Fr. Font's diary of the Anza expedition one finds this note:

We set out from the Village of La Rinconda [the Chumash village at the mouth of Rincon Creek] at nine o'clock in the morning, and at three in the afternoon halted at a place called The Vicinity of the Villages of Mescaltitan [the shore of ancient Goleta slough], having traveled some nine leagues, about six west by north, two northwest, and finally a short league to the southwest.

A direct pass through the mountains would have been a great advantage for the colony. Unfortunately, nature arranged otherwise. The route progressed more than thirty miles along the coast before Gaviota Pass afforded easy access to the Santa Ynez Valley. It is noteworthy that even today no primary road crosses the mountains directly north of Santa Barbara. Crude trails, probably evolved from Indian paths, did exist in colonial times, but they were not suited to heavy traffic. In 1861 Brewer described the condition of one such "trail."

Such a trail as we found that day! The worst I had traveled before was a turnpike compared to that. Now following along a narrow ledge, now in a brook over boulders, now dismounting and jumping our mules over logs, or urging them to mount rocks I would have believed inaccessible

291

The plaque which commemorates the Santa Barbara Mission Aqueduct, dating from 1806.

... The trail ran up by zigzags, at an actual angle of thirty degrees average, and in places over forty degrees! We measured one slope of several hundred feet where the trail was at an angle of thirty-seven degrees, the slope itself much steeper.

With the difficulties of overland travel limiting commerce to occasional inter-mission trade, the Santa Barbara colony turned to the sea for outside contacts. The maritime situation, unfortunately, was only slightly more favorable. During the calm periods of summer and autumn the slight indentation of the coast at Santa Barbara offered safe anchorage. But during the tempestuous months of winter and spring ships were obliged to anchor three or four miles offshore and transfer their cargoes in lighters. This presented an additional problem, since it was hazardous to land lighters through the surf.

The Franciscan colony at Santa Barbara thus enjoyed scant overland contact and fared little better by sea. Because of headwinds it took ships fifty to one hundred and fifty days to reach San Diego from San Blas, and from San Diego to Santa Barbara it took another three or four days. Under such conditions it was imperative that the community early achieve a high degree of self-sufficiency.

A noteworthy aspect of colonization at Santa Barbara was the submissive attitude of the Indians. At no time during the period of exploration or the early phase of colonization does it appear that they actively resisted the Spanish. On the contrary, there are numerous accounts of their having offered material assistance. The explorers were met with a welcome that at times became oppressive. After having presented the Portolá party with generous gifts of food, the natives proceeded to entertain the explorers until, as Fr. Crespí relates, "they were sent away, charged with emphatic signs not to return in the night and disturb us; but it was in vain, for as soon as night fell they returned, playing on some pipes whose noise grated on our ears." In the face of growing military abuse, an insurrection was attempted in 1828, but by this time the foundation of the colony was secure.

It goes without saying that such an attitude hastened the process of conversion. In the absence of hostility, the padres could easily induce the Indians to join their community. This was usually accomplished by offering them gifts such as glass beads, pieces of cloth or, more rarely, food. The presidio was able to recruit labor in the same manner, although in later years the inducement included tobacco and wine. Natives "hired" by the presidio were free to leave after their task had been completed, but the situation at the mission was quite different. Here the "contract" on "conversion" was a lifetime affair. The Indian who fled was regarded as a fugitive, while the neophyte population as a whole was subjected to close surveillance.

At the outset there was disagreement as to whether a neophyte village should be established at the mission. To save expense Neve urged that the padres should administer to the Indians in their villages, but the missionaries protested that by this plan the neophytes could not be controlled. Neve's plan was abandoned, therefore, in favor of congregating the neophytes at the mission. In time, as the neophyte population increased, it became impossible to accommodate all the converts at the mission and a number were permitted to commute from their villages.

Owing to the submissive attitude of the Chumash and the presence of a large number of potential converts, the growth of the neophyte population was very rapid. The mission register indicates that only three converts had been secured by the end of 1786, but six months after the founding of the mission the number had increased to 70, and by the end of 1788 the population had grown to 307. A year later a total of 425 was recorded, and ten years later a total of 864. An absolute maximum of 1,792 was achieved in 1803, but thereafter the ravages of disease fostered a numerical decline fully as striking as the preceding rise.

To what extent did acquired culture traits set the mission neophyte apart from the ordinary Indian? The question can be answered in part by consideration of what incorporation into mission life involved. The convert was obliged to change his name, his clothing, his housing, and to a lesser extent his diet, livelihood and language. Under the supervision of the padres he was, in effect, transformed from an acorn gatherer to a farm laborer, from a mat maker to an adobe brick maker, and from a relatively free and mobile being to one subject to rules of movement. The conversion process as it was conceived and put into practice reflected economic requirements as well as a desire to erase pagan ways. In short order some of the neophytes were trained in crafts, such as weaving and wood working, while others were put to work in the fields.

Yet there were occasions for modification in each of these regards. It is unlikely that the neophytes were completely dependent upon mission food. Neophytes living apart from the mission were allowed to continue the old livelihood, including long fishing voyages in their plank canoes. Among the mission neophytes native food always provided a dietary supplement and in times of crop failure was their main sustenance. As Fr. Olbés remarked:

> Besides what the Mission gives them, the neophytes are very fond of
> what they lived on in paganism, as the meat of deer, rabbits, rats, squir-
> rels, or any little animal they can catch, while those on the seashore have
> a craving for whatever the sea produces.

Furthermore, it does not appear that native dialects were abandoned or that native ceremonies were completely ignored. It is
known, for example, that Mission Indians offered sacrifices to the
pagan god "Chupu" when an epidemic of pneumonia swept over
the area in 1801.

Nevertheless, the mission neophyte received a veneer of European culture. He learned to attend mass and acquired a lively taste
for Spanish wine. However superficial it may have been, his
acceptance of the white man's ways set him apart from his still
pagan brother.

With the beginning of the nineteenth century the pioneer phase
of Franciscan colonization at Santa Barbara came to a close. The
colony still faced vexing problems: self-sufficiency had not yet
been achieved, water supply remained a difficulty, and the mission
and presidio continued to compete with each other for native
labor. But by and large the foundation of the colony was secure.

During the period of pioneer activity the native landscape was
partially transformed. Near the site of the Indian village of
"Yanonalit" a presidio was built. A mile and a half northward the
buildings of the mission rose out of the foothills — first as makeshift huts, then as elaborate structures. At the turn of the century
the mission was beginning to reflect the orderliness of a well-exe-
cuted plan. The central unit consisted of a church and a complex
of store rooms, work shops, and living quarters, constructed of
adobe and sandstone, pine timbers and tile. Directly south of the
main unit was the neophyte village, which in 1802 consisted of 113
small adobe huts arranged in a uniform grid. Immediately to the
east of it the Mission Creek aqueduct irrigated a small vegetable
garden, while corn, beans, wheat and barley were dry-farmed on
the neighboring slopes.

The environment, too, was beginning to show signs of an invasion. Travelers at the turn of the century viewed a landscape subtly but significantly different from that which greeted the first explorers. Although large scale deforestation and the scars of over-grazing were not yet clearly visible, both trends were under way. The stands of pine on the crest of the mountains and the thickets of trees along the intermittent streams had begun to thin. Through-out the lowland the gradual depletion of native perennial grasses heralded the advent of a new era of annual weeds.

To this extent the Spanish had made their mark upon the land-scape. But it must be remembered that the "intruders" were still a numerical minority, and that in a large part of the area their fea-tures were of a secondary, "novel," character. In the strictest sense Spanish control was limited to the area directly influenced by the mission and the presidio. The dominant cultural feature in the remaining portion of the lowland was still the Chumash village.

At the close of the eighteenth century the cultural pattern of the Santa Barbara area exhibited a duality expressive of the interaction taking place. The Spanish had made an indelible impression upon the landscape, but there remained a substantial area in which the native pattern had not yet begun to fade.

The Caring Colony:
Alta California's Participation
in Spain's Foreign Affairs

BY DAVID J. LANGUM

ONE OF THE PERSISTENT HISTORICAL IMAGES of Spanish California, 1769–1822, is that of peaceful, carefree isolation from the rest of the world and its cares. Historian Charles E. Chapman called Spanish California "out-of-the-world" and suggested that "the Californians had little idea of events or conditions in the world outside." Generally, historians have agreed with this interpretation. One of the earliest American historians of California, Franklin Tuthill, wrote in 1866 of the Spanish Californians that "without disturbance, without bloodshed, with scarcely a ripple on the calm surface of their simple society, these occupants of a wild and unknown portion of the continent drifted through two generations. While America, on her eastern border, was convulsed with a war that was rending from England her thirteen colonies, nothing disturbed the quiet of this priest-ruled region." More recently in 1973 T. H. Watkins described Spanish California as "caught in this vacuum of neglect and isolation . . . ," and floundering "in a backwash of time." "From the beginning," wrote Leonard Pitt, "California had been little more than an outpost of empire, a remote frontier. Since the province lay at the farthest reaches of New Spain, itself a Spanish colony, California's colonial status was twice removed. This geographic and political isolation bred provincialism."

While it is inconceivable to suggest that Spanish Califomia was near or even well within the mainstream of historic events, still the prevalent notion of early California as completely isolated, care-free and unconcerned by the major events of the day, is overdrawn. News did take some time to travel to California. However, when it did arrive, the Spanish pioneers showed concern, took appropriate action, and thereby demonstrated an understanding and care for old Spain and broader world events in which Spain was engaged. This proposition can be demonstrated by an examination of the California reaction to the wars in which Spain was engaged during the years beginning with 1769, the year of California occupation, until 1821 when the province became Mexican. There were other signs of Californian involvement in world events, such as war scares and defensive responses, and of course the religious and civil ceremonies which accompanied changes in Spanish mon-archies. However, most significant is the California reaction to the five actual wars of Spain: two with England, 1779–83 and 1796–1802; two with France, 1793–5 and the Peninsular War of 1808–13; and the Spanish American Wars of Independence, 1810–21.

WAR WITH ENGLAND, 1779–83

A courier from Mexico notified Governor Felipe de Neve of Cal-ifornia's first foreign war in August 1779. Beginning immediately thereafter, letters were exchanged and circulated as to contingency plans in the event of an attack on California.

However, of more immediate impact on Californians was the call by King Carlos III in the same month for a war levy, in the form of a contribution but in reality a tax, of two pesos per adult Spaniard (over eighteen years) and one peso per adult Indian. Some 4,216 pesos were ultimately collected from Alta California for the Spanish cause, of which the missions contributed between 20 percent and 25 percent, and toward which total Governor Neve personally contributed 2,000 pesos, or half of his annual salary. The most interesting contributions are from the presidios, Mon-terey, Santa Barbara, and San Diego, providing respectively 833, 249, and 515 pesos. The contributions from San Francisco were unfortunately lumped in together with those of two missions so a separate stating is impossible.

The artist serving with the expedition of La Pérouse, the first French party to visit California in 1786. The scene is at Mission San Carlos Borromeo near Monterey. *Courtesy Bancroft Library.*

The approximate number of soldiers at these three presidios at this time, including officers and those attached to the presidios but assigned to mission stations, were: for Monterey, 53; Santa Barbara, 34; and San Diego, 54. The average per capita contribution of soldiers on behalf of themselves and their families, necessarily approximate, is therefore in the area of sixteen pesos for Monterey, seven pesos for Santa Barbara, and nine pesos for San Diego. The significance of these figures will be seen shortly.

By an earlier order of June 24, 1779, the king had commanded that in both Spain and the Americas "public prayers be offered up for the prosperity and success of our Catholic armed forces." This command was not received in Alta California, however, until June 13, 1780. Notwithstanding the delay with which the message was received, Fr. Junípero Serra, the Father President, wasted no time in compliance and by circular letter to all the missions dated June 15, 1780, he implored his fellow padres "that as soon as you receive this letter you be most attentive in begging God to grant success to this public cause which is so favorable to our holy Catholic and Roman Church . . . Our Catholic Sovereign is at war with perfidious heretics." He then followed with the specifics of the prayers to be used each Sunday including "the psalm, verses and prayers which the Roman Ritual prescribes in times of war . . ." and specifically indicated that the request be included: "That Thou wouldst be pleased to humiliate the enemies of our Holy Church."

These prayers were repeated at least weekly in every church and presidio chapel in California. Therefore, every person in California who attended church at any time during the next three years — and that must be almost everyone — needs have become aware of the war, and at least to that extent aware of the international events of the day.

WAR WITH FRANCE, 1793–5

In October 1793, California learned that another war had been declared, this time with revolutionary France, and a call made for contributions. By March 1794, California had raised 740 pesos, but this was declined with thanks by the viceroy in Mexico. How-

A view of the Monterey Presidio in 1790. Courtesy *Museo Naval, Madrid.*

ever, in the next year Viceroy Branciforte renewed this request and suggested contributions on the basis of two pesos per Spaniard, one peso per mixed, and one-half peso per Indian. Unlike his predecessor, Serra, the new Father President, Fermín Francisco de Lasuén, refused to allow mission contributions and a total of 3,881½ pesos were raised from the soldiers and settlers, including a personal contribution of 1,000 pesos from Governor Borica. If we assume a population of the non-Indian *gente de razón* of about 1,500 in 1795 and an average family size of ten, that would indicate an average contribution of around nineteen pesos per family or per breadwinner, after exclusion of the large gift of Borica.

Even though Lasuén did not contribute funds he sent a circular letter charging all the missionaries:

... whenever the occasion arises, to impress on your subjects the absolute justice of the decision of His Majesty in regard to France. And I charge both your Reverences and all others to help the levying of this war with the contributions of which you are capable, that is to say, with fervent prayers, begging the God of Armies that the troops in Spain may win glorious victories, and that in the struggle they may win victory with honor, for on their side are justice and true zeal.

Likewise, at the conclusion of hostilities, every mission and presidio celebrated a Solemn Mass in honor of peace. It was in this manner, through the church, that many Californians were constantly reminded that their nation was at war or peace with other nations in the world.

WAR WITH ENGLAND, 1796–1802

Upon outbreak of war with England, the missions again contributed the usual prayers urging the Spanish cause, but no funds. One new aspect of this war was the increased activity of the missionaries to propagandize their Indian subjects which therefore meant that necessarily there was more talk and anxiety at the missions concerning this war than the two preceding it. This effort was inspired by the order of Governor Borica that the missionaries be prepared to supply Indian labor to build fortifications if needed. Fr. Lasuén advised the missionaries in circular letter on March 14, 1797:

In order to attain this objective, it will be very fitting, and will be even necessary, that we should take advantage of any occasions that seem opportune to us in order to continue to influence the minds of our poor neophytes. And in my opinion the best method will be to make them understand as well as they can and in any way that is possible the reason for the proclamation, that it was for their welfare and that of their country that our great King has found himself obliged to declare the English the enemies of all the Spaniards, and to order that they be treated as such.

Early in the war there was a serious fear of English invasion, and although this fear proved to be groundless it was nevertheless real in the minds of the Californians. A paraphrase of fevered letters in the period March 1797 to June 1797, gives the sense of this anxiety:

March 28th, April 10th, . . . Goycoechea to B., [Borica] Santa Barbara defenses in a very bad state to resist attack. Is suspicious of the Indians to whom the British have given beads. Families to be gradually removed to Angeles. . . . March 31st, Sal to B., all care taken. Provisions to be destroyed and not allowed to fall into the hands of the foe. . . . March 31st, April 6th, May 11th, Grajera to B., a sentinel on the beach at San Juan Capistrano, Invalids of Angeles, San Gabriel, and Nietos rancho ready. If the Presidio has to be abandoned, shall it be destroyed or not? . . . April 24th, B. to Goycoechea, Target-shooting every Sunday. Indians must be imbued with anti-English sentiments, taught that the foe is hostile to religion, violators of women. . . . April 25th, B. to commandants, economize, for the supplies of 1798 cannot come. . . . April 30th, Alberni to B., Indians refuse to go to Bodega from fear. . . June 8th, B. to commandants. If Presidio is abandoned, guns to be spiked and powder burned.

Contributions were again taken and again only from the soldiers, settlers and small amounts from Mission Indians. Neither the missions nor missionaries contributed. A total of 3,460 pesos was collected, including another 1,000 personal contribution of Governor Borica. With an estimated gente de razón population of 1,800 and further assuming the Indian contribution amounted to no more than 300 pesos and an average family size of ten, the average contribution per family, or per earning unit, was approximately twelve pesos.

We have previously estimated per family contribution of nineteen pesos per earning unit in the 1793–5 war with France and using more accurate figures from individual presidios estimated contributions for the English War of 1779–83 at between seven and sixteen pesos per breadwinner.

The significance of these average per family contributions is seen dramatically when compared to the list of fixed prices in effect in California beginning with the proclamations of Governor Neve on January 1, 1781. Although modifications were made thereafter it remained essentially intact through 1803 and was generally enforced. Some of the significant maximum prices fixed by this regulation included: bull for slaughtering, five pesos; ox, trained to the yoke, six pesos; wheat, per *fanega* (roughly two and one-half bushels), two pesos. Thus, if an average Californian family's war contribution in each of these wars was approximately twelve pesos, this is an economic equivalent, for each war and each family, of two and one-half bulls for slaughter; two oxen trained to the yoke; or fifteen bushels of wheat. Therefore the degree of economic participation of the average Californian family in Spain's foreign wars was quite high in real purchasing-power equivalents.

War with France, 1808–13

The Peninsular Wars were echoed in California in the same familiar vein. Lack of proper defenses caused concern but there does not appear to have been any invasion scare of the degree felt in 1797. The padres repeated the usual prayers and included special sentiments for the safety of the Spanish king while he was a Napoleonic captive in France.

A call for contributions was again made and although the total figures are unknown, 1,689 pesos were collected solely from the presidios in 1809. As there was a total military force in California in 1810 of approximately 320 men, excluding invalids at the pueblos, this would indicate a per soldier contribution of some five pesos, lower than before, but still generally confirming the economic value of the average war contribution.

WARS OF SPANISH AMERICAN INDEPENDENCE, 1810–21

Analysis of events in California during the Wars of Spanish American Independence similarly supports the view that California's political and cultural isolation has been overdrawn. Curiously, however, it is to this very period that many historians point as evidence of California's isolation. Charles E. Chapman wrote:

> In the main, the people of the province were ignorant of the reach and importance of the series of wars which were being fought throughout the Americas. They received but little news, and were constantly under the impression that the revolts were nearly over. They never doubted that the King would win. Down to 1818 they themselves were not called upon to take part in the struggle...

John W. Caughey opined that "California...was so effectively isolated from Mexico that Hidalgo's 'Grito de Dolores,' which reverberated through most of Mexico, did not find an echo in this province," while John Francis Bannon concluded that "California was spared contacts with the independence movement until 1818." Hubert Howe Bancroft was the most emphatic:

> The fact that Mexico was in trouble, and either could not or would not aid this distant province with money or supplies, was the sum and substance of the rebellion so far as it had effect in California. From a political and military point of view, the "grito de independencia," and the fierce waves of contention that followed it, died out in the south, nor sent so much as a faint ripple of popular excitement to this distant north-western shore.... Yet mail communication was comparatively uninterrupted, and it is hardly possible that the friars and officers were not constantly informed in private letters of the course events were taking in Mexico. All were strong in their allegiance to Spain. There was as yet not the slightest indication of any popular feeling in favor of independence.

Yet the evidence belies these conclusions of blissful unconcern. Many inflammatory papers urging rebellion reached California during the wars, and at least one group of revolutionary agents, traveling in the guise of actors, attempted to proselytize Californians. More concretely, an actual conspiracy developed in 1811 among as many as sixty soldiers and officers to seize the San Diego

305

Presidio. Five men were imprisoned in chains, including Sergeant José Pico, the father of the future California governor, Pío Pico. Two of the five were released quickly, but of the remaining three, two died after several years' confinement in irons (literally and in addition to their imprisonment), and the last was not released from his chains and prison until Mexican independence was established. Certainly these men, and they are only symptomatic of underlying discontent elsewhere, thought their actions somewhat more than Bancroft's "faint ripple of popular excitement" or Caughey's "echo."

Although Californians were called upon to engage in actual fighting only in connection with Hippolyte Bouchard's raids on the California coast, that very incident offers revealing evidence that many Californians were fully aware of the political implications of Mexico's revolutionary struggle. When the Argentine privateer attacked Monterey in November 1818, the shore battery did considerable damage to the two insurgent ships in the early stages of the fighting. However, the gunners were suddenly ordered to cease firing, under circumstances that might lend support to a belief that a sympathetic officer (Manuel Gómez as artillery commander is usually singled out) was in fact aiding the insurgents.

But whether yea or nea, the important point is that many Montereños contemporaneously believed that their city had been handed over. As the insurgents entered Monterey a steady stream of refugees poured out of the California capital. A man named Inocente García had a house along the line of retreat and his comments are revealing:

Many of the fugitives, some on horseback, others afoot filed past my house and gave me reports of what had happened, and I would put all of this down .... They told me that there was some understanding between the officer who commanded the artillery and the insurgents; that the governor had ordered that they sink the ships at all costs. Jesus Vallejo had a culverin under his charge and shot it with such true aim that he made some gaping holes in the black frigate which was the larger, and put it in danger of sinking, when he got the order to cease fire. The order was brought to him by his own father, Sergt. Ygnacio Vallejo, from the commander of artillery. This same officer would not accede to the plans being

306

made to prevent the landing of the insurgents, and thus they came ashore and destroyed everything.

The point is not whether these accounts of betrayal were true or not, although the accusers included men much calmer than these rumor-ripe refugees. It is rather that the fleeing populace would never have even thought of treachery and betrayal on the part of their own soldiers unless they were fully aware that this was no simple looting adventure of a mere pirate, but rather an expression of an ideological and civil conflict which could in fact generate sympathy and cooperation among at least some Californians. That people were all too well aware of what was involved in the wars for independence is the only explanation for the fears of Padre Olbés of Santa Cruz, in October 1818, after warnings of the impending raid had been received. He reported great public activity at the mission and at nearby Villa de Branciforte in anticipation of Bouchard, "not to fight, but to join them, for such is the disposition of the inhabitants."

SUMMARY

If a colony is vitally concerned about its mother country's foreign and civil wars, then to that extent it is not politically or culturally isolated, regardless of physical distance or difficulty in communicating with the homeland. The evidence suggests that Spanish California was as involved with Spanish and European policies as it could be, given its actual distance from the primary scenes of activity. Californians were frightened of invasion and made contingency plans if that event occurred; were reminded of the current foreign wars every Sunday; were aware of the nature of the revolutionary wars and at least some motivated to active support of the insurgents; and more directly, most paid war levies four times in thirty years and in an amount which constituted a significant economic impact for an individual family. It is impossible to reconcile all this to the image of carefree California, dreaming in a backwash of provincialism. As war alarm succeeded war alarm and each new tax succeeded the last, and certainly as they were

307

cursing their betrayers in flight from burning Monterey, Californians might well have preferred, had they the choice, to be still more isolated and far less concerned.

No Settlement Without Women: Three Spanish California Settlement Schemes, 1790–1800

BY SALOMÉ HERNÁNDEZ

Twenty pair of young eyes turned eagerly eastward searching the horizon for a glimpse of the shoreline of what would be their future home. Their owners, a female companion and nineteen orphans "recruited" as future artisans and settlers of Alta California, looked anxious to touch terra firma after two months on board the Concepción.

THIS SCENE, although not described in any document, is not a far-fetched theoretical scenario for the orphans' arrival on August 24, 1800. The orphans were part of the last formal group of settlers sent to California by Spanish royal officials in Mexico City. During the last decade of the eighteenth century, officials also backed two lesser-known settlement attempts by individual artisans and convicts. With these settlers ended the large scale official settler recruitment response to the foreign encroachment which José de Gálvez, the inspector general of New Spain in the 1760s, had begun decades earlier.

This narrative will attempt to tell the story of the female recruits who were such an integral part of these settlement attempts. It will be shown that women played a major role in these individual schemes and by inference in the major settlement ventures of the Spanish borderlands. Like the males, the female recruits who remained in California added to the *gente de razón* population which reached about 3,000 persons by the turn of the century. They would in turn add more to the numbers as they bore offspring.

When Gálvez began implementation of his military and settlement response to foreign threats to Spanish authority in the 1760s, there were no settlements in California. Indeed, California had languished forgotten for almost two centuries after the discovery of San Diego Bay in 1542. Nonetheless, the much desired settlement process began modestly with the arrival in San Diego of the four-pronged Portolá/Serra expedition of 1769. It must be noted, however, that this was a military venture and no women participated in the effort.

From the beginning of California's mission and pueblo period frontier officials, missionaries, and Spanish subjects had repeatedly petitioned the crown for settlers. Even after Gálvez's departure and the recession of foreign threats, it was obvious that the presidios needed reinforcements and, second, the region needed inhabitants. Military men and royal officials alike agreed with officer Miguel Costansó that the poor California soldiers were "condemned to a perpetual and involuntary celibacy."

Late eighteenth-century requests specifically asked for artisans to teach Indians of the missions, to help presidio soldiers, and to supply civilian needs in towns. California's future depended on the skills of these artisans to build forts, churches, and homes; but the frontier also needed families. Even the missionaries added their encouragement of the recruitment of women. They hoped to bring in the families of the artisans, most of whom worked at the missions. They also hoped that the presence of Hispanic women would serve as a civilizing agent upon the lonely soldiers who often accosted the Indian women. For these reasons the convict and the artisan, with his family, became sought-out additions to the newly established colony.

Officials hoped to send families to California by land because the sea routes from San Blas to San Diego were long and difficult. In addition the ships which plied the coast were small and did not allow for the transportation of large numbers of settler families. Before the families could be sent, however, an overland route to California accessible to military and civilians alike had to be found. Juan Bautista de Anza opened such a route with a group of veteran soldiers in 1775. When he arrived in the new province, not only did he see evidence of the California soldiers' sad condition but he also became convinced that the needs of the region dictated the recruitment of both men and women. Thus Anza seconded the requests for settlers already received by officials in Mexico City.

At the turn of the century, there remained officials who also held Gálvez's concerns and believed that settlement was the correct response to the foreign presence on Spain's frontiers. Men such as Viceroy Branciforte of New Spain took a personal interest in the settlement process in which women became increasingly important and indeed indispensable. Anza and Fernando Rivera y Moncada learned from their own experiences and those of earlier settlers in New Mexico, Texas, Arizona, Sonora, and other provincial regions. They also responded to circumstances in California. Six years after the Portolá expedition, the recruitment for the Anza and Rivera y Moncada expeditions of the 1770s and 1781 included women. Although many of the expedition volunteers were soldiers, they also brought their families. Often, women and children came to outnumber the male recruits in these settlement expeditions.

Rivera y Moncada guided his very first recruits along the Baja California route, via Loreto, while Anza opened the Arizona/California overland route. A few years later, in 1775, Anza led a contingent of 250 persons to California using his newly discovered route. Anza's recruits included twenty-nine wives of soldier/recruits. Six years later, Rivera y Moncada united 174 recruits in Sonora. He sent part of the group via Loreto and part by sea. The larger portion journeyed overland via Tucson and the Colorado River.

Both Anza and Rivera y Moncada took special care to screen the women in order to find suitable female settlers. It did not suffice for a woman to be the wife of a male recruit. Acceptable female

A sketch of a *Californio* in 1790. The artist was with the Malaspina expedition.

A Californio lady as sketched by the artist serving with
the Malaspina expedition in 1790.

recruits were not forced to travel, they had to be willing participants in the expedition. Women had to be of good character and
blood since they and their daughters were potential wives of the
frontier soldiers.

Even before the expeditions reached their destination, the settler ranks increased. Rivera y Moncada's single recruits married in
order to fulfill their promise to their commander and thereby
increased the number of families. The offspring of various Anza
recruits also married and formed new families. Most importantly,
the women also bore children while enroute to their new home.

Although officials were somewhat disappointed in the final tally
of volunteers for the Anza and Rivera y Moncada expeditions, the
experienced leaders were convinced they had good recruits. They
eventually led more than 300 persons to California. These settlers
would increase the Hispanic population in California and later
provide the participants of new settlement ventures within
California.

In a similar manner, the women of the artisan, orphan, and convict groups, as we shall see, also contributed as individuals to the
settlement of Alta California. This is especially true of the
orphans, most of whom remained in California to become known
as the Lorenzanas. Indeed, it must be noted that many of the artisans and most of the convicts had no wish to remain on the frontier
and tried every manner possible to assure their prompt return to
more settled regions. The petitions of the latter group were often
approved, since their actions had often proved them to be undesirable subjects. Since this study looks primarily into the females'
settler/recruit status, future studies must be made to trace the
recruits' later participation in California history.

There is no doubt that the women contributed to the success or
failure of the settlement ventures. In the first group, the wife
became a desired companion to the skilled laborer. In the second
group, the female orphans were equal partners in the scheme. In
the third, only the courage of a devoted wife, who volunteered to
go to California with a convict-husband, made the program
possible.

In the case of the orphans, officials debated at length before making a conscientious decision to include female orphans in the settlement scheme. It became clear that there could be no settlement without women. In the case of the convicts, women had to petition the *oidores* to allow their husbands to exchange a prison sentence of hard labor in San Blas or Cuba for exile in California, on the condition that they would join them. As for the artisans, officials could only hope they would bring their families. Observers believed that the presence of women would influence the married artisans and convicts to remain in California.

Since settlers were needed, Manuel Carcaba, quartermaster for California working under the orders of the viceroy and the military commander of California, coordinated the recruitment and assignment of the diverse groups to the fledgling settlements in the 1790s. The initial recruitment of artisans and their families did not go as smoothly as officials had hoped. When authorities searched for enthusiastic settlers, they found few volunteers who wanted to leave their homes. But the search continued. Recruiters searched for married men because the Spaniards thought a bachelor could not contribute fully to the settlement endeavor. So important did this effort become that the expedition coordinator, Manuel Carcaba, was moved to state that he felt proud to have played "a small role in all the efforts necessarily made to get the families of the artisans" to California.

Although individual artisans and their wives had entered California in previous years, the 1790s heralded the implementation of a formal recruitment policy. California officials specifically asked for more skilled Spanish subjects. Santiago Ruiz, a mason and carpenter, was among the initial recruits in 1791. He took his wife with him. In 1794 authorities in Mexico also recruited Manuel Reyes, a carpenter, for Mission San Carlos, and Antonio Domingo Enríquez, a weaver, for Mission La Purísima Concepción to teach the Indians. In the years that followed other individuals or groups of artisans left for the towns and presidios of the frontier.

On orders from the viceroy, Carcaba renewed his recruitment endeavors in 1795. Among those he recruited was Joaquín Botello, a Spanish tailor, who lived in Mexico City with his wife and six children. Two other artisans, Mariano Tapia, a pottery maker and

315

tile layer, and Mariano Mendoza, a weaver, enlisted and planned to leave their wives Josefa Leonarda Benítez and Antolina Soto behind in the capital with a monthly stipend of ten pesos to be taken from their 500-peso wage. Manuel Muñoz, a bachelor ribbonmaker, also enlisted. Two years later José Faustino Arriola and José Arroyo, both blacksmiths, arrived in the company of Pedro de Alberní. All these men arrived in California with a minimum of delay.

On occasion, women accompanied the artisans. For example, in 1798 José Reyes, a chairmaker, enlisted to teach the Indians his trade. He agreed to leave on the next available ship, with his wife and family, and to remain three years in California. The contract promised a wage of ten *reales* a day from the day of his departure, and a military ration for the trip. His wife also received a military ration for the round trip.

Most contracts lasted from two to six years. The salary likewise varied according to the skill of the individual. Artisans could also look forward to taking advantage of some special rights and privileges, including a possible land grant. In addition to providing wages, officials assisted the recruits and their families during the waiting period, departure, and journey. For the most part, the early- and mid-1790s contracts ended at the turn of the century. Officials could persuade few of the artisans named in the previous paragraphs to renew. In fact, many, like Arriola, requested and received a license to terminate their contracts early. Attrition forced viceregal officials to seek new recruits.

One exception was Manuel Ruiz, a mason, who completed his four-year contract in 1795 and requested an extension. He had begun work on the San Carlos mission church and preferred to work to its completion. He asked that his wife and family be brought from Guadalajara to join him. Father Francisco Fermín de Lasuén, a California missionary, endorsed the request but added that the mason would pay the transport costs out of his wages.

Recruits continued to arrive in California. In 1797 the frigate *Concepción* brought nine new artisans to Monterey. Five had families, but only three wives, Victoria Luna, Felipa Estrada, and María Gertrudis López, planned to accompany their husbands.

316

The Monterey Presidio as sketched by José Cardero in 1791. *Courtesy Museo Naval, Madrid.*

Ultimately, Victoria Luna traveled with five children and Felipa Estrada with none. María Gertrudis decided not to go with her husband while another woman, María Cirila Argüello, made up her mind to go with hers. Each member of the group, including the bachelors and the wives, received ten pesos for the journey from Guadalajara to San Blas.

A special effort was made to encourage the recruitment of artisan families "of clean blood and a good upbringing to establish and propagate civilization among the natives of the land." A skill was desirable, but as in the Anza and Rivera y Moncada expeditions, a wife and family were just as important, because officials believed married men were more apt to remain on the frontier. In the same manner, these leaders gave careful consideration to choosing women of pure blood lines so that they would have the option of marrying members of the troops.

Once in California, women, who were indispensable to the recruitment process, took on added roles. Artisans had their hands full with the duties of their contracts. Thus the responsibility of cultivating the land fell to women. Officials hoped that the families, especially the women, would dedicate themselves to such endeavors as tending garden plots, working on farms, and raising stock to help maintain themselves and their families. Sometimes women made an arrangement with another neighbor or paid laborer to work in their garden. Some wives also helped out in the missions.

Some years later, the governor of California, Diego Borica, lauded the wives of Spanish soldiers and muleteers who worked while their husbands were away on patrol. These wives cared for and worked in their homes, ranches, fields, and gardens and conducted other activities to help the family, and therefore the settlement effort. Another Californian noted that women had shoe shops in their homes where they made their footwear.

Officials wanted such industrious women to travel to California with their husbands. To this end officials expended energy and money to bring women with the artisans but to little avail. By the end of the century another California governor, José Joaquín Arrillaga, complained that not one artisan "had established himself and I do not believe that one will." This lack of success forced officials to search for other means to provide settlers for California. Officials eventually focused their attention on the recruitment of apprentices for the short-term artisans who would be in California. As early as January 1797, Carcaba began considering the vice-regal suggestion that young orphans be evaluated as likely prospects to aid the ailing artisan program.

Soon thereafter the bishops of Mexico City, Puebla, and Guadalajara received a letter from the royal authorities asking that they search orphanages for young boys to be apprenticed. Bishops, who operated many of the orphanages as a religious charity and paid paternal attention to anything that influenced the welfare of the orphans, showed an interest in the selection process. Initially, viceregal officials asked that only boys over six years of age be considered due to the difficult journey. They also determined that "no blacks or mulattos be chosen, but only Spaniards, Indians, and mestizos." The restriction of castes was to prevent "the contamination of the good castes of natives of that peninsula."

Carcaba, already noted for his role in recruiting artisans, again proved instrumental in selecting and sending orphans to California. After personally going to the Mexico City orphanage, he wrote in 1797, "I would hope that the choice of orphans be extended to include the females." The orphans were to be distributed among the settlers and other new inhabitants, particularly those lacking children, to be reared and educated according to local customs so that they would become productive subjects.

Since authorities had a twofold task of finding apprentices and increasing the population, they began to consider young female orphans as recruits. Once this decision had been made, officials acted to prevent a loss of potential female candidates. The viceregal court set a moratorium on the custom of placing female orphans of serviceable age in private homes. The bishops of Puebla and Guadalajara stopped parceling out the young orphans. The court fiscal, as a representative of the viceroy, then asked orphanage administrators if there were any eligible girls, and if so, how many. The archbishop and the bishops permitted Carcaba to search for the young females.

319

The Monterey Presidio in 1790. *Courtesy Museo Naval, Madrid.*

Carcaba found no children available in Guadalajara, but the Puebla orphanage had two girls and six eligible boys. The majoriy of the boys were over eleven and already had marketable skills. Although the young recruits had been identified, it was only after the bishops were satisfied as to the details of the transfer that they gave orders to allow the children to be transferred to Mexico City. Delay followed delay, however, and the bishop complained of the difficulties of keeping the boys and girls. He also noted the excessive cost of feeding and clothing the youngsters. Eventually six of the eligible boys ran away, and those that remained were underage or mulatto. The outlook, however, was brighter in Mexico City, where the orphanage had more individuals from which to choose. Unfortunately, of more than one hundred children, only nine males and eleven females qualified. Authorities eventually selected another twelve girls between six and ten to go as female recruits.

Although the Mexican orphans had been identified, nothing was done for a while. When officials finally acted two years later, many of the children were no longer available because they had run away or died. Carcaba suggested that those children who were still available be sent to the hospice (poorhouse) where they would be under better supervision. This transfer was completed in November 1798. Optimists hoped that during the delay more individuals of both sexes would be found and transported, but unfortunately this proved not to be the case. Carcaba recommended that the children be sent off to California immediately, but the departure did not take place until 1799.

To care for the youngsters, Carcaba suggested the use of long, narrow carts with two wheels and a tilt, called *carros matos*, as best for transportation and protection against inclement weather. After a lengthy investigation, government officials found the building of wagons, renting of mules, hiring of muleteers, and paying of escort too costly and therefore asked for bids to transport the group as inexpensively, safely, and comfortably as possible to San Blas. Francisco Barrón, a merchant, made the lowest bid at 4,000 pesos. After much negotiation, Barrón agreed to return the cost of unused food and charge only 3,600 pesos. Although pressed for time by the sailing season, he refused to discuss lowering the estimate to accommodate for runaways and any deaths that might occur. He argued that the cost would be the same "for twenty individuals as for sixteen." He also offered to find a doctor, to supervise the boys himself, and to find a woman to care for the girls.

Custom required that a woman be contracted to accompany the girls. She was to be a woman of experience, judgment, and good conduct, who would accompany them on the whole journey and protect them from the actions of their youth or from the insults of the muleteers. The escort also had to be made up of men of honor and good conduct. Barrón also offered to feed the orphans three times a day with "decency and frugality, and not with heavy foods that would endanger their health." He likewise promised that all the orphans would be cared for according to the needs of their "age and sex." In regard to the young women, Barrón stated, "I will take the women, most of them young girls," in a four wheeled covered cart pulled by mules.

The children, who became known in California as the Lorenzanas because they took the name of the archbishop of Toledo who was their benefactor, are listed below.

Both Carcaba and Barrón drew up lists of the children. The lists contain but small discrepancies. A third extant list is almost identical to the first except María Gertrudis is listed as a Spaniard and Carlos as a mestizo. Carcaba gives an older age for many of the orphans, which may be explained by his wish to fulfill the age requirement, but it is not clear why he would underestimate the age of the older girls. The report of the final disposition of the orphans in 1803 supports Barrón's higher age estimates for the older girls.

The list includes four mestizos and two mestizas, two Spanish boys and eight girls, and two Indian boys and one girl. Descriptions of complexion seem to bear out these racial classifications. For example, Mariana is described as being of "clear rosy tint"; Valeriana with "red hair and complexion"; Felipe de Jesús of "rosy color"; and José Victor as of a "dark color, that tends toward a mixture of Indian and mulatto." By contrast the well-known early eighteenth century Texas Isleño expedition was comprised of

CARCABA LIST			BARRÓN LIST	
Name	*Age*	*Caste*	*Name*	*Age*
José Victor Lorenzana	10	mestizo	José Victor Cano	8
Juan Vicente	10	Indian	Juan Vicente Vásquez	7
José María Macedonio	10	mestizo	Macedonio Suárez	12
Manuel Felipe de Jesús	10	Spaniard	José Ma. Felipe Jesús	8
José María de Dolores	10	Spaniard	José Ma. Dol. Avilés	9
José María Jacinto	10	mestizo	José Jacinto Ortiz	10
Domingo Tomás	10	mestizo	Domingo Tomás Cisneros	7
José Timoteo	10	mestizo	José Timoteo Fernández	7
Carlos Lorenzana	10	Indian	Carlos Téllez	7
[Not in Carcaba list]			Ma. de Jesús Torres	22
Ma. Francisca Ignacia	15	Spaniard	María de Francisca	17
Ma. Josefa Pasquala	14	Spaniard	María Pasquala	19
María Vicenta	13	mestiza	Vicenta	13
María Margarita	10	Indian	Margarita	9
María Toribia	10	Spaniard	Tadea	9
Ma. Jesús Valeriana	10	Spaniard	Valeriana	10
María Ana Josefa	10	Spaniard	Mariana	10
María Alexa Josefa	10	Spaniard	Inez	10
Polinaria Ma. Guadalupe	10	Spaniard	Apolinaria	7
Leonarda Joaquina	10	Spaniard	Leonarda	11
María Gertrudis	12	mestiza	María Gertrudis	18

Canary Islanders. Recruits for the Anza and Rivera y Moncada parties were of a varied racial mix, but the mestizo predominated. Anza and Rivera y Moncada had made an initial effort to recruit Spaniards but Spanish volunteers were not so easily found especially in the borderlands. Ultimately these leaders had to settle for hard-working mestizo recruits.

For a while, it seemed all obstacles had been overcome, but officials had not counted on the recruits and problems they might cause. Viceroy Miguel José Azanza soon received a letter from Juan Marquez de las Amarillas written on behalf of the orphan Doña María Gómez, a young woman who had been raised in the home of José Díaz de Rivera, deceased secretary of the ecclesiastical *cabildo*, and who had been selected as a recruit. Since the Mar-

323

quez had promised the deceased guardian to care for the girl, he argued that he planned to place her in the Colegio de Belen to study music and other skills and eventually supply her a dowry to enter a convent, something he still wanted to do. The Marquez also argued that her delicate health made an arduous journey to California impossible. The fiscal answered that the Marquez had no legal rights in the matter, and thus his request could not be approved without leading the way for similar petitions that would endanger the program.

The petitions did come as the fiscal had foreseen. A second orphan, María de Jesús Torres Lorenzana, initiated her own request to remain in Mexico. She asked the viceroy for protection from the dangers to which her honor and soul would be exposed if sent on this voyage. She also wrote that she and her two sisters had a religious vocation and should be given dowries to enter the convent rather than be sent to a far-flung frontier. The fiscal countered her arguments by stating that she obviously had not been instructed as to the objective of the recruitment and the wishes of the king or she would not have refused to go.

As an orphan, María de Jesús knew she might be forcibly recruited. Realizing that she could not prevent the inevitable, she hired on to care for the children. Arriving at the poorhouse on November 29, she wrote to the viceroy of the long journey and the need for clothing. She and the other orphans had two changes of clothing, and they were fearful of being left "naked." The fiscal found her request for clothing reasonable and promised to take action.

A third orphan became the subject of an exchange of letters with Doña María del Rosario, widow of Simón Recio. Doña María asked that María Josefa Pasquala Lorenzana, whom she had cared for since infancy, be returned to her for proper medical care. Since orphanage officials hoped to employ her in one of the many tasks of the institution, they insisted on keeping her. When the chaplain told her that the orphanage physicians could better care for the young orphan's epileptic condition, Doña María desisted from her request, on the condition that María Josefa be given a thorough medical examination.

Officials would soon answer the requests of both women. Indeed, orphanage administrators had already arranged for Doctor José Vicente de Peña to evaluate the health, constitution, and strength of the orphans and to certify their ability to make the land journey to San Blas and the sea voyage to California. Dr. Peña believed all the orphans were basically fit to travel, except for María Josefa Pasquala. He also believed all the orphans had inherited the weak character of the parents who had abandoned them. He feared that even if the orphans departed in good physical condition, they would only fall ill. Other medical experts agreed only with Peña's positive evaluation. They also disagreed that Pasquala should be prevented from joining the others. They recommended she be given special care and "be bled without delay," and frequently thereafter, to avoid future mishaps. Relying on these opinions, the viceroy decided against any further delays.

To follow up on María de Jesús's request for clothing, officials asked for a report of the quality and quantity of the orphans' clothing. As a result of the study, officials budgeted some 981 pesos to clothe the orphans. Female inmates of the hospice were to sew shirts, skirts, ties, and other simple white pieces from material in stock, but a tailor would have to make coats, pants, and overskirts. At the same time, the purveyor would supply the orphans with such goods as knapsacks, shawls, stockings, shoes, and hats.

The boys received one knapsack, two coats, ties, a pair of pants, four handkerchiefs, and a pair of shoes. Three received cotton stockings. The girls' wardrobe was more ample. It included one knapsack, two blouses, ties, bedsheets, half-handkerchiefs, from two to four housecoats, four small handkerchiefs, a pair of shoes, and four to seven skirts of wool and local cloth. In addition, some girls received pillows, shawls, stockings, and blankets, depending on their needs. The fiscal ordered that all articles, including the knapsack, be marked with each child's name.

After this initial financial outlay, the treasurer gave Barrón 100 pesos for miscellaneous expenses, including tobacco. Although women smoked in colonial Latin America, one would suppose that the cigars carried as part of the supplies would be primarily for the older boys. Interestingly enough, officials ordered the tobacco for seven young women, whom they said smoked cigars excessively. By supplying them, authorities hoped that the women would not have to ask the soldiers, coachmen, and peons for cigars. In addition, all of the orphans, especially the young boys and girls, were to receive refreshments and fruits. In total, officials spent some 1,000 pesos to feed, clothe, cure, and educate the children after they had been united at the hospice.

The orphans remained at the hospice from November 7 until January 28. There they were fed and clothed. The girls' fare — which included beef at noon and in the evening and chocolate in the morning and afternoon — seemed to be better than that of the boys, suggesting that the girls were considered more fragile and in need of better nourishment for the journey.

As the orphans awaited their departure, Barrón continued to make necessary arrangements. To further insure the safety and comfort of the children, Barrón received *cartas auxiliadoras* that instructed local authorities to give the group any aid they might require, including housing and escorts. Letters in hand and just eight days after taking charge of the children, Barrón escorted the children out of Mexico City, eager to be on his way and fulfill the terms of his contract.

Although little detail is available on the first leg of the journey, probably all went well. On arrival in San Blas, Barrón immediately sent a letter stating that the orphans had arrived ahead of schedule and without any mishap. Since he agreed with local officials that the higher and cooler climate in Tepic was safer than tropical San Blas, and in order to save money on room and board, he kept the "tender innocents" in that inland city. Meanwhile José García, the subdelegate of San Blas, completed arrangements for their embarkation from the port.

Barrón left his charges in the hands of Antonio de Santa María, the subdelegate of Tepic, who in turn gave him a receipt for twelve girls and nine boys, "all well, healthy, and robust with their respective wardrobes." Santa María took the opportunity to question the orphans about their treatment. They all responded in one voice that the treatment had been good, because Barrón readily supplied them with the necessary foods and "likewise with fruits, wine and other things they might request, for which reason they remained very appreciative."

Despite the orphans' positive response, the subdelegate noted the sad state of the children's clothing. Indeed, the young girls were ashamed to come before the official because of their clothing. This situation gave rise to the accusation that Barrón and María de Jesús had failed to discipline the youngsters sufficiently because they tore their clothing while playing with each other. Clearly, however, since normal activity had caused deterioration of the clothes, officials petitioned for the royal authorities to resupply the worn apparel.

Because of these problems, additional expenses were incurred to clothe, feed, and board the children, and eventually buy their passage. Daily expenses were incurred for such items as wood, brooms, grills, grinding stones, cigarettes, soap, candles, laundry, and food. The total bill included the salaries for a woman who cooked — for five pesos a month and the *tortillera* — three pesos. An errand boy received three pesos. These persons worked until June 9 when the children left for San Blas.

Before their departure, María de Jesús wrote a letter praising Barrón's "great care and diligence," but she also took the opportunity to repeat her request for permission to return to Mexico City to be with her real sister. The royal minister argued that she could not abandon the children whom she had helped raise and who loved and respected her "as a mother." He considered her request impossible since it would necessitate a "separation precisely when they [the orphans] needed her vigilance and care, that is, during the period of the sea journey." The young girls needed her even more, he continued, to help them "avoid the sufferings that might result from some disgrace with a sailor." He asked that she remain with them until each would be given a destination in California. Royal officials knew her worth and the difficulty in replacing her and asked a San Blas official, José García, to convince her to continue her work. The parish priest and the local commander both tried to persuade her to remain with the orphans. María de Jesús remained unconvinced and wrote another letter soon after her arrival in the port on June 14. She stood fast despite receiving no answer to her first petition.

In this third letter she stressed "her great love" for her real sister, who was not with them, and petitioned to be freed from the exile she endured. She also spoke of the illness of two of her "orphan sisters," Apolinaria and Inez. But with a tone of resignation, she ended her letter stating she would continue on to California with her sisters. With this goal in mind, she sailed off with the orphans to California.

All but one orphan, who died before disembarking, arrived in Monterey on the *Concepción*. This left twenty people to deal with and, as Apolinaria later stated, "distribute like dogs." While the group remained in Monterey from August 24 to October 6, Macedonio and Timoteo were placed in the homes of two presidial soldiers. Five females remained under the care of presidial quartermaster, Hermenegildo Sal. Twelve other orphans departed for other ports, including Los Angeles and Santa Barbara. Sal continued supplying the women under his care with food, candles, shoes, soap, and other items. Despite the hopes of many, the results proved disappointing. Raymundo Carrillo, the orphans' protector, complained that female orphans generally lacked those skills appropriate to their sex, such as cooking and sewing. This lack of home skills caused suffering to the female orphans since Carrillo found it more difficult to place them.

Since many of the children were too young to marry immediately upon their arrival, they had to go live with different families. Carlos, Jacinto, Tadea, and Margarita were placed in Santa Barbara homes. Six of the other young men and women lived in temporary homes in San Diego and others went on to Los Angeles. By 1803 three young girls were married. A fourth, Gertrudis, was a widow.

To help the orphans during the initial stage, officials spent additional money to pay for food and the wages of the San Carlos Mission Indian who assisted in the kitchen, brought wood, and even washed the orphans' clothing. Carrillo complained they did not apply themselves to anything unless pressured to do so. Despite the problems, another officer saw that some were "of marriageable age and although their stay might not be a short one, they will be given all the help and security possible."

One of the unskilled orphans who found difficulty being placed, was twelve-year-old Mariana Díaz Lorenzana. She continued to live in the commandant's house without being placed or employed, because she did not know how to cook a meal or sew a garment. Ten-year-old María Valeriana Lorenzana likewise had not found employment because of "her uselessness." In time they would learn because the image of the California women required that women be good future mothers. Foreigners in California would later be touched by the "beauty, grace, kindness, and above all the virtue of the Hispanic ladies," including the offspring of the Lorenzanas.

The older girls soon fulfilled their goal of becoming settler mothers by marrying California soldiers. For example, by November 1800, María Pasquala had married Joaquín Juárez, and María Francisca had married Juan María Hernández, both presidial soldiers. A year later María Inez and María Leonarda married the Catalonian Volunteers José Palafox and Juan Álvarez. Sal supplied them with new clothing because he judged their attire unfit for a wedding. In August 1802, María de Jesús married Miguel Brito, an artilleryman, but left California on the frigate *Princesa* that same year. Her departure left only Apolinaria in the Carrillo home. As the organizers of this effort had wished, the other girls had gone on to become brides.

María Gertrudis's case exemplifies the settler role thrust upon the female orphans who had not volunteered. She married José Truxillo, a Catalonian Volunteer who died on February 15, 1803. After his death she immediately petitioned for a license to return to Mexico City. Officials in Mexico City countered that she erroneously "believed that merely by marrying and becoming a widow she had fulfilled her destiny," but such was not the case. The objectives proposed by the Superior Government when they sent her and others of her class, were more encompassing. If she were allowed to leave, "the rest will do likewise using the same or another excuse." Official opinion noted that she was merely sixteen years old and could marry again and contribute to the population of the peninsula. She would not be abandoned but would receive monetary aid. Thus, women were clearly to remain in California. At the same time this case also illustrates the reluctance of some women to endure life on the California frontier.

Until the receipt of María Gertrudis's petition, viceregal officials had paid little attention to the orphans after their arrival in California. Except to order the director of the hospice to send "an annual remittance of young orphans of both sexes" to California, which was not done, the orphans seemed to have been forgotten. In 1803, responding to María Gertrudis's case, the officials requested reports from California on the final disposition of the orphans. Concerned officials expressed the wish that orphans of both sexes be raised, educated, and, in the case of the boys, be taught such trades as carpentry or weaving. Because of later criticism of the young girls, California officials also suggested that the girls should learn to weave or sew.

Unfortunately, no more orphans were sent. In addition, artisans still in California did not remain for long. Worse still, it was difficult to enlist new professionals. For this reason, orphans were not able to learn trades. Several of the boys turned to crime and forced officials to place them "with honorable citizens, who could keep them in line and instruct them in the principles of religion." Although the young girls did not become delinquents, their obvious lack of skills meant that they were not very useful, except as prospective wives to the settlers. Because of the problems with the orphans, officials saw the continued need for more new settlers. Since families and youngsters of Mexico City could not be persuaded to go northward, officials decided to try another segment of the population.

Carcaba believed the time was appropriate to implement an alternative plan presented in 1791 and contacted the Audiencia of Guadalajara about the feasibility of turning sentenced criminals into settlers. Since guilty prisoners were often sentenced to hard labor in Havana and Veracruz, Carcaba hoped to "send prisoners that did not have bad habits," along with their families, to California as settlers. On receipt of Carcaba's request, the judges began entertaining requests presented by convicts' wives who informed the oidores that they would join their husbands as settlers in California, if the sentences could be served in California rather than elsewhere in Mexico. The women hoped that they would be united with their husbands, and the whole family would be free, albeit on some far-off frontier. Officials decided that both the convicts and their wives were to be selected only if they were "robust and of suitable age." The convicts were also to remain behind bars until they left for their destination.

An example of a convict/recruit family was that of Juan Antonio Hernández and María Antonia Sandoval. When María Antonia heard that her spouse had been sentenced to ten years in a Havana prison, she courageously asked the court for mercy, begging instead that he be sent to Alta California or sentenced to labor in the public works of Guadalajara. In her petition María Antonia mentioned her husband's advanced age and emphasized that he had a large family, with five young maidens who could possibly be wed in the province, and vowed she and her family would accompany him. How she and other wives learned of the possibility of commuting the sentence and what to emphasize in their petition is now unclear, but possibly local authorities approached them. The oidores unanimously approved the change of sentence, which specifically stated that "the wife and children were obligated to follow him according to the sentence." The entire family was to leave for Monterey.

The Hernández family received aid for expenses incurred on the journey. The older children, Magdalena, Serafina, Luisa, Juana de Dios, and José Bustillo, received eighty pesos. In addition, while in San Blas, officials also gave the parents ten pesos for the younger children and gave each family member a ration worth one *real* a day. When the Hernández family boarded the *Concepción*, their oldest daughter, Magdalena, had deserted and could not be found. Despite the loss of one member, the family was not reprimanded and continued to receive its rations on board as well.

They arrived in California, where Juan Antonio's drunk and riotous ways would have justified further imprisonment. Governor Arrillaga, however, set him free and allowed him to return to his home because of "the innocence of his family who had followed him to this fate." Ten years later, after completing his sentence,

331

Juan Antonio requested a license to return to San Blas. His "scandalous" comportment made it easy for Arrillaga to grant the request. Since several of the offspring had left, only part of the family and two grandchildren accompanied María Antonia and her wayward husband.

Upon their return to San Blas, the Hernández family complained that the captain of the ship gave them only four rations instead of the six due them. They also accused the California presidio officials of refusing to aid them and thus forcing them to make use "of their best clothing and of furnishings" to sustain themselves. The captain defended his actions by stating that the family accepted these conditions rather than wait for another ship. The commander argued that the government had not obligated itself to pay for the return journey. Ultimately, both officers were exonerated.

Juan Antonio Hernández turned out to be a heavy responsibility. It seems obvious that had it not been for his suffering wife, he would have been put in jail even in California. Other recruit families who volunteered to go to California on June 20, 1801 were not as much a burden to the California officials. The group included María Luz de Fuentes, who agreed to serve a sentence with her husband, Martín Vela. Still another woman, María Apolinaria Galván, offered to go with her husband, Cristóbal Pimentel. Each individual, male and female, received his ration/wage of ten pesos. The recruits and their escort arrived in Monterey on August 9, having lost one member through desertion.

In another case, María Gregoria de Ramírez offered to accompany her husband, Rafael Ramírez, and her young son if her husband's sentence for involuntary manslaughter were changed. The judges reviewed the Ramírez file and accepted María's proposal. Soon thereafter, the audiencia agreed that the sentence was to be carried out in California rather than Havana and the family left.

Interestingly enough the audiencia denied some pleas for commutation of sentence, including that of José Severino de Navarro and his wife, María del Carmen, an Indian from the Zapotlán mission. José had escaped from Veracruz to be with his wife after she had been left without protection upon the death of his mother. His petition read, "to present my petition, I kneel before the feet of the Audiencia with the aim that they might grant my petition to complete my sentence in the Presidio of Monterey, and that I might have the privilege of taking my wife, who is all that I love." Despite this moving statement and his offer to serve four extra years, his request was denied. The preceding requests were from wives who appeared personally before the judges. It is not clear whether these were the only cases the judges accepted.

These cases illustrate the dedication of authorities to find families to populate California. Even with the convicts, officials took care in selecting the families. A convict's case would not be heard unless the wife volunteered to go with her husband. Married men were sought, as they were on the Anza and Rivera y Moncada expeditions mentioned briefly in the introduction. In contrast to the previous settlement efforts, no single men and women convicts were recruited. Officials interviewed the men and their wives, cared for them before their departure, and gave them rations and/or wages. Even the children were entitled to aid. Interestingly, neither the artisan nor the convict was a truly voluntary settler who wished to make a new life in California. They generally wanted to return to Mexico, and often did so, with their families.

Thus when the California military commander, José Joaquín Arrillaga, received a letter asking for an evaluation of the convict/family recruitment program, his reply was negative. Arrillaga sent the questionnaire on to his subordinates. From Monterey, Raymundo Carrillo stated that "the conduct of those sent is scandalous. The majority of them brag about their ugly crimes and even worse, do so without thinking seriously about reform." Pedro Alberní, another California officer, ill and unable to write a full report, agreed with Carrillo. Both wanted to build the region with good, upstanding subjects. In view of the failure of the program, Governor Pedro Fages requested "useful men, not those who have committed criminal acts."

These officers also described the sad condition of several convicts, whom, they agreed, were weak rather than vicious men. Father Fermín Lasuén added that the convict did not have "a quality, ability, art, or skill that was needed" in California. Ultimately the bad behavior of the convicts and their lack of skills outweighed the positive influences of their settler families. Thus, no more convicts were sent.

Because of the basic flaws in the convicts, the convict system and the artisans' short-term contracts, two of the attempts to populate California seemed doomed to fail from the beginning. Convicts and artisans petitioned to leave California. Nonetheless these individuals or their offspring, although small in number, increased the population of California. Their reluctance to stay probably stemmed from the most important difference between these recruits and those of the Anza and Rivera y Moncada expeditions — they were not volunteer settlers. Although the convicts were forced to bring their spouses, few stayed to make a new life in California. The role of women is noteworthy in each group. Some of the artisans brought wives and families to keep them company. These women became active members of the frontier society. Wives and families augmented the family income through their work raising stock or harvesting crops. The women also bore children who increased the population. Thus the presence of women was equally vital to two of these settlement attempts. Women were settlers in their own right. Without women, the settlement activity would not have been successful. Their experience was as much a part of the military/settlement plan Gálvez began implementing as was the men's experience. They were an integral part of the response to the petition for settlers which was echoed by administrators, military and missionaries.

Just as Anza and Rivera y Moncada took special care to screen the women in order to find suitable female settlers, so did Barrón. In his selection of the females, uppermost in his mind was their future role as wives and mothers. Except for the orphans, either male or female, who had little to say about their future, willing female recruits of good character and blood were sought.

Of these three expeditions, the orphans — male and female — had the longest-ranging effect on California's future. Although neither the males or females succeeded in completing an apprenticeship program, even a superficial look at mission, pueblo, and presidio marriage and birth records demonstrates their participation in a successful completion of the second goal — helping to populate the region. Despite the female orphans' apparent lack of domestic skills, they married and bore many children, thus contributing to the settlement of Alta California. Indeed, of the female orphans, only Apolinaria remained single to serve God, king, and fellow citizens in southern California. She became known as the *Beata* for her work. Doña Juana Machado, a contemporary to Apolinaria, notes:

She dedicated herself to the service of the Church and to the care of the padres at mission San Diego. There in the mission she taught girls, whose parents asked the favor, to read and write. She did not have a formal school, but devoted what time she could to it. She went by the name of Doña Apolinaria de la Cuna. She was godmother to a large number of children of civilized people as well as of Indians.

Apolinaria stated herself, "I, who had no daughters, had to care for the children of all." Although her contribution is unusual and extraordinary, all the women contributed to help build and strengthen the frontier. Luis Martín studied the *beatas* in Lima and there are many similarities between Apolinaria's activities and those of women in Peru. One historian's description of the unmarried female teachers seems appropriate:

. . . just as George Washington, though childless, is hailed as the "Father of this country," so she has permitted no one to beckon her into a life of devotion in a single home, but has remained the "High Priestess" of an ever-growing Spanish American group. . . She has been peacemaker, and to hundreds of young people "A Mother Confessor."

APPENDIX A:

ARTISAN CONTRACTS, 1794
Province of Californias

News of the artisans which are found here, with data on their names, titles, trade, wages, length of their contracts, date of the contract, expiration date, and place they are to be found.

Title	Trade	Name	Time of Contract	Daily Wage	Date of Contract	Expiration of Contract	Place
Mtro.	Bricklayer	Manuel Ruiz	4 years	18 reales	1/23/1791	1/23/1795	Mission San Carlos
Ofcl.	Cantero	Salvador Rivera	"	12	"	"	Mission San Luis
Ofcl.	Cantero	Joaquin Rivera	"	10	"	"	Monterey
Mtro.	Carpenter	Jose Aᵗᵒ Ramírez	"	10	1/1/1792	1/1/1796	Mission San Carlos
Mtro.	Bricklayer Cantero	Santiago Ruiz	"	14	1/4/1792	1/4/1796	Monterey
Mtro.	Blacksmith	Pedro Gzlz García	"	14	"	"	Mission San Luis
Mtro.	Miller Carpenter	Cayetano López	"	11	"	"	Mission San Luis
Ofcl.	Cantero	Pedro Alcantará	"	7	"	"	Mission San Carlos
Mtro.	Weaver	Antonio Henríquez	"	12	2/1/1794	2/1/1798	Mission Sta Cruz

Signed Monterey, December 13, 1794
Diego de Borica

APPENDIX B:
ARTISAN CONTRACTS, 1797
Province of Californias

News of the artisans which are found here, with data on their names, titles, trade, wages, length of their contracts, date of the contract, expiration date, and place they are to be found.

Title	Trade	Name	Time of Contract	Daily Wage	Date of Contract	Expiration of Contract	Place
Mtro.	Weaver	Antonio Henríquez	4 years	12 pesos	2/1/1794	2/1/1798	Mission San Carlos
Ofcl.	Bricklayer	Toribio Ruiz	"	1 peso	11/10/1795	11/10/1799	San Diego
Mtro.	Tailor	Joaquin Botello	5 years	1,000 pesos/yr	10/22/1795	10/22/1800	Monterey
Mtro.	Ribbon-maker	Manuel Muñoz	"	500 pesos/yr	"	"	Monterey
Mtro.	Weaver	Mariano Mendoza	"	600 pesos/yr	"	"	Mission San Juan
Mtro.	Bricklayer	Manuel Ruiz	6 years	14 reales	1/25/1791	6/31/1797	Mission San Carlos

Monterey, January 1, 1797, Diego Borica

337

APPENDIX C:

LETTER OF MARÍA DE JESÚS LORENZANA TO VICEROY

Exmo. Sr. Dn Miguel Joseph Azanza: Venerado Padrecito de mi mayor respeto: es cierto que VE [vuestra excelencia] siempre haze reminiscencia de sus vasallos que le dan el beneplácito de obedecerle en lo que VE les manda; más es ignorancia mía recordarle mi regreso breve por que ya me lo prometió, y me lo cumplirá; pero para tener el gusto de que ya lo tiene comunicado quiero tener un pasaporte para mi defensa.

Los conductores nos llevaron a este pueblo con el mayor esmero y cuidado y todos estamos buenos, y saludamos a VE con el mayor rendimiento y por consiguiento lo pasamos bien al cuidado del Sr. Subdelegado.

Dios Nro. Sr. guarde a VE los Años que le desea esta su humilde criada que SPLB.

María de Jesús Lorenzana,

Tepic, March 14, 1800,

Archivo General de la Nación, AGN/CA-41/31134-v.

The Economy of the Alta California Missions, 1803–21

BY ROBERT ARCHIBALD

ON JUNE 26, 1803, Father President Fermín Francisco de Lasuén died. The following day he was solemnly buried at the foot of the altar in the chapel of Mission San Carlos near his missionary companions, Juan Crespí and Junípero Serra. Lasuén and Serra, opposites in personality, had firmly planted Spain upon the soil of Alta California. The affable and yet firm Lasuén had inaugurated the "golden age" of the California missions. Staple crop production had reached limits undreamed of by the pioneers of Serra's day. During Lasuén's tenure as Father President nine new missions were begun, bringing the total to eighteen. Under the firm prodding of the gentle Basque priest, older missions implemented systems of irrigation, orchards were planted and buildings were improved. Technicians were imported from New Spain who taught the secrets of their crafts to Indian neophytes. By Lasuén's death in 1803, the mission chain was well supplied with competent weavers, masons, carpenters, blacksmiths, leather workers and even ribbon-makers. Some experiments had faltered; notably hemp culture and a fur-trade monopoly. Serra, the founding pioneer, had laid the basis for the missions and Lasuén, gentle and conciliatory, had brought them to their peak of development.

The years from 1803 to 1821 witnessed turmoil, revolution and bloodshed throughout Hispanic America as disgruntled Creoles took advantage of the discomfiture of the Spanish monarchy at the hands of Napoleon, and the consequent turmoil in Spain. California had no Hidalgo, Bolívar or San Martín. It was little affected by the ideology of revolution, although the revolution itself profoundly affected the area. The decline of Spain's power since the halcyon days of Charles III had little by little opened the gates to foreign intruders. The years from 1803–21 were to see what had been a trickle become a flood. The process was given much impetus when normal trade channels were interrupted by revolution signaled by the "Grito de Dolores" of Father Hidalgo in 1810. Foreigners became an increasingly familiar sight along the California coast. The interruption of pay and supplies for the presidios made them dependent upon the food surpluses and manufactured items which only the missions could supply. The missions became the economic mainstays of California.

The relative wealth of the missions in this time of scarcity eventually led to attacks upon them and growing demands for their secularization. The presidial soldiers and even commandants who were deprived of food, clothing and pay by the interruption of the San Blas trade, were embittered by the apparent unwillingness of the missions to share the bounty which was theirs.

Without a doubt the most difficult area of the mission economy to assess during the period from 1803 to 1821 is the impact of smuggling operations. This trade, which was blatantly illegal, finds slight mention for obvious reasons in mission reports. The problem of smuggling was common to all of Spain's colonies in the New World during the period. The trade, although illegal, was profitable to both parties. Spanish mercantile restrictions gave the missions no legal outlet for excess trade items. The problem had been recognized and a solution proposed by Naval Lieutenant Don Francisco de Paula Tamariz. Tamariz, in an 1814 memorial to the king, proposed that California might be open to trade with other Spanish possessions since it could supply much food. He reminded the king of the largess of the California missions which had no legal outlet. He noted that weekly the missions butchered, for the maintenance of the neophytes, 350 or 400 cows. In one year the missions slaughtered close to 19,000 head of cattle. An equal number of hides were available for export, in addition to 26 or 30

340

thousand *arrobas* of tallow and fat. The hides were discarded since they lacked a market and the tallow and fat was worth 4 to 6 *reales* of silver per *arroba*. Tamariz noted the smuggling which was already prevalent. Some 2,500 to 3,000 furs came into the hands of the missions annually. Few of them were remitted to San Blas because China-bound "Boston Men" appeared each year to purchase the furs. The missionaries, he added, had no scruples about engaging in this nefarious business. In spite of the lieutenant's entreaties, a faltering Spain was unable to take advantage of the production which California had to offer.

After 1800 the connection with San Blas ceased to be an adequate outlet for the burgeoning mission economies. California furs, which were carried to China via San Blas, followed a laborious and expensive route. The San Blas vessels took skins from California to San Blas where they were loaded on mules and sent off to Mexico City. From there they were returned to Acapulco where the Manila Galleon loaded and transhipped them to the Philippines where the Chinese completed the last leg by taking them to the mainland. Obviously the extent of the trade was severely limited by cargo space and profits were limited by what could at best have been astronomical expenses.

The problem of insufficient supplies and a limited market was a recurrent theme. In 1806 Father José Senán at Mission San Buenaventura complained that during the year 132 skins of tallow weighing 741 arrobas, 200 dressed cowhides and 64 sheepskins had been consigned to an agent in Mexico, but that the agent had not settled the mission account in two years. In 1808 Senán claimed that mission production had been so great that it was impossible to ship at a profit. San Buenaventura had that year produced 200 skins of tallow weighing 1,428 arrobas which were sold to an unnamed purchaser in Mexico who was to pay the Syndic at Tepic. The same purchaser also contracted for fifty skins of lard weighing 321 arrobas. The lard and tallow had brought the mission 1,956 pesos, 2 reales. The core of the problem preventing the marketing of mission surpluses was transportation. Shipments from each mission were accepted on a prorated basis. This was due to the limited cargo space of the San Blas supply vessels and the fact that ships' officers tended to speculate on the tallow trade on their own and hence take up valuable space. Even hemp, which was produced by order of the king to supply cordage for ships, ran into the problem of inadequate transportation. By 1810 Señán complained that 450 animal skins remained unsold at Mission San Buenaventura. These pelts would have yielded 3,000–4,000 pesos. Further, he argued, hemp was produced for the king's account, yet its export was limited by the capacity of the San Blas vessels.

An inadequate market for mission products was compounded by the uncertainty of payment which made illicit trade with its immediate and certain rewards more attractive. The missions were frequently called upon to contribute surpluses to the presidios, and in return they received a credit entry in the account book of the *habilitado*. When the balances mounted up a draft was issued on Mexico City. At best two years passed before the profit on grain sold to the presidios could be realized. Since a bill of credit was of no use in California, it was left to the Procurator of the College of San Fernando in New Spain to purchase with it items of utility to the missions. Added to the fact that the presidios paid low prices in the first place were the transportation charges on goods shipped to California. This was in contradiction to the suggestion by former governor Felipe de Neve that grain should be paid for in the form of merchandise needed by the missions at Mexico City prices. Even though furs were shipped to San Blas it was done reluctantly since risks incumbent in shipping and storage were borne entirely by the missionaries. Fray Martín Landaeta at San Francisco complained that a shipment of furs remained in the hands of the *comisario* because they had not been registered. What doubly disturbed him was the possibility that they would be treated poorly while in storage.

The restrictions placed upon the missions by the prevailing system of mercantilism, the low prices, uncertainty of payment and hazards of shipment combined to make illicit trading attractive to Califomia missionaries. The official attitude of the Spanish government between 1800 and 1810 was one of benign neglect. Possibly due to a lack of money and manpower, laws relating to illegal trading in California were never strictly enforced. California became a smuggler's paradise and the missions benefited.

In 1803 Fray Landaeta warned his superior of the attractiveness of trade with Americans. He explained that he was remitting four sea otter pelts but that three American ships had cast anchor in the course of the summer and that they were willing to pay 8 to 10 pesos per pelt. Discreetly, he added that "even if they had paid much more, I would not have engaged in smuggling." Despite the holy father's protestations, Americans found the pious Franciscans very willing to barter on the side.

William Shaler, a true Connecticut Yankee, found the missionaries to be willing accessories in smuggling. From 1803 to 1805 he was a frequent, although clandestine visitor to the missions. In his journal of 1804 he gave welcome advice to all who would follow:

For several years American trading ships have frequented this coast in search of furs and they have left annually in the country about $25,000 in specie and merchandise. The missionaries are the principle monopolizers of the fur trade. Anyone acquainted with the coast can easily obtain abundant provisions.

Shaler was able to find provisions for his vessel, the *Lelia Byrd*, with remarkable ease. By the time he finished canvassing the missions, some twenty, or at least one-half of the pious padres owed him money. Of these, only four had honored their notes, proving to be no more prompt in bill paying than the Spanish government which they criticized.

Although in contravention of the Nootka Sound Convention, Shaler was not the only trespasser on the Spanish domain. By 1810 the Yankees became bolder as the interruption of regular supplies increased demand for clandestine trade. For example, in 1812 George Eayrs was trading with the padre at San Luis Obispo. In return for 58 otter skins, grain and meat, the mission received $1,384 worth of goods.

The eruption of the Mexican independence movement in 1810 inaugurated more than a decade of turmoil which was resolved only by absolute independence from Spain. Although peripheral to the struggle, the balance of power in California was altered. The missions found themselves in the seemingly enviable position of having a virtual monopoly on technical skills and the food supply. Smuggling now became a necessity of life. Presidial soldiers whose families were improperly clothed and poorly fed were embittered by the missionaries who supplied them meagerly and reluctantly.

The supply shortage forced the missionaries to begin production of such items as clerical habits, sandals and a host of other items which had previously come from Mexico. In addition, attempts were made to increase food production to meet presidial demands. To supply items for trade, more encouragement was given to Indian neophytes to hunt otter. Inevitably the padres began to depend more heavily upon illicit trade for those items which they could not produce. Adelbert von Chamisso, the naturalist aboard the Russian ship *Rurik*, noted that only the smuggling trade, which Governor Pablo Vicente de Solá attempted to suppress, had been able to supply indispensable articles. Trade was carried on with Russians, Americans and Peruvians. The *Flora* and *Tagle* from Peru brought cloth and articles to barter. Trade was carried on with Fort Ross and in 1813 amounted to $14,000 worth of goods. Father President Señán complained in 1819 that the province no longer enjoyed its former connections which once supplied necessities. He bemoaned the reliance on foreign supplies because of the outrageous prices which they extorted. The Peruvians had raised the premium which they charged on goods from 15 to 50 per cent. Although the Franciscans nostalgically longed for the "good old days" the impact of the Mexican independence movement had few poor effects, and may even have bolstered the mission economy.

With the passage of time the quarrel over presidial supplies assumed ominous proportions and contributed to the propaganda urging mission secularization. The ability of the missions to sustain their military counterparts testifies to their economic strength. At times the presidios served as middlemen who exacted a profit from the trade carried on between missions and foreign merchants. In 1815 Governor Solá demanded that Mission San Juan Bautista deliver 150 arrobas of flour along with some wool and tallow. The merchandise was sold to a Spanish corvette and in return the mission obtained some plowshares, pickaxes, crowbars, iron and copper kettles.

The supplies of food and other items requisitioned by the presidios from the missions brought little benefit to the missions. In exchange for goods delivered, the missions received from the *habilitados* drafts on the treasury in Mexico City. Although padres and military officials squabbled over prices, the arguments were academic since few of the drafts were ever honored. As early as 1811 some $14,000 worth of mission drafts had accumulated with no money in the Royal Treasury with which to redeem them. Six years later, in 1817, outstanding habilitados drafts in favor of the missions had reached the staggering sum of $400,000. The missions pleaded poverty, but the evidence suggests that they were far from poor.

The variety of items supplied to the presidios provides an idea of the ability of the mission economies to diversify and prosper. In 1815, among other items, San Carlos supplied *serapes*. San Buenaventura contributed mules and leather bags. In 1816 Mission San Buenaventura supplied *sombreros*, tallow drippings (*manteca*), soap, blankets and cloth. Other missions supplied shoes, hides, saddles, mules, knapsacks, muskets, leather shields, cartridge pouches, garters and lances. Obviously some of these articles, such as muskets, were not made at the missions but most were. In 1815 Governor Solá decided to outfit the four presidios with lances and the missions were called upon to furnish the iron, steel and even the blacksmiths and tools. The missions supplied the necessary articles and in return received worthless drafts on Mexico. In addition to the manufactured items, the usual food supplies, cattle, horses and mules were furnished.

The contribution which aggravated the Franciscans the most was cash. This was understandable since in what was essentially a barter economy, cash was a precious commodity and was badly needed for trade. For the most part the only source of cash was foreign trade. Generally the governor would present the demand for cash to the Father President who would then apportion it among the missions on the basis of their cash reserves and general prosperity. In 1814 Mission La Purísima contributed $800 in cash to the habilitado of Santa Barbara by order of Governor José Argüello. One of the largest assessments came in 1821 when the missions donated $3,000 for an arsenal at Monterey. Each mission contributed from $25 to $200. Mission cash reserves were relatively large. A conservative estimate was given by Father Mariano Payeras in 1821 in a protest against Governor Solá's interference in the temporalities of the missions. Most missions, he said, had from $100 to $1,000 in cash and a few $3,000 to $4,000. Despite protests, the missions had the only cash in Alta California.

While the outside world suffered the violence of revolution, the missions of California were able to further increase and diversify mission production. The extent of the production of the mission workshops is difficult to estimate because no reports were required. It is certain, however, that this type of production increased in importance as it became essential to have items with which to barter for necessities from passing foreigners. A critic of the missions, Tamariz, went so far as to claim that the missions were so involved in commercial production that they ignored the needs of the Indians.

Wine production assumed significant proportions between 1803 and 1821, although the basis had been laid as early as 1780. At one time or another grapes were grown at all of the missions, but because of the variable factors of climate and soil, leadership in wine production went to San Gabriel, San Fernando, San Buenaventura and San José. Techniques of grape growing and wine harvesting were archaic. The land was poorly cultivated. Visitors and missionaries disagreed over the quality of mission wine and the disagreement itself proves that it was simply a matter of personal preference. Of all mission wines San Gabriel was commonly agreed to have the best. Don Francisco de Paula Tamariz observed in 1814 that the mission vines had multiplied fruitfully and that they were of the best quality.

After a faltering start in the late eighteenth century, hemp production began to be increased for use as an item of trade. In 1801 hemp production was inaugurated with official encouragement. In that year Joaquín Sánchez, sergeant of marines and an expert in the manufacture of hemp, was sent from Mexico. In 1804 he distributed seed to Mission San Luis Obispo, Purísima, Santa Inés and San José. Hemp was sown in April and harvested in August. The government agreed to pay $4.00 per arroba. The industry seemed to flourish, especially in the south. Bancroft claims that the industry declined after 1810 with the severing of the connection with San Blas and the lack of money to pay for the hemp. Evidence suggests that while hemp production may have declined somewhat, it was traded to foreign vessels for other items.

Hide production was a function of increased presidial demands for shields, saddlery and shoes in addition to the demands of foreign traders. Boston men in particular demanded hides for the developing leather industries of New England. The Spanish were generally unfamiliar with the finer points of tanning and as a result the mission product was suitable only for crude shoes, rough saddles and saddle pads. Hides were poorly scraped and placed into a vat of tanning liquor where they remained until cured. Tallow, another by-product of the cattle industry, had been shipped to Mexico but the slack in the trade was eagerly taken up by Americans after 1810. Tallow was also used at the missions to produce soap for local consumption. Tallow and leather production stimulated the construction of brick vats for tanning and the making of soap, while Indian neophytes provided a cheap labor source.

Generally the period from 1803–21 was a time of elaboration and expansion within the mission system. New buildings were constructed, granaries and houses for neophytes were built. Indians made blankets, coarse cloth and their own clothing with wool shorn from rapidly increasing flocks. Langsdorff observed that the neophytes cleaned and combed the wool in addition to spinning and weaving. The implements and looms were of moderate quality, and the process of fulling was poorly understood. The product was a cloth of ordinary quality. The missionaries refused to wear the products of their own looms until the exigencies of short supply forced them to. Father Señán made a plea in 1812 for clothing for the missionaries lest it become necessary to make them out of the domestically produced sackcloth. He admitted the shortcomings of the mission cloth which he said at times turned out light gray and sometimes whitish or dark. Because of the lack of combs and fulling equipment, the cloth was flimsy and lacked durability.

Masonry and tiles were used to construct aqueducts and reservoirs to supply water for irrigation. Forges became common sights throughout the mission chain. Rude tools were made at the missions, while more sophisticated tools such as molds, saws, files and chisels were purchased from foreigners. In one letter, Señán complained that a diamond point for glass was missing from a recent shipment. This and the fact that glass windows were coming into use point to the development of glass manufacture. Storage buildings were constructed for tallow, corn, peas, soap, butter, salt, wool and hides. Workshops for making tallow, for all types of smith work and for cabinet makers and carpenters appeared. For most of the goods produced, the mission was the only source in Alta California.

The production of agricultural staples remained relatively stable from 1803–21. The pressure for secularization, although increasing, had not yet forced the missionaries into either falsifying annual reports or ignoring agriculture. The fact that agricultural production remained static reflects declining yields and backward technology. The Indian population remained relatively stable, but at the same time the demand from presidios for food for the table and for provisions to trade for manufactured items decreased mission food supplies. This, it seems, would indicate a declining dietary standard for the mission residents.

In consistency with trends established in prior years the missionaries emphasized wheat at the expense of corn. In keeping with Spanish preferences, wheat production was always encouraged wherever it could successfully be grown. At Mission San Carlos wheat and corn harvests were both 200 fanegas in 1803. By 1821 720 fanegas of wheat were harvested and only 80 of corn. The phenomenon was repeated at San Buenaventura where during the same period wheat increased from 1,000 to 4,500 fanegas while corn decreased from 450 to 366 fanegas. San Diego, which had always had problems retaining agricultural self-sufficiency, saw a gradual increase in the production of both wheat and corn. With few exceptions the same process is evident at all of the missions.

Severe droughts hit the missions in 1807, 1809, 1817 and 1820.

Naturally the southern missions suffered most. In the early days of California such events would have caused extreme suffering, and Indian neophytes would have been released to fend for themselves as best they could. The missions of 1810 were much more highly developed institutions than those of 1775. By this time several alternative measures had been developed to insure survival in case of crop failure. The increase in the number of missions decreased the chances that all would simultaneously have a food shortage. The general productivity of missions like San Juan Capistrano and San Gabriel insured that surpluses would be available to aid institutions like San Diego which suffered chronic food shortages. Systems of irrigation also proved to be hedges against drought. Earlier droughts had taught bitter lessons. At San Diego, after the droughts of 1801 and 1803, an extensive system of irrigation works was constructed. This included a dam with an aqueduct which carried water to the mission and fields. The aqueduct was constructed of tiles resting on cobblestones in cement and was approximately one foot deep and two feet wide. The third expedient which could be relied upon in lean years was the storage of surpluses from years of plenty. In 1806 Langsdorff noted that Mission San José had granaries which held 2,000 fanegas of wheat and a proportionate quantity of maize, barley, peas, beans and other grain. At Mission San Francisco, he observed magazines for storing tallow, soap, and ox hides, in addition to facilities for the storage of corn, peas, and beans. While crop failures were indeed serious, the devastation which they caused was not comparable to that of earlier years.

The productivity of the mission gardens continued although no exact statistics were kept. The usual garden herbs and vegetables which had been common since the early days were still grown. Fruit trees had by this time matured and were producing fruit, although success varied from mission to mission depending on climate. At San Francisco, for example, fruit often failed to ripen properly because of the fog.

The period after 1810 began a time of precipitous rise in the death rate caused, among other things, by an alarming infant mortality. In 1818, out of a total of 64,000 neophytes baptized, some

41,000 died. This total includes baptisms for both adults and children and suggests high mortality for both groups. At San Buenaventura the number of deaths exceeded the total number of Indians resident at the mission for the first time in 1809. The same point was reached at Mission Purísima Concepción in 1808, while it was reached as early as 1790 at San Carlos. In 1809 deaths exceeded the total population at San Juan Bautista and continued thereafter. Surprisingly, because of a rapidly increasing number of baptisms, the total population of the missions declined only gradually throughout the period. The signs of future decline were clear. As soon as the rate of baptisms began to decline, so would neophyte populations and with them the mission as a viable institution.

The reasons for the rapid increase in the death rate appear to be variations on those familiar throughout the New World. The Indian was exposed to various alien European diseases for which he had developed little or no tolerance. The first of these was measles whose devastating effect was felt time and time again by the natives of the Western Hemisphere. Langsdorff noted in 1806 that measles had killed thousands of Indians and he went on to add that almost all pregnant Indian women who contracted measles, miscarried as a result. The gathering of Indians at missions simply magnified any epidemic because of the rapid spread of contagious disease among people living in close quarters. A high incidence of inherited venereal disease also took its toll. Several other factors must have aggravated the accelerating death rate. According to William Shaler in 1804, the padres did not seem to know even the rudiments of medicine. Added to this, as mentioned previously, the diet of the mission Indians probably decreased in nutritive value. While the missions still enjoyed an outward appearance of prosperity, the germ of future decline was present.

The mission period in Alta California extending from 1803 to 1821 is unique. In this compressed period of time, the California mission closely approximated the ideal of "the mission as a frontier institution," while in the same two decades those forces which would eventually undermine and destroy the system were gathering. From the outside liberal forces were gaining force in Spain and Mexico and would soon find the mission system incompatible with liberal ideals of equality, liberty and justice. No one could foresee that the California Indian, ill-equipped to compete in western culture, would be destroyed by those very ideals.

The Franciscan padres of California unwittingly participated in the destruction of the very system to which they were so devoted. The mission as an institution was a part of the old regime and its life depended on the absolutism and paternalism of the Spanish monarchy. Mercantilist economic restrictions were an integral part of this scheme. The free trade which the missionaries espoused in their dealings with foreigners was a part of the new liberalism given force by the French Revolution. Free trade would ultimately lessen the economic ties with Spain and eventually break those with Mexico.

Smallpox Immunization in Alta California: A Story Based on José Estrada's 1821 Postscript

BY ROBERT J. MOES, M.D.

ON AUGUST 28, 1821, José Estrada of Monterey wrote a letter to his friend José de la Guerra, in Santa Barbara. The letter had a brief postscript which is tantalizing in the limited information it gives. The postscript states: "The Russian surgeon has brought vaccine and today has vaccinated 54 persons, I being the first."

One cannot readily allow this terse note to a letter to rest without further pursuit. Such pursuit requires evaluation of other information relating to the vaccinations so briefly mentioned by Estrada. Additional understanding of the episode also necessitates consideration of the history of smallpox inoculation and vaccination.

The term "inoculation" (variolation is synonymous) refers to introduction of material from a smallpox lesion into a healthy individual with the intent of producing the disease, hopefully in a mild form, and with resulting lasting immunity. Vaccination, now applied to many types of immunization, originally referred to the production of active immunity against smallpox by inoculating the patient with cowpox virus or with the fluid or "lymph" obtained from a cowpox lesion produced in man.

The development of active immunity by direct or indirect exposure to a disease or to its lesions goes far back in history. No doubt even primitive man observed that contracting certain diseases would safeguard against further affliction with the same condition. This led to purposeful exposure to a disease with the intention of producing lasting immunity; as time went on such exposure being made to less severe forms of the disease.

Ultimately, inoculation was undertaken with the transfer of material from the lesions of smallpox to those who had not had the disease. The procedure was carried out in antiquity, notably in India, China, Persia, and among the Arabs. Understandably, a multiplicity of methods was used. Understandably, too, the process was often surrounded with mystical or religious significance. Frequently the actual inoculation was preceded and followed by a rigidly prescribed period of diet and hygienic management.

An esthetically unsatisfactory Chinese practice involved introducing the dried crusts, or even the liquid pus, of smallpox into the nostrils of the person being inoculated. Commonly, however, the smallpox material was introduced into or beneath the skin. The Brahmins did this by using active friction over a small area of skin until there was a slight oozing of blood and then strapping the smallpox material to the abraded area. It is said that they were able to control accurately the number of smallpox lesions which the patient subsequently developed.

More often the material was introduced by the point of a knife or was rubbed into or bound upon a superficial laceration. One or more sites might be used, here again often a matter of necromantic or religious significance. Interestingly enough, inoculation was often performed on the dorsum of the web space between the thumb and index finger, a site which would seem unsatisfactory from the viewpoint of the patient's comfort as well as that of the resulting restricted use of the member.

The substance used in inoculation varied with the availability of the lesions and with the preference of the operator. On the whole fresh liquid from the content of a smallpox vesicle appears to have been the most desirable and most efficacious. However, the liquid was often collected on lint or on threads and was either used dry or moistened with water. Fresh or dessicated crusts of the lesions were frequently employed.

354

It appears that inoculation was first practiced in Great Britain and in Europe during the early part of the eighteenth century. Presumably the procedure was introduced into England by Lady Mary Wortley Montagu, the wife of the British Ambassador to the Ottoman Court, whose young son had been inoculated in Constantinople. Lady Montagu wrote in a letter to a friend in 1717:

I intend to try it [inoculation] on my dear little son. I am patriot enough to take pains to bring this useful invention into fashion in England; and I should not fail to write to some of our doctors very particularly about it, if I knew any one of them that I thought had virtue enough to destroy such a considerable branch of their revenue for the good of mankind. But that distemper [smallpox] is too beneficial to them not to expose to all their resentment the hardy "wight" that should undertake to put an end to it. Perhaps if I live to return I may, however, have courage to war with them.

She did persist, and in England, in 1721, her three-month-old daughter was successfully inoculated. Other inoculations followed. The practice was given its greatest impetus by the decision of the Princess of Wales to have it performed on her two young children, the procedures being carried out successfully and without particular complication.

Certainly Lady Montagu was not very flattering in her opinion that physicians would be reluctant to take up inoculation because of the loss of revenue from treating smallpox. In any event, this proved to be erroneous in the sense that a number of individuals made a great deal more money inoculating than they could possibly have accumulated in any other form of medical endeavor. Notable amongst these men was Thomas Dimsdale, M.D., who inoculated the Empress Catherine of Russia and her son, the Grand Duke Paul. Dimsdale is said to have received a fee of £10,000, £2,000 for traveling expenses, and an annuity of £500 for life. In addition, he was made Baron of the Russian empire and was appointed Councillor of State and Physician to Her Imperial Majesty.

Inoculations had numerous disadvantages which periodically restricted its use or caused it to be banned. Often it resulted in a case of smallpox as virulent as one contracted under normal contagion. Of greater import was the fact that an inoculated person might become the source of an epidemic of the disease in a region otherwise unexposed. A recently published letter written by Edward Jenner, on April 17, 1805, stated "Allow me to add, Sir, that I hope and trust the mischievous practice of the inoculation of the smallpox will henceforward be totally prohibited at the hospital, for while this is permitted we shall never be able to extinguish the smallpox in the Metropolis."

Nevertheless, the overall mortality rate following inoculation was markedly less than that of natural smallpox, a situation particularly true when the material used was attenuated or diluted. This has been emphasized by one writer who strongly minimizes Jenner's work on vaccination.

In spite of the problems arising from it, the practice of inoculation was occasionally continued, often advantageously, until recent years. A long-time medical associate once told me that in his youth in rural Tennessee (ca. 1890) inoculation was still performed, using crusts from smallpox lesions which were dried in the sun for a few weeks and then rubbed into scratches made on the recipient's arm.

The native population in the parts of the New World conquered by Spain were largely destroyed by disease. Smallpox was introduced into New Spain (Mexico) early in the sixteenth century, certainly as early as 1520. It was the major disease responsible for the annihilation of much of the aboriginal population. A Spanish historian chooses a somewhat different approach to this decimation of the natives stating,

There exist recent investigations that confirm that large population centers, including entire Mayan cities, had disappeared before the arrival of the Spaniards, victims of (pre-existing) epidemics. It is true that smallpox invaded America with the arrival of the Spaniards, with some slaves utilized during colonization being the principal vehicle of transmission, and yet, it should be proper to recall that this import was not brought in Spanish hands and that it was the Spaniards who, through their quarantine measures impeded the dissemination of epidemics and who liberated the American continent from smallpox for all time.

One doubts if the *Conquistadores* did much to impair the dis-

semination of epidemics. Certainly Spain was not wholly responsible for liberating "the American continent from smallpox for all
time." Nevertheless, by the latter part of the eighteenth century,
there was considerable evidence of Spanish interest in the prevention and control of the disease including the use of inoculation.

The primary concern in this essay is with the extent to which
these efforts were transmitted to and carried out in Alta California. One should note, first of all, the improbability that smallpox
existed in that area prior to 1828, whereas the disease was rife in
Mexico and in the more adjacently situated Baja California. This
was due to a number of factors. Likely, the most important was the
geographic isolation of Alta California and the resulting length of
time required for either land or sea voyage, the latter normally
from San Blas. Furthermore, the military, missionaries and settlers who made the long trek were chosen for health and physical
fitness. In addition during the Spanish period, foreign ships were
forbidden from landing or engaging in trade, and there was no
overland travel by foreigners. Finally, Alta California authorities
were aware of the methods of quarantine and hygenic management, applying these measures, at least reasonably well, on the
few occasions that possible smallpox cases came to the area.

The first official instruction concerning the prevention and
management of smallpox reached Alta California in 1786. On September 15 of that year Commandant General Jacobo Ugarte y
Loyola of New Spain, in keeping with a royal decree, wrote Governor Pedro Fages and forwarded twenty copies of a book for distribution in Alta California. This handsome little volume of 164
pages was printed in Madrid in 1784 and was written by Don
Francisco Gil, who is listed on the title page as surgeon of the
Royal Monastery of San Lorenzo and a member of the Royal Academy of Medicine of Madrid. A well-preserved copy of this book is
in the Santa Barbara Mission Archive-Library and no doubt has
been at that mission since its receipt there.

Gil's book is almost a medical history of smallpox. It considers
the opinions of the medical greats of antiquity as well as those of
the leading physicians of his own time. The methods of prevention
offered in the book are largely those of quarantine, fumigation and

357

DISERTACION
FÍSICO - MÉDICA,

EN LA QUAL

SE PRESCRIBE UN MÉTODO SEGURO

PARA PRESERVAR A LOS PUEBLOS

DE VIRUELAS

HASTA LOGRAR LA COMPLETA EXTINCION

DE ELLAS EN TODO EL REYNO.

·SU AUTOR

D. FRANCISCO GIL,

CIRUJANO DEL REAL MONASTERIO DE S. LO-
RENZO Y SU SITIO , É INDIVIDUO DE LA
REAL ACADEMIA MÉDICA DE MADRID.

MADRID MDCCLXXXIV.

POR D. JOACHÍN IBARRA , IMPRESOR DE CAMARA DE S.M.

CON SUPERIOR PERMISO.

This book by Francisco Gil was sent to California in 1786. It introduced the technique of inoculation against smallpox. Photo by William B. Dewey. *Courtesy SBMAL.*

358

proper management of fomites. However, Gil does cover inoculation both historically and practically, but reserves its use for epidemics not readily controllable.

A severe epidemic of smallpox in Guatemala and southern Mexico led the viceroy, the Conde de Branciforte, to issue, on February 28, 1797, a set of instructions concerning the prevention and
management of smallpox, a copy being sent to Governor Diego
Borica of Alta California. This document has been translated. For
our purpose, only Article 8 of the instructions will be reproduced.

When the latter [the epidemic] becomes widespread because of the
inability to stop it in the beginning by the appropriate methods indicated, it will be desirable to put inoculation into practice, pointing out to
those concerned, in order that they may adopt it voluntarily, its advantage and the great success constantly obtained in Oajaca, Tehuantepec
and other towns, where the results have been exceedingly favorable to
mankind. The house or professional hospital should then be enlarged to
receive and treat poor persons who have been inoculated, or to inoculate
those who, although they desire it, shall decline to be inoculated on
account of their great poverty.

This instruction again makes it obvious that inoculation was
advised as a means of restraining the spread of smallpox if there
was not early success in the use of quarantine and standard
methods of control. Of considerable interest is the fact that the
Spaniards realized that inoculation itself might be harmful or
might spread the disease. This is evident in the advice that the
smallpox isolation house or provisional hospital be enlarged to
receive and treat poor persons who had been inoculated.

Dr. Pablo Soler, the surgeon general at Monterey from 1791 to
1800, was the only physician in California during this period. He
was reputed to have been a hard working, highly skilled physician
and surgeon and with excellent training, being a graduate of Barcelona. Soler, over the date May 17, 1798, wrote a document, coun-
tersigned by Governor Borica, which was circulated throughout
Alta California. It was concerned with the method of performing
inoculation against smallpox.

It is probable that this document was a further development of

A view of Mission San Carlos Borromeo in 1790 as depicted by the artist serving with the Malaspina expedition. *Courtesy Museo Naval, Madrid.*

the 1797 instructions of Viceroy Branciforte. It is also possible that its issuance related to the arrival at Santa Barbara on May 3, 1798, of the *Concepción*, the regular supply ship from San Blas. Governor Borica had information that there was smallpox aboard the ship and sent orders to Captain Felipe Goycoechea, the commandant at Santa Barbara, concerning quarantine and isolation. These orders were not strictly followed, for the passengers and crew were required to remain aboard for only thirteen days. However, despite Governor Borica's great concern, smallpox, if indeed it had existed aboard the ship, was not transmitted, and California continued to remain free of the disease.

Dr. Soler's instructions have also been fully translated. The paragraph relating to the actual techniques of inoculation states:

... wet the point of a lancet or similar instrument with smallpox pus; introduce the lancet thus anointed beneath the skin in the web between the index finger and the thumb, so superficially that hardly any blood appears; then place the finger on top of the wound when removing the lancet so that the pus will remain. Do not apply a bandage until the blood has dried.

The translator adds the comment, "There can be no doubt that this instruction was prepared for use by the missionaries or that they actually performed inoculations." I quite agree with the first part of this statement.

However, there is no evidence that inoculation for smallpox was ever performed in Alta California during the Spanish period. It is improbable that it was carried out even in later times. The information previously presented should make it clear that the Spanish authorities did not advise inoculation as a primary prophylactic measure and that, furthermore, there had never been even an aborted epidemic in the area. In addition, lacking the acute disease, the smallpox "pus" used in inoculation was not available, and it is certain that it was not so available following the incident of the *Concepción* at Santa Barbara in 1798. Smallpox cases on that vessel, if any existed, were recovering and were without active lesions from which the liquid "pus" might be obtained. The possibility of crusts or other dried smallpox material having been

361

brought to California for use in inoculation may be discounted by the reasons previously given, including concern over the development of iatrogenic smallpox.

Vaccination for smallpox, originally referred to as inoculation with cowpox, was developed almost entirely from the magnificent work of one man. Nevertheless, there were minimal earlier activities in the field.

As previously noted, there existed the very old and common observation that certain diseases conferred immunity. Cross-immunity had also been observed in the protection against smallpox conferred by human infection with cowpox, a disease with relatively mild systemic manifestation. The dairy farmers and milkmaids of England had long known of this and were aware that the milkmaid who developed a pustule on her hand after milking a cow whose udder was infected would not contract smallpox if later exposed to that disease.

However, prior to Jenner almost nothing was done to utilize the knowledge and nothing at all to publicize it. Benjamin Jesty, a farmer of Dorsetshire, who had had cowpox, gained a niche in medical history in 1714 by inoculating his wife and two children with cowpox material with their resulting immunity to smallpox. Peter Platt of Holstein, aware of the alleged protection afforded by cowpox, successfully vaccinated his employer's three children in 1791. Neither of these individuals proceeded further in the matter.

Edward Jenner was born at Berkeley in Gloucestershire in 1749. When he was eight years of age, he was inoculated against smallpox, and he long remembered the unpleasantness of the occasion. He later said that for six weeks he was bled and purged and kept on a low diet and dosed with medicines and was then removed to one of the so-called inoculation stables and haltered up with others in a terrible state of disease. Understandably, this made a strong impression on Jenner and possibly influenced his investigations on the prevention of smallpox.

When thirteen years of age, Jenner was apprenticed to a surgeon at Sodbury in Bristol and continued his apprenticeship for six years. During this period his attention was drawn forcibly to the nature of cowpox when a young countrywoman came to him to seek advice. The subject of smallpox was mentioned, and she immediately observed, "I cannot take that disease for I have had cowpox."

Following the apprenticeship at Sodbury, Jenner became a house pupil of John Hunter. This famous younger brother of William Hunter has been called the "Father of Modern Surgery." He was professor at the famous Great Windmill Street School of Anatomy. His investigative mind led him to dissect "everything from bees to whales," and he inculcated Jenner with the necessity of observation and investigation.

Jenner returned to Berkeley and to the life of a general practitioner, but with the extra qualities imbued in him by Hunter, with whom he continued to correspond. During this period he inoculated a patient against smallpox and observed that the inoculation did not take, the man having previously had cowpox.

Cowpox broke out on a farm near Berkeley in 1794 and allowed Jenner to culminate his investigations. A dairymaid named Sarah Neames contracted the disease and, on May 14 of that year, Jenner took matter from a cowpox sore on Sarah's hand and inserted it by superficial incisions into the arm of James Phipps, a healthy boy about eight years of age. The inoculation succeeded and produced a lesion similar to that which would have resulted from smallpox inoculation. Six weeks later Jenner inoculated the boy with smallpox matter and without producing that disease.

He confirmed his observations by means of further cowpox inoculations and in June 1798, published his medical milestone, *An Inquiry into the Causes and Effects of the Variola Vaccinae, a Disease Discovered in some of the Western Counties of England, particularly Gloucestershire, and known by the name of the Cowpox.*

Obviously, there were faultfinders and doubters, but, nevertheless, the practice of vaccination spread rapidly, all countries being anxious to prevent the ravages of smallpox. The ties of the young United States with England were such that vaccination was employed in New England even prior to its use in Europe.

Dr. John Coakley Lettsom, Jenner's friend, in 1799 sent a copy of the *Inquiry* to Dr. Benjamin Waterhouse, Professor of the Theory and Practice of Physick, Harvard College (later University) in

Massachusetts. Ultimately Dr. Waterhouse obtained a supply of cowpox matter from England and vaccinated seven of his own children. Furthermore, their immunization against smallpox was confirmed by later inoculation with active smallpox matter. Dr. Jenner himself provided Dr. Waterhouse with a further supply of vaccine which reached him in the spring of 1801. In turn, Waterhouse forwarded some of the matter to President Thomas Jefferson in whose hands it completely succeeded. The President did not think it beneath him to set an example to his fellow citizens and in the course of July and August 1801, he, with his sons-in-law, vaccinated in their own families and in those of their neighbors, nearly 200 persons.

Even this limited description of the early dissemination of vaccination in the United States makes it questionable that it was entirely the Spaniards who liberated the American continent from smallpox for all time.

The practice of vaccination spread into Spain from Paris during the latter part of 1800. Dr. Francisco Piguilem, a physician of Puigerde, obtained some virus which was successfully used in December of that year. An announcement of this appeared in the *Gazeta Real* of Madrid on January 6, 1801. Thus, "the Spanish government from the first evinced a degree of energy in promoting the practice of vaccination which did not usually mark its other proceedings."

The vaccine reached Russia by way of Breslau in October 1801. The Russian Court was at that time in the ancient capital (Moscow) because of the coronation of Czar Alexander. The Czarina Dowager zealously promoted the new practice. She desired that the name of Vaccinoff might be given to the first child who received the infection. The young Vaccinoff was then conveyed to St. Petersburg in one of Her Imperial Majesty's coaches and placed in the Foundling Hospital, and a provision (pension) was settled on her for life.

As one might anticipate the earlier vaccinations were not entirely successful. Contamination of the lymph or vaccine was not unusual, and the material consequently produced infection, often of severity. There were mountebanks who sold strips of shirt on which drainage from a vaccine lesion had long since dried. Others purveyed materials from furuncles, or even from the actual lesions of smallpox, as being true vaccine. Understandably infection, spurious vaccination, and even smallpox itself developed.

There was also a considerable early problem based upon preservation and transportation of the lymph in an active state. Originally it was conveyed on the point of a lancet. The use of the common steel lancet was soon abandoned in favor of silver, gold or ivory, and ivory became considered the most suitable. It was on an ivory point that the vaccine was sent from Breslau to Moscow for its use under the supervision of the Russian Empress.

On longer journeys, particularly in hot climates, these methods did not suffice and the lymph became dessicated and without efficacy. Means used to prevent this included sealing the vaccine in thin gut or in vials or glass tubes stoppered with wax. Better yet lint or threads impregnated with the vaccine were secured between glass plates, and the whole dipped in wax until a solid ball was formed and this, in turn, being carefully packed.

A more cumbersome means of maintaining and propagating the virus was that of arm to arm vaccination. This required a number of persons, usually children, the number being based upon the length of the voyage being contemplated. The first individual was successfully vaccinated. When the content of the lesion was suitably liquid, usually on the eighth or ninth day, it was used to vaccinate the next person. This was continued "from arm to arm" as long as required or while subjects were available. However, even this method was not entirely certain and could fail because of an immune reaction or by the inadvertent rupture of a lesion in the subject's sleep.

All of his leads us to the consideration of vaccination in New Spain and, in turn, Alta California. Although somewhat out of chronological sequence, consideration should be given to the possibility of pre-Jennerian vaccination in California. This possibility is presented by one historian who states, "The first vaccination, according to Governor Arrillaga's statement to Langsdorff, was made in 1786 with vaccine derived from cowpox in the Monterey district." The possibility is not denied by two other writers, one of whom interprets Langsdorff as suggesting "the possibility that vaccinations were performed in California as early as in the Eastern United States, if not earlier."

Dr. Georg H. von Langsdorff was a peripatetic German doctor of medicine who graduated from Göttingen in 1797. In 1806 he served as personal physician to Rezanov, Russian diplomat and Imperial Inspector, accompanying his employer on a voyage from Sitka to San Francisco. Langsdorff reports a conversation with the governor of Alta California in this fashion:

Gobernador Arrillaga imparted the important information that vaccination had been introduced into Mexico from Europe and that a surgeon there had already vaccinated a great many people. He assured me that for some time cowpox had been seen often in the country south of Monterey and that it had been successfully used for inoculation by many people. But for more than 20 years smallpox had not appeared here and people had therefore forgotten the dreadful devastations it had made, the precaution of vaccination was by many considered superfluous and hence rejected. It may be remarked that distemper among the cattle in Nueva California seems to manifest itself chiefly in the Spring and abates when the grass is dried by the heat in June and July. I took especial pains to find the disease myself but did not succeed."

One may note, first of all, Governor Arrillaga's knowledge of widespread vaccination in Mexico, the beginnings of which will shortly be mentioned, and the implication that the practice had not reached Alta California. Secondly, and of more import, is the question of possible pre-Jennerian inoculation with cowpox in Alta California. The governor, reported by Langsdorff, stated that cowpox had been present for "some time," and that it had been successfully used for inoculation by many people.

It is highly improbable indeed that there was a Benjamin Jesty in California. Alta California was sparsely populated and was not a dairy country. It is unlikely that the transmission of cowpox to a milker occurred with sufficient frequency to make it a matter of common knowledge. Finally, and conclusively, smallpox had not developed in Alta California, and there was no fashion in which it could have been observed that human infection with cowpox would have protected against smallpox.

One may be certain, however, that prior to 1806 the Californians were aware of Jenner's work and consequently of the efficacy of inoculation with cowpox. Communication from Spain to Mexico and from the latter to Alta California required considerable time but was carried on regularly. Information regarding vaccination was an important topic in the journals of the early nineteenth century, and one only need recall that an announcement of successful vaccination appeared in the *Gazeta Real* of Madrid in January 1801. Obviously this information could not have reached Alta California at a time sufficiently early to have allowed for cowpox inoculation there prior to the performance of vaccination in the United States.

New Spain, Guatemala and the South American Spanish colonies were constantly faced with the possibility of epidemic smallpox. Consequently, on becoming aware of vaccination and its benefits, they made considerable and persistent efforts to obtain vaccine, but it does not appear that any of the material reached Mexico until December 1802. At that time the new viceroy, Don José de Iturrigaray, arrived in Mexico City from Spain and was accompanied by a professor, first class, of the Royal Fleet, Don Alexandro Arboleya, who brought with him small vials of vaccine fluid (presumably from Spain). Supplement No. 12 of the *Gazeta de Mexico* relates that the material was promptly used in inoculating children from the Home for Abandoned Children, but "... His [the viceroy's] interested and laudable intentions of seeing it done went unfulfilled for the time being, since the matter had no effect on any of them, doubtless because it had lost its efficacy in passage."

Nevertheless, the efforts of the viceroy and of Arboleya ultimately became successful. Active vaccine was obtained from Vera Cruz where it had been brought on the frigates-of-war *Anfitrite* and *O* from Havana, which latter city had received viable vaccine from Spain. On the evening of its arrival in Mexico City, and on the following day, vaccinations were performed with the desired results.

A remarkable document of twelve pages, a second supplement to the *Gazeta de Mexico*, gives a bit of the history of vaccination, covers the methods of obtaining and transporting the vaccine, meticu-

367

lously describes the technique of vaccination, and concludes with an extensive primer of questions and answers. Finally a plate of illustrations shows the type of lancet used and the appearance of the vaccination on the fourth, eighth, and tenth or eleventh days, as well as the appearance of a false vaccination. Illustrated, too, is a child with multiple vaccinations, a method used in Mexico even in recent times and based, no doubt, on the premise that other spots might take if one site of inoculation was unsucessful.

A paragraph from the first *Gazeta* supplement serves very well to introduce the major effort devoted to smallpox immunization in Spanish America:

The anxiety which these results [the early failure of Arboleya] caused in the mind of His Excellency [Iturrigaray], especially since he found himself commanding such dominions in which when they suffer from the natural pox it causes the most lamentable ruin, always leaving an unfortunate and painful memory, was mitigated by the receipt of the Royal Decree which notified His Excellency of the great Philanthropical Expedition which His Majesty was pleased to have sent to the Americas at their Majesties expense without stinting any cost at a time which due to the late wars the Crown finds itself heavily laden with debts; consideration of which weighs less in the august and most pious heart of His Majesty than the conservation of the health and lives of his beloved subjects, wishing to make us participants with Europe in the imponderably good and singular discovery of the vaccine.

The Philanthropical Expedition referred to in the *Gazeta* was the Royal Maritime Vaccination Expedition. This magnificent undertaking has not had the general attention it deserves, although it has been excellently and thoroughly covered in two studies.

I do not believe that one could possibly improve on the evaluation which follows:

Seldom, perhaps never, in the history of medicine has there embarked an expedition so grandly conceived, so well executed, so uniformly successful as that of Balmis. Certainly no new therapeutic procedure of similar magnitude has even been made available by a single agency to such a wide segment of the world's population. By it the discovery of Jenner was made available to the population of the West Indies, Mexico, Central America, much of South America, Philippine Islands, the East Indies and China. Through this one act on the part of the corrupt and decadent government of Spain, more lives probably were saved than were lost in all the battles of Napoleon. Yet this magnificent experiment in social welfare and public health has gone substantially unnoticed and unrecorded by both medical and political historians.

Dr. Francis Xavier Balmis was Surgeon Extraordinary to Carlos IV. The latter had a personal interest in prevention of smallpox inasmuch as his daughter had suffered from the disease. He consequently responded to petitions from the New World for the vaccine, and it was determined to equip and dispatch an expedition to bring vaccination to these possessions. Balmis was appointed director. The ship left Corunna on November 30, 1803.

Arm to arm vaccination was considered to offer the best possibility of reaching distant destinations with viable vaccine, and twenty-two orphan children who had never undergone smallpox, were selected for the preservation of the vaccine fluid by transmitting it successfully from one to another during the voyage. The children were very well cared for and were constantly supervised so that the vaccinated area would not be damaged or premature cross-vaccination occur. No doubt vaccine lymph, preserved in one of the fashions previously described, was also on board. Consideration had been given to bringing cows infected with cowpox, but this was not done.

The expedition stopped at the Canary Islands and then proceeded to Puerto Rico and Caracas. Here it was divided into two branches. Don Francis Salvani, the sub-director, went to South America and notably to Colombia and Peru. Balmis proceeded to Havana and from there to Mexico City by way of Vera Cruz.

Balmis' work was not easy nor entirely happy. He was an imperious man and was insistent on the privileges and the degree of cooperation which he felt were due him as the medical representative of the king. Furthermore, he was disillusioned by successful vaccination having occasionally preceded him, as has been noted in respect to Vera Cruz and Mexico City. Nevertheless, he and members of the expedition were able to vaccinate and leave the basis for future vaccinations throughout New Spain and Guatemala.

Balmis then took ship from Acapulco to the Philippines, on this part of his voyage carrying twenty-six children, candidates for arm to arm vaccination, with him from New Spain. It had been planned originally that the expedition's function would terminate in the Philippines, but this did not satisfy Balmis. When he had accomplished his purpose in the Philippines, he sailed to Macao, vaccinating in that Portuguese colony, and then went on to Canton where he introduced vaccination to the Chinese. Returning to Macao, he embarked on a Portuguese ship and reached Lisbon on August 15, 1806. On the way he stopped at St. Helena, and strange to say, was the first to induce the British inhabitants of that settlement to adopt the antidote, and this even though it had been discovered in their own country and sent them by Jenner himself.

A copy of the *Madrid Gazeta* forwarded to Jenner in November 1806, announced the safe return of Balmis and stated that he had the honor of kissing His Majesty's hand on Sunday, September 7.

Balmis made a second official trip to New Spain in 1810 and remained there for approximately a year. His stay, and his activity in revitalizing the vaccination program, was marred by political unrest and personal frictions. A set of regulations for the propagation and perpetuation of the vaccine in New Spain was printed in Mexico City over the date of October 10, 1810, and the name of Francisco Xavier de Balmis. One may be certain that this document reached Alta California as did the previously noted supplement to the *Gazeta de Mexico*. However, none of the personnel or disciples of the Royal Expedition came to California at any time, the northernmost point of their efforts being in what is now southern Texas. This apparent dereliction was likely based on the limited population of Alta California as well as upon the absence of smallpox in the area.

Hubert H. Bancroft records that "Vaccination proper does not seem to have been introduced [in California] until 1817 when some lymph was brought by a Spaniard named José Verdia and a little later by the surgeon of a Russian war vessel. Again in 1821, the surgeon of a Russian war vessel, the *Kutusoff*, presented the Governor with some vaccine matter which he had brought from Lima." The information regarding Verdia has been routinely repeated during the intervening years, but I cannot find any other reference to this man, his activities or from where he brought the lymph.

At this point let us return full circle to José Estrada's letter which, you will recall, was written by him in Monterey on August 28, 1821, and was sent to his friend, Don José de la Guerra, in Santa Barbara. Recall, too, that the brief and intriguing postscript to this letter stated, "The Russian surgeon has brought vaccine and today vaccinated 54 persons, I being the first."

José Mariano Estrada was born at Loreto, Baja California, in 1784 and, at the time of his letter was *habilitado* (paymaster) and sometimes acting commandant at Monterey. His friend, José de la Guerra y Noriega, born in Spain, had served in the Monterey company but at the time of the letter was captain of the Santa Barbara company and active in political affairs.

The body of the letter deals with articles for sale which were brought by the Russian ship, notably linens, woolens, dress material and tobacco. Of the latter Estrada writes, "The tobacco to the amount of one *quintal* [hundredweight] is for each Presidio. If you want more, I have here 40 pesos that Sergeant Pico has given me for which two quintals can be bought and the price has risen to 20 pesos. Truthfully, the price is cheap, but it is not of very good quality." The letter also noted that the Russians were slow and had not taken aboard a fifth part of their cargo.

One may be certain that this Russian ship was the *Kutuzov*. This vessel, named after a Russian general, famous in the Napoleonic War, had been purchased by Russia from the French following the final defeat of Napoleon.

We know but little of the 1821 voyage of the *Kutuzov* in which vaccination was carried out during the ship's stay in Monterey. Bancroft remarks that the "*Kutuzov*, Russian ship, from Callao [the port of Lima] arrived at Monterey in July; paid $4,121 in duties at San Francisco in September; made a second visit to Monterey on September 10th." Perhaps the Russians hurried with loading their cargo, only a fifth accomplished on August 28th, or perhaps they completed loading on their return to Monterey.

It is a reasonable presumption that in 1821 the *Kutuzov* was duplicating a previous and relatively famous voyage. On that ear-

A view of the Monterey Presidio in 1791 as sketched by José Caldero, who was with the Malaspina expedition. *Courtesy Mueso Naval, Madrid.*

lier journey the ship, and an accompanying vessel, the *Suvorov*, were captained by a man with the impressive name and title of Fleet Captain-Lieutenant Cavalier Leontii Andrianovich Hagemeister, commander of the fourth Russian round-the-world expedition. The vessels made the long voyage from St. Petersburg out of the Baltic, across the Atlantic and around the Horn. The *Suvorov* arrived in Sitka on July 23, 1817, and the *Kutuzov* not until November 20th of that year. En route both vessels called at Lima, but the *Suvorov* proceeded directly from there to Sitka. The *Kutuzov* put in at several coastal points in Peru and then stopped at Bodega Bay and San Francisco where a large stock of food supplies was purchased for the chronically undernourished Russian colonies in Alaska. It is possible that this voyage was the earlier occasion, suggested by Bancroft, on which a Russian warship brought lymph to California.

It is not pertinent to the subject of this inquiry, but one should know a bit more of the earlier voyage of the *Kutuzov*. This further information relates largely to Aleksandr Andraevich Baranov, who was chief manager and governor of the Russian colonies in America for twenty-eight years and was the founder of Novo Arkhangel'sk (present-day Sitka). Following the arrival of the *Kutuzov* from San Francisco, his post was assumed by Hagemeister, and Baranov left Sitka aboard the ship on November 27, 1818, to return to Russia and a well earned rest. The *Kutuzov* passed the Sandwich Islands and made an effort to stop at Manila but was prevented in doing so by adverse winds. The ship put in at Umata Harbor on Guam for fresh provisions on January 28, 1819, and reached Batavia on March 7, remaining for thirty-six days. Baranov became sick there, an illness attributed to the tropical climate, and died while the ship was in the Straits of Sunda on April 16, 1819. Baranov was seventy-two years of age.

The *Kutuzov*, of course, continued on its world girdling voyage and returned to St. Petersburg. The archives of the Russian American Company, dating from 1810–17, were in Baranov's possession and, with his death, there was no further care of these records. The historically valuable documents vanished without trace when the ship arrived at St. Petersburg.

Estrada's letter tells us of the items which the *Kutuzov* had aboard for trade or barter. No doubt the linens, woolens, and dress material were of Russian origin. It is possible that the tobacco was obtained in Peru or Mexico but more probable that it had been brought from Russia and that then, as now, tobacco of this origin "was not of very good quality."

Our present interest, of course, is not so much in these items of commerce as in the origin of the lymph which was used to vaccinate Estrada. No doubt this vaccine was on board the *Kutuzov* primarily for the purpose of immunizing the population in Russian America; the Russians, as we have seen, having a considerable early interest in the control of smallpox. It is highly improbable, however, that the vaccine was of Russian origin inasmuch as there would have been little chance of preserving it during the long voyage of the *Kutuzov* from St. Petersburg to Sitka.

There is evidence that the surgeon of the *Kutuzov* obtained the vaccine in Lima. It is probable that there was an ample store of the material in that city, thanks to the work of Balmis' lieutenant, Salvani. A letter from Governor Solá to Captain de la Guerra, recorded under the date of September 25, 1821, states "that more than 90 children of both sexes were vaccinated but the desired effect was not produced, because the pus (which was brought by a physician from Lima on the Russian frigate Kusorof [*sic*]) had lost its virtue."

An earlier entry, relating to a communication from Governor Solá to the Fathers of San Juan Capistrano, makes it evident that the vaccine was well cared for by the Russian surgeon, being carried by him in "small crystal vials." Perhaps it was ineffective when it was obtained in Lima, or perhaps it "lost its virtue," during the approximately four months prior to the vaccination of the "more than 90 children."

I see no necessary discrepancy between the 54 persons of whom Estrada stated he was the first and the more than 90 children noted by Governor Solá. Estrada's postscript implies that adults were vaccinated on August 21, and the governor's communication to de la Guerra suggests that the children were vaccinated after the return of the *Kutuzov* to Monterey on September 10. One might speculate that the vaccine lost its virtue in the interim and that Estrada and his group may have experienced the desired result.

Cook, in consideration of Governor Solá's description of more than 90 children, noted that, if the statement was correct, "then a large proportion of the white children must have been immunized for the population of Monterey was quite small at the time." It appears to me that Indian children, too, would have been vaccinated and conceivable also that Estrada's 54 included Indians. The above noted letter of Governor Solá to the Fathers of San Juan Capistrano expressed his hope that chiefly Indians would be vaccinated. Of lesser interest is Cook's reference to the *Kutuzov* as the *Rusa*, an error resulting from confusing the Spanish adjective for Russian with the name of the frigate.

In conclusion, one is certainly led to speculate as to the reasons for the interest in vaccination in Alta California of Estrada's day and particularly so in a sparsely populated area which had not known epidemic smallpox and had suffered but little actual threat of it. Primarily, however, the population was not indigenous, and people had strong personal memories of the ravages of smallpox in Mexico, Guatemala and Baja California. Furthermore, as we have seen, Spain had long inculcated them in the methods of smallpox prophylaxis and in a resulting desire to control the disease by establishing immunity.

Spain deserves much credit for this and for her considerable part in endeavoring to rid "the American continent from smallpox for all time." It is evident, too, that the provision of vaccine by Russian ships was an important factor in smallpox vaccination in California, a role which was controlled for several years following 1821.

Nevertheless, Estrada's vaccination, contributed to by Spain and Russia, related chiefly to the medical milestone developed by one man, the *Inquiry* of Edward Jenner.

Contributors

THE ARTICLES that are published in this anthology were authored by the following individuals. The contributors are listed in alphabetical order. Following each brief sketch, bracketed information is provided to identify the volume number, year, and inclusive pagination for each of the articles reprinted. Without exception, all of the articles published in this volume were footnoted. However, as previously stated in the Introduction, these notes have been omitted in this anthology. Any curious reader interested in the documentation may turn to the original issue of the *Quarterly* to consult the omitted notes.   —*The Editor*

ROBERT ARCHIBALD earned his doctorate in history from the University of New Mexico in 1975, before embarking on a teaching career in the groves of academia. His dissertation explored the somewhat neglected area of the economic development of the missions in Hispanic California, a study that was subsequently published by the Franciscan Academy of History, Washington, D.C. [LVIII (1976): 227–240.]

IRIS H. W. ENGSTRAND is professor of history in the University of San Diego, where she serves as chair for the department. She earned her M.A. and Ph.D. degrees from the University of Southern California. A specialist in the history of California, she has published extensively in that subject area. She is also an authority on Spanish scientific explorations along the Pacific slope. [LXVII (1985): 281–290.]

WILLIAM E. EVANS, a native of southern California, graduated from San Diego State University and embarked on a professional career as a teacher. Long interested in the history of his native state, he contributed articles on that subject to the *California Historical Society Quarterly* and the *Peabody Journal of Education*. [LI (1969): 85–96.]

377

EDUARDO GARRIGUES LÓPEZ-CHICHERI is a career diplomat in the service of Spain, having served his government in a number of important diplomatic posts, and is currently the Consul General of Spain in Los Angeles. He has a keen interest in cultural affairs, history, and creative writing. He has published a number of books and contributed numerous articles to Spanish newspapers.

MAYNARD J. GEIGER, O.F.M., one of California's distinguished historians of the Hispanic period, was born in Lancaster, Pennsylvania, in 1901, but spent most of his life in the Golden State. He entered the Order of Friars Minor in 1919 and was ordained to the priesthood in 1929. After taking a doctorate in history at the Catholic University of America, he returned to Mission Santa Barbara, where he spent the rest of his life, serving as archivist/historian to the Province of St. Barbara until his death in 1976. An indefatigable researcher, he authored a definitive biography of Junípero Serra, among other invaluable works. [XLVI (1964): 109–124; L (1968): 33–42.]

FRANCIS F. GUEST, O.F.M., received his Ph.D. in history from the University of Southern California. He has spent his priestly career as a teacher and pastor. On the death of Maynard J. Geiger, O.F.M., in 1976, he was appointed archivist for the Santa Barbara Mission Archive Library. He has published extensively in the mission era in California history, including a biography of Fray Narciso Duran as well as a volume of his letters that he translated and edited. [LXVII (1985): 223–261.]

SALOMÉ HERNÁNDEZ was born in Mexico. She came with her family to San Diego when only six months old. She received her B.A. from the University of San Diego in 1971, the M.A. in history from Arizona State University in 1975, and her Ph.D. from the University of New Mexico in 1979, after spending a year researching in Spain on a Ford Foundation Fellowship. In 1980 she began a career as a Foreign Service Officer with the U.S. Information Agency. [LXXII (1990): 203–233.]

HARRY KELSEY, a doctoral graduate of the University of Colorado, spent his professional career in the field of historical curatorship, first with the Colorado State Historical Society, then the Michigan State Historical Society, before his appointment as chief curator of history in the Los Angeles County Museum of Natural History. He has published widely on a variety of subjects and is the author of the definitive biography of Juan Rodríguez Cabrillo. In retirement he continues to research and publish his findings. [LXI (1979): 313–336.]

DAVID J. LANGUM took his B.A. from Dartmouth College, his J.D. from Stanford University, and subsequently an M.A. in history at San Jose State University. After admission to the California Bar, he entered private practice, first in San Francisco, later in San Jose. In 1978 he accepted appointment to the faculty of the Detroit College of Law and is currently a full professor in the Cumberland School of Law, Samford University, Birmingham, Alabama. He has received a number of awards for his scholarly contributions and recently coauthored a biography of Thomas O. Larkin (University of Oklahoma Press, 1991). [LXII (1980): 217–228.]

WILLIAM M. MASON is a member of the History Division, Los Angeles County Museum of Natural History. He is exceedingly well versed in the early history of Baja and Alta California, with particular expertise in family history. In addition, he has devoted much attention to the history of Afro-Americans in California, particularly Los Angeles. His publications range across these fields of interest. [LXX (1988): 235–263.]

MARVIN W. MIKESELL is unidentified in the *Quarterly* issue within which his article was published. However, in another contribution, it would appear that he was a geographer by profession and may well have held an academic appointment. [XXXVII (1955): 211–222.]

ROBERT J. MOES, M.D., a midwesterner by birth, received his

B.A. and M.D. from the University of Nebraska, Lincoln. He undertook his internship and residence in Los Angeles, which became his home for the rest of his long life. He was a surgeon of distinction and repute. Long interested in the history of medicine, a field in which he was a notable book collector, on retirement from private practice he began to research and write on the history of medicine in early California. In all he published six brilliant essays on this subject prior to his death at age eighty-three. [LXI (1979): 125–145.]

NORMAN NEUERBURG is professor emeritus of art history in California State University, Dominguez Hills. Among several specialties in which he has established his scholarly reputation is his interest in California mission art and architecture. He has published a growing body of work in that respect and continues to research and write on those subjects. In addition, he is often called upon to be a consultant on mission-related restoration projects. [LXVII (1985): 263–280.]

DOYCE B. NUNIS, JR., became editor of the Historical Society of Southern California's quarterly publication in 1962. Under his editorship the publication was rechristened the *Southern California Quarterly*. A resident of Los Angeles since 1938, he received his B.A. from the University of California, Los Angeles, and his M.S. in Ed., M. Ed., M.A., and Ph.D. in history from the University of Southern California. His professional teaching career has been spent in the environs of his adopted city, including appointments at UCLA, 1959–65, and USC, 1965–89. A widely published scholar, he is now professor emeritus but continues to be active in historical research and publication.

DONALD A. NUTTALL received his Ph.D. in history from the University of Southern California. He subsequently joined the Department of History at Whittier College, where he has spent his professional career. An authority on Spanish California, he has made many notable contributions by publishing studies in a number of scholarly journals. [LIII (1971): 185–198.]

MANUEL P. SERVÍN received his Ph.D. in history from the University of Southern California where, for several years, he taught courses on the history of California and the American West, before switching to the field of Latin American history. He subsequently taught at Arizona State University and later at the University of New Mexico before his retirement. For a number of years he was editor of the *California Historical Society Quarterly*. He is deceased. [XLV (1963): 109–121.]

THEODORE E. TREUTLEIN, a doctoral graduate of the University of California, Berkeley, spent his professional career in the Department of History, San Francisco State University. A recognized authority on the history of the American Southwest, particularly the Borderlands and Mexico, he was also well versed in the history of the Spanish era in California. Author of numerous books and articles, he was elected a Fellow of the California Historical Society. [LV (1973): 1–7.]

RICHARD S. WHITEHEAD had a distinguished career in city planning in Santa Barbara County. He had a longtime association with the Santa Barbara Trust for Historic Preservation and was keenly interested in the restoration of the Santa Barbara Presidio. To this end he undertook in-depth research on the subject and labored long and hard on it. [LXV (1983): 67–94.]

RAYMUND F. WOOD was born in London, England, but was educated in California and Washington. He obtained his first master's degree from Gonzaga University, in medieval philosophy, which he followed some years later, after service as an officer in World War II, with a doctorate in medieval history from the University of California, Los Angeles. He also obtained a master's degree in library science from the University of Southern California. He has authored several books concerned with Mariposa and Kern counties, as well as Mission San José, among others. He has contributed many articles to scholarly journals in the field of history and librarianship. He is professor emeritus of librarianship, UCLA. [LI (1969): 185–209; LIII (1971): 199–234.]

Index

Entries are filed word-by-word. Spanish personal names are indexed by primary surname (for married women, by husband's primary surname), according to Hispanic practice. *Italic* page references indicate photographs or illustrations. The abbreviation "pass." (for *passim*) denotes scattered references to a subject in the page sequence cited.

Index

Juan Rodríguez (ship), 7, 12
Juárez, Joaquin, 329

Kino, Eusebio Francisco, S.J.,
  29, 282
Kotzebue, Otto von, 126
Kutusov, or *Kutusoff* (ship), 370–75

La Pérouse, Comte de, 119, 125–26
La Pérouse expedition, xxii, 262, 299
Land Act of 1851 (U.S.), 247
Land grants, xi, 237–38, *240*, 244–46;
  legal foundation, 238–40, 242
Landaeta, Fr. Martín, 342
Langsdorff, Georg Heinrich von, 126,
  231, 347, 349, 350, 365–66
Lasuén, Fr. Fermín Francisco de, 258,
  261, 262, 316, 333–34; defense of
  mission system (Refutation of
  Charges), 94, 99, 102, 106; favor of
  clemency toward Indians, 97, 102,
  125; justification of keeping
  Indians at missions, 99–100, 106–7,
  120–22; solicitation of money to
  aid Spain in war, 302, 303;
  supervision of improvements to
  missions, 204, 339
Las Casas, Bartolomé de, *see* Casas
Laws of the Indies, 98, 112, 240–44,
  245, 250
Lelia Byrd (ship), 343
Libraries in early California, 249–62
Limerick, Patricia, xi
Lithographs, *see* Artworks
Lobera, Juan de, 11
López, Cayetano, 336
López, María Gertrudis, 316, 318
López de Villalobos, Ruy, 9, 12, 13
López de Zúñiga, Diego, 9, 10, 25
"Lorenzana," Apolinaria María
  Guadalupe 323, 328, 329, 335
"Lorenzana," Carlos (Carlos Téllez),
  322, 323, 328
"Lorenzana," Domingo Tomás
  (Domingo Tomás Cisneros), 323
"Lorenzana," José María de Dolores
  (José María de Dolores Avilés), 323
"Lorenzana," José María Jacinto (José
  Jacinto Ortiz), 323, 328
"Lorenzana," José María Macedonio
  (Macedonio Suárez), 323, 328

"Lorenzana," José Timoteo (José
  Timoteo Fernández), 323, 328
"Lorenzana," José Victor (José Victor
  Cano), 322, 323
"Lorenzana," Juan Vicente (Juan
  Vicente Vásquez), 323
"Lorenzana," Leonarda Joaquina, 323
"Lorenzana," Manuel Felipe de Jesús
  (José María Felipe Jesús), 323
"Lorenzana," María Alexa Josefa
  ("Inez"), 323, 328, 329
"Lorenzana," María Ana Josefa
  ("Mariana"), 322, 323
"Lorenzana," María de Jesús (María
  de Jesús Torres), 323, 324–25,
  327–28, 329; letter to Viceroy
  Azanza, 338
"Lorenzana," María Francisca Ignacia,
  323, 329
"Lorenzana," María Gertrudis, 322,
  323, 328, 329–30
"Lorenzana," María Josefa Pasquala,
  323, 324–25, 329
"Lorenzana," María Margarita,
  323, 328
"Lorenzana," María Toribia ("Tadea"),
  323, 328
"Lorenzana," María Valeriana, 322,
  323, 329
"Lorenzana," María Vicenta, 323
Lorenzanas, 314, 322–23;
  see also Orphans
Los Angeles pueblo: early buildings,
  217, 218, 223–24; early ranchos
  near, 237–38; founding, xxi,
  139–40, 243; original name, 49,
  142–46; settlers recruited, 140, 143
Lucenilla, Francisco, 29
Lugo, Antonio María, 232, 238
Lugo, José Carmen del, 232–34
Luna, Victoria, 316, 318

Machado, Doña Juana, 335
Malaspina expedition, 312, 313,
  360, 372
Maps as decorative prints,
  see Artworks
Marques, Gabriel, 24
Marquez de las Amarillas, Juan,
  323–24
Marroquín, Francisco, Bishop, 11, 12
Martín, Luis, 335

Index

1780, 300; rebellion plotted, 305–6
San Fernando, College of (Mexico
City), 37, 38, 119–20, 253–54,
256–61, 342
San Francisco (ship), 7, 19
San Francisco presidio, 34, 174, 268;
contribution of money to aid Spain
in war, 298; layout and design,
176, *177*, 178, *179*, 180, *181*, *182*,
193–94, 217, 219–21, 232
San Francisco pueblo, 34, 231–32
San Jorge (ship), 7, 12
San José (ship), 61–66 pass.
San Jose pueblo, xxi, 139–40, 142, 243
San Juan de Letrán (ship), 7, 12
San Marín (ship), 7
San Míguel (ship), 6, 7, 8, 19
San Salvador (ship), 7, 8, 9, 12, 19
Sánchez, Joaquín, 346–47
Sánchez, Fr. Miguel, 200, 201
Sanchez, Nellie Van de Griff, 88
Sancho, Fr. Juan Bautista, 105, 259
Santa Barbara presidio, 174, 221, 229,
268, 270, *280*, *283*; and Indians,
284, 293; contribution of money to
aid Spain in war, 298; detriment to
community, 282, 284; excavations
and reconstruction, 195–97;
founding, 282–84; layout and
construction, 188, *189*, *190*, *191*,
195–97 pass., 217–18, 284–85;
number of soldiers c. 1780, 300
Santa Barbara Trust for Historic
Preservation, 196–97
Santa María, Antonio de, 326–27
Santa María, Fr. Vicente de, 106
Santiago (ship under Pedro de
Alvarado), 7, 12
Santiago (ship under Juan Pérez), 71, 72
Scurvy, 42, 44, 80, 82, 84
Sea-otter fur trade, 210, 225–26,
339–44 pass.
Sebastián (Fr. Garcés' Indian guide),
152, 157, 158, 160, 162
Señán, Fr. José, 95–96, 341, 344
Serra, Fr. Junípero, *93*, 107, 119, 124,
261, 264, 268, 272, 273, 300, 339;
and Sacred Expedition of 1769, 34,
35, 40–44, 66, 68; attitudes toward
Indians, 89, 93–94, 95, 101, 105–6,
112, 118, 127; confirmation dispute
with Gov. Neve, 131–37, 250; days
at Carmel, 69, 71, 74; education

and teaching in Majorca, 36;
founded Mission San Carlos, 68;
founded Mission San Diego, xx,
33–34, 44, 83; founded Mission
San Francisco de Velicatá, 34, 42;
myths about, 33–35, 56, 75;
takeover of Jesuit missions as
Franciscan father president, 38,
39; voyage from San Diego to
Monterey, 34, 35, 66, 68
Settlers, *see* Colonists
Seven Cities of Cíbola, *see* Cíbola
Shaler, William, 343, 350
Shinn, Beryle, 27
Shipbuilding in early New Spain, 3–6
Smallpox: epidemics in New Spain,
356–57, 359; historical
development of inoculation,
353–56, 362–65; prevention and
management in New Spain,
357–75; Royal Maritime
Vaccination Expedition, 368–70
Smuggling in early California, 210–11,
226–29, 236, 340–44
Solá, Pablo Vicente de, 175, 344, 345;
on punishment of Indians, 107,
125; on smallpox vaccination,
374–75
Soler, Pablo, 359–61
Solórzano Pereira, Juan de, 92, 95
Somera, Fr. Angel, 199
Spanish American Wars of
Independence, 245, 248; attack on
Monterey, 306–7; conspiracy in
San Diego, 305–6; sedition in
California, 305, 307; supply
shortages in California, 231, 340,
343–44
Stevenson, Jonathan D., 251
Suárez, Macedonio (José María
Macedonio "Lorenzana"), 323, 328
Suvorov (ship), 373

Tagle (ship), 344
Tallow production in early California,
284, 341, 345, 347
Tamana (ship), 210, 227
Tamariz, Francisco de Paula, 340, 346
Tapia, Bartolo, 210, 226
Tapia, José Bartólome, 238
Tapia, Josefa Leonarda Benítez de, 316
Tapia, Mariano, 315

Index

393

Six hundred copies
designed by Ward Ritchie
were printed by
Premier Printing Corporation
and bound by
Roswell Bookbinders.

Two hundred copies
are reserved for
the Consulate General
of Spain
in Los Angeles.